Blacks, Indians, and Spaniards in the Eastern Andes

Ciudad la Villa de Mizque. Villa. Guaman Poma. Courtesy of Fondo de Culture Económica del Peru

LOLITA GUTIÉRREZ BROCKINGTON

Blacks, Indians, *and* Spaniards *in the* Eastern Andes

Reclaiming the Forgotten in Colonial Mizque, 1550–1782

University of Nebraska Press   Lincoln and London

Portions of chapter 2 were previously published
as "La dinámica de historia regional: El caso de
Mizque (Cochabamba) y 'la puente' de 1630"
in *Historia y Cultura* (Lima: Museo Nacional
de Arqueologia, Antropologia, e Historia del
Peru, Instituto Nacional de Cultura, vol. 22,
1993), 75–104.

Portions of chapter 5 were previously published
as "Trabajo, etnicidad y raza: El
Afro-boliviano en el corregimiento de Mizque"
in *Anuario*, 1996–1997. Sucre: Archivo y
Biblioteca Nacional de Bolivia. 107–122, and
"The African Diaspora in the Eastern Andes:
Adaptation, Agency, and Fugitive Action,
1573–1677" in *The Americas*, vol. 57, no. 2
(October 2000), 207–224.

Library of Congress Cataloging-in-Publication
Data

Brockington, Lolita Gutiérrez.
Blacks, Indians, and Spaniards in the Eastern
Andes : reclaiming the forgotten in colonial
Mizque, 1550–1782 / Lolita Gutiérrez
Brockington.
p. cm.
Includes bibliographical references and index.
ISBN-13: 978-0-8032-1349-4 (cloth : alk paper)
ISBN-10: 0-8032-1349-2 (cloth : alk paper)
1. Mizque (Bolivia : Province)—History.
2. Mizque (Bolivia : Province)—Race relations.
3. Blacks—Bolivia—Mizque (Province).
4. Indians of South America—Bolivia—Mizque
(Province).   I. Title.
F3341.M58B76 2006
305.800984'23—dc22   2006045688

To my family, especially Don

Contents

List of Maps and Tables   *ix*

Acknowledgments   *xi*

Introduction   *1*

Part One: Reclaiming Mizque's Forgotten

1. The Landscape and Its People   *15*

2. Re-creating a Region for a Colonial Market   *43*

Part Two: The Emergence of a New Interregional and Intraregional Center

3. Transforming the Land into Landed Estates   *77*

4. Harnessing the Resources   *101*

Part Three: The Human Face of Mizque: The Actions and Interactions of Africans, Indians, and Spaniards

5. The Africans and Their Descendants   *129*

6. Indian Affairs   *181*

7. Town, Countryside, and the Social Construct   *234*

Conclusions   *275*

Glossary   *289*

Notes   *293*

Bibliography   *323*

Index   *333*

Maps and Tables

Maps

1. South America   3
2. Corregimiento de Mizque, ca. 1620   52

Tables

1. Prices of Hacienda Products   82
2. Tax Appraisal for Turque Slaves, 1635   145–147
3. Inventory of Hacienda Chalguani Slaves, 1767   153–156
4. Ethnic Groups on Mizque Chacaras   218
5. Yanacona and Ethnic Count in the Padrones and
   Percentages of Huidos   221–225

Acknowledgments

This book has been a long time in the writing. Its germinal stage originated at a particular professional and intellectual juncture in my life through a series of coincidences. The result of these unexpected turns of events found me, a dedicated Mexicanist, slowly making my way up the four flights of wide marble steps, to stop at the top to catch my breath once more, and then enter the reading room of the Archivo Histórico Municipal de Cochabamba (AHMC), Bolivia, 8,600 feet above sea level. Before me was a sight that others have also commented on, expressing awe mixed with more than a hint of horror. There, atop several tables, in helter-skelter heaps and stacks, cobwebbed and dust—laden beyond recognition, lay masses of jumbled documents—in short, centuries of regional history.

Bolivia was destined to be my home away from home, my family away from family, for years to come. Fortunately, previous archival experience and the natural sleuth that energizes most historians, coupled with sheer obstinacy, bore results. My research, which would soon focus on the Mizque Collection, was greatly helped by the steady organizational transformation and improvement taking place in the archive over the years. Today it is a brightly lit, dust-free, temperature-controlled (in the stacks), inviting repository. Under the directorship of Itala de Mamán, and despite some nearly overwhelming obstacles, the archive continues its ongoing organizational efforts, including the restructuring of its catalog system. The new system, I have been told, will be compatible with the one I use in this work. I could not have begun this work, let alone reached its conclusion, without the many people who came to my assistance at the AHMC over the years with an unfailing generosity of spirit, goodwill, and cooperation. I thank each and every one.

Continued research took me further up the Andean chain of verticality, first to the Archivo Nacional de Bolivia in Sucre (colonial La
Plata) to study the other half of the Mizque Collection. There I had
the immense good fortune and honor to consult with the late, deeply
respected Don Gunnar Mendoza during several months of intense research. His exemplary, well-organized archive, his advice, and his guidance were absolutely essential in the direction and focus of my investigations, and I owe him my deepest gratitude. I also wish to thank his
staff of the time for their amiable cooperation, especially Judith Terán
Ríos, whose patience and help with the paleographical knots and traps
I encountered reading early colonial rural notarial records made for
clearer understanding of documentary context. I will always appreciate
her assistance! And I thank the current director of the archive, Marcela
Inch Calvimonte, for her prompt response in granting me permission to
reprint parts of articles written earlier in the archive's journal, *Anuario*.

I continued my vertical climb up the mountains to the most famous
peak of them all—Potosí. There, in the Archivo de la Casa de la Moneda, director Edgar Valda Martínez and his staff facilitated my access
to the truly awe-inspiring, leather-bound, gold-embossed, five- and six-
inch-deep (and very legible!) treasury accounts of the Cajas Reales. My
gratitude goes to this hardy group as well. Having flown dozens of
times between Cochabamba and Sucre and traveled by autobus from
Sucre to Potosí and back, I can assure the reader that the mountainous
terrain is as otherworldly and impressive as it is breathtaking—literally
and figuratively—and intimidating. That the colonial settlers and residents made this trip on horseback, in carriages, and driving mule teams
is a testimony to the guts, courage, and foolhardiness that must have
been a driving force for many of those early regional residents. And a
good number of the travelers did not survive, as the eerie paintings in
the Casa de la Moneda museum in Potosí bear witness.

The word *thank-you* cannot begin to convey the enormous gratitude and cariño I have for my Cochabambino colleagues and friends.
They have supported and encouraged my efforts over the years. Their
observations, their suggestions, and the many ideas exchanged over
such an extended period of time fueled much of the thinking that went
into this work. Some of them also allowed me access to their extended

libraries, while others invited me to present papers, or made contacts for publishing articles, or helped make contacts for ongoing and future research, to name just a few of their acts of generosity and professional consideration. I thank Father Mauricio Valcanover of the Franciscan order for introducing me to Mizque (both the place and archive indices) and for placing at my disposal invaluable transcripts of related documents he personally collected in the Archivo de Indias in Sevilla; Josep M. Barnadas, founder and executive secretary of the Academia Boliviana de Historia Eclesiástica; David Pereira Herrera, director of the Museo Arqueológico, Universidad Mayor de San Simón, and museum staff members Ramón Sanzetenea Rocha, María de los Angeles Muñoz, and Walter Sánchez; and José M. Gordillo Claure. I also wish to thank project assistants Freddy Zurita and Aida Tancara, who worked with me to decode and transcribe the extensive estate censuses used in the study.

And finally, my Cochabamba thank-you's would be incomplete without extending my warmest gratitude to others—families and friends who offered not only unflagging support but also the most welcomed and heartwarming hospitality that so characterizes "lo Cochabambino." They especially include the Araujos, Barnadas, Henkels, Millers, Muñozes, Pereiras, Rothes, and many others whom space does not allow me to list here. They know who they are, and they too have my fuertes abrazos. To all, un millón de gracias!

North of the equator, equally important acknowledgments are in order. The many months of intense archival research could not have been done without a Travel to Collections grant from the National Endowment for the Humanities as well as a Fulbright Research award. A year of writing was generously supported by an additional National Endowment for the Humanities Fellowship for College Teachers and Independent Scholars. And I thank Freddie Parker, former chair of the History Department at North Carolina Central University, for arranging a reduced teaching load to allow time for writing. Many people read and constructively commented on papers and chapters or attended meeting sessions where these works in progress were presented, including Woodrow Borah, Patrick Carroll, Franklin Knight, Jane Landers, Lydia Lindsay, Colin Palmer, Freddie Parker, Matthew

Restall, John TePaske, Ben Vinson III, Carlton Wilson, and the co-participants in the annual Carolina-Virginia-Georgia Colonial Latin American Seminars. I thank them all, and also William (Sandy) Darity, director of the Institute of African American Research, of which I am a fellow, for his support and encouragement. Thank-you also to Teresa Chapa, Latin American/Iberian Resources bibliographer, Walter Davis Library, the University of North Carolina at Chapel Hill; and Carlos Maza, general manager, Fondo de Cultura Económica del Peru, not only for his swift response granting permission to use the Guaman Poma frontispiece but for additional suggestions regarding the illustration. Thank-you also to Donald L. Stevens, editor of *The Americas*, for permission to use portions of "The African Diaspora in the Eastern Andes" in this work; and to Jerry Gershenhorn, Nicholas A. Robins, and Richard W. Slatta for their indispensable advice. My thanks also to Peggy Ellis for her patience, humor, and editing, processing, and typing skills over the years; and to Stacy S. Miller, who masterminded the ready-for-press copy of the manuscript. And finally, I extend a most appreciative bow to every editor and manager at the University of Nebraska Press who helped guide this book to fruition. Their hard work, encouragement, and understanding were indispensable.

Two very important people, John J. TePaske and Colin A. Palmer, deserve an additional portion of deeply felt gratitude and appreciation. I once again thank them for their stalwart support and encouragement for this project and their sound, critical, and extremely helpful advice at the many steps along the way.

And last but far from least, I want to thank my now considerably extended family for enduring the many years this work took with patience, wit, and humor. For Don, my archaeologist husband, soul mate, best friend, and critic/editor (don't forget the diacriticals, Lolita!), I save my deepest gratitude and love. It has been one fine adventure!

Blacks, Indians, and Spaniards in the Eastern Andes

Introduction

Spain's conquest of Peru brought together three peoples—Indian, African, and European—and propelled reconfigurations of land and labor systems to combine Old World arrangements with those of the New World. Imperial economic policy was based on a mercantilism that would intensify with the explosion of mining activity after the resounding 1545 silver strike in Potosí. Suffice it here to note that historians and economists continue to examine and debate this nearly legendary metallurgic production, which recent scholarship indicates a probability of even greater output than was previously held.[1] The force of this silver flow would manifest itself far and wide, in Europe and in the viceroyalties and *audiencias* (regional courts and jurisdictions) of South America. Like the conquest itself, directly and indirectly, silver's impact would bear upon indigenous, African, and European social, political, and economic structures and institutions. Depending on the circumstances of time, place, and market (both internal and external), it would reshape old and create new networks of trade and transport just as it would reshape traditional systems and create new ones of labor and production. Furthermore, neither conquest nor mining was a simplistic, one-dimensional cause-and-effect phenomenon vis-à-vis the victors and the vanquished, the masters and the slaves, the bosses and the exploited. New World peoples, those carriers of European imperial policy, would in turn respond to ongoing change, often reshaping their own social, economic, and political institutions to form their own part of what has been described as a new, hybrid, post-conquest world.[2]

This work is part homage and part thank-you to the late Thierry Saignes, whose poignantly titled *Los Andes orientales: Historia de un olvido* inspired the direction the book would take in its long journey into "the forgotten," those vast valleys, piedmonts, and lowlands of the eastern Andes. With much due respect to Saignes, I took the liberty of adding a further dimension to the concept of *olvido*. I included an additional group of people, African slaves and their descendants—*negros*, *mulatos*, *pardos*, *zambos*, and *morenos*—whose history in the region has been largely ignored, hidden, or in the words of Michel-Rolph Trouillott, "silenced." Their smaller numbers belie their importance, and theirs is the most forgotten history, without which the colonial history of the eastern Andes is incomplete.[3] Thus, in keeping with the spirit of my title, *Reclaiming the Forgotten*, I put Africans first in the sequence of population groups this work examines.

Further, the project exists within a larger theoretical and interpretive framework. My approach postulates that within the construct of a political economy that brought together the three population groups there existed an intersection and cross-fertilization of values, mores, and other sociocultural measurements that were present and identifiable in the workplace, in the legal system (including the courts), in the church, and in private lives. This phenomenon directly and indirectly influenced interrelations and identity in terms of race, ethnicity, class, and gender. It was a combination of forces that in turn interfaced with deeply conflicting notions (African, indigenous, and Spanish) of territoriality and power. The results manifested themselves in a colonial reality of massive contradictions and ambiguities in which in order to survive—and many did not—people reclaimed or reinvented themselves and prevailing institutions. While the larger picture acknowledges the political economy of region and empire, it also takes into consideration a moral economy that fueled a racism—itself laden with contradictions—that seeped into the region's societal fabric, the residues of which remain in place today.

The focus of this study is the multi-ecologically zoned province of Mizque, an early colonial settlement (designated a frontier) southeast of the Cochabamba Valley in the audiencia of Charcas. The administrative center for the jurisdiction was referred to as the Villa de Mizque long before it gained official status and recognition in 1603 as la Villa de Salinas del Río Pisuerga. However, as often as not the documents continued to refer to it as el pueblo or la Villa de Mizque, the name

South America. Geography and Earth Sciences Department, North Carolina Central University

by which it is called even today. This should not be confused with the Indian community el Pueblo de Mizque.[4]

In the past, a good part of the traditional literature pertaining to the early viceroyalty of Peru placed emphasis on a Pacific coast-to-highland trade-and-transport axis geared primarily for the Potosí silver-mining market, allotting little attention to the slopes and valleys of the eastern Andes. Prompted by growing evidence indicating considerable agricultural and commercial activity early on in these eastern reaches of the viceroyalty, both South and North American scholars began asking different questions regarding the area's prehistoric and colonial past.[5] Further, in recent decades a new wave of colonial and postcolonial scholarship, focused on region and based on rigorous methodology, has emerged from Cochabamba's Universidad Mayor de San Simón.[6]

More specifically, and central to the present discussion, historical economist Gustavo Rodríguez Ostria urged investigators to give closer scrutiny to regional networks and diversities. Rodríguez presented a somewhat different paradigm for the scholar who seeks more innovative explanations for historical processes involving the regions east of the Andean highlands. Here, he suggested a harder look at the equally important yet up to now relatively untapped intraregional systems. It is at the regional or local level, argued Rodríguez, that "local economies functioned independently from the 'locus' of Potosí."[7] While Rodríguez addressed nineteenth- and twentieth-century political and economic processes, his paradigm—as with all sound paradigms—is not bound by temporal or spatial limitations. Instead, his model can apply to an earlier time and place—specifically, sixteenth- and seventeenth-century Mizque—to explain a far earlier version of an active, important intraregional commerce, trade, and market system.

A careful search through the Archivo Histórico Municipal de Cochabamba and the much larger Archivo Nacional de Bolivia in Sucre disclosed an impressive array of documentation pertaining to sixteenth-, seventeenth-, and eighteenth-century Mizque. Yet this region, despite a number of local efforts,[8] remains in the shadow of the more systematically researched Lima-Potosí sphere. Current generalist Andean literature gives colonial Mizque a passing nod at best. Close scrutiny of the documents, however, reveals that Mizque—villa, jurisdiction, and region—deserves far greater attention than it has thus far received.

Cochabamba's municipal archive, for example, houses thousands of historical documents dating from the region's earliest colonial years up to the 1920s. The data relating to colonial Cochabamba surpass that of Mizque by some four to five times. Not surprisingly, the preponderance of historians and archivists investigating the Cochabamba material reflects this ratio. To date, far more scholars seek to explain Cochabamba's history than that of its neighbor. Yet the sheer volume of the Mizque documentation clearly indicates that this region, too, played a vital historical role in the geopolitical and economic axis under Spanish imperial rule. Careful examination of the Protocolos Notariales and Expedientes Coloniales richly underscores Mizque's significance.[9]

Compared to Cochabamba's municipal archives, the national archives in Sucre (formerly La Plata or Chuquisaca, seat of the colonial audiencia) hold an equally large—if not larger—body of documents pertaining to Mizque. This collection is referred to as the Archivo de Mizque and, along with the material collected in Cochabamba, provides most of the documentary evidence for this work. These sources are surpassed only by the Ramo de Tierras y Indios and Expedientes, also located in the National Archive, wherein land disputes, indigenous affairs, royal orders, and decrees relating to Mizque can be found. Both the Cochabamba and Sucre holdings are notarial in nature. They consist of dowries, last wills and testaments, partnerships, rental contracts, freight and transport contracts, and bills of sale, including the sale of African slaves. In addition, the collections contain the data-laden census records of rural estate residents as well as those of Indian communities. The long-term accounts of propertied orphan children under state-appointed guardianship also appear in these notarial documents, as do a wealth of court litigations. Many of these categories are serial in content and provide discernible patterns of change over time. These rich sources render a plethora of social, political, economic, and demographic history.[10]

The bountiful documentary resources reposited in the above archives notwithstanding, some caveats require explanation. First, in the course of my investigations, the subject of African slaves, their descendants, and all related data had yet to be afforded a separate section or branch in either archive. The National Archive now has a card catalog section specifically on this subject. Cochabamba's municipal archive does not, however, and immense time and effort are required to cull through countless documents to find any data pertaining to this group. Further, as rich in data as the court cases may be, they can be as frustrating as they are fascinating. For some of the litigations, many of which go on for years, the outcome is not available. Either the documentation was incomplete, the case was dropped, or the litigants settled out of court. Fortunately, most of the cases used in this work found resolution in the courts. Finally, the documents have gone through countless filters. The first round of filtering could occur at the time of the document's creation. Words, perceptions, labels, and intentions could be subtly (or not-so-subtly) altered by the scribe, the interpreter, the defense, or the prosecution, to name a few.[11] Then there is the selection process. Who decides which document or group of documents is preserved or discarded, and to how many of such selection processes are the documents submitted? It is little wonder that serial documentary runs and cross-references are so gratefully welcomed by the researcher.

Equally important for this work, we now know that Mizque's past extends far beyond the parameters of European contact and colonization. Indeed, current archaeological excavations and anthropological and ethnohistorical studies dramatically underscore the region's significance long before the arrival of the Europeans. Archaeologists and anthropologists often raise questions similar to those posed by social historians. The difference rests in the fact that the former must look elsewhere than the written word and seek answers from markedly different sources. The end results both inform and enrich the historian's task.

Chapter 1 sets the stage. It explains vast and complicated geography of the *corregimiento* (colonial province or jurisdiction) of Mizque, which contains many ecological niches. Here I examine the creation of a highland-lowland duality which itself became a misleading dichotomization and a two-dimensional stereotyping that ultimately led to an all-encompassing and dismissive perception of the eastern slopes, valleys, tropics, and plains, or in Thierry Saignes's timeless words, "the forgotten." Based on archaeological, ethnographical, and ethnohistorical studies, the chapter identifies the region's many indigenous ethnicities and chronologies and explains the advent of the Inca, soon to be followed by the incursions of the Spaniards. I then discuss the many Spanish expeditions into the eastern Andes, a temperate and fertile region that Spaniards soon realized contained immense economic potential to be exploited for themselves and Spain. Early explorations and pacification occurred unevenly and sometimes disastrously. The

Europeans (including the first missionaries) had no concept of the diversity of these ethnic groups or of their aggressive determination to resist pacification. These groups were eventually quashed sufficiently to permit the emergence of a European settlement.

Chapter 2 describes the founding of Mizque in 1603, officially renamed the Villa de Salinas del Río Pisuerga. It explains the rationale for the region's settlement and development and the extension of its territorial boundaries. This chapter discusses the settlement process, the activities of the Roman Catholic Church, and the reconfigurations of labor and land use to better serve the Spaniards' political economy. It closes with a detailed explanation of a major bridge-construction project, significant in several ways. It reveals the political and economic drive of the area's leadership, discloses the actual machinations of how a civic plan for a larger good is transformed from a vision to a reality, and provides a rare glimpse into how a regional town center actually functioned.

Chapter 3 is a continuation of the preceding one, but with a closer look at the area's resources and agricultural potential, of which the Spaniards promptly took advantage, as the hacienda, vineyard, livestock ranch (essential for any successful colonial agribusiness enterprise), sugar plantation, coca field, and mining transactions and litigations testify. Here the full impact of the region's multiple ecological zones becomes apparent, as realized in the diversity of its products and the rapid increase in agricultural production units. The latter came in all sizes, including some very large, actively functioning estates that comprised several units of production. The units were not necessarily contiguous but were created instead for the ecological environment best suited for production. One salient issue pertaining to the estate system in the eastern Andes was the nearly total absence of the *mayorazgo* (entailed estate retained by family for several generations). However, rapid land turnover did not prevent the emergence of a European propertied class, which, in the restructuring of social and political traditions, was able to exert its will over the majority. This chapter also discusses the labor force required in the region's production activities, including African slaves and their many descendants, and of course, the indigenous population.

Chapter 4 looks closely at production itself—planting and harvesting, processing goods for market, and transporting these goods. It also gives *mayordomos* (the hacienda or chácara overseers) the voice that is not often heard. In Mizque, the marked turnover of estates existed alongside an equally notable turnover of mayordomos. Through a sampling of available estate records I was able to arrive at not only a list of market prices (itself an invaluable measure for the general cost of living and ultimately for living standards per se) but also market destinations, both intraregional and interregional, for area products. The chapter further underscores the necessity of available livestock, and purposefully includes some of Viceroy Toledo's decrees on the subject to make the point. Coca production continues to receive attention here as elsewhere throughout the work. This plant's impact on the history and culture of the region has acquired a magnitude far beyond the proportion its benign, mildly stimulating little leaf would indicate. This chapter also explains local mining activities, a discussion that will no doubt raise more questions than it answers. An enigma exists concerning area mining, since we have numerous references to this activity yet no documentation on actual yield.

Chapter 5 deals extensively with the African slaves and their descendants. While this population group is referred to in every chapter, consistent with the conceptual organization of this book and its division into three thematic parts, I wanted to devote a separate chapter to a detailed account of their history. By doing so I highlight the fact that they were another integral group in the eastern Andes—recognizable and functional—as was the indigenous population, and as the Europeans would also become. I have borrowed a term related to the subject from recent Mexican scholarship, which I have used in another work, as well as on occasion in the pages to come. The presence of Africans in Mesoamerica is referred to as Mexico's third "root." I think the analogy is excellent. It is a fact that harbors no ambiguity or ambivalence. It connotes recognition and does not allow for silencing or forgetting. That is how I wish to present the history of Africans in the region. To do so, in this chapter I briefly trace the dual diaspora of Africans. First, they assisted in Spain's military conquest of Peru, and more specifically in the campaigns to explore, pacify, and settle the eastern reaches of the Andes. In the second diaspora, kidnapped, enslaved Africans were involuntarily transported from Africa to the port of Buenos Aires and ultimately sold into the Corregimiento de Mizque, where they were needed to meet a growing market demand now juxtaposed with a shortage of indigenous labor. I go on to explain the population mixture that began within the first generation of imported Africans, to emerge as a mostly African-indigenous group that grew exponentially. Freedom was attained less due to manumission and more because the children of these mixed unions were born out of slavery—that is, they acquired by law the legal status of the mother, sometimes mixed, often indigenous, and often free.

Chapter 6 focuses on Indian affairs. This ordering of the chapter sequences is not intended to imply a lessening of the enormous significance of the indigenous populations and their contributions to New World cultures. The vast and still-growing body of scholarship on the subject belies any suggestion to the contrary. While this chapter gives less weight to the Mizque and Pocona Indian *repartimientos* (larger administrative units of tribute-paying Indian laborers), it does elaborate on the less-explored lowland ethnic warrior groups, touching upon their lifestyles and even more on their resistance to Spanish rule. The Yuma, Yuracaré, and others were a perpetual thorn in the side of the imperial plan through the mid-1700s. From there I move on to a discussion of coca's history and its place in the area's moral economy. I am able to demonstrate that the Spanish imperial economic pressures were far more egregious and life-threatening to the indigenous population than any economic system imposed by their Inca predecessors. Royal decrees calling for better treatment went unheeded. However, as with other controversial colonial issues, that of coca production also was rife with contradictions. Yet the fact remains that members of the indigenous community paid the highest toll in the name of coca. Royal tribute demands consistently exceeded community Indians' ability to pay. Little wonder that people fled their communities and attached themselves to the *haciendas* (large agricultural estates) and *chácaras* (smaller agricultural units), only to leave these production units frequently and at will. I then discuss landholding claims brought by indigenous communities and how these were handled by the litigants and their representatives. The Europeans almost always won their claims on indigenous lands, although the Indians occasionally received some modicum of justice, however slight. The chapter moves on to discuss the significance of *curacas* (indigenous leadership) and the several role transformations experienced by Mizque's native elite. This is followed by an analysis of the controversial issue of indigenous ethnicity, which is discussed mostly within the context of hacienda and chácara labor, where a wide range of ethnic groups—albeit in modest numbers—were represented. The Mizque chácaras also provide innovative data concerning *forasteros* (outsider labor), or more specifically the absence until the mid-1600s of the designated term so widely used elsewhere. The forasteros, like the local Indian community population, came to the haciendas in droves and departed in equally impressive numbers.

Chapter 7, the final chapter of the text, adds a human profile to the thousands of actors, victims, carriers, implementers, and exploiters of the political and economic forces—African, indigenous, and Spanish—that determined the course of people's lives in the Corregimiento de Mizque. I focus here on the experience of African slaves and their descendants. I then take a closer look at diseases—particularly malaria, but others as well—that struck the local populations unsparingly, except for a respite during part of the seventeenth century, only to rebound in the eighteenth century and resulting in yet another demographic transformation, due not only to high mortality rates but also to people fleeing to healthier zones. This reactive movement should come as no surprise, given the local cultural tradition of movement that is revealed throughout these chapters. The chapter also explores issues of day-to-day life, looking into family life, treatment in the workplace, and civic and political participation in terms of regional development. Most of all, this final chapter explains how people of all races and combinations thereof interacted with each other, as is vividly illuminated in their wills and testaments, litigations, and court cases. In these instances they acquire their own personas as redemption seekers, generous providers, witnesses, victims, defendants, and accusers. The larger issues of control and resistance lurk behind many of these cases; yet just when it was least expected, justice was occasionally served. The chapter continues with an assessment of slave treatment and slave response, usually in the many forms of resistance. This resistance is detailed here in terms of fugitive action, but in fact it culminated with the ultimate and usually (but not always) irrevocable form of resistance: freedom through birth and the attainment of the mother's legal status. This serves to explain the large mixed population of African origins that inhabited Mizque's corregimiento in the late eighteenth century. It also provides the context of the final discussion on the region's colonial subculture of livestock ranches, ranch owners, cowboys, and other ranch hands, many of whom were black (slave and free) and mulato (almost always free). Here I demonstrate yet another form of agency and assertion, this time via occupational roles and the additional mobility and independence inherent in these roles.

Before launching into the first chapter, I wish to make some important clarifications relating to geographic locations, racial appellations, the use of Spanish words and phrases, and other related issues. First, geographic locations and place-names in this region can be confusing. In some instances a name can refer simultaneously to a particular hacienda and a particular town or community. It can refer to an area that traverses multiple ecological niches that are not necessarily contiguous. Thus I might refer to the town of Pocona, the Indian community of Pocona (contiguous), and the coca fields of Pocona located in a discontiguous, distant, and ecologically distinct zone. I try to make these distinctions as clear as possible in the text.

Spanish labels for race will be used in the text as they appear in the documents and will use the Spanish spelling, particularly when I am drawing from or referring to specific documentary evidence. I think this is historically more accurate. Many of these and other Spanish terms eventually made their way into the English language, but I think it is important to know their origins. Thus I use the term *negro*, which refers to a black slave and later (somewhat ambiguously) to a black person of uncertain legal status (to be discussed in the text). I also use the Spanish terms *mulato* (no doubt derived from the occupational role of the all-important mule team driver, filled by some African slaves but mostly by their descendants), *pardo*, *zambo*, and *moreno* to identify various mixtures of the African, European, and indigenous populations as perceived by the Europeans at the time (also to be discussed in detail later). These terms are italicized upon first citation in the text and are immediately defined. They also appear in the glossary. Subsequent appearances of these terms are left in non-italic type but retain the Spanish spelling throughout. Otherwise, I use the term *Africans* when referring to the first generation of imported slaves. Sometimes I will use the phrase "people of partly African origins" to indicate that they mixed with other groups. I occasionally use the English *black*, as I do *Indian*, but for the latter I more often use the Spanish *indio* or *india* or the terms *indigenous* or *native*. The purpose here is to be contextually true to the documents without distracting the reader with unnecessary repetition.

I have tried to be consistent with other frequently used Spanish terms for which English translations are neither adequate nor true to the important nuances of language and culture. I use *hacienda* and *chácara* (respectively, complex and relatively more simple units of production) interchangeably, exactly as they are referred to in the records. Other units of production discussed at length include *viñas* (vineyards) and *estancias* (livestock ranches) in the *corregimiento*, a term I also use frequently and which refers to the entire, far-reaching territorial jurisdiction that was colonial Mizque. Finally, when the Andean term *curaca* (indigenous elite leadership) appears in the documents, I use it in the text. If the Spanish-imposed word *cacique* is used for the same leadership, I use that. Otherwise, I will use curaca when referring to regional indigenous leaders.

In addition, direct documentary quotes are presented in their original form in uncertain spelling, abbreviations, and no added accents or other diacritical marks. Otherwise the text itself uses modern spelling, full names, and required diacriticals. For example, although usually written in lowercase in the colonial documents, the titles for lady and gentleman—Don and Doña—will be capitalized in the text. Further, italicized English words in the text indicate my emphasis. Finally, the majority of references to currency in this work involve the *peso corriente* (the silver peso of 8 reales), which I simply refer to as the *peso*. When the *peso ensayado* (the silver peso of 12 reales) is used, I make specific note of it in the text.

I

Reclaiming Mizque's Forgotten

1. The Landscape and Its People

THIS CHAPTER EXPLAINS the economic and political significance of the Corregimiento de Mizque's geographic and ecological conditions dating from pre-Inca sequences. It discusses the indigenous ethnic groups and their response to Inca and soon European imperial incursions, the latter of which sometimes resulted in disaster. The Europeans had little concept of the diversity of the ethnic peoples they hoped to pacify and even less of the latter's determination to repel pacification. The Spanish warriors-cum-pacifiers persisted in their campaigns, amassing *encomiendas* (entrustment of Indians for tribute and labor purposes) and key political posts, setting the stage early on for the corregimiento's emergence as an important regional trade center.

Mizque's Geography and Prehistory

The eastern flanks of the Andes cover vast regions of distinct geographic and ecological zones. Here the eastern mountain ranges—the Cordillera Oriental with its bleak altiplano and puna of scrub and grass—sweep downward to yield many fertile subpuna valley systems boasting open plains and temperate climates. The best known of these valleys, Chuquisaca and Cochabamba, lie roughly 9,000 to 8,600 feet above sea level, respectively. Another, less-known valley system, and the subject of this study, is the valley of Mizque ("sweet" in Quechua), referred to in the colonial period as the Corregimiento de Mizque. This region ranges from 1,000 to 7,000 feet above sea level and is located southeast of the valley of Cochabamba. Today most of this colonial jurisdiction has been redistributed into various districts and departments, including Cochabamba, Campero, Carrasco, Mizque, and parts of Santa Cruz, to name a few. These eastern reaches also contain much steeper, tropical river valleys called the *yungas* (hot lowland areas) located near La Paz and also in the Cochabamba-Mizque valley regions.

Moving beyond the subpunas and their adjacent tropics, the terrain continues to change into the *pie de monte* or *montaña* (loosely, foothills). From there the landscape again changes to become flat, open plains: to the north the Llanos de Mojos and its extensive environs, and to the east-southeast the Llanos del Chaco, which includes the Santa Cruz region, also pivotal to this work. These latter plains, in turn, extend from the Santa Cruz zone beyond what today would be recognized as the borders of Brazil, Argentina, and Paraguay and include the vast Pilcomayo River basin.[1]

Until recently, little was known about the history and archaeology of these eastern reaches, the furthest of which remained shrouded in mystery and legend long after the arrival of the Europeans. We do know that borders and concepts of frontiers and territoriality are recent impositions, having little or nothing to do with the reality of much earlier inhabitants and their territorial holdings. The works of Alfred Métraux and, later, Thierry Saignes's continue to open many doors to historians, archaeologists, and anthropologists. We now know that the Inca conquest, although it occurred relatively late in the Inca's campaign of expansion, extended deep into the eastern lowlands—far beyond limits assumed in the literature. Saignes also effectively demonstrated the dual nature of the Andean world and the essential role of its "tropical other." This eastern other was occupied by the Guarani, as well as the nearly legendary Mojo, Chuncho, and Chiriguano, whose fearful reputations were established long before the arrival of the Spaniards. Métraux in particular established a strong Guarani-Chiriguano line of descent and subsequent subjugation of the more numerous Chané people. Saignes amplified the discussion, arguing that the early chroniclers had no notion of indigenous ethnicity and must be held accountable for lumping these distinct groups together as one and making their designated names synonymous with "Chiriguano," or "savage" (in its most pejorative sense).[2]

This duality became so entrenched, continued Saignes, the either-or mentality so fixed in the Andean worldview, that no viable term for the "in between" subpuna valleys existed in either Aymara or Quechua to name this intermediary "no man's land." Nor did the subsequent Spanish conqueror-invaders manage to find appropriate terms in Castilian. There were no explicit words to ascribe to the lower slopes and valleys of a mountain range. The not entirely appropriate term *pie de monte*, Saignes argued, was in itself somewhat pejorative, simultaneously all-encompassing and dismissive of the eastern slopes, valleys, tropics, and plains. I will use the term *montaña*. To confuse matters more, this pervasive and misleading dichotomization, particularly in earlier influential works, served only to perpetuate the two-dimensional stereotyping. Thus, the peoples of the central Andes are designated a historicity of which the "marginal" peoples of the Amazon are unworthy. Saignes argued that this bipolar division and its attendant mythology can find its roots in Inca territorial policy and the drawing of enemy lines. The Spaniards merely reinforced what already existed. Meanwhile, that intermediate area between the two opposing poles—the eastern Andes—has been completely overlooked and designated the "olvido."[3]

Fortunately, Saignes's "lost" eastern Andes are now the focus of important, ongoing studies. In a burst of investigative activity, local and foreign archaeologists, historians, and anthropologists are searching for answers to questions raised by Métraux, Saignes, and others. For example, archaeological evidence now supports cultural traditions in the present-day Cochabamba and Mizque valley systems dating back to 10,000 BC if not earlier. This predates the later altiplano Tiahuanaco and Inca states or empires. The pottery-making agriculturists lived in stratified, hierarchical societies and maintained regional networks and exchange systems. These very early coexisting cultures appear to have been ethnically homogeneous and enjoyed stable economies. The evidence also indicates they were influenced by people of both the montaña and the Amazon regions. Further, they also had contact with highland cultures and beyond, all the way to the Pacific coast. Clearly, they were active participants in an ongoing dynamic of migration and exchange and in all likelihood served as intermediaries for the various groups with whom they had contact.[4]

From yet another temporal/spatial perspective, anthropologist-ethnohistorian Raimund Schramm, looking specifically to the Cochabamba-Mizque valley systems, questioned European-imposed classifications of indigenous ethnicity, territoriality, and frontier. He found that several peaceful and warrior ethnic groups, often interconnected, existed in Mizque's eastern montaña long before Inca imperialism propelled its conquering armies eastward. Further, some of these groups interacted with later peoples brought in as *mitmaqkuna* (colonizer/laborers) under the Inca's expansionist colonization policy. These bold bow-and-arrow people resisted Inca conquest, particularly in the montaña zones and in the more tropical lowland reaches of the region known today as the Chapare. Further, many of these groups migrated out of the "jungle" and made their homes elsewhere, sometimes permanently. Moreover, European-designated frontiers and boundaries marking specific rivers or mountain ranges as territorial divisions did not exist in earlier times. More critically, the concept of frontier did not exist. Instead, these lines of demarcation materialized in the 1580s and later, as the present study will establish.[5]

In fact, archaeological investigations indicate that many of the fortresses, boundaries, and so-called frontiers were only recently created by the Inca rulers to protect their nearby conquered colonies. These territorial demarcations imposed by the Inca often resulted in ongoing rebellions by the above local groups resisting the Inca and defending their own territories. Later, rather than succumb to the tribute exactions imposed by the Spaniards, they fled deeper into the Chapare, with which they were quite familiar.[6] It is also clear that although many ethnic groups resisted the Inca entirely, others who were subjected to colonization and relocation found ways to derail imperial policy. They chose *la huida* (flight) and simply returned to their places of earlier origin.[7]

By 1500 Inca troops had conquered the outlying valleys of Cochabamba, Pocona, and Mizque. To these three locations they transferred the Cavi, Cota, and Chuy, respectively, to guard against the "savages." Subsequently, they pushed on to establish outposts in the plains of Guapay (today Santa Cruz). This massive reorganization and relocation of ethnic groups also served to fend off the Chiriguano. (Viceroy Toledo's later reorganization was not new to the local ethnic populations.) Not all the ethnic groups returned to their origins, which would account for the presence of the Churumata and the Charca in Totora (then part of Mizque) and of the fierce Moya in Aiquile. But as most scholars concur, the Inca were not always successful in their expansionist strikes and colonization efforts, particularly in the eastern zones. Clearly, inhabitants of the slopes resisted the Inca troops and held out against repeated attacks until the arrival of the Spaniards in 1532. In fact, the landing of the Europeans caught the Inca off guard, forcing them to hastily abandon all military expansion and fortress building. The Inca, of course, had their own complicated history, as the growing body of revisionist literature postulates. Ethnohistorian Catherine Julien's interpretations of this literature puts to rest a number of traditionally held misunderstandings concerning the nature of the Inca "empire" and thus the nature of Inca history. Her cautionary alert to the "filters of language and culture" serves the scholarship well.[8]

Underscoring the fragility of Inca defense in these southeastern territories, scholars have discussed the impressive Paraguayan Tupi-Guarani invasions. For example, mounting a campaign of thousands of warriors, they easily broke through Inca defenses, entered through Tarabuco/Pocona, and sacked all of the state-run enterprises. Clearly, this particular historical "segment" (Julien's term) of the empire had peaked and was stretching its limits, itself the victim of an expansionism now "too rapid and superficial."[9]

Thus, counter to the traditional portrayal of the east as a "no man's land" beyond which lay a vast wasteland, the reality was quite the opposite. The eastern valleys, slopes, rain forests, and plains were inhabited by a broad range of peoples. Some were very powerful and influential non-state groups, others less so. Individually or collectively they traversed the entire region by choice or by force, crossing back and forth across the Cordillera, making their way up or down the eastward range of ecological stations, arranging themselves (or being rearranged) according to internal needs and external forces. They would carry out patterns of multiethnicity, movement, migration, and interregional contact as their ancestors did thousands of years before them and as their descendants continue to do up to recent times.

The Arrival of the Spaniards
The Spaniards under Francisco Pizarro brought the Inca's imperial machine to an eventual halt, but not without resistance. The conquerors invaded from the north and captured the doomed Atahualpa in his

highland domain of Cajamarca in 1532. Yet the Spaniards themselves faced Indian sieges, civil wars, rebellions, and assassinations of most of the key conquest leaders and other important figures. This chaos continued almost unabated for at least twenty years.[10]

Yet at the same time, despite the constant turmoil, European explorations and settlements proceeded virtually unchecked. In 1534 the Spanish king, Charles I (who also reigned simultaneously as Charles I of the Holy Roman Empire), divided the Inca empire into two parts, one (New Castile) to be governed by Francisco Pizarro, the other (New Toledo) by Diego de Almagro. Later in the year, Spanish headquarters moved from near Cuzco in the highlands down to Lima on the Pacific coast. In July 1535, Pizarro and Almagro, perhaps caught up in the full implications of the future potential that the conquest of the Inca empire offered, set aside their growing antagonisms and jealousies. Almagro was dispatched on an *entrada* (expedition) to explore New Toledo and to reach Chile. It would be on this ill-fated expedition, as Josep M. Barnadas points out, that the Europeans first set foot in that vast and complex eastern region, soon to be named Charcas. But, as this historian argues, others were already approaching Charcas from an entirely different direction.[11]

Along with the continual history of ethnic invasions and wars emanating out of the Paraguayan/Amazonian front, a new genre of invader emerged. Paraguayan Europeans were competing for territorial gains and personal wealth against their Lima-Cuzqueño counterparts, who, driven by the same forces, were coming from the opposite direction. The Paraguayans would see their future in the "west," the Lima-Cuzqueños saw theirs in the "east." During the early years, both sides aimed to establish outposts in the fabled plains and rain forests. According to Barnadas, the first known person to make it up the Paraná River to the mouth of the Paraguay (1526–30) was Venetian explorer S. Gaboto. This, of course, was two years before the Inca were defeated at Cajamarca. Gaboto not only managed to get along with the Indians but also established a fort near present-day Rosario. Propelled by tales of vast silver yields and other wonders, others followed, and over the ensuing decade they would traverse further distances from departure point Asunción (founded in 1537). The Paraguayans continued westward explorations, entering and establishing outposts in the Chiquitos and Mojos region by the 1540s.[12]

By the 1550s, Ñuflo de Chávez, a particularly astute and ambitious Paraguayan, had a grander scheme in mind. In 1559 he founded Nueva Asunción on the eastern banks of the Rio Guaypay (soon to be known as the Río Grande, which will figure prominently in later discussions), and early in 1561 he established a second city, Santa Cruz de la Sierra. Still hungry for more territorial appropriations, Chávez pushed deeper into the Charcas region, greatly worrying royal authorities in Lima. While Paraguay laid claim to the Chiquitos, Mojos, and Santa Cruz regions and made attempts to colonize, Viceroy Cañete skillfully incorporated these regions into the Audiencia de Charcas and placed the ambitious Chávez (by now in the process of breaking off his Paraguayan connections) in charge. Most scholars agree that regardless of his loyalties and self-interests, Ñuflo de Chávez was responsible for opening up and colonizing the region. While most Paraguayans continued to perceive Santa Cruz as an extension of Asunción, the Peruvians saw it as part of Charcas and the audiencia's crucial line of defense against the unyielding Chiriguano and other aggressive ethnic groups.[13]

Looking again to the Lima-Cuzco nexus, as noted earlier, regardless of ongoing warfare on virtually all sides, Pizarro remained determined to gain access to all Inca wealth near and far. Thanks to Almagro's fortuitous return from the failed Chilean entrada, the siege under which the Inca held Pizarro and his men (1536–37) was ended, the Spaniards were rescued, and the Inca were defeated. Yet the old enmity between Pizarro and Almagro resurfaced, and a fierce battle erupted between the two and their respective followers (War of the Salinas, 1537–38) from which the Pizarro faction emerged victorious (temporarily), the Almagro faction defeated (temporarily), and Almagro the senior dead (permanently).

All the while, Pizarro continued to send forth entradas. In July 1538, according to Barnadas, his brother Hernando and two hundred men, facing again impressive Indian resistance, made their way toward Lake Titicaca. This was the expedition that came across the first silver mines, giving credence to the nearly legendary Inca wealth, and of things to come. The third Pizarro brother, Gonzalo, took over command of this expedition (Hernando returned to headquarters), only to face a severe setback when completely surrounded and cut off by aggressive Charcas warriors. Brother Hernando and six hundred additional troops came to the rescue: the siege was broken, and the Indians were defeated.[14]

Within a few months, efforts at occupation and settlement gained momentum. Charcas was conquered and Chuquisaca (La Plata) was founded in 1538, Huamanga in 1539, Arequipa in 1540, Huanuco in 1542 (the same year Francisco Pizarro died on the battlefield), and La Paz in 1548. As soon as the Spaniards caught on to Potosí's vast mineral potential in 1545, the silver rush was on and Potosí mushroomed. Yet the Villa Imperial did not function as an official town until 1561, a pattern we shall see elsewhere in the settlement process. Cochabamba and Tarija gained official recognition in 1572 and 1575, respectively, although the Cochabamba region was conquered much earlier, in 1538, causing many of the area's ethnic groups to flee into the montaña.[15]

All the while, one after another, expeditions fanned down the eastern slopes despite the nonstop turmoil in the highlands—or perhaps, as some have argued, because of it. The entradas also served as a safety valve for the defeated parties, who quickly departed from the area of conflict heeding the beckoning calls of the fabled "El Dorado," the origins of which can probably be traced back to the waves of migrating Guaraní coming out of the Amazon (Paraguay/Brazil) and making their way into Charcas territory, where they eventually became known as the Chiriguano. They never abandoned their belief in the garden of Eden, known to them as "Paititi," a myth their descendants passed along to the intrepid Europeans.[16] Thus began the three-hundred-year search for El Dorado that spanned the entire hemisphere and came to rest, finally, in the great gold rush of California.

Of the many entradas in the fruitless search for treasure in the eastern wilderness, only two were successful. The discovery of the Carabaya mines in the lowlands north of Lake Titicaca led to the settlement of San Juan del Oro in 1538. These would be the only mines found in ongoing quests for the elusive ores. The only other successful expedition was the one led by Chávez out of Asunción. Apparently, of the forty-five known expeditions into the montaña between 1537 and 1635, only six originated in the Rio de la Plata/Asunción region, and these were among the earliest. The Paraguayans obviously gave up the search for their fabled garden of Eden early on. The Peruvian groups continued unabated—sometimes yearly, sometimes every couple of years or so—and launched some forty expeditions down into the Amazonian montaña. All of these expeditions originated in Charcas.[17] The failure rate was impressive, which makes equally impressive the determined perseverance, for almost one hundred years, to explore and attempt to settle the region. The military led thirty-one of these forays, the missionaries nine. While one-quarter were search-and-return missions, the remainder fell into other categories: military combats/defeats, settlement/destruction, settlement/abandonment, and Indian massacres. Six of the expeditions at least managed to establish way stations if nothing more.[18]

Other forces working against the Spaniards, including unbearable heat, dehydration, starvation, insect bites, and getting lost, only added to the hazards of relentless Indian warfare. But equally important, two other major obstacles played into the equation and seriously impeded European success in their push into the montaña. First, they brought along with them their characteristic internal rivalries, jealousies, and competitiveness established in the early days of conquest and cemented in the civil wars—almost a pathology in this hostile wilderness. Some expeditions disintegrated because of internal rife and factionalism; others succumbed to out-and-out warfare, with rivaling expeditions competing for the mythical lost Edens. These destructive rivalries were not restricted to the more remote eastern reaches; even the more temperate zones of Pocona and Cochabamba bore witness to internecine conflict as late as 1546.[19]

Further, the ethnic montaña groups had a history of conflict among themselves and—of particular relevance to the present discussion—an ongoing enmity with the highland Indians that predated the arrival of the Europeans. Thus arose an unexpected negative outcome of the Peruvian entradas into the montaña: thousands of highland Indian auxiliaries accompanying the Spaniards lost their lives to their longtime lowland "savage" enemies.[20]

In addition, many of the Indian groups manipulated the entrada efforts of both the military and the ecclesiastic groups. They aligned themselves with whichever expedition served their own political interests, then disengaged from these liaisons with equal ease when Spanish backup no longer served its purpose. For example, in terms of the missionary endeavors, indigenous people adhered to some of the Christian doctrine when it suited them, but they often used the missionaries for their own political purposes. For the most part, the missionaries came up shorthanded in the montaña. The Indians benefited from the material goods proffered by the padres, but they were never "pacified" in the manner accomplished during that same time period in northern Mexico.[21]

The search for Paititi would lose its pulse over time, even for the determined Peruvians. For them the quest for gold had proved fruitless, but the search for El Dorado and the attempts at settlement and Christianization were not entirely futile. In the process, other key but lesser-known areas—the *valles internos* (interior valleys) of the montaña—emerged as regions ripe for settlement. And here is where we will move away from the polarizing highland-lowland dichotomy and give a close scrutiny to a major component of Saignes's "no man's land," specifically, the valley region of Mizque.

While the explorations lost momentum during the post–civil war years, pacification continued unabated. Imperial administrators had two objectives in mind. Concern over containment of the so-called Chiriguano remained paramount. "Chiriguano" now became the label under which early colonial authorities lumped together all Indian "savages" who posed a threat to colonization.[22] A related and equally important mission fueled royal efforts to control aggressive Indians: settlement and colony building. These goals were best reflected soon after the civil wars in the *encomienda* (entrustment of Indians) and settlement policies implemented by Pedro de la Gasca (1547–50) and Viceroy Cañete (1556–60).[23]

Among those who best reflect the established profiles of the early *encomendero* (holder of the entrustment)-cum-settler, three families stand out: the Chavezes, the Cazorlas, and the Paniagua de Loaysas.[24] All three, in one way or another and to a greater or lesser degree, had some kind of involvement in the Mizque region. And because these families were instrumental in the shaping and evolving of what became, first, an important colonial frontier in the eyes of the Spanish state, and soon a significant regional center, their histories of adventures, exploits, and achievements are relevant to this study.

The Ñuflo de Chávez Family

General Ñuflo de Chávez's pacification and settlement efforts in the eastern regions in the 1550s and 1560s—Chiquitos and Mojos, and, in particular, the founding of Santa Cruz—and his subsequent murder in an Indian camp are all well documented.[25] Less well known are the feats and exploits of his sons Álvaro and Francisco. In a 1585 testimony petitioning reward for service to the king, Álvaro states that, following the lead of his father and his older brother, he too had launched a military career to serve the crown. At the age of sixteen he was already participating in pacification campaigns in the Santa Cruz area. Joining forces with Santa Cruz governor Lorenzo Suárez de Figueroa and, later, with another patriarch, Hernando de Cazorla, Álvaro conducted several attacks against the Chiriguano.[26] Clearly, his campaigns, like those noted in the testimony of others requesting rewards, were as fierce, bloody, and ruthless as the raids mounted against the Spaniards by the Indians.

Álvaro and his many witnesses boasted of how he, like his counterparts in rank and status, not only volunteered his services to the crown but personally financed his campaigns as well. He not only recruited his own soldiers but also fed and equipped them. In one of his accounts, Álvaro describes how, in one retaliatory maneuver, he and forty soldiers caught an entire Chiriguano settlement off guard one night. He single-handedly killed the cacique, Caripuy, who apparently had earlier led a particularly ferocious attack against the Europeans. Álvaro and his men then proceeded to massacre as many Indians as they could, seized their European weapons, and took fifty Indians captive. They also took with them some Indians who had been enslaved by the defeated Chiriguano as well as "un negro." Finally, Álvaro and his group destroyed their crops and burned the settlement to the ground, leaving behind only a few, mostly wounded victims. It was during these *entradas* that Álvaro rose to the rank of captain.[27]

Álvaro's older brother Francisco, also a captain, posted similar testimonials of his brave deeds. He had joined forces with General Don
Gabriel Paniagua de Loaysa to fight Indians in the Santa Cruz region.
He dutifully responded to calls for help to chase English corsairs ("los
luteranos") off the shores of Lima *and* to go after and capture the
runaway black slaves ("los negros cimarrones") who had aided and
abetted the invaders. These exploits alone had taken a good two years,
not to mention a serious toll on his health. He, too, had financed all of
these exploits out of his own pocket. He, too, felt deserving of reward
for his heroic deeds.[28]

Heroism, of course, is relative. In discussing European atrocities
against the rebellious native population, Barnadas underscores his argument by citing friar T. de San Martín, who wrote to the king in 1550.
According to this account, one F. de Chávez (brother Francisco?) under
orders from Francisco Pizarro to retaliate the slaughter of an avaricious
and abusive Spaniard, allegedly rounded up and killed, one by one,
about six hundred Indians. In response, the children of the slaughtered
Indians asked to be baptized and of their own accord, upon reaching
the place of baptism, deliberately tried to drown themselves in the wa-
ters. To which the horrified friar added, "He was rewarded with an
encomienda!"[29]

In fact, the whole purpose of Francisco and Álvaro's litany of services they and their father had rendered to the crown was to seek
what the family considered adequate reward. All three, they repeatedly claimed, had not only contributed their services but had also borrowed heavily from their own resources in the pacification of the new
colony. Each son apparently had been compensated, but according to
their testimonies it was not nearly enough. The crown already had
awarded Álvaro 500 pesos in yearly *renta* (fixed income) and Francisco 1,400 pesos in Indians.[30] Francisco died in Lima, apparently having never regained full health after chasing after Englishmen and runaways. Álvaro persisted, now being the sole (and relatively young)
provider for his widowed mother and two sisters. Key to the larger
theme here, throughout his testimonials Álvaro and his witnesses continually refer to his reward of the Corregimiento de Mizque granted
by the king in 1586. They also consistently play down this post as

somewhat impoverished and insufficient to compensate for all that the Chávez men had done for the crown. This became a more immediate issue after Francisco's death. And indeed, Álvaro finally convinced the authorities of his family's meritorious conduct, and the crown further rewarded him with a 5,000-peso fixed annual income. Alas, he died in Madrid, the newly acquired *merced* (grant of land) actually in hand, while apparently preparing his return to Peru.[31]

The Fernando de Cazorla Family

The following profile of the Cazorla family reveals another dimension of Mizque's emergence as a significant regional center. Fernando de Cazorla Narváez, grand old patriarch and possibly one of the last survivors of the earliest civil war days, submitted an impressive list of accomplishments in his testimonials.[32] Between 1587 and 1590, in requests for recognition and reward for fifty years of service to the king, he reminded the authorities that he had paid for all of the expenses that those many years of participation had involved. He fought Indians at the Isla de la Puna in retaliation for their killing of Bishop Valverde. This was no doubt the same Bishop Valverde famous (or infamous) who, as required by the Spanish king, accompanied Pizarro and his men into the battlefield at Cajamarca. There, facing the Inca Atahualpa and his unarmed warriors, the bishop released Pizarro from any obligation to protect the king's "vassals," thereby unleashing the forces of conquest that brought the Inca empire to its knees. Cazorla answered other calls to battle whenever needed, joining up with other notable warriors such as the aforementioned Captain Francisco de Chávez. He established settlements. He traversed dangerous enemy territories to meet his obligations. And to Fernando de Cazorla, the enemy threat was twofold, comprising not only hostile ethnic groups but also the followers of Gonzalo Pizarro. In fact, in revenge for his loyalty to Viceroy Blasco Ñunez Bela, on one occasion Fernando barely escaped garroting in the hands of Pizarrists. Another time, these same rebels forced him into exile. He managed to return, only to be severely wounded in another battle.[33]

Apparently, Fernando de Cazorla was on close terms with the viceroy and was frequently at his side when not waging battle with the enemy forces, be they Indian or Spanish. The testimonies refer to the many rewards the viceroy had already bestowed upon Cazorla for the above and many other deeds. After the civil wars, Cazorla gave his nearly undivided attention to the Indian campaigns and pacification of the Mizque–Santa Cruz region, including the yungas. Either voluntarily or by orders from Viceroy Francisco de Toledo, he launched his own forays or fought in league with others. He and his men joined in major battles alongside the likes of the Chavezes (Ñuflo as well as son Francisco), Andrés Manso, or Gabriel Paniagua de Loaysa as they attempted, in consecutive battles, to break down Indian resistance. Cazorla's two young sons, Luís de Narváez and Fernando de Narváez, also in the line of duty to the crown, often accompanied their father in these campaigns. In fact, the former, when just twenty years of age (a *moço*, or lad, in his father's words), lost his life in an Indian ambush.

In addition to the loss of Luís, the accounts repeatedly refer to two of Cazorla's black slaves, together worth 2,000 pesos, who were killed in one of the Indian skirmishes. The reiteration of the loss of his very expensive black slaves in an Indian ambush in the Mizque region underscores an early presence of people of African origin in the area. They were active participants, voluntary or otherwise, in a militaristic, horse-and-gun culture here as elsewhere throughout the New World during this phase of conquest and exploration. Some of them and their descendants, as we will see, remained in the region working, slave and free, as cowboys and ranch hands. Over time they formed unions with more recently arrived slaves and soon their descendants, brought in to work in other agricultural sectors. They would also over time mix with the indigenous population to form a fast-growing population of color. Others would soon emerge as ranch owners themselves, demanding their rights and taking the likes of Gabriel Paniagua's mayordomo to court. Cazorla was not the only warrior-cum-encomendero to bring his black slaves into those early campaigns of pacification. Little wonder that his exploits, as he claimed, cost him easily 120,000 gold pesos out of his own coffers.[34] Over the years he had earned the rank and title of *maese de campo general*, one of the highest positions a field commander could achieve. His surviving son, Fernando, rose over time from the rank of *alférez real* (advanced ensign) to captain. Further, in

1587 Viceroy Toledo appointed Cazorla *corregidor* (governor of the corregimiento or province) of Cochabamba, no doubt the result of his convincing petitions and testimonials. Cochabamba by then was already in the process of becoming the foremost breadbasket to supply the voracious Potosí market.[35]

Thus, Cazorla's appointment as corregidor should be viewed as a generous one. Clearly, he had been recognized and rewarded over the years to some degree. Equally clearly, in his old age he, like his counterparts also seeking recompense, considered the earlier awards insufficient and incommensurate with the magnitude of the services rendered. To compensate for this perceived oversight, Cazorla petitioned for an annual income of 8,000 pesos ensayados through encomienda or other suitable means in compliance with inheritance laws. On August 13, 1587, the royal audiencia of La Plata passed on a recommendation to the king that Fernando de Cazorla Narváez (and his family) be granted an annual income of 5,000 pesos ensayados through an encomienda of Indians from Pocona, no doubt the Cota discussed earlier.[36]

Cazorla's petitions and testimonies reveal far more than mere good deeds and acts of service, more than grandiose narratives of battles won or lost. These documents also provide direct insight into Mizque's regional development. While Cazorla's post as corregidor of Cochabamba may have lasted five years, this cannot be proven with the available data. On the other hand, by his own testimony as well as those of his dozens of witnesses, his ties to Mizque were as indisputable as they were solid. Not only did he own considerable property in the jurisdiction, but his valley haciendas supplied the troops involved in the region's Indian campaigns with literally all the necessary food, equipment, weapons, horses, and lodging.[37]

One particular foray calls for a closer look. In 1584, Cazorla organized a contingent and joined with the governor of Santa Cruz to fight the persistent Chiriguano. As with all of his campaigns in the Mizque–Santa Cruz region, his valley hacienda served once more as a base of operations. Drawing from his own resources, he outfitted and provided for 110 soldiers, including African slaves, as well as local Indians and 914 horses. Specifically, he supplied all the food (plus the necessary firewood and cooking utensils) for everyone. Cazorla not only provided the horses just mentioned but also furnished their feed. He supplied money, clothing, weapons including *arcabuses* or harquebuses (fifteenth-century matchlock heavy guns requiring support for firing), swords, ammunition, and armor. He offered lodging when needed, not only to the soldiers but to anyone traveling through the region, whether on campaign-related matters or not. Significantly, in this particular mission the Indians were recruited specifically to tend to the needs of the soldiers (not to mention the horses, which required care, food, and water); they did not participate in battle. Cazorla not only fed them but also paid them. When the approaching winter forced the campaign to a halt, Cazorla himself did not fare as well. This was the mission in which his young son Luís lost his life. On June 14 of that same year, Cazorla organized another expedition in the valley of Pojo. They departed for Santa Cruz with 99 soldiers (87 of them were *arcabuseros*, or those who handled the heavy guns, and 30 of them were cavalrymen). They also brought with them 68 *negros* (usually synonymous with black slaves) and *mulatos* (people of mixed African and indigenous parentage) and 100 *yanaconas* (indigenous Andean servants or laborers). In yet another attempt to mount a campaign, this one apparently out of the valley of Mizque, Cazorla recruited 75 soldiers and more than 1,000 allied Indians accompanied by 150 Chiriguano turncoats (traitors?), but apparently they met with bad weather at every turn. Hostilities would resume the following year, and again Cazorla rounded up men and gear and returned to the Santa Cruz battlegrounds.[38]

By most accounts, Cazorla did more than his share of subduing and pacifying the local ethnic groups, either by massacre or intimidation. He masterminded and cooperated with others in the relentless offense against the regional Indians. Many credited him with having made the entire region safer for travel and settlement. It should be added, however, that these same ethnic groups, though diminished in force and size, did not easily abandon their aggressive behavior. As I will elaborate in chapter 2, their now more sporadic but still frightening forays into the European and Indian settlements near and around Santa Cruz as well as the eastern reaches of Mizque continued well into the eighteenth century.[39]

Heroism aside, Cazorla's own best interests were served by quashing aggressive ethnic groups. He had a huge stake in pacifying the region. As mentioned, he personally financed and supplied the above campaigns, many of which lasted months and often took place in areas of difficult terrain far removed from his valley base. These missions obviously required a considerable reservoir of resources, both monetary and material. His Mizque hacienda had to be operating in full swing. For example, 914 horses make up a sizable herd to have at one's disposal on a given occasion. They require corrals, water, feed, and all else necessary to maintain healthy horses. What about equipment and gear? Leather becomes a key material here, which of course would have to come from hides, no doubt from his own livestock. Then there is the food factor. He had a lot of mouths to feed. In keeping with the *hacienda-chácara* (large to smaller agricultural units) tradition of the region, most if not all of his supplies came from his own properties.[40]

Expanding the scenario of a well-propertied *hacendado-chacarero* (holder of agricultural units), Cazorla won unanimous acclaim from his witnesses for his impressive vineyards. His last will and testament further supports his advantaged position. The Cazorla documents provide a clear portrait of a well-connected, prosperous warrior-cum-encomendero, settler, and property owner. Further, he served as treasurer as well as benefactor (after his death) of the Franciscan church and monastery in Mizque. Although Cazorla was born in Spain, his exploits from early youth on took him through most reaches of the viceroyalty. Even though he served as corregidor of Cochabamba, Mizque was his chosen home. His last will and testament, in 1592, states unequivocally that he wishes to be buried alongside his deceased wife in the chapel of the Franciscan monastery in Mizque, his soul prepared for the ever after by the resident Franciscan priests.[41]

The Gabriel Paniagua de Loaysa Family

Finally, the third profile adds further insight into the nature of Mizque's earliest European settlers and their complicated family connections. It also provides a closer view into the dynamics of opening up a "no man's land" and reinventing frontiers. Of the three families in question, the testimonials and petitions of the Paniagua de Loaysa clan offer more kinship and genealogical data than the Chávez or the Cazorla documents. The sheer bulk of these documents testifies to an extended, very powerful family.

According to a 1612 petition of Antonio Paniagua de Loaysa, the family's history begins with the most senior of the clan, his grandfather Pedro Fernández Paniagua de Loaysa. Born in Spain, Pedro Fernández fought in the Comunero revolt of 1520 in which the people of Castile rebelled in resistance to Charles I's economic pressures.[42] He fought on the side of the king and as a reward was made a knight of the order of Calatrava. He married a noblewoman and with her had three sons and three daughters. He lived quite comfortably, enjoying the fruits of his *mayorazgo* (entailed family estates) and living in a town house in the city of Plazencia, where he held the post of *regidor* (councilman). He also, according to James Lockhart, enjoyed some very well placed connections. One cousin served as a president of the Council of the Indies, another became the archbishop of Lima. He also had ties to the illustrious Carvajal family. For some reason, possibly because of the Lima connection and in apparent rejection of this seemingly bucolic life, Pedro Fernández made a complete break. Leaving his wife and younger children behind, and taking with him his oldest and apparently much favored son Alonso (*hijo natural*, a child born out of wedlock), he set sail for Peru with Pedro de la Gasca in 1547.[43]

Upon arriving, Pedro Fernández was appointed *embaxador* (mediator) to negotiate with Gonzalo Pizarro's followers, which he did. Apparently he also conducted some negotiations with Pizarro himself, placing himself at considerable risk in the process, as he became a target of Pizarro's vengeance. Pedro Fernández nevertheless pursued negotiations with the Pizarrists, persuading many of them to abandon Pizarro and reestablish their loyalty to their king. He also fought in many battles during the last phase of civil wars, including the famous battle of Xaqui Xaguana (Jaquijahuana) in 1548, in which Gonzalo Pizarro met his final defeat. Customary of the time, in this as in all of his activities in service of the crown, Pedro Fernández personally financed his part in the fierce battle, supplying and outfitting his own soldiers, grooms, servants, black slaves, and horses and providing arms and ammunition. For all of the above efforts he was awarded an encomienda of Indians—no doubt Chuy—in Pojo, in the valley of Mizque.[44]

Pedro Fernández, elderly now but a warrior to the end, died in 1554 in the Battle of Pucura during the Francisco Hernández Girón rebellion.[45] He bequeathed his encomienda in Pojo to his oldest legitimate son, Gabriel Paniagua de Loaysa, then about eighteen years old and residing in Peru. His favorite son, Alonso, the hijo natural, stayed by his father and shared the exploits, escapades, and all the battles, including the one against Francisco Hernández Girón. He also fought civil wars and Indian campaigns in the Santa Cruz region, alongside not only his father but often with his brother Gabriel, where they confronted the Chiriguano and Diego de Mendoza and allegedly helped to settle the Manso-Chávez affair. According to the testimonials, Alonso fought hard and financed all of his own activities and war efforts, but apparently he died with no rewards, estateless, and with no dependents. Pedro Fernández's son Gabriel would carry on the family legacy and prove himself capable of the activities and services for which the clan had by now gained fame (or infamy, depending on one's perspective).[46]

Don Gabriel Paniagua de Loaysa, another maese de campo general, lived fifty-four years in the viceroyalty of Peru. His service to the king in the civil wars and Indian campaigns is well documented and beyond dispute. He participated in and contributed to many of the military missions of his father and his brother, of Fernando Cazorla, and of other prominent leaders. He also financed and led his own war and pacification efforts. Apart from inheriting the Pojo encomienda, he acquired others in Mizque as well. He also amassed properties in the valley and subvalleys early on and established, as did his counterpart Fernando Cazorla, a system of haciendas, estancias, and chacaras in the jurisdiction of Mizque that would serve him well. His Mizque properties supplied all provisions required to sustain his troops and support his ongoing military activities (most of which took place in the Santa Cruz region), including cattle, horses, mares, cows, sheep, food rations, equipment, feed, and more. The crown rewarded his many successes with the ultimate rank and title of maese de campo general and with three more repartimientos, in Mizque, Aiquile, and Pocona. This last encomienda, like Pojo, was strategically located near the then highly profitable coca-producing yungas.[47]

Viceroy Francisco de Toledo further rewarded Gabriel Paniagua de

Loaysa by appointing him as the first corregidor of the city of Cuzco. Keeping in mind Toledo's relentless drive to establish his newly created reforms and policies, this appointment acquires considerable weight and prestige. Don Gabriel as well as his heirs and witnesses describe his duties at length. The first appointment was for three years, during which he was responsible for selecting the new officials that the reforms and restructuring required. Further duties required that he monitor the new tribute and tax laws leveled at the Indian population, particularly in relation to coca production. Not only did he have to search for new corregidores, but he also had to find people capable of filling the newly created posts of *protector* (legal defender) of the Indians. Further, he administered the redistribution of local Indians into *pueblos* (towns where Indians were congregated for administrative and indoctrination purposes) and repartimientos, which served his Mizque interests well. He also bore the responsibility of setting church-state relations in motion.[48]

By all Spanish accounts, Don Gabriel was an excellent corregidor and maintained "peace and harmony." This appraisal should come as no surprise, since he stood to benefit (as did his entire estate) if the Toledano reforms were effectively implemented and harmony established throughout the viceroyalty. The three-year appointment expired in time for him to head another royal call to arms. This time he, like others of his rank and status, financed yet another contingent in the usual costly manner—troops, servants, supplies—to pursue Francis Drake and his buccaneers, hovering threateningly near. Witnesses testified that Don Gabriel and his men assisted in the defense of the port cities of Lima and Callao, again engaging in battles and risking lives. Viceroy Toledo rewarded him by renewing his appointment as corregidor of Cuzco, this time for six years. Obviously the viceroy approved of his administrative abilities. This time, Don Gabriel moved his entire family and household belongings with him and left his Mizque house and haciendas under the stewardship of a majordomo. At the end of the six-year appointment he retired to La Plata, where he lived out his last three or four years. All evidence underscores the fact that the Peruvian elite regarded Gabriel Paniagua de Loaysa with considerable respect and admiration.[49]

But the Paniagua de Loaysa clan is only half the story. Gabriel Paniagua de Loaysa's two sons, Antonio (who provided some of the testimonials on grandfather Pedro's many deeds cited earlier) and Gabriel junior, raised yet another hero to their pantheon of conqueror-cum-encomendero settlers. With the same laudatory enthusiasm they brought to the Paniagua cause, the two younger men dealt with their maternal grandfather, Antonio Álvarez Meléndez. Antonio Álvarez must have arrived in the colony while very young, since according to his grandsons he lived some seventy-six years in the region. He married Doña Mayor Verdugo de Ángulo and had one legitimate child, a daughter, Doña Leonor Álvarez Meléndez, who became the child bride of Gabriel Paniagua de Loaysa. He first served the crown in Nicaragua and also served with Pedro Arias Dávila, although the capacity in which he served and the nature of his activities in the central American zones remain unspecified. Somewhere along the way he built for himself an impressive retinue of servants and black slaves, all of whom he equipped with weapons and horses. Apparently he cut quite an illustrious figure. Seeking to serve his king (and no doubt his own fortune as well), he arrived in Peru just in time to join the Spanish forces and rescue Fernando Pizarro from the massive Indian siege of 1536–37.[50]

Antonio Álvarez subsequently became enmeshed in the chaotic civil wars. Not once but twice the Almagrist forces captured him. The second time they imprisoned him in Cuzco, where he was almost beheaded. He escaped and fled on foot across difficult, unpopulated terrain. He found safe haven in Vilcas and returned to Cuzco, now under royal banner and accompanied by local troops. Apparently the authorities recognized Antonio Álvarez's activities by granting him a repartimiento somewhere in Charcas. However, according to his grandsons, due to the confusion of the ongoing civil wars, no one had any idea of the location, let alone the details of this reward. He was also named the governor's lieutenant and captain general of Charcas.[51]

The relentless civil wars caused yet another twist in Antonio Álvarez's personal life. Apparently he and Gonzalo Pizarro had been close friends. More significantly, they had also been business partners and shared an ownership of what were then the richest, most productive gold and silver mines of Porco. The grandsons were able to produce the partnership contract signed by both men, which detailed, among other things, the considerable investment each had contributed to this joint enterprise. Both agreed to provide their respective shares of Indian and African slave labor (the use of African slaves in the mines was not yet in disfavor) and to appropriate equipment and draft animals as well as other goods and materials necessary for the mines to function successfully. They signed their first contract in 1539 and signed related contracts in 1540 and 1542. Friendships, business partnerships, and hugely profitable investments notwithstanding, the Gonzalo Pizarro rebellion and attendant imprisonment of Viceroy Blasco Nuñez Vila irrevocably reversed relations. Antonio Álvarez responded immediately and was one of the first to take up arms against his former friend and partner.[52]

The loyalty of Antonio Álvarez was never in question. Kept at bay by Pizarrist forces, he and his men hid out in the hills for a year, living off wild plants in order to survive. They finally joined Pedro de la Gasca and fought with him in the final defeat of Gonzalo Pizarro in the earlier-mentioned battle of Xaqui Xaguana. Like his counterparts already discussed, Don Antonio financed all of his service activities out of his own pocket. But his military obligations prevented him from taking care of his mining activities, resulting in serious losses in gold and silver. However, after Pizarro's defeat, de la Gasca did reward him with a repartimiento of Indians in the Carrangas region, conveniently located to supply labor for his Porco mining and for other activities in La Plata. Antonio Álvarez would return once more to the battlefields and would again face imprisonment, this time not alone but accompanied by none other than Pedro Fernando Paniagua de Loaysa—two stalwart grandfathers! The seemingly endless civil wars continued. Antonio Álvarez, quite elderly by now, received further recognition of his lengthy, ongoing service to the crown, and according to his grandsons he was named not only lieutenant but also *alcalde* (mayor of a town or city; presides over town council) and placed in charge of "all of these provinces" and in particular the city of La Plata and the mining town of Potosí. He assumed the responsibility and, with his own soldiers, restored and maintained order, again entirely at his own expense.[53]

These profiles reveal several layerings of historical experience. First, the documents bring the lesser-known conquerors, warriors, Indian campaigners/pacifiers, and encomendero-settlers into focus. These were flesh-and-blood people who begat progeny and whose escapades and adventures (or misadventures, depending on one's interpretation) cost or nearly cost them their lives as they chose to live them. The course of their lives in turn affected directly or indirectly the lives of many others, from immediate kin, partners, and peers to Indian groups and Africans, slave and free. Some of these early warriors united their families through marriage, and their descendants would follow in their footsteps, participating in the last vestiges of civil war and Indian pacification wherever they could. However, the chance for military achievement and its attendant advancement in rank and status grew dimmer as relative order replaced the many years of chaos. Now, as the weapons of war were laid aside, land and labor assumed primary importance. Here again, the Paniagua de Loaysa clan provides additional information pertaining to the European opening up and settlement of the eastern "frontier," specifically the region of Mizque. It is understood that these Spaniards were merely the latest group to move in and out of the area in an attempt to establish hegemony and territoriality. They staked a claim to the area early on, surely anticipating the official recognition that eventually occurred in 1602.

In 1604, Antonio and Gabriel junior's father, Don Gabriel Paniagua de Loaysa, close to completing his six-year appointment as corregidor of Cuzco, renewed his quests for further compensation. His petition and testimonials from this year further underscore the significance of those hegemonic claims established earlier. To support his petitions, he argued that his brother Alonso had fought beside him in several civil war battles and Indian uprisings and attacks. His brother was along to help settle matters between Ñuflo Chávez and Andrés Manso. He also joined Gabriel in a number of Indian campaigns, covering all related expenses from his own resources. Yet brother Alonso was never rewarded for his service. Gabriel continued by pointing out that he was his brother's only possible successor and that everyone in his family— not just his brother, but his father, his father-in-law, Antonio Álvarez Meléndez, and his own son (hijo natural) Captain Francisco Paniagua de Loaysa—had served the king. The latter had served all over the viceroyalty in every military capacity possible, including chasing after the English buccaneers, yet he died in Spain, never receiving recognition for his many self-financed exploits.[54]

Don Gabriel reminded the authorities that he still held the post of corregidor in Cuzco but that his own properties had been sorely neglected. Compared to the rewards the crown had given both his father and his father-in-law, he considered himself greatly undercompensated for his many services and asked for more. First, Gabriel Paniagua de Loaysa had four repartimientos in his possession, all in Mizque. He held Pojo, which Pedro de la Gasca had given to his father, Pedro Fernández, in 1548, and which he subsequently inherited after his father's death, probably around 1554. The other three had been awarded to him by Viceroy Luís de Velasco: Pocona (which, like Pojo, was part of the coca production complex), Mizque, and Aiquile. Complaining that all four repartimientos had decreased in value over time, Don Gabriel requested that the authorities grant him possession of these encomiendas for another lifetime. He also requested that his mother-in-law's repartimientos also be extended another lifetime. He noted that his mother-in-law, Doña Mayor Verdugo de Ángulo, wife of the celebrated Antonio Álvarez Meléndez, was considerably younger than he—as was her daughter, who by all accounts must have been a child bride when the much older Don Gabriel married her. Since Doña Mayor Verdugo had the advantage of youth on her side, she would clearly outlive son-in-law Don Gabriel. He would not live long enough to enjoy Álvarez Meléndez's two repartimientos—the profitable, well-located Carrangas and Totora (located in Mizque)—both now in the hands of his mother-in-law.[55]

By requesting an extension of all the above repartimientos, Gabriel Paniagua de Loaysa hoped to provide security for his sons, Antonio and Gabriel junior. He knew that Antonio, as firstborn son, would surely inherit his encomiendas, so he also requested an annual fixed income of 6,000 pesos for his younger son Gabriel. Gabriel, he explained, unlike his predecessors, did not have the same opportunities to seek his fortunes through service to the crown. Locally, relative order now predominated and the military activities of the earlier days were no longer needed. His son could go to Chile and conduct campaigns there, but according to Don Gabriel, it was very far away, over rough terrain that included treacherous mountain ranges. Carrying out military service in Chile required vast resources that Gabriel junior did not have and which he, now living in La Plata and so deeply in debt (over 80,000 pesos), could not provide. Leaving his Mizque house and haciendas in the hands of careless mayordomos had also resulted in financial losses, and Don Gabriel declared he could not even provide dowries for his two maiden daughters.[56]

Gabriel Paniagua de Loaysa died sometime between 1604 (the date of his last petition) and 1608, when his two sons resumed petitioning for greater recompense in honor of the clan's extended history of loyal service. Gabriel senior did indeed die before his mother-in-law, Doña Mayor Verdugo, and never benefited from the Totora and Carrangas repartimientos that he was to receive after her death. While Antonio inherited his father's Pocona, Pojo, Mizque, and Aiquile repartimientos, he continued to complain that these had dropped in value. Basically, what he clearly wanted was his grandmother's holdings in Carrangas and Totora, but Antonio feared that this apparently feisty dowager would outlive him, just as she had outlived his father (her son-in-law). Everyone concurred that Antonio was not well, that he had aged far beyond his forty years. His eleven-year marriage had produced no children (would-be successors to the many repartimientos; as noted earlier, Antonio was the firstborn son). Further, if we are to believe his petitions, he too had fallen into debt. He had drawn from most of his wife's 50,000-peso dowry to cover living in the grand style to which the family was long accustomed, and now he was in debt as well. He insisted that he had, at one time, every right to the repartimientos so tenaciously held by his grandmother. By law, since his father, Gabriel senior, had married Álvarez Meléndez and Doña Mayor Verdugo's only daughter, Leonor, the repartimientos should be passed on to Antonio, their firstborn son, rather than to the grandmother. However, recent laws now prohibited people from holding more than one inherited set of repartimientos, and according to Antonio, his father chose to keep those he had inherited from his own father, Pedro, forgoing the holdings of his in-laws. In fact, by law Antonio now would not be eligible for his grandmother's repartimientos until their third *vida* (lifetime).[57]

Antonio's persistence concerning the repartimientos calls for further explanation. First, Gabriel Paniagua de Loaysa and his two sons consistently downplayed the worth of all the clan's holdings. Grandfather Álvarez Meléndez's repartimiento in Carrangas, according to them, was easily worth 20,000 pesos in 1548 when Pedro de la Gasca awarded it to Pedro Fernández de Paniagua. Now, they claimed, it would yield at best a mere 3,000 annually. Pojo also originally brought in some 20,000 pesos, with Indian labor alone worth 10,000 a year. Now, they complained, this former coca-producing region, having lost a good part of its workforce, was worth little more than 1,500 pesos a year. The value of Mizque and Aiquile fluctuated from petition to petition, ranging from about 900 to 1,500 pesos annually. Curiously, neither Pocona nor Totora was evaluated in these papers, suggesting that all parties concerned agreed on both the worth and the status of these two repartimientos. After his father's death and subsequent inheritance of his repartimientos, Antonio came to terms with the fact that his grandmother Doña Mayor Verdugo would indeed probably outlive him. Since he had little chance of obtaining the relatively profitable Carrangas repartimiento—with its convenient proximity to the Porco mines—he and his brother adjusted their requests a bit more realistically. They still insisted on compensation. In Antonio's last petition, recorded in La Plata in 1613, he asked for another lifetime for his grandmother's Carrangas repartimiento; another lifetime for his Mizque and Aiquile repartimientos (no mention of his grandmother's Totora or his Pocona and Pojo holdings); knighthood for both himself and younger brother Gabriel; and finally, for Gabriel, 6,000 pesos in a new repartimiento, or fixed annual income, plus a decent corregidor post.[58]

For all the claims of devalued repartimientos and income loss, one overriding theme rings clearly throughout these petitions and testimonials. The Paniaguas lived quite well; indeed, as a clan they held high government positions and possessed ample holdings: lavish houses and furnishings, servants, African slaves, horses, repartimientos, land, haciendas, chacaras, estancias, and the like. They wanted further rewards because they wished to maintain their affluent lifestyle and still be able to pay off their family debts, accrued (according to them) mostly as a result of the many generations of service rendered to the crown. Antonio and Gabriel junior estimated this would require upwards of 10,000 pesos a year. In Antonio's last recorded petition, cited above, he again did not request extensions on the family's Totora, Pocona, and Pojo repartimientos. Clearly, these must have continued to operate acceptably, and the family sought to maintain them at a status quo. Interestingly, both Antonio and Gabriel also complained about the system by which repartimientos had been distributed in the past and the nature of land acquisition during their own time. However, it is important to note here that the Paniagua petitions, like the others cited, bear a particular formula of supplication and do so consistently. The requests all acquire a tone of humility and, of course, economic deprivation bordering on complete destitution, even though, as we know, they were quite wealthy. Nevertheless, close examination of their observations reveals more than the usual sour grapes and lamented impoverishment expected under the circumstances, and their petitions may have contained more than a touch of truth.[59]

Repeatedly, the Paniaguas declared that the family had never been properly compensated for their many contributions and services. But the brothers elaborated even further, arguing a number of times that Pedro de la Gasca was less than fair when handing out repartimientos. Both claimed that de la Gasca went out of his way to coddle the former Pizarrists and that he gave larger awards, greater salaries, and more generous repartimientos to them than he did to staunch loyalists. After all, the likes of grandfathers Don Pedro and Don Antonio came to Peru specifically to serve their king in a time of need, not to mention their own father, Gabriel, whose services also had become legendary. The brothers maintained that de la Gasca essentially bought the loyalty of former Pizarrist rebels and a guarantee that no further civil wars would occur. Some scholars see seniority as a key factor in explaining the acclaim and recognition royal authorities granted the humblest conquest and civil war participants. However, in the light of the Paniagua brothers' perceptions of recognition, seniority in this instance would only partially explain royal generosity and prestigious acknowledgment of "even those who were on the losing side of the civil war battles."[60] Further unstated but implicit in the brothers' observations was that they and others like them paid the price for this "bought" loyalty.

Gabriel junior added a further complaint. He stressed not only that he could no longer support himself, carry on military service, or participate in distant Indian campaigns, as his forebears had, but also that he no longer had fair access to land. According to the youngest son (who would inherit none of the Paniagua–Álvarez Meléndez holdings), people who held earlier repartimientos were now aggressively pushing their way into vacant lands and usurping everything available, without the viceroy's permission. He could not possibly compete under these circumstances.[61]

Indeed, competition was part of the larger equation. By the early 1600s, if not earlier, many hacendados and chacareros would recognize the region's potential as a trade and transport link and as a producer for local and regional markets. The Chavezes, the Cazorlas, and most of all the Paniagua de Loaysas did not establish their houses, haciendas, estancias, and chacaras there some fifty to sixty years earlier out of ignorance. Nor did they petition vehemently to renew their old repartimientos (or, as in Gabriel junior's case, ask for new ones) out of sheer whim. The old warhorses did succeed in their service to the king (and to themselves). They pacified the region by quashing its former inhabitants, the so-called Chiriguano, who now are recognized as the Amo, Raché, Yuracaré, and mixtures thereof, to name a few. And they focused their energies into turning their perceived frontier into a settlement, and a settlement into a regional center. As the following chapters will illustrate, Mizque the pueblo, Mizque the villa, and Mizque the region became key factors in the dynamics of intraregionalism and interregionalism. Further, this former "no man's land" would mock its earlier mislabel and become a critical link between the viceroyalty's easternmost hinterlands and its fast-growing Andean highland centers.

2. Re-creating a Region for a Colonial Market

As we have seen, the Indian campaigns were part of a larger imperial plan to settle and develop the Corregimiento de Mizque for local and interregional markets. The goal was aggressively pursued by private interests and actively encouraged by the crown. This chapter explains the region's prominence long before it achieved official recognition, by which time reconfigurations of land and labor systems were also under way. We will examine in detail a major infrastructure project initiated locally and encouraged by the state—the building of a bridge that physically and symbolically linked this "no man's land" to the highland markets.

Official Founding and Renaming of the Villa

On September 19, 1603, the town of Mizque gained full legal status and recognition. On that day, in an austere ceremony, it became officially known as the Villa de Salinas del Río Pisuerga. According to the local scribe, the government representative commissioned by Viceroy Luís de Velasco to officiate in the founding ceremonies, Don Francisco de Álfaro, did so "with great Christianity and prudence."[1]

On the site of the former Indian *reducción* (forced resettlement of diverse groups), "voluntarily" given up by its inhabitants, in front of an "exhilarated" crowd of Spaniards and Indians, Don Francisco called upon God's blessings and with pomp and ceremony took over the town in the name of the viceroy. He proceeded to appoint *cabildo* (municipal government) members. Don Antonio Troche del Vallejo and Maese del Campo Joan de Paredes received their bars of office as town magistrates. Pedro de Céspedes y Abrego became official town herald. Significantly, Don Gabriel de Encinas—a name that will emerge in the documents somewhat later than the venerable Paniaguas, Chavezes, or

Cazorlas but is no less prestigious—was named chief constable. Álfaro also named four councilmen: Captain Juan Dávalos de Zárate, Juan de Vargas de Toledo, Captain Francisco Perero Barrantes, and Pedro de Torres de la Calancha. Francisco Macías Torrico received the post of general attorney, while Pedro Lascano Argumedo became *alcalde de la Santa Hermandad* (magistrate or deputy in the rural constabulary) for the rural districts. All of these men were *vecinos* (permanent local residents) and *hacendados* (landowners) in the jurisdiction of Mizque. I provide their names and appointed posts here because they were prominent players in Mizque's early political and economic development; as such, many of them will reappear in different contexts in this work, as will those who over time filled these same posts. In his letter to the audiencia, Álfaro explains that many people were dissatisfied with the selections for the government posts: "There were many contenders for few posts and not everyone could be satisfied. Only one vote per family was allowed. Since families are large, they are not happy with the results of this order but this was the only justifiable way to handle matters and my own wish was to have no doubts as to my decision." Finally, in order to get off to a good start, the cabildo discussed a number of service-related issues pertaining to God and king. In a display of formal, official civil accord, the cabildo swore to "bow humbly at the feet of Your Highness in hopes that you will look favorably upon this town, now part of the royal crown, particularly in terms of growth, which we all hope for as we promise obedience in service of your royal personage which may God our Lord protect and make prosperous."[2]

Old habits are hard to break, however. Despite the rather cumbersome new appellation, Villa de Salinas del Río Pisuerga, the town remained informally known in the documents as the Villa de Mizque. As early as 1557, in the official Visita a Pocona (inspection of Pocona), it was referred to as the Villa de Mizque. Yet a 1561 document called it the "Villa de Mizque, termino y jurisdición [within the boundaries and jurisdiction] de la Villa de Salinas." The term "Pueblo de Mizque" referred to the earlier-cited corporate Indian community. It frequently appears in references by the 1580s as "el Pueblo y Villa de Mizque," "el Pueblo y repartimiento de Mizque," "el Pueblo de Mizque de la encomienda de Paniagua de Loaysa," and "el Pueblo de Mizque." The immediate area was referred to as "el Valle de Mizque," although on more than one occasion the term "el Valle y Distrito de Mizque" (1586) entered the documents. And of course, the much larger, far-reaching configuration became the Corregimiento de Mizque.[3]

Regional Expansion and Territorial Shifts

Not surprisingly, Mizque's eventual emergence as a regional hinterland center was reflected elsewhere in the Charcas interior. In Spain the growing significance of the Charcas province was taken most seriously. In the summer of 1563, authorities in Madrid gathered to discuss the options of transforming other provincias in the viceroyalty into audiencias. The voices of a bevy of well-connected, seasoned Peruvian residents summoned to testify in support of or against these major changes further the point at hand. All of the people interrogated knew their hinterland well, having lived in and traveled the vast eastern regions of the viceroyalty as governors, merchants, leaders of Indian campaigns, and the like. In a 1584 account of his Indian campaign in the region, Gonzalo de Martín provided a wider geographic perspective to reveal a shift away from the Pacific coast-to-highland trade-and-transport axis and a growing economic interest in the hinterland. His letter represented the views of the many who wished to see Charcas recognized legally as an audiencia and who hoped to underscore the importance of the hinterland-highland trade routes. Writing to the crown, he observed:

> The road between the *gobernación* [administrative province] de Tucumán and the Ciudad de los Reyes [Lima] is treacherous. There are many mountains, bad weather and [poor conditions]. The merchants of Tucumán would much rather do business transactions [coca, livestock, food products] in the audiencia of Charcas rather than the Ciudad de los Reyes [because it is a much easier trip]. The same [applies to] the natives, who all prefer Charcas. In fact, the vecinos and *naturales* [Indians] of Tucumán all prefer [dealing] with Charcas rather than the Ciudad de los Reyes which is some 200–300 leagues [600–900 miles] further.[4]

The others unanimously concurred with Gonzalo de Martín, each adding strength to the prevailing arguments in accordance with their respective knowledge and experience. For example, Don García de

Mendoza testified that as governor of the "provincia de los Tucumanes, Juriés y Diaguitas and Comechingones [*sic*]," he had constant contact with military men and other travelers. They all agreed, as did the general population, that they would much rather conduct transactions with La Plata than with Lima. First, La Plata was much closer than Lima, or Chile for that matter (Spain at that time was also considering the possibility of changing the gobernación de Chile into an audiencia). Also, continued Mendoza, there were no rough mountain ranges to cross and one could travel year-round. Further, while the terrain produced no gold or silver, it did yield abundant supplies of food (including meat), honey, wax, cotton goods, and *quascas* (Quechua for hides), for which Potosí was the obvious market. Referring again to Chile, the governor felt that although there might be locations geographically closer to Chile, the snow-covered mountain ranges were impassable six months of the year. Further, once one got past the mountains there remained a vast, uninhabited terrain and some 500 miles before reaching any area halfway hospitable for establishing an audiencia. Mendoza was also of the opinion that the vecinos and naturales of the Mojo and Chuncho provinces would be much happier doing business with the audiencia of Charcas.[5]

Baptista Ventura, native of Madrid but well traveled throughout Peru, concurred with Mendoza, noting that travelers could find plenty of food, water, and wood for cooking and heating. The road to Lima was terrible, the weather hot and miserable, he claimed. Further, while some people may have business with the city, most people traveled there only because of the viceroy. Were it not for the viceroy, he insisted, few if any would choose to travel to Lima; they would all take their business to Charcas.[6]

Finally, Sebastian de Rivas agreed with the others, but he added an indigenous dimension to the argument. He contended that the Indians of Cuzco were probably better served looking to the audiencia of Charcas for their transactions. The roads were better and travel was easier. Further, they had a better advantage buying, trading and selling coca and basic provisions as well as their other harvests in Potosí. And finally, the naturales had trouble adjusting to Lima's hot climate and often fell ill or prey to other problems while there.[7]

Another witness, Diego de Meneses, a vecino of Madrid who had lived in Peru for twenty-six years, took the descriptions of the dangerous roads to Chile a step further. He elaborated that, unlike the road to Charcas, the one to Chile was snowbound, bitterly cold, and "impassable most of the year, *where many españoles, indios and negros,* as well as their horses, have died from exposure and from lack of food and water" (emphasis added).[8]

Many others testified as well, often recommending names of still others who would be willing to come forth and discuss their opinions of and experiences in the viceroyalty of Peru. Of particular concern, of course, was the audiencia of Charcas and regional trade. One wonders how the Spanish court was able to round up the dozen or more Peruvian observers in Madrid that summer of 1563. But Charcas had been changed from a provincia to an audiencia just two years earlier, and the issues of Peruvian boundaries and alignments were of considerable importance. In fact, the Spanish court, in its push to gather information, went to some length to seek out sources. At one point during the month-long inquiry, the commissioner sent scribe Juan Pérez de Calahorra to the royal jail to question one Licenciado Altamirano, a judge in the audiencia of Lima. Why Altamirano was being held prisoner is not explained, but his eleven years as a judge in Lima clearly carried weight.[9]

On August 29, 1563, King Philip issued a royal decree proclaiming that "said governance of Tucumán, Juries y Diaguitas and the province of los Mojos y Chunchos, and all that was settled by Andrés Manso and Ñuflo de Chávez and all that will be populated in those parts and all the land that lies between said city of La Plata and Cuzco including said city of Cuzco . . . are now subject to the said Audiencia [of Charcas] and not the Royal Audiencia de los Reyes, nor the Governor of the said province of Chile."[10]

The royal commission had achieved its purpose, and the territorial boundaries of the audiencia of Charcas (or La Plata—they would now be one and the same) had been broadened considerably. Having now gained recognition, Charcas would continue to expand, with or without Cuzco within its boundaries. The region and its many fertile valleys indeed had demonstrated an economic "buoyancy" of their own.[11]

And Mizque would accommodate itself accordingly. One need only look at a map to understand government interest in defending, populating, and developing the fertile Mizque area. First, it was far closer to the La Plata–Potosí market than were its competitors along the Pacific coast and in the Tucumán region. Further, it served as a crucial link in keeping Santa Cruz in check and as a corridor for Santa Cruz products intended for highland consumption.

Acceleration of the Settlement Process

Regardless of ongoing Indian raids, particularly along the eastern perimeters, which will be discussed at length later, this vital region became increasingly active. In fact, some scholars argue that Mizque's course of growth in some ways paralleled that of neighboring Cochabamba.[12] And according to other authorities, the prominence of Mizque was underscored during a good part of its colonial experience by serving as the official seat of the Bishopric of Santa Cruz. Further, these same scholars suggest that Mizque's civic and economic progress actually surpassed that of Cochabamba.[13]

Clearly, Mizque played a significant role early on in imperial Spain's adaptations to Andean concepts of verticality and reciprocity so well articulated in the now-classic works of John V. Murra. Murra's model, variations of which remain in place today, depicts pre-Columbian Andean groups controlling other "colonies" or "islands," often at considerable distance from the "center," in order to acquire products needed or desired that could only be produced at different ecological niches in different altitudes or elevations. This "vertical control" also involved a reciprocal relationship in which goods were exchanged between the central area or seat of power and the various settlements, or "archipelagos."[14]

Even before the advent of Viceroy Francisco de Toledo, by the early 1550s the Corregimiento de Mizque was undergoing its own rearrangements of political administration and land, labor, and production systems imposed by colonial rule. Encouraged by the crown, European entrepreneurs moved into Mizque's more temperate zones to control, indirectly or directly, agricultural production for the increasingly demanding markets of Potosí *and* the fast-growing Chuquisaca or La

Plata. The region was conquered in the late 1530s. The Paniagua de Loaysa family was among the very first to be granted encomiendas. They, along with Diego Centeno and Lope de Mendoza, received their awards in 1548.[15] Wasting little time, the Paniaguas put their vast holdings and encomiendas to use. In a litigation dated 1558 over property rights the Paniaguas claimed hundreds of *fanegadas* (a fanegada is the amount of land needed to sow 1.6 bushels of grain) as legally theirs, stating they had been under cultivation for many years.[16] Others would soon follow these first encomenderos. Schramm informs us that by the 1570s a corregidor for Mizque and Pocona, Pedro de Quiros, was already in place. Moreover, by 1577 and 1578 the onslaught of Spanish land usurpers had taken its toll, much to the provocation and consternation of the increasingly displaced local ethnic groups.[17]

While the neighboring Cochabamba valley system retained the Inca tradition of grain production, Mizque did not. Mizque Indian communities and private entrepreneurs (European and Indian), with the benefit of having access to multiple ecological niches—the indigenous groups having enjoyed this advantage long before the arrival of the Inca and the Spaniards—diversified early on. Soon they would be producing an impressive array of agricultural products as well as all manner of livestock for local and highland markets. No doubt anticipating future markets, by the early 1560s royal authorities strongly urged increased settlement of Mizque in order to counter the economically disruptive incursions by the "Chiriguano" and others.[18] In addition, it was during this period that the crown continually ordered the prominent encomenderos Chávez, Cazorla, and Paniagua de Loaysa to form militias and lead campaigns against the aggressive ethnic groups.

By 1560 the Roman Catholic Church sent priests to Mizque to indoctrinate the local Indians (priests had entered the coca-producing yungas in the Pocona area at least by 1557, if not earlier). In 1571, Alonso Paniagua de Loaysa (brother of Gabriel senior, discussed in chapter 1) founded a *hospital* (combination hospital, infirmary, and temporary asylum for the poor and the transient). By 1598 at least five hospitals existed in the audiencia-Mizque, La Plata, Pocona town, Pocona yungas, and Potosí. Mizque, like the rest of the hemisphere, would be plagued with epidemic disease from the 1550s on. Indian community livestock was used toward the purchase of medicines and supplies for the hospital. We also know that Viceroy Toledo's mandates had taken hold, and by 1573 royal authorities were assessing the Indian communities to determine how much tribute they could provide to support the priests sent in for religious indoctrination. These same authorities also sought to resettle the Indians into reducciones "because there are not enough lands for all and they [the Indians] will cause less problems for the chácara owners."[19]

In 1581 the old patriarch and maese del campo Captain Fernando de Cazorla and his wife, Doña Isabel Osorio, volunteered as benefactors, and Franciscan father Francisco de Alcozer petitioned the audiencia in La Plata for permission for the Cazorlas to found a church (with elaborate religious decorations and icons) and a convent for the Franciscan order. Clearly, the indoctrination of the Indian population continued as a driving force for the Franciscans, but of equal importance was the order's need to increase its activities to serve the growing Spanish population. They needed more clerics, a larger house, and an orchard. As patrons and benefactors of this endeavor, the Cazorlas and all of their relatives and descendants would enjoy the privileges that accompany such largess—pews of choice, indulgences, burial plots, and the like. By 1582, three of the above-mentioned hospitales were already in place in the region: one in Mizque and the two Pocona units.[20]

In further acknowledgment of Mizque's growing significance, on October 2, 1586, Don Álvaro de Chávez's persistent rounds of petitions and testimonials (cited in chapter 1) finally paid off. In recognition of his and father Ñuflo's heroic deeds and brave campaigns against the Chiriguano, Álvaro was named "Corregidor of the valley of Mizque, Pocona, and the Indians and repartimientos of Mizque, Pocona, Aiquile, Totora of Joan de Guzman and Totora of Doña Maior, and the yanaconas in all of the chacaras [throughout] the corregimiento, all of which are in the province of Charcas."[21]

Administrative Challenges and Civic Projects

The detailed instructions of Don Álvaro's responsibilities (matters concerning Indian treatment are discussed in chapter 6) can be briefly summarized as follows. First and foremost, Don Álvaro was required to maintain "peace and justice" among all Indians (reducción, repartimiento, or otherwise) and Spaniards ("and others") in his assigned corregimiento. He also had to stay informed of all civil and criminal matters and keep careful record of the same. Also, he was to keep very careful record of tribute collection and keep Spaniards out of Indian communities and repartimientos. Apparently, Don Álvaro also was to be on the lookout for Spanish bigamists or deserters—men who left wives behind in Spain and formed unions with Indian women or who simply abandoned their wives in Spain. He should allow no one to build a church or monastery without explicit permission from the viceroy, nor allow any person to practice law without a permit. Further, no magistrate or ecclesiastic had the right to arrest a layperson without royal authority. The post yielded an annual salary of 1,000 pesos plata ensayada to be paid every six months, but only after all the corregimiento's biannual *tasas* (collections of taxes, tribute, etc.) had been completed.[22]

As the European population grew, the native population had already begun to decline. The earliest Indian census for the jurisdiction is that of Pocona in 1557. Within roughly one hundred years, its native population dropped by 87 percent. Disease played an important role in Mizque's history and remained the primary cause of Mizque's population loss (see chapter 7).[23] Shrinking Indian communities notwithstanding, native and European producers together established Mizque as a valuable source of market goods. In a measure that seemingly contradicted the 1573 orders, a royal decree issued in 1590 ordered that the eastern reaches of the corregimiento, between Mizque and Santa Cruz de la Sierra, be populated. As decreed by Viceroy Toledo, "it is agreed to give large quantities of land to the Indians for planting and for livestock. What is left over give to the Spaniards, providing the Indians are given what they need."[24]

Not only did Mizque produce a wide variety of agricultural products, but the region also produced thousands of head of livestock, mostly cattle, sheep, and goats, but also horses and mules. Further, for transport, many of the larger chácaras and haciendas possessed their own *recuas* (pack teams, usually mules) of twenty-five to forty-eight beasts each. By 1595 at least sixty privately owned estancias, chacaras,

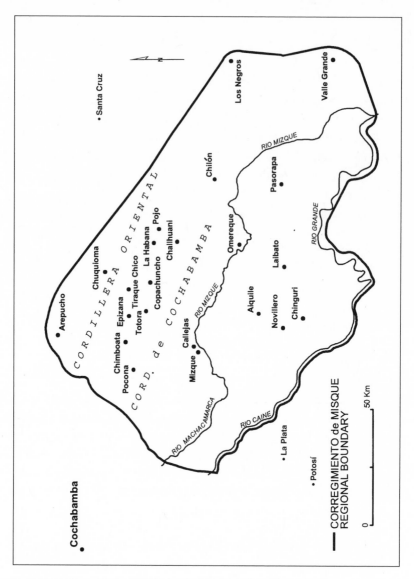

Corregimiento de Mizque, ca. 1620. Geography and Earth Sciences
Department, North Carolina Central University

and haciendas of all sizes existed in Mizque (many of which can be located on Map 2), with most producing some if not all of the products
listed above. Significantly, regional indigenous leaders also had large,
productive landholdings more than comparable to the Spanish land

possessions, reflecting indigenous land-tenure practices dating to pre-Inca times.[25]

On May 6, 1611, authorities in La Plata requested that Mizque cabildo scribe Pedro de Lara (the same scribe who notarized the founding ceremonies) submit a listing of owners of inhabited homes in the Villa de Salinas. Apparently, the villa had gotten off to a sluggish start. Further, the evidence strongly suggests that many of the vecinos were spending much of their time on their haciendas when they were not enjoying their lavish abodes up in La Plata. For whatever reason, in a move to encourage construction, local residency, and general growth, the royal government decreed *alcabala* (sales tax) exemption for people involved in these latter activities. At least fifty-two houses were identified as furnished and occupied. One would assume these were located adjacent to or close by the main square. Apparently, however, some abandoned houses or buildings in stages of disrepair also existed. The scribe suggested that these could be rented out and renovated. The names of many now-familiar persons appear on the list of residences: encomenderos, founding fathers, ecclesiastics, government officials, merchants, professionals, and the like. The Paniagua de Loaysas still had a house and several lots in town, as did the prominent mother-in-law in the clan, Doña Mayor Verdugo. Maese del Campo Juan de Paredes, Pedro Argumedo, Gabriel de Encinas's heirs, Captain Pedro de Torres de la Calancha, Álvaro de Abreu's heirs, and other notable hacendados also claimed residency.[26]

Just a few months later, in 1612, a very angry mayordomo of the Villa de Salinas, Francisco Gómez Arnalde, vented his frustration in a blistering attack on the manner in which others were running the town. His report "on the development of the Villa and of that which is necessary for the good and growth of the Republic" comprised a numbered of tenets or observations (and complaints). The following were among the issues he raised:

1. First, the *mita* [draft labor] Indians waiting in the main square on Monday mornings are there for town house and building construction, and no other purpose.

2. The *juez poblador* [development magistrate] is not doing his job and is not seeing to it that the Indians are channeled into said construction.

3. Those empty lots of the wealthiest vecinos must be developed and if not, taken away from them and given to someone who will build up the property.

4. More houses are needed for the cabildo. Construction has stopped and there is no place for the corregidor to live except in the Indian pueblo [a town where Indians were congregated for administrative and indoctrination purposes] as he does today and this is great harm against the good and benefit of the Republic, and the prisoners need better accommodations.

5. Because there has been little follow-up from above, not all viceregal construction orders have been carried out.

At this point, in the margins of the document are scribbled in minuscule lettering observations and admonitions such as "has been done," "do as required," "there's not enough money," "If things are done properly money will be sent down," "do what's supposed to be done and Indians will be available," and so forth.

6. The vecinos of this villa must not be charged more than 200 pesos ensayados for their share of alcabala collection. Any more would be unfair.

7. That the cabildo scribe stay at his job and be less absent which is quite detrimental for the vecinos and forasteros who require his services for lack of other scribes. Or obtain another [royal] scribe. . . .

9. That the cabildo keep regular hours.

10. Better meat control. The lamb and veal are very poor quality.

11. A strongbox with three keys for cabildo archives is not in place as required.

12. Roads, streets, and irrigation ditches need attention. Pigs loose in the streets must be slaughtered as ordered. They cause much damage, especially in the irrigation ditches. . . .

14. We need a *procurador* [prosecutor] with a stated salary and responsibilities who will work for this villa and not against it.

15. We don't have enough cedar for our own building needs, but outsider lumber dealers are cutting down our trees and selling the lumber in the Villa de Oropesa or elsewhere. Please order them to sell the wood in this town and not elsewhere. To the contrary results in great harm and it is only fair that this be remedied.[27]

The remaining tenets consisted of a string of complaints concerning irresponsibility and lack of attention to civic affairs. Worse, mayordomo Gómez Arnalde accused Captain Juan de Tablares, the current corregidor and *justicia mayor* (deputy of the corregidor), of possessing very poor judgment. The mayordomo claimed that Tablares had little ability to choose adequate people to oversee the maintenance of the countryside, *tambos* (roadside inns), weights and measures, branding procedures, roads, and other matters. This corregidor had given his young and very inexperienced son-in-law too much responsibility in these affairs, and almost nothing had been accomplished. Nor had the current procurador general fulfilled his commissions; he was yet to return after having been out at his haciendas for many days.[28]

Clearly, the mayordomo echoed some important concerns regarding Mizque's failure to live up to its potential. Misuse of Indian labor, slackness in town construction, inertia regarding urban and rural improvement projects, and administrators' failure to perform their duties were only a few of his grievances. However, the concluding complaints perhaps expose the core of the problems. The mayordomo held the present corregidor (a political rival, a personal enemy, or maybe simply a terrible administrator) personally responsible for Mizque's shortcomings. Judging from the many comments scribbled in the margins of the documents, the mayordomo's observations seemed to carry some weight and were at least given consideration by others. Possibly some were even carried out. The following events more than underscore Mizque's role as a significant agricultural producer and regional transport-communication link.

Villa Leadership, Community Action, and Building a Bridge

On December 28, 1629, Don Cristobal de Sandoval y Rojas (knight of the Court of St. James and corregidor of the Villa de Salinas), Francisco de Rivera, Matías de Betancourt, Juan de Saldaña, Juan Ruíz de Herrera, and other administrators and attorneys came before the cabildo. They launched a proposal that a bridge be built across the Río Grande, which served as a boundary separating the jurisdictions of Mizque and La Plata. This was no idle dream. These men were not only dead serious, but they came well prepared to argue their case and see it through, as the more than 168 documents pertaining to the bridge, its construction, and the aftermath indicate. These documents, immensely rich in detail, provide a rare, behind-the-scenes view of how the lesser-known colonial trade centers functioned and how they related *to* as well as *with* each other in their own intraregional contexts.[29]

In the following months (December 1629–July 1630) many people came forward to offer strong support for the bridge. Apart from the cabildo members, notable vecinos served as witnesses, including some of the highly regarded first settlers, as they still proudly called themselves. Fundamental issues were recorded repeatedly in various legal tracts—reviews, reports, writs, warrants, testimonies, bids, contracts, and decrees—as efforts mounted to convince the viceroy, via the audiencia in La Plata, that the bridge was an absolute necessity. It would, they all argued, contribute to the common good of the entire viceroyalty.[30]

In support of their case, the proponents of the bridge spoke of the long, hazardous trip between La Plata and Mizque, calculated to be about a twenty-four-league (seventy-two-mile) passage that included the infamous, highly dangerous white-water crossing of the Río Grande. The consensus was that the customary crossings in boats and *balsas* (rafts) were not only costly but also extremely risky. Every year, particularly during the rainy season (which usually began in November and ended in March), for lack of a bridge, "many people are drowning and there are many losses of goods, so much so that merchants and other travelers are reluctant to trade and travel [to the region] . . . to the detriment of all . . . [there are] losses in royal taxes and [all of this is] harmful to the general welfare, especially in relation to trade with the province of Santa Cruz and the Villa de Cochabamba and vicinity whose losses are so notorious that they recognize the utility and advantage of constructing said bridge."[31]

Indeed, the lives of countless Spaniards, Indians, and blacks had been lost in those crossings, not to mention the loss of mule teams, horses, and other livestock. As often as not, goods that were not swept away by the strong currents were damaged beyond repair, accounting for additional losses. On one occasion, one of the witnesses, Maese de Campo Juan Nuñez Lorenzo of the villa's Santa Hermandad, recalled being completely stranded in the middle of the river with mule teams and more than twenty men. They had lost their boat as the river rose rapidly, and they could not get to either embankment. With the assistance of some Chiriguano Indians who had "left their province of Sta. Cruz" (suggesting they were of peaceful intent and not organized warriors), and using makeshift rafts, he was able to extricate himself. The others were less fortunate and apparently perished. He suffered major losses in the disaster. Clearly, Nuñez Lorenzo concluded, the bridge had been needed for a long time.[32]

Another witness, Don Juan de Llano, vecino and alcalde de la Santa Hermandad of this same villa, recalled his own brush with drowning four years earlier. He and six others had boarded one of the boats on the La Plata side with the intent of crossing the river to reach the Villa de Salinas side. The boat struck a large piece of timber and sank about four and a half miles downriver, taking five passengers with it. These deaths, added de Llano, like most of the others, could have been avoided had there been a bridge. Concurring with de Llano and the others, still another witness, Don Antonio Calderón, vecino and regidor of the villa, added a further dimension to the litany of drownings and property losses. The only time the sugar shipments could be brought up from Santa Cruz for transport across the river was during the rainy season, the worst possible time for crossing, even by boat. The shipments invariably got wet, causing considerable loss, as was "widely known."[33]

Rodrigo Peraza Betancourt, vecino of the villa, testified that for more than thirty years he had frequently crossed the river in order to travel back and forth between the Villa de Salinas and the Ciudad de La Plata and that it was always a difficult trip, especially the river crossing during the rainy season when it was particularly hazardous, be it by horseback or by raft. Peraza Betancourt confirmed the other witnesses' reports of the drownings of many "españoles, indios y negros" and of goods lost in transport, especially when there was turbulence and the strong currents swept everything along the way. These losses would never have occurred had there been a bridge. And in fact, declared the witness, building a bridge was a very small price to pay. Considering the great losses thus far accrued the bridge would all but pay for itself in no time.

Peraza Betancourt emphasized the far-reaching implications of building the bridge. This crossing was a major transportation and communication point that served not only the Villa de Salinas and the Ciudad de La Plata but also the gobernación de Santa Cruz, the Villa de Cochabamba, and the Villa de Potosí. Even Cuzco and Lima would gain by improving this important trade route. In fact, the entire provincia de Charcas, the Frontera de (the frontier or border of) Tomina, and the new settlement in the Valle de Chilón, whose residents continually crossed the river for trade, business, and communication purposes, would benefit. In short, Peraza Betancourt merely reflected the prevailing consensus that constructing a bridge would be in the best interests of the entire region.[34]

So eager were these community leaders to see the bridge built that by January 4 they had already selected what they considered the best location for its construction. They chose the "Angostura del Río Grande"— the narrowest stretch of the river located at the most convenient point for both Mizque and La Plata, situated about thirty-six miles from the former and forty-five miles from the latter. Here there would be six yards between the water and the bridge and nine yards from bank to bank. Further, the chosen site was also near a wooded area, which would provide the lumber needed—long, thick beams—at little cost. Regarding expense, everyone involved appeared to agree that the total cost would not exceed 16,000 pesos ensayados.[35]

Just how the bridge would be paid for had also been carefully calculated, and here again emerges a detailed disclosure of the internal workings of an intraregional network. In the following months another group of witnesses, complying with a viceregal decree, appeared before the cabildo. Two of them were particularly noteworthy. As first settlers and founders of the villa—their signatures appear on the original founding declaration in 1603—their word obviously carried weight. On March 20, 1630, Pedro de Torres de la Calancha, a vecino, town founder, and councilor, testified that since the founding of the town twenty-six years ago, the only source of income for town expenditures on construction and repairs had come from *penas de camara* (judicial fines) and *gastos de justicia* (court fees). However, continued Torres de la Calancha, these funds were no longer so readily available because they were being managed through La Plata and more widely distributed for repairs and construction elsewhere, all for the "bien de la republica" (larger public benefit). Now, public funds available for the villa came from only two sources, the tile factory and the *carnicerías* (slaughterhouses). The tile factory leased out in return for six *indios de mita* (rotational draft Indian labor) and the carnicería was leased for four indios de mita, which together yielded 400–500 pesos. Yet even this sum was insufficient to pay for repairing and cleaning the canals and irrigation ditches and for other essential repairs without which the villa could not function. The only other means that Torres de la Calancha knew of came from a yearly 22-peso fee from the Gonzalo de Solís estate. Neither of the above sources amounted to much.[36]

This same witness noted that when the town was first established, a considerable sum was spent building the main canal leading from the river to town, an expense that, everyone agreed, was necessary and unavoidable. Ongoing construction and repairs continued to cost money that the town obtained by drawing from the alcabalas registered in the cabildo. In fact, Torres de la Calancha had heard from cabildo members that the villa owed the crown 1,000 pesos ensayados but did not have the means to pay. Yet he recalled that when he was a member of the cabildo and they needed additional funds for the canal and a much-needed fountain, they petitioned the crown for permission to impose a *sisa* (excise tax). He also heard that then-Viceroy Enríquez de Guadalcassar had recommended approval of the tax to the audiencia president, Don Diego de Portugal, but that the issue apparently was dropped. Certainly now more than ever, permission to enact a sisa was imperative, especially since they no longer had access to the earlier funds from various fines and fees.[37]

Torres de la Calancha continued to press for a sisa. Not only did they need to raise money for the canal system, town repairs, and the bridge, he said, but there was also the issue of the fountain. Voicing the opinions raised by other town leaders, he argued that along with the projected bridge, the Villa de Salinas also needed a fountain in the town square. A water fountain would greatly improve the appearance of the town and create public goodwill, which was certainly something to consider with the bridge going up. But even more important, a water fountain would benefit the entire community, rich and poor alike, especially the poor who, due to lack of water, had not experienced growth. They needed access to more water for their households and for the orchards that sustained them. The construction of the fountain and installation of the necessary pipes should cost around 4,000 pesos. The villa could raise this sum within five years by imposing a sisa on retail meat and wine: 1 peso per *botija* (4–5 liters) of wine, one-half real per *arroba* (25 pounds) of beef, and one-half real per arroba of lamb. The cabildo would determine the going rate on a yearly basis depending on local ability to meet these taxes, which, according to Torres de la Calancha, should bring in 600–700 pesos annually.[38]

Several days later another prestigious founder and vecino, Captain Gabriel de Encinas, came forward. On March 26, 1630, under oath, he concurred with the others that the town's current income was insufficient to take care of present needs—cabildo construction and operations, running the royal jail, and yearly repairs on the canals and bridges after the winter floods. Therefore, Encinas too appealed to the viceroy for permission to impose a sisa in order to raise 15,000 pesos, 3,000 of which would pay for the proposed fountain and *encañada* (water pipes), the remaining 12,000 to be earmarked specifically for the bridge. He noted that approving the building of this bridge would no doubt be the most important accomplishment the viceroy could achieve in his lifetime. He added that there had been a dire need for a bridge since the discovery of these lands, a need that had been ignored while most available moneys were spent on La Plata. Yet La Plata was very difficult to reach, and countless losses occurred in transit; moreover, the vecinos of La Plata did not seem to care one way or the other, even though they too stood to benefit, especially when the bridge could be built at so little cost. Further, the inevitable delays in the transport of goods resulted in higher prices for the people in La Plata and Potosí. A sisa on meat and wine would bring in at least 1,000–2,000 pesos each year. Thus, the bridge could be paid for within twelve to thirteen years.[39]

But in order to accelerate the raising of funds and build the bridge as quickly as possible, Encinas had another idea, which in fact had the support of the cabildo. Would the viceroy consider allowing the corregidor to exercise his due authority over this town—Villa de Salinas—as well as the others under his jurisdiction, such as Santa Cruz and the Valle de Chilón, and collect voluntary contributions? That way, with each vecino contributing in accordance with his ability and on a voluntary basis (the newly settled Chilón need contribute only 400 pesos), the villa could quickly raise nearly 6,000 pesos toward paying for the bridge.[40]

By March 26, 1630, cabildo members—governor and corregidor Cristobal de Sandoval y Rojas, chief constable Captain Diego Gaitan de Mendoza, official standard-bearer Diego Hidalgo de Paredes, councilors Antonio Calderón and Pedro Ortíz y Mayda, and public trustee Juan de Saldaña—convened and issued their joint opinion in support of all the testimonials presented during the preceding days. In addition to strongly urging the sisas and the voluntary contributions of local vecinos, the town leaders also proposed other measures. They argued that La Plata, Cochabamba, and San Lorenzo, gobernación de Santa Cruz, should also share the costs of installing the bridge. La Plata, in particular, would reap the most benefit of all. Therefore, it seemed only fair that La Plata pay for one-third of the cost. The Villa de Salinas, while not as prosperous or as populated as La Plata, because of its proximity to and obvious need for the bridge, would be willing to pay another one-third of construction expenses. And lastly, one-third could be shared by the Villa de Cochabamba, Ciudad de San Lorenzo, and Valle de Chilón, since they were all more distant from the bridge. Further, Mizque would be willing to contribute ten Indians who lived near the intended site of the bridge. These Indians were experienced construction workers, having served as draft labor on the Pilcomayo bridge near La Plata. Certainly the bridge under discussion was of no less importance. Indians also could be drafted from other neighboring vicinities, such as Copabilque, Pachatarabuc, and Cochabamba, to make up the remainder of the thirty needed for construction.[41]

The many months of rigorous preparation and petitioning by Mizque's town leaders paid off. On July 1, 1630, a *memorial* (writ) was issued from the audiencia in La Plata. It acknowledged Mizque's petitions for the bridge and named two *diputados* (deputies) to investigate the selected site and verify all the costs involved. The memorial also agreed that too many people, local and outsiders, had drowned and that a bridge was urgently needed. Further, it stated that considering the transportation, communication, and commercial activities involving the Ciudad de La Plata, Gobernación de Santa Cruz, Villa de Cochabamba, and all the other neighboring districts, all interested parties needed to contribute toward the construction of a road at both the entrance and the exit of the bridge. It also called for the various cabildos—La Plata, Cochabamba, and so forth—to determine whether they wished to cooperate with the plan as set forth by the Villa de Mizque. If so, these other cabildos were to submit the appropriate papers and state how much sisa they would need to impose and on which goods in order to raise their share of expenses toward the bridge's construction. Any interested cabildo failing to comply with the stated procedures would incur in a 500-peso pena de camara each.[42]

Clearly, the project met with approval at the highest government levels. From early July on, the documents reveal the most minute details on exactly how a community went about completing a public works project, every step of which was monitored by the audiencia in La Plata. In fact, interested parties had already begun to bid for the bridge contract as early as February. A document penned July 4, 1630, in La Plata noted that on February 20, master carpenter Joan de Andrada had notified all of the cabildos that he would be willing to undertake the construction of the bridge as well as open up a road between Aiquile to the Angostura passage (toward Charobamba) and from there to La Plata, all for 12,000 pesos. Others submitted their bids as the audiencia gave its final approval and established stipulations and instructions concerning the construction process.[43]

First, according to the audiencia, all of the interested communities were to raise 4,000 pesos each, to be deposited promptly so that work could begin. One-third of these funds—4,000 pesos—would be paid out at the beginning of the project, another third halfway through, and the final third would be delivered when the bridge and roads were completed and had met all the stipulated requirements. These payments would include the cost of *peones* (day laborers) and all materials. Further, the work was to be completed within one year of signing the contract, and preferably not during the rainy season.[44]

The bridge itself was to be made of wood—thick, sturdy beams measuring at least a half a *vara* (yard) thick and as long as necessary for a safe, solid structure. It would measure thirteen to fourteen feet in width, not including the guardrails, which should measure some two yards high and be sufficiently strong and well made that neither people nor recuas would ever again fall into the river and drown. Further, the wood itself, available nearby, was of the very best quality and should be expected to hold up well for at least fifty years. And finally, the audiencia reiterated that this bridge would benefit all the communities involved and that as beneficiaries, each community was to pay its fair share of all costs. This last statement was no doubt prompted by the cabildo in La Plata, which appeared to be backing down somewhat in its commitment to the project.

> . . . and for this reason we are writing to make known the extreme difficulties this city [La Plata] is [already] having in covering the huge costs of the Pilcomayo bridge which it has taken on by itself, with no help from the other municipalities. [But] on behalf of this city, once the bridge is built, we will then see to it that a road is built as conveniently as possible from this city and through its jurisdiction to wherever shall be necessary, for which there is no foreseeable difficulty in carrying through with this project, as important to this province as it especially is to that república over which our Lord looks after.[45]

Despite master carpenter Joan de Andrada's early February bid for the contract, the town of Mizque was obligated by law to announce the upcoming project by *pregón* (public proclamation) via a *pregonero* (town crier) for thirty days in succession. The pregonero was almost always an African slave or a former slave (discussed further in chapter 5). In compliance with the law, the pregonero stood in the main square of the villa, in front of the cabildo, and called out the news of the intended plan for all to hear. Between July 9 and August 30, 1630, two black pregoneros announced the pending bridge project: Juan negro, a milkman, slave of the wealthy hacendado and plantation owner Bartolomé Cortés, and the *mozón* ("robust youth") Simon negro.[46]

Not surprisingly, other architects and carpenters appeared and submitted their bids to the Mizque cabildo. In an effort to underbid the others, each swore to do more for less. The competition appeared to be reduced to two bidders, architect Andrés de Melo, vecino of Mizque, and master architect Juan Toledano, another local resident, who both agreed to do the job at 3,500 pesos per installment, reducing the total cost from 12,000 to 10,500 pesos. In his bid for the project, Melo criticized his competitor Toledano, claiming the conditions as provided in the latter's bid were incomplete and unnecessary for the intended tasks. Toledano eventually backed down and asked that his bid be removed from consideration. He claimed that he had more jobs in Mizque than he could handle and that under the circumstances he probably would be unable to finish the project within the designated time—officials, supplies, and rainy season notwithstanding. He nevertheless remained available for consultation and auxiliary assistance.[47]

Andrés de Melo, on the other hand, clearly wanted the job. He promised to finish everything, including the roads, within three months of signing the contract. He also agreed to feed twenty draft Indians needed for the project, pay them 3 reales a day, and hire a mason. Further, he would construct two level, stone-paved, reinforced *plazuelas* at the bridge's entrance and exit, sturdy enough to handle the heaviest of recuas. He also said he would open a road between Aiquile and Villa de Salinas. All of this, he said, would be completed before the rains began. And finally, he agreed that before receiving his payment, which was to be paid him two months in succession after finishing the project, he would have two diputados appointed by the cabildo to inspect his work in order to verify that he had complied with all of the specifications in the contract.[48]

No sooner had Melo presented his bid than another competitor appeared. Joseph Gil Negrete, vecino of the town, offered to build a stronger, better bridge for 3,450 pesos per payment, 50 pesos less per payment than Melo was asking. Further, he claimed that he could do a more efficient job with less Indian labor and at no risk whatever to their lives. Along with his bid, Negrete included a draft of the bridge he planned to build and very detailed instructions. By September 9, no decision had been made and complaints began to surface that further delay would jeopardize the entire project. So Juan Toledano was sent to assess the proposed site one more time and make a final evaluation.

On September 11 he reported back that in his experienced judgment the site was appropriate and that given certain conditions, there was no reason why Mizque's share of the costs should exceed a little more than 3,000. Under these circumstances, he saw no reason why he should not undertake the project himself. Not to be outdone, Melo, begging for justice, also lowered his fees by 450 pesos.[49]

On September 12, the cabildo of Villa de Salinas met and unanimously agreed to accept Andrés de Melo's bid for the bridge contract. Another African pregonero, Luís negro (referred to as "boy slave of Don Francisco Matienzo"), was called upon to publicly announce the conditions of Melo's bids. After several public proclamations to which no one responded, Melo agreed to everything stipulated in the contract and in accordance with the law, and signed the papers. He promised to begin work within two weeks, and by September 13 he was completing the necessary labor arrangements for the road work and bridge construction. In addition to the seventeen mita Indians provided by Melo, the town agreed to contribute twenty more, whom Melo would also feed and pay 3 reales each. All of the Indians drafted belonged to the two local *ayllus* (clans) named after their respective *caciques* or *curacas* (indigenous elite/noble leadership).[50]

All the while, the cabildo had not only been negotiating bids and contracts for the bridge but had also been seeking voluntary donations for its construction. Starting on September 8, 1630, the contributions (*mandas*) from Mizque vecinos began to flow in. Vecinos from Santa Cruz, Chilón, and Cochabamba were expected to do the same. Those who could not contribute toward the building expenses would have to pay a toll for each crossing. The following is the list of Mizque contributors as presented in the document, complete with abbreviations and spelling errors.

don Gabriel Paniagua de Loaisa	200 pesos corrientes	
don Gabriel de Encinas	200 "	"
don Diego de Paredes Hidalgo	200 "	"
don Álvaro de Mendoça Altamirano	100 "	"
Francisco Sanchez de Orellana	100 "	"
Capt. Medinilla	50 "	"

Ju⁰ Xiᵐᶻ de Obeido	50	"	"
Frᶜᵒ de Ribera	100	"	"
don Frᶜᵒ Matienzo	50	"	"
don Xpoval de Salazar	50	"	"
Frᶜᵒ Herⁿᶻ Maraver	30	"	"
Augustin viejo	8	"	"
Herman Mᵃ Carrasco	100	"	"
Miguel vaquero	30	"	"
Frᶜᵒ Diaz Rravelo	10	"	"
don Antonio Calderon	100	"	"
don Frᶜᵒ Turumaya	100	"	"
Ju⁰ Rodriguez de Herrera	50	"	"
Frᶜᵒ Delgado	100	"	"
Ju⁰ de _____?	20	"	"
P⁰ Arias Cotima	50	"	"
Salvador Garcia	50	"	"
Alejo _____? de la Torre	50	"	"
Ju⁰ de Çuñiga	50	"	"
Ju⁰ de Xaramillo	50	"	"
Matias de Betancor	30	"	"
Capt. Ju⁰ Muñez Loro	30	"	"
Xpoval Mim de Briambre	30	"	"
Miguel de Molina	25	"	"
Ju⁰ Trejo	10	"	"
Joseph Gil Negrete	30	"	"

don P⁰ Cabello de Guzman　　7 large jugs of wine from the Charchari vineyard delivered to this villa

P⁰ Ortiz de Maida　　70 pesos corrientes

Ju⁰ de Castilla　　100　"　"

el Venᵈᵒ Ju⁰ Flores de Paredes sent the half of what he earned presiding over the burial of an Indian named _____ tonanco.　　20 pesos more or less

Ju⁰ Diaz de Nava	40 pesos corrientes
Xpoval de Aguilar	50 " "
P⁰ Al͎ᵒ Rubio	40 " "
Dom⁰ Salgado	20 pesos in wine plus 8 pesos
Miguel de Ocana	20 pesos corrientes

In the chacara of Tuiron of Ju⁰
de Valençuela said person on the
14th of October 1630 contributed
toward said bridge   20   "   "

In Chaluani on the 16th of same
month and year Capt. Ju⁰ de
Godoy Aguilera contributed 100 pesos
in vatted wine delivered to the
Villa for its worth in
cash   100   "   "

In Tiraque on the 18th of October
of said year F͎ᶜᵒ de Andrade _____
contributed   12   "   "

Immediately followed by
Al⁰ Ruiz Morezon   4   "   "

In Pocona on the 19th October of
said year Ju⁰ López Franco   10   "   "

On the Turquillo chacara of Pablo
M͎ᵗ͎ᶻ de Asurduy Dom⁰ Hurtado   20   "   "

In the chacara in Ayquile of
Pablo M͎ᵗ͎ᶻ de Asurduy said
Pablo M͎ᵗ͎ᶻ although I
(escribano Miguel Gar͎ᵃ Morato)
and don Xpoval de la Pila
alcalde de la herm͎ᵈ
came to see the completed
bridge [and] we urged
him to contribute a

considerable amount
since he _____ so interested
in having his very fine
haciendas so near the
bridge on this side [yet]
he refused to contribute more
than 50 pesos corrientes.

13th of November of 1630	50	"	"
Juº de Bargas de Toledo	8	"	" 51

The first five people on this list were all prominent vecinos and landowners, some of them among the original founders of the villa. The hefty (within the current economic context) contributions of 100 or 200 pesos reflect their stake in the bridge project. But of equal significance is the seventeenth contributor on the list, Don Francisco Turumaya, one of the several Mizque caciques to figure prominently in the documents used in this work. He controlled the ayllu located in the Pocona region of the jurisdiction (see Map 2), a major coca-producing zone. His contribution of 100 pesos demonstrates not only that he was a man of means but that his economic interests (as with those of wealthy caciques cited throughout this work) lay squarely with his equally well-to-do European neighbors. Further research may reveal that others on the list also share Indian lineage. On the other hand, both Augustín viejo (the old) (8 pesos) and Miguel vaquero (30 pesos) were most likely of African ancestry, since the use of a descriptive nomenclature rather than a native or European surname usually indicates an African connection.[52]

Apart from the names listed above, two promissory notes appeared on August 19 and September 2, 1630, from vecinos in Omereque (an important area for livestock and wine production), both of whom were clearly anxious to contribute their share of 100 pesos each, to be forthcoming. Although the signature on one note was illegible, the other was signed by Pedro de Lara, the long-standing cabildo scribe who actually notarized the founding of the villa. Obviously, he had a stake in Mizque's development. All of the above contributions brought the sum total collected for the bridge in voluntary donations to at least

2,845 pesos, and in all likelihood more. Through voluntary donations alone, Mizque was able to contribute almost its entire share toward this obviously important *obra de república* (public project).[53]

Construction proceeded according to plan. As the work neared completion, the cabildo assumed its responsibility to make certain that all was in compliance with the contract. On November 6, 1630, three people were selected to pass review on the project, now all but finished. Not only were the bridge and road work to adhere exactly to the written stipulations, but the team was also to see that Melo did not overwork his Indians (his history of Indian abuse and other questionable behavior must have been widely circulated by now). In short, there was to be no fraud. On November 10 at eight o'clock in the evening, Santa Hermandad constable Don Cristobal de la Pila (who submitted the following inspection reports), public scribe Miguel García Morato (who penned the reports), and Joan Ximénez de Obeido arrived at the Mizque side of the bridge, where Melo was waiting for them. By the light of the full moon, the bridge looked quite good to them as they crossed it to the Chuquisaca side and back, but they reserved judgment until the following day when they would be able to continue the inspection in full daylight.[54]

The next day the team scrutinized the bridge as closely as possible, above and, in some instances, below the water. Among other things, they examined the quality of the wood, took exact measurements of the beams or girders, and determined whether each one had been properly squared off and securely fitted on the corbels (support beams or brackets), which were also carefully examined. They studied the *cal y canto* (stone and mortar work), the fortifications, and how securely the bridge was anchored into the opposing riverbanks. These cabildo representatives also examined the stone-paved entrance and exit for the bridge as well as the road work that Melo had promised on the Villa de Salinas side.[55]

The inspection reports were decidedly mixed from the beginning. While all three reviewers agreed that the entrance and exit appeared to be well constructed and paved, what followed does not emerge as a unanimous consensus. The non-official member of the group, Joan Ximénez de Obeido, although without title to indicate social, military, political, or professional position (usually an indication that none existed), spoke with considerable authority when he assessed the construction. Among other things, he was critical of the girders: they were not properly seasoned or finished (according to Ximénez de Obeido) or squared off; they were not properly aligned; several did not meet the standard length as prescribed in the contract; and some of the beams were even laid out in the wrong direction. Further, they had not been fitted properly into the corbels on either bank of the river. [56]

The men agreed that Melo had done a good job of extending the stone-paved road on the Chuquisaca side, up a slope about half a block to where the terrain leveled off. Further, the road extending from the bridge on the Mizque side was even better and wider, and it included a *placetilla* (small plaza) covering the entire entrance to the bridge. Moreover, it was understood by all that there was still work to be done, not just on the bridge but also along the road the investigators had traveled to reach the bridge, and upon which they would return to the Villa de Salinas. Rather than a real road, it was actually more of a beaten path of nine miles or so. While it was quite passable now, during the rainy season it would be difficult if not impossible to travel on it. Therefore, Melo was instructed to open up another road, already approved and decreed by the cabildo. This road would go by the slope near Don Antonio Ramón's estancia, Yuturi, which was actually on the construction site. Melo had already sent Indians to find the area. [57]

Despite Ximénez de Obeido's criticisms, Constable de la Pila filed a very favorable report. First, he noted that the bridge entrance and exit points were well constructed, as were the fortifications extending from bank to bank across the river. The bridge itself was firm and sturdy, well and evenly built with no indication of slack. He added that he had been informed that if one were to compare wooden bridges, such as the one over the Quiquijana River, twenty-seven miles from the city of Cuzco, or the one five leagues further on in the pueblo of Urobamba in the Yucay valley, both built by the Portuguese Manuel de Andrada, Melo's work was far superior. This bridge was sturdier, with no sign of shaking or swaying, and the wood was solid as the ground upon which one walks. The bridge measured fifteen feet wide (his own feet served as a measure), and all the beams were of satisfactory length, fitting well into their respective corbels. In short, it was a good, solid bridge and Melo should be paid promptly. De la Pila urged "His Royal Majesty" to honor Melo with a merced and to grant him other, even larger, projects. As to whether Melo had complied with the stipulated construction measurements, that was a matter for the cabildo to decide upon reviewing all the relevant documents. Nevertheless, as far as de la Pila was concerned, after having crossed the bridge many times on foot and muleback, in his judgment, "his conscience and God allowing," the bridge was a good one—unless, he added, someone more experienced in these matters judged otherwise.[58]

Which is precisely what happened. Both García Morato and Ximénez de Obeido thought that some of the girders were not quite as thick or as long as they should be. Although the bridge was satisfactory at the moment, it might not hold up on a long-term basis. However, they too agreed that it was a matter for the cabildo to resolve. They concluded that if these smaller beams and other perceived shortcomings were acceptable, then Melo must be paid.[59]

On November 14, the cabildo met and decided that Melo had not followed their instructions. Several violations were cited. Among the many concerns was the issue of the girders. They had not been properly finished and still needed to be debarked and squared. Already smaller than stipulated in the contract, they would shrink over time and be entirely unacceptable. The girders lacked sufficient corbels for support, the existing corbels were undersized, and the girders were not securely anchored on either embankment. Further, instead of using the required stone and mortar, Melo had substituted mud for the mortar, which of course would not hold up over time. For these reasons and more, the cabildo issued orders for another bridge site visitation and added Juan Rodríguez de Herrera, apparently an authority on roads, to the inspection team. Other experts were encouraged to participate. This time, armed with specific warrants, they were to see that Melo complied promptly with all of his obligations, including the road work. Only then would he be paid for his work. Otherwise, he would be fined and forced to pay for all public and private costs and losses incurred during the project.[60]

Post-Bridge Conflicts and Regional Interests

The written orders, signed statements, reports, edicts, and testimonies that emerged in the following days not only reveal the intricacies of a local bureaucracy at work on a local project but also offer a glimpse of the very human side of affairs, as real then as they are today. As the cabildo pressed for further inspections, an increasingly indignant Melo swore he had indeed fulfilled his end of the bargain. Accusations flew from all sides. The cabildo appointed investigators to actually dismantle sections of the bridge, much to Melo's outrage. By law, however, he was under obligation to cooperate. Not to be outdone, while the cabildo continued to refuse to pay Melo for his work, additional construction costs, and Indian salaries, Melo made good his threats to take the entire case before the royal court of appeals of the audiencia in La Plata.[61] Unfortunately, we do not know how this case was resolved. However, given what I know of Andrés de Melo's history, legal battles, and convictions of guilt, I am inclined to believe that the cabildo won its case (Melo will reappear in chapter 7).

Disputes and settlements aside, the above discussion serves to underscore exactly how community leaders, professionals, and profiteers together—or, as often as not, in conflict—functioned to create and build upon a very important intraregional network. As soon as the local need for and the potential broader benefit of the bridge were acknowledged by the highest officials in the viceroyalty, Mizque's cabildo moved quickly to put the plan into action and the bridge was built. Further, the building of the bridge reveals far more than merely a local construction project; it also provides insight into broader historical concepts. First, the large body of documents pertaining to the case reflects the centralist, authoritarian Habsburg system of attempted control, even on the most minor issues, over its colonists and indigenous populations. Everything pertaining to the bridge project—from the justification of its construction, to costs, bids and contracts, materials used, Indian labor, and more—all had to be written and notarized by an official royal scribe and presented to the audiencia in La Plata. By law, prescribed written procedures, stipulations, and instructions had to be followed and were carefully monitored by the audiencia, with the approval of the viceroy. Any failure to comply with audiencia rulings on this public work resulted in fines, often sizable. The extent of this control becomes even more significant when one realizes that the royal government was *not* paying for the bridge and road work. La Plata's response to the contributions it was expected to provide toward the bridge construction makes this point very clear. Having paid for the construction of the Pilcomayo bridge with no assistance whatsoever from neighboring jurisdictions, La Plata was unwilling to follow up with another major expenditure of this nature. For the general welfare of the viceroyalty, however, it promised to do its best to meet its obligations. Not once did Mizque's cabildo suggest a royal subsidy for the bridge.

All of this points to another significant and, for the purposes of this ongoing regional study, key issue. Despite the centralized Habsburg state, regional leaders, when they deemed appropriate, seized the initiative and combined their collective efforts to achieve their own regional goals. Of equal importance, prominent curacas participated in that leadership, reinforcing definitions of a new, hybrid post-conquest world.[62] Along with their European counterparts, indigenous leaders too were hacendados. I would also add here that much of the curacas' wealth was inherited, handed down through generations, and still represented a continuity of their pre-Columbian status. The bridge would serve their economic interests as well. Thus, at least in the earlier years the wealthy curaca not only enjoyed his traditional role as leader of his people but was also an equal partner in regional decision making that would result in his own economic well-being in the nontraditional world. The Mizque case emphatically underscores Rodríguez's argument that local economies developed separately from the Potosí "locus." While the pervasive traditional wisdom holds that Potosí was, over an extended period of time, the economic lifeline of the Peruvian viceroyalty, present indications point to an equally valid alternative, or perhaps more accurately, supplementary explanations. This is not to deny Potosí's economic impact, which I underscore emphatically elsewhere. Rather, this work simply reflects an important regional or local perspective of a larger symbiotic relationship. These hinterland, subpuna valley products, after all, did serve the mines. Of utmost importance here is the fact that as the proponents of the Mizque bridge argued their case, Potosí's significance as a part of the relevant commercial network under discussion palpably diminished. According to the documents, Chuquisaca, rather than Potosí, would be the key beneficiary of the new bridge. When the final plans were drawn for sharing by thirds the project costs, Potosí was never mentioned because Potosí did not directly participate. Potosí's silver flow notwithstanding, regional *self*-interest was the guiding force.

Mizque's cabildo established its regional leadership and set the plan into action. The municipal government and town leaders pleaded for what they knew was an economically beneficial cause. They requested permission to impose local taxes and, more important, were willing to supplement the greater part of construction costs out of their own pockets. Finally, and equally important, Mizque's spokesmen prompted their neighboring regional jurisdictions to follow their lead. Mizque—the jurisdiction and its township, Villa de Salinas del Río Pisuerga, or Villa de Mizque, and eventually Ciudad de Mizque—had carved its niche in the so-called periphery of the eastern Andean frontier. After the bridge was built, the area continued to grow and enjoy considerable prosperity, so eulogized in the earlier traditional accounts and histories.[63] It would later suffer a devastating decline attributable to a number of causes, including disease, environmental issues, and, in my opinion, draconian political and territorial reconfigurations (all to be discussed in later chapters), to become an almost eerie ghost town, the ravages of which remain even today.

II

The Emergence of a New Interregional
and Intraregional Center

3. Transforming the Land into Landed Estates

EARLY ON, THE SPANIARDS took full advantage of the resources and agricultural potential of the Corregimiento de Mizque. In so doing, they quickly established their power base as a propertied class. This chapter explains in detail how the outsiders amassed and exploited their land acquisitions in a burst of diversified agricultural activity. This could not have occurred without the multiple ecological zones that so favored the region. Nor could the Europeans have acquired their elite status without importing African slaves to supplement the labor pool required to sustain their economic well-being.

The corregimiento, as we now know, functioned as an active, productive agricultural region long before its municipal center was officially recognized by the royal government in 1603 as the Villa de Salinas del Río Pisuerga. Others would soon join the Paniaguas, Cazorlas, and Chavezes. Names such as Abrego, Encinas, Hernández Robles, Álvarez Meléndez, Paredes, and many others, including prominent curacas—themselves established area landholders before the European arrival—would begin to figure notably in extensive inventories and accountings of their holdings and possessions. They too were ready to exploit the area's considerable resources.

With its multiple ecological zones, the region yielded a great diversity of products: wheat, corn, barley and other grains, a large variety of fruits, beans, chickpeas, peas, potatoes, *ají* (chili), garlic, cotton, lumber, cheeses, honey, sugar, sorghum, peanuts, yucca, coca, and wine. The latter two products frequently appear in the late-sixteenth- and seventeenth-century tribute lists.[1] Further, like the Santa Cruz region, the eastern reaches of Mizque also produced considerable amounts of sugar and sugar by-products for local consumption as well as the regional markets of La Plata and Potosí. The later-eighteenth-century productive vineyards and sugar haciendas owned by the Jesuits—Habana and Chalguani (not to be confused with the Mojos mission itself)—were part of an already long established agricultural tradition.[2]

The Proliferation and Rapid Turnover of Estates

By the early 1600s, the countryside was flourishing with production activities from landholdings of all possible sizes. When referring to these holdings, people frequently interchanged the term *hacienda* with *chácara*. *Viñas* (vineyards) were specified as such, and *estancia* consistently referred to a livestock ranch. The estancia and hacienda called Leibato, for example, typifies some of the larger operations in the region. Exactly when it was first established cannot be ascertained. Property turnover occurred with astounding frequency here. Apparently, its most recent owners, Pedro Velazco and his wife, María González, had purchased much of the Leibato properties from Pablo Martínez. However, they had also purchased twenty-one fanegadas of planting fields from two separate parties, and El Pongo, their estancia, from a third party, Pedro de Lescano. Altogether, these properties were valued at 39,600 pesos, by no means inexpensive but certainly consistent with property values of the time.

In 1607, Velazco and his wife were putting half of these collected properties—"the estancia [Leibato], chácaras and lands with their produce, tools, and equipment, and livestock large and small"—up for sale.[3] The buyer, Pablo Pérez, a permanent resident of the town of Mizque as well as its treasurer and city attorney, agreed to a seven-year purchase transaction that would involve numerous set payments to cover the *censo* (loosely, a mortgage), which usually was obtained at an annual interest rate of 5 to 7 percent, tribute payments for the yanaconas, and similar expenses. Pérez also agreed to maintain the properties and keep them in good running order at his own expense. Further, he swore under oath not to parcel out for distribution in any way or to sell under any condition his newly acquired properties until they were fully paid for, according to the seven-year plan.[4]

The sale included Leibato and half of the livestock estancia El Pongo. A steady supply of livestock was essential for successful vineyard activities as well as sugar production. Pérez's share of this estancia included hundreds of head of cattle, sheep, hogs, and mares. This suggests, of course, that prior to the division the estancia was producing at least twice that number of livestock. The deal also included eight acres of wheat fields. Lastly, the properties involved in this transaction included half of a vineyard in Omereque, which for Pérez came to eighteen thousand *cepas* (grape vine stalks). Twelve African slaves apparently came with the chácara Omereque.[5] As will be later discussed, African slavery was almost synonymous with vineyards and wine production.

In the colonial Mizque valley and adjacent valley systems, land transactions often turned into petty squabbles if not serious disputes involving attorneys, witnesses, cosigners, and considerable legal fees. Such was the case of Leibato. Accusations and counteraccusations ensued as each party—the sellers, Pedro Velazco and his wife, and the buyer, Pablo Pérez—tried to prove the other guilty of fraud, cheating, and theft. Pérez accused the couple of charging him more than the value of the property, claiming that "they had deceived him into paying much more than the fair price for his half of the properties . . . [and] cheated him out of 4,500 vinestalks."[6]

The sellers countered by saying that Pérez was already 14,000 pesos in arrears for not making his mortgage and tribute payments. Pérez insisted that these payments were not his responsibility and that he had worked very hard over the years and had made needed improvements in the properties, all of which he had paid for out of his own pocket. He was not about to come forth with excessive payments for properties he had to work on to bring them back into decent condition. In turn, Velazco and his wife challenged Pérez to pay them the 10,500 pesos he still owed them on the asking price of 16,234 pesos for land parcels they had sold him (not to mention the 14,000 pesos of censo and tribute payments). And finally, Pérez was to receive only five of the African slaves pertaining to the vineyard in Omereque. By 1614 the sellers were saying "it really is a hacienda" (possibly meaning the properties could not be divided), which Pérez also refuted, claiming that all eleven slaves belonged to him now.[7]

The embattled parties eventually came to terms, and they swore under oath to maintain their respective obligations and agreements. While on May 27, 1614, they all "swore before God and on the cross with the fingers of their left hands" to abide by these agreements, the additional provision that "anyone who caused more problems would be fined 4,000 pesos by the royal chamber of penalties" surely reinforced all good intentions.[8]

Meanwhile, true to his word, Pérez had definitely made the improvements he had claimed. By 1613, Leibato and its related properties were growing wheat and producing thousands of *botijas* (five-liter clay containers) of wine annually. At the going wholesale prices in Mizque, La Plata, and Potosí at the time, his wine harvests could have easily resulted in an income of 20,000 pesos from his Omereque vineyard alone. Further, Pérez's ranches now handled hundreds of head of livestock, including cattle, sheep, and horses. By this time his properties were collectively valued at 39,000 pesos, just a few hundred pesos short of the 1607 selling price. By most standards this was more than satisfactory.[9]

Another representative hacienda/chacara complex belonged to General Álvaro Abrego (often spelled Abreu in the documents) y Figueroa. While he is not referred to as an encomendero, his military title and the timing of relevant documents suggest that Abrego was a contemporary of the old-guard warrior-encomenderos discussed in chapter 2. Apparently, either a daughter or a granddaughter of his was once married to Ñuflo de Chávez.[10] His chácara/viña, named La Calleja, was certainly in existence in the late 1500s, during which time he rented it out for a three-year stretch at 300 pesos a year. By 1608, La Calleja apparently had the capacity to produce at least eighty-three *tinajas* of wine (over 11,000 liters; one tinaja is 133.5 liters).[11]

La Calleja's records for 1611–13, by which time Abrego was deceased, indicate that the hacienda produced annual lots of wine ranging anywhere from 500 to 940 botijas (2,500 to 4,700 liters). After Abrego's death, Don Joan Pinelo de Ayala served as estate administrator and *tutor y curador* (guardian) of Abrego's minor children. Under the vigilance of the audiencia in La Plata, Pinelo handled all of the estate's financial affairs, as he had done since 1610. For the period between 1611 and 1613, according to the guardian, La Calleja made 13,086 pesos from wine alone, paid off debts large and small, and still cleared 1,257 pesos. Interestingly, legal and administrative debts for the period under discussion amounted to 2,875 pesos, a sum by no means unfamiliar to these hacienda/chácara complexes in Mizque's valleys.[12]

At this time, most regional chácaras rented out at an average of 300 pesos a year, while a rented house in the Villa de Mizque, completely furnished and with servants, cost 110 pesos a year. A large city house, complete with courtyards, several entrances with street access, and occupying one entire city block sold for 1,000 pesos. A corner store, owned by a cacique and strategically located on the main plaza, rented out at 30 pesos a year.[13] It helps to remember that the 6,000- and 10,000-peso annual incomes allotted the Paniaguas for their services to the crown were considered quite comfortable. (For the price of wine and other goods produced on the chácaras, haciendas, and estancias, see Table 1.)

It would appear that wine production was the primary agricultural activity at La Calleja. Unlike Leibato and its numerous related properties, this chácara did not engage in livestock production. In fact, the records show that administrator Pinelo purchased four slabs of salt and one cow every Christmas and Easter for the chácara's yanaconas. During stomping season, he also had to supply the grape stompers with beef, which they apparently consumed at a rate of one-fourth of a cow weekly. Not only did he have to buy meat, but on a number of occasions he also had to purchase corn. The chácara produced corn only for its own use, and under Pinelo's watch corn harvests fell critically short of family, staff, and workers needs. Corn production suffered for a number of reasons. First, the crop itself yielded less than expected. Further, La Calleja's yanaconas were too ill to harvest the crop one season, no doubt victims of one of the epidemics that scourged the region periodically. In order to feed his charges, the chácara administrator had to purchase 69 *cargas* (414 bushels; one carga equals six bushels) of corn between October 1610 and January 1611. The following year he reported having planted some eighteen cargas of corn saved from the previous year's crop, again to meet hacienda needs and distribute among the yanaconas.[14] Clearly, the chácara was not mass-producing corn, and throughout this period the administrator continually purchased additional cargas of corn from outsiders.

Table 1. Prices of Hacienda Products

1602–1610	
Wine	4–7 pesos per botija (top quality, 14 pesos
Oxen	30 pesos per pair
Sheep	6 reales 1 pesos each
Wheat	2–5 pesos fanega (12 reales carga, 9 pesos carga?)
Cows	8–9 pesos each
Horses	14–16 pesos each
Suet	2½ pesos per arroba
Lamb	1 peso 2 reales each
Aji	1 peso per cesto
Corn	2 pesos per carga
Yanacona clothing	20 pesos each
Mules	60 pesos each, outfitted
1628	
Mules	16 pesos each
Burros	60 pesos each
Sheep	5+ reales each
Cows	4½ pesos each
Mares and colts	4 pesos each
Horses	8 pesos each
Oxen	11 pesos each
Cane sirup	6 pesos per botija
Coca	6 pesos per cesto
1633	
Wine, aged	6 pesos per botija
1634	
Wine, good	7 pesos per botija
Wine, poor	3 pesos per botija
Mules	30 pesos 4 reales each
1635	
Cane sirup	8 pesos per botija
1678	
Wine	6 pesos per botija

Sources: AHMC-M, Vol. 1599–1629, Vol. 1624–1676, Vol. 1597–1607, Vol. 1629–1676, exp. 38.

The emphasis on wine production must have paid off. Over the years, La Calleja would acquire a good number of African slaves. By 1624 its most recent owners had put it up for sale, apparently not for the first time. The inventory, among many other things, included thirty *pieças de esclavos* (pieces or units of African slaves). The addition of thirty slaves within a ten-year period is of considerable significance and no doubt reflected a major investment in an agricultural activity that was doing well.[15] The available data offer no specific explanation on why La Calleja was again up for sale, but the general pattern emerging from the documents is one of frequent property turnover in the Corregimiento de Mizque, as the following will demonstrate.

The vineyard at La Calleja would change ownership many times after the death of General Álvaro Abrego y Figueroa. In 1629, General Bartolomé Cortés, on his deathbed in San Lorenzo de la Frontera, listed among his extensive holdings La Calleja, located in the valley of Mizque. The general appears to be something of a self-made man. He died at the age of forty, which suggests he was second generation rather than the earlier European-born frontiersmen-encomenderos discussed in chapter 2. He came from Peru, where he maintained ties up to the time of his death. Apparently, three of his slaves had driven a twenty-eight-mule team to Peru, where their presence was recorded.

According to Cortés, he and his first wife started out virtually penniless, but over time they came to acquire many properties and became quite wealthy. His second wife, Doña Luisa Ponce de León, also from Peru, specifically Cuzco, brought considerable wealth of her own to the union. Because of his poor health the general could no longer travel to his widespread holdings, so he remained on or in the region of his sugar plantation "en el distrito de los chanes" (the ethnic group of the Santa Cruz/San Lorenzo region), where he also had a sugar refinery and all the necessary equipment: many oxen, work horses, carts, and at least a dozen slaves. Another five slaves worked and resided at La Calleja, where the general's second wife supervised production activities. By his accounts, La Calleja still had livestock and now boasted a good number of untamed mules, as well as a forty-mule recua, rather large for the time and place, as most teams consisted of between twenty-four and thirty-two beasts. The general's inventory lists extensive, often lavish, personal belongings: jewelry, clothes, accessories, furnishings, cooking and eating ware, and other items considerably beyond the category of bare essentials.[16]

The inventory that Doña Luisa compiled after her husband's death reveals a somewhat different set of circumstances. La Calleja now belonged to her, as did the five slaves and the expensive wardrobes and jewelry she brought into the marriage and the 12,000 pesos that apparently remained as part of her dowry. The vineyard's estancia now had hundreds of head of sheep and goats. The bodega (wine cellar) housed twenty-four tinajas, "large and medium"—it can be safely said that tinajas came in many sizes—of wine. The general's widow had returned to Cuzco and was now looking for a reliable mayordomo to oversee La Calleja. The vineyard's story will continue to unfold in chapter 4, as the chácara's mayordomo tells it very differently.[17]

A Closer Look at Successful Hacienda Enterprises

Turning to yet another productive valley agricultural enterprise, the lengthy, highly detailed accounts pertaining to the haciendas (viñas and chacaras) named Oloy serve the present discussion well. These diversified units were owned by Captain Gabriel de Encinas, mentioned in chapter 2 as one of the original founders of the Villa de Salinas del Río Pisuerga (formerly the Villa de Mizque and often referred to as such in the documents) and a regional power broker. At the founding in 1603, the captain was appointed to the office of chief constable. He also served many years as corregidor of the town (other close relatives would follow suit), and he also served in the audiencia of La Plata. He had important connections, and important people were in his debt.

The particular set of documents examined here is identified as "Cuentas de los Menores de Encinas" (Accounts of Encinas minors). Normally, this kind of accounting is reserved for under-age orphans of deceased, propertied parents. Encinas's heirs—a daughter, Doña Ana, and two sons, Don Marcos and Don Diego—were not orphaned, and their father was alive and involved in numerous political and economic activities. No mention is made of a mother. For whatever reason, all matters pertaining to Oloy were the financial affairs of his children and were written specifically for them.[18]

A guardian was appointed to administer these affairs, and his sole responsibility was taking care of the children's estate. Apparently, at least three administrators had served at Oloy. One of them, Francisco Encinas Saavedra, no doubt a relative of Captain Encinas, acted as guardian from 1602 to 1604. He was followed by Augustín Ferrufino, another prominent community figure who served in a number of public posts, including that of corregidor in 1620. Ferrufino assumed the role of guardian for all the Encinas heirs shortly after his marriage to Encinas's daughter, Doña Ana, who must have been considerably younger than her husband. Although this particular set of documents goes back only to 1600, another set of data, *padrones de chácara* (chácara or hacienda censuses), is from somewhat earlier. These records were kept by census-taking officials and their attendants, who traveled throughout the region periodically to take inventory of yanaconas residing on each chácara for tribute-collecting purposes. The padrón documents indicate that by March 22, 1597, the "chácara" (as the census takers called it) of Captain Gabriel de Encinas in the valley of Oloy listed 179 yanaconas—men, women, and children of all ages. Of this population, 49 were able-bodied, adult male laborers. In short, Encinas's hacienda operations reflected full-fledged, healthy production activities.[19]

Oloy not only produced and sold all manner of livestock, grains, and wine but also boasted another source of hefty income. Captain Encinas was in the censo business, lending money at 5 to 7 percent interest, and could count on considerable yearly income from numerous people paying their debts. In just one brief period, 1601 to 1603, the estate acquired 11,654 pesos in censos. It could easily have been more than double that amount. One Teodoro de Pareja apparently owed 5,474 pesos in back censos, but through some land transactions and other deals with Encinas he managed to make good on his debt or at least reduce it substantially. Also, Encinas had an ongoing litigation with Álvaro Abreu of La Calleja, who owed 728 pesos, and the general maintained litigations with several other people who were not keeping up with their censo payments. Significantly, when Augustín Ferrufino took over as guardian of Encinas's heirs, he noted that he did not think the censo accounts of his predecessor, Francisco Encinas Saavedra, were complete. The earlier administrator apparently had spent most of the two years of his guardianship in La Plata dealing with legal problems relating to the minors' properties. Another set of estate earnings, *cobranzas* (collections), also appears in these records. In this instance, in 1604, Diego de Quintela Salazar went on record as having paid the children's estate 2,556 pesos in partial payment of some 3,000 pesos he owed.[20]

The serial detailed listings, as well as summaries of same, of yearly harvest, incomes (where the above censos and cobranzas appear), and expenditures yield extremely useful data. Through these daily, monthly, and yearly accounts one can obtain an invaluable view of regional history and microhistory. The Encinas papers, like the documents of other estates still to be discussed, provide considerable information along these lines. The only difference here is that Oloy operations were not necessarily more diversified than other Mizque valley enterprises, but only more extensive. Thus they simply provide a broader database with which to work.

For example, a 1602 inventory reveals that Oloy had in stock at that time thousands of sheep and hundreds of cows, calves, mares, pigs, and goats. The hacienda also had twenty-five pairs of oxen, indicating extensive or intensive agricultural production. It produced hundreds of botijas of wine plus hundreds of cargas and *costales* (large sacks no doubt equivalent to a carga, since the terms are used interchangeably) of corn. The chácara administrator, Encinas Saavedra, was able to sell all of the wine. He sold 545 botijas in La Plata and in Potosí, and the remaining 75 botijas paid for the *diezmo* (10 percent state-church tithe). All of the corn and wheat (with the exception of the diezmo payment) went to feed the household and yanaconas. The following year, while wine production was down (possibly a poor harvest), corn and wheat production increased notably. By 1604 wine production was the highest to date, with the usual percentage allocated for the diezmo, household needs, and *limosna* (alms). Encinas Saavedra sold 710 of the remaining botijas. This same year, Oloy produced considerably less corn and somewhat less wheat than it had the previous year. By the end of 1604 the administrator had sold thousands of head of livestock and now reported a markedly reduced inventory. He also reported having to purchase mules specifically for the recua because twelve of its mules had been stolen.[21]

Under the stewardship of Encinas Saavedra, Oloy earned at least 27,516 pesos for the Encinas heirs between 1602 and 1604. The administrator sold 1,551 botijas of wine, sometimes receiving up to 14 pesos per botija, which, at three times the going price, suggests it was of excellent quality. The wine sales alone earned the estate nearly half of its income for this period. The sale of all manner of livestock brought in more than 2,000 pesos, while the sale of hundreds of cargas of surplus corn and wheat added to estate coffers. Odds and ends consisting of winemaking equipment, a silver plate, and suet rendered another several hundred pesos.

While income of 27,516 pesos from operations alone is substantial for the two-year period in question, this sum acquires significance only when it is measured against the expenses accrued for the same period. According to Oloy accounts, total expenditures from 1602 to 1604 and some of 1605 amounted to 24,882 pesos. By far the most costly of all expenses related to censo payments and other similar debts, which come to 9,834 pesos, and family expenses follow at 6,320 pesos. The latter category included all clothing and accessories (linens, soaps, etc.) for the three heirs, and it also included the boys' schooling as well as Doña Ana's wedding.

Production costs for these two years came to 4,022 pesos. Next in terms of costs came legal fees, which amounted to 1,979 pesos. These fees included a constant flow of money to scribes, accountants, attorneys, solicitors, court costs, and related matters of lesser significance, all relating to the children's estate. This brings to mind the earlier comment of Doña Ana's husband and guardian, Don Augustín Ferrufino, who wondered if his predecessor's accounts were complete, since Encinas Saavedra had to spend a good part of his two years as guardian running back and forth to La Plata to take care of legal matters. According to the accounts, Encinas Saavedra had at least seven different litigations or investigations going on at the same time, which certainly offers some insight into the complexity of running these diversified operations.[22]

Maintenance, repairs, equipment, and day-to-day activities of the hacienda also swallowed up their share of estate earnings. Ferrufino reinvested 1,323 pesos into Oloy over the period in question. Two other categories, payroll (490 pesos) and yanacona service (1,519 pesos), should really be viewed in this context as a single economic unit. At least five mayordomos were hired (for what seem to be short-term periods) and paid off, but they were essential to running the chácara, as were, of course, the yanaconas. While the yanaconas were not paid salaries, by law they had to be clothed and allowed to harvest their own crops. However, as noted earlier and apparently not uncommon to the economically active agricultural enterprises in the Mizque region, the yanaconas were kept continually occupied tending to hacienda-related production activities. This, in turn, required that Oloy provide them with corn and wheat and pay Indians from surrounding towns to come in and work on hacienda repairs and the like. The yanaconas' clothing alone came to 1,274 pesos, and the *tasa* (head tax) on them came to 245 pesos.[23]

Together, then, hacienda service, salaried and otherwise, came to 2,009 pesos, considerably more than hacienda maintenance costs and quite sizable when one considers that the owners did not have to pay their yanaconas a salary. While in 1603 the administrator paid 550 pesos for fifty outfits for the male and female yanaconas, one year later he was paying 644 pesos for sixty outfits. Encinas Saavedra also provided one "Pablo negro" not only with clothing but also with a hat (the yanaconas were not issued hats). Whether Pablo was a slave is not indicated, but no doubt he was, as indicated by the ascriptive "negro" and the fact that the estate was clothing him. Lastly, church-related expenses, censos, diezmos, and other contributions amounted to relatively little—a mere 222 pesos.[24]

Oloy, then, paid for itself—its maintenance, all of its production activities, feeding the entire household, staff, and workers, its debts in censos and other investments, and all of the children's needs (schooling, journeys, wardrobes, and even expensive weddings). Furthermore, two sets of inventories reveal just how well they lived in Oloy, which will be explained in chapter 7. All this considered, Oloy still managed to clear 2,634 pesos at the end of the 1602–4 accounting period.

One final note concerning Captain Encinas's properties: he also owned houses "in the Villa de Mizque," according to one inventory, or "en el Pueblo de Mizque," according to another.[25] Either one suggests that Encinas owned these houses before the official founding of the Villa de Salinas del Río Pisuerga. It has also come to light from an entirely different source that several years later, in 1633, he was somehow enmeshed in a land dispute with Andrés de Melo of the bridge affair. The properties in question ("Las tierras de Zulpe") were quite extensive and involved 20,000 pesos and African slaves and mulatos.[26]

Moving to another family and another set of accounts, the "Cuentas de Joan Álvarez Meléndez" provide a broader view of agricultural activities in the Mizque valley and extended environs. Joan Álvarez Meléndez, whose papers date back to at least the 1580s, died sometime around 1596. Heirs or minors are not evident in the available data for this estate. Instead, his brother Cristoval Álvarez Meléndez served as the estate's *albacea* (executor). As such, he became accountable for all possessions and properties and production activities related to his brother's multiple holdings scattered throughout the valley and beyond. Here the Paniagua Loaysa clan reappears, in this instance to purchase or rent a good portion of Álvarez Meléndez's properties. Thus the need for careful accounting.

The documents yield exceptionally detailed inventories for each unit of production. These units were located strategically in the diverse ecological zones for which Mizque was well known. Accordingly, Álvarez Meléndez's chácara Copachuncho, located in the temperate valley region, produced the wheat (about 1,500 cargas) and corn required to feed the many households, staffs, and laborers these multiple operations involved. It had a number of houses and *rancherías* (hamlet-like clusters of huts where the workers lived). The main house, not surprisingly, was well furnished with many household accessories and even a number of books.[27]

Further, the Copachuncho inventory listed two mills. One of these was on the property, while the other was located in nearby Tiraque and came with walled-in houses. The records indicate the presence of more than a hundred head of livestock: sheep, goats, pigs, mules, workhorses, oxen, and a recua consisting of twenty-two mules. Further, the padrón of February 28, 1597, listed sixty men, women, and children yanaconas present, of which twenty-four were able-bodied adult males. Separately from Copachuncho existed the *estancia de vacas* (cattle ranch) Episana. This estancia had more than a hundred head of cattle, mares, and colts and apparently an additional thousand head of sheep.[28] Over time, Episana would become increasingly important in livestock production.

In addition to the above production units, Álvarez Meléndez owned a sugar plantation in the yungas of Chuquioma, part of the more tropical, coca-producing lowlands (to be discussed in detail later). This plantation, which had no name, contained an *ingenio* (refinery) and a mill for grinding the sugarcane, as well as all manner of tools and equipment required for sugar production. It also had a number of houses, including those making up the ranchería for the yanaconas. The main house was modestly furnished. Most staples and supplies—corn, *charque* (dried meat or jerky, possibly llama), flour, soap, and the like—were brought in. According to mayordomo Estevan Griego, the plantation was producing 1,000 arrobas (25,000 pounds) of milled sugar at the time of Álvarez Meléndez's death in 1596. He also recorded seventy-two botijas of miel (cane syrup), of which he sold at least sixty-two. By this time, Mizque lowlands and Santa Cruz provided sugar and related products for most of Charcas.

Finally, Álvarez Meléndez also owned five coca-producing chácaras in the same yungas region no doubt near or on the sugar plantation, which during the taking of the inventory had produced 136 *cestos* (about 20 pounds). Also in the same plantation area, he owned another chácara that produced bananas, pineapples, and oranges. Significantly, the same eight African slaves appear repeatedly in the inventories, but they seem to be associated specifically with the sugar plantation.[29]

The papers of Álvarez Meléndez do not include the usual detailed estate earnings and expenditures so useful in production analysis, but the inventories do provide considerable insight into other, related matters. For example, in his final accounting, brother and executor Cristoval ascribed a monetary value to the deceased's remaining belongings that did not include his many landed properties or what was left of them. Gabriel Loaysa and Doña Mayor Verdugo, as mentioned earlier, had purchased or rented Copachuncho, if not other landholdings as well. The remainder of Álvarez Meléndez's possessions were valued at 1,957 pesos. Payments of his remaining debts, including alcabalas, the funeral, legal fees, and other expenses, came to 2,498 pesos.[30] Yet certainly the earnings and/or value of his many other landed properties—the tropical sugar plantation, chácaras of coca, livestock ranch, and fruit-producing chácara—netted, or had the potential to net, considerable income.

Another hacienda complex—Bartolomé Cortés's Turque and its related estancia Tuyota, its vineyards, plantation, and other properties—provides an additional perspective to the present discussion. Its most recent owners, Juan de Rivera and his wife, María Durán (neither is titled), died in 1628 and 1634, respectively. However, in this case the relevant documentation includes not only the usual inventories but also a *tasación* (appraisal for tax purposes) of all properties, holdings, and belongings pertaining to Rivera's estate. The documents concerning these complex and far-reaching holdings are themselves extensive and detailed. No doubt the government-appointed tax appraisers took greater pains to ensure as thorough and accurate an accounting as possible. Unlike the traditional notary, they did not have to rely solely on what family members wished to inform. Thus these papers offer an even broader spectrum by which to assess agricultural production in the Mizque valley systems.[31]

To begin with, appraisers Don Antonio Calderón Alejo García de la Torre and Miquel García Morato (the latter also served as the official scribe for the Villa de Salinas at the time) made note of the extra effort involved in their task. In particular, they wrote of the greater distance between Turque and the Villa de Salinas. Apparently, because of the distance, while some of the hacienda workers were registered as having been born and raised on the Turque hacienda, they and their families lived on the closer livestock estancia Tuyota. At the time of appraisal the estancia had more than a thousand head of sheep, over a hundred horses (male and female), mules, burros, and oxen, whose total worth at the market price of the time amounted to almost 3,200 pesos. Tuyota also registered the usual livestock-related equipment.[32]

The estate possessed two large, fully furnished houses at the *casco* (main unit), referred to as Turque Arriba (Upper Turque). The older of the houses also had a nearby, newly constructed chapel. Together these two properties were appraised at 400 pesos. A new house, not quite finished, built by Juan de Rivera's son Gabriel was also worth 400 pesos. The estate also possessed two vineyards, one containing 36 grape stalks, the other 7,500 stalks. Together the vineyards were appraised at 20,671 pesos. The vineyards came with their wine bodega, which at the time of appraisal contained 39 tinajas holding 1,232 botijas valued at 1,203 pesos. In addition, there were 4 other tinajas of poorer-quality wine yielding some 30 botijas. The wine alone was worth 1,248 pesos. The accounts also make note of the tools and equipment required for wine production.

Further, the estate held several fields not under cultivation, which were valued at 600 pesos, a number of draft horses at 40 pesos total, plus of course the required recua, this one made up of thirty-five mules, appraised at 1,070 pesos. In addition, the casco properties included a large orchard with fruit-bearing orange, lime, pomegranate, quince, and guava trees valued at 600 pesos. The household furnishings, accessories, and personal belongings (including tooled silver) in the main house in Turque Arriba were valued at 2,625 pesos.[33]

The estate had its own sugar plantation at Turque, complete with its mill and processing equipment. It also possessed at least sixty-eight slaves—male and female—of all ages, each identified by age, often place of origin, name, special characteristics, abilities, or skills, and respective economic worth—in short, how much they cost. And finally, Juan de Rivera's estate also owned a full city block of houses and plots in the town proper. The houses were completely furnished.[34]

In terms of production, between 1628 and 1633 the vineyards yielded 2,671 botijas of decanted wine. Between 1629 and 1633, after the children and the diezmos were paid off, the estate had 347 arrobas (8,675 pounds) of sugar and 61 botijas of cane syrup. Looking at the larger picture, over the years after Juan de Rivera's death, measuring estate earnings against its debts, one could safely say, given the data available, that like most of the Mizque operations discussed here, the haciendas, estancias, and plantations pretty much broke even, and perhaps better. Although the estate earned 18,067 pesos between 1628 and 1633, it paid out 20,569 pesos, 2,502 pesos less than its income. Yet one year later, in the 1634 accounting, deceased Juan de Rivera's brother Gabriel, now tutor for Rivera's wife and four minor children, reversed this trend. For that year the estate's operations brought in 8,097 pesos but spent only 4,769, thus clearing 3,328. If all things worked in its favor, the estate could easily pay for itself and still have surplus finances. This was not an unenviable position considering the precariousness of agricultural production and the market.[35]

In terms of sheer magnitude, however, the estate of Maese del Campo Juan de Paredes provides a nearly panoramic perception of the region's potential. Paredes, one of the signing founders of the Villa de Salinas in 1603, served at that time as the regional magistrate. His documented land transactions appear by 1595, and it is likely that he had begun to acquire his holdings even earlier. By 1610 his estate at large comprised a variety of holdings. It was usually referred to as Tucuma. The main house apparently was located on the holding sometimes called Tucuma Alta (Upper Tucuma), while the chácara/viña was established on Tucuma Baja (Lower Tucuma). In its entirety, then, the estate involved the main residence, vineyards, corn and wheat fields, a mill for grinding both grains, houses, bodegas, *vasijas* (large containers), rancherías, estancias, and the like. Tucuma Baja, where the vineyard was located, had a hundred oxen and related equipment, eighty-nine pack mules, and an impressive number of wine-filled tinajas. Clearly, this vineyard operated on a relatively large scale. The estancia El Novillero (possibly formerly owned by Gabriel Paniagua) held an additional hundred of head of sheep, cows, horses, and mules.[36] Further, in the accounting (and thinking) of the time, slaves were always listed with and as property and objects. In this case, in El Novillero were listed, along with the livestock, four black slaves whose descendants would later populate this estancia in greater numbers. The maese del campo also owned "great amounts of properties" downriver from Mizque as well as "some houses" in La Plata next to the church of San Sebastian. His house, presumably in Tucuma Alta, was well furnished with the usual chairs, beds, tables, and weapons. The inventory also refers to silver medals that were to go to his nieces and nephews upon his death.[37]

The debts owed to Paredes were also quite impressive. At the time of the writing of his last will and testament, nine debtors owed him a total of 9,880 pesos. Unlike Encinas, who was in the censo business, debts owed to Paredes did not involve censos. Some were quite hefty individual debts, with two involving 1,000 pesos each and another of 5,000 pesos.[38]

Paredes's inventory also sheds considerable light on the family history and the origins of the chácara/viña Tucuma Baja. The founder and original owner was Juan's older brother Alonso, who had died some twenty years earlier (around 1590) in Spain. Upon his death, this older brother bequeathed his Mizque properties to his younger brother Juan, his sister María de Paredes, and her two children. The hacienda had been averaging about 6,000 pesos yearly, adding up to 120,000 pesos over twenty years, so each of the four family members had 30,000 pesos coming in inheritance, a sum that could purchase a sizable piece of useful land. Alonso also founded a chapel in the main church in the town of Majacela, Castile, Spain, where they were born. The chapel was created in the name of the family members buried there, for whom daily masses were still being offered at, of course, a cost. It was not unusual for the earlier, often first-generation Spaniards to send their newly acquired wealth back to their inheritors in Spain. In this case, Alonso was taking care of the souls of his predecessors. Lastly, the inventory papers make it quite clear that the Paredes family made every effort, and put it in writing, to keep their extended properties within the family. This, in 1610, is the first hint of a traditional mayorazgo to be found in the countless Mizque property-related documents examined in this study thus far.[39] The attempt to keep the properties in the family did not succeed, as will be discussed below.

Considerably later, in 1679, the Inventario (inventory) de Bienes Robles appears. These accounts not only shed light on the dynamics of property holding in the countryside but also provide some insight into the ownership of town properties in the Villa de Salinas (formerly Mizque) itself. In 1679, Secretary Felipe García de Robles, public scribe of the royal crown and of the cabildo of Villa Salinas del Río Pisuerga, died intestate in Santa Cruz. Again, the only documents available are inventories, which involved a number of participants and witnesses. These included Roblès's legitimate sister, Doña Josepha de Robles y Palma; her son, Don Juan González de la Torre; and local officials Don Antonio Polanco y Velasco and Mayor Don Juan Francisco de Morales. The corregidor, Maestro del Campo Don Bernardo la Sierra, oversaw the proceedings. Robles did have a brother, Bachelor Juan García de Robles, prominent ordained priest now serving in Potosí. He also had four minor illegitimate children (*hijos naturales*). There is no mention of a wife or legitimate children.[40]

Apparently, Robles owned at least three houses in town. One had three large rooms—a living room and two equally large adjacent rooms—a large patio, an orchard with its attached or nearby *torrecilla* (turret) with four bedrooms, completely walled in, and with tiled roofs. The house also had a *pulperia* (small general store) with its own small courtyard, or *patio*. All had doors with keys, and the window frames, ledges, and sills were made of cedar. The orchard consisted of all manner of fruit trees—quince, pear, apple, orange, peach, fig, and lime— all in good condition. There appears to have been another house, of which Robles's sister owned the second story, and a third, purchased by Robles from his niece, which had several rooms, one of which could be used as a kitchen. This property, like the first, had a bountiful fruit orchard and thirty-nine *alfoncigos* (pistachio trees) as well as a large, walled-in courtyard. It had a little passageway leading to the main street of the villa, with a large front door with key. Doors with keys were obviously much sought after, no doubt for security as well as reasons of prestige. According to the inventory, some thirty *magueyes* (century plants) were found on the property.[41] The number of these plants suggests they may have been used for industrial purposes.

While the first house was furnished with only a very large wooden cupboard, the third dwelling had considerably more furnishings: chairs, tables, trunks, buffets, and the like, all of cedar. The property contained two storerooms, one of which, the inventory takers concurred, could have been converted into a kitchen.[42] At least two of these properties must have been quite large to have contained the orchards and large courtyards referred to in the inventories. They could easily have taken up a good portion of a city block (if not an entire block) as exists in Mizque today.

In addition to his houses in town, Secretary Robles had taken possession of "la hacienda de Tucuma." This hacienda would be, of course, the casco of the former Paredes estate, "located within the parameters of the Villa de Mizque itself,"[43] that the Paredes family had tried to keep intact. In these later years, Tucuma appears to have evolved into a relatively modest agricultural unit with more than a hundred head of cattle (most of which were branded), horses, mules, and a few burros. That there were fourteen oxen at Tucuma suggests modest but ongoing planting and harvesting. The inventory team learned that more cattle belonged to the hacienda but that they had strayed back to Pocona, where they were originally purchased. The hacienda's mayordomo (or *agente*, as he is called here) had taken off in pursuit in an attempt to return the strays to Tucuma. The main house, while large, was now in considerable disrepair, as was the neglected fruit orchard. They took note of the additional lands purchased as well as all of the tools and equipment used on the hacienda.[44] Compared to the other inventories, this one is sparse, with no mention of the worldly goods noted in the Encinas, Álvarez Meléndez, and Paredes accounts. Perhaps the furnishings and such were in the possession of the still-nameless mother of his four children; even more likely is that they remained in the possession of the estate and the Paredes descendants. As a scribe, Secretary Robles was in high demand and constantly on the road (he died in Santa Cruz) from one town to the next, one hacienda, chácara, or estancia to the next, meeting the myriad responsibilities required of a public notary. Yet even he had acquired a good sampling of Mizque properties over his lifetime. And the detailed descriptions of his town houses and rural properties provide an almost physical sense of the doors, walls, windows, corridors, main halls, patios, orchards, courtyards, and wheat and corn fields. Many of those houses are still in place today, just as they were more than four hundred years ago.

The Caciques and Their Properties

The Europeans were not the only property owners in the Mizque region. Of equal if not greater significance were the cacique holdings in the same area, no doubt dating from long before the arrival of the Spaniards. Of the six randomly selected cacique last wills and testaments I studied in the course of this project, their individual chacara holdings amount to a collective total of forty-two. One cacique alone, Don Pedro Chirima, *cacique principal* (lead chieftain) of the Cota (ethnic origins will be discussed in chapter 6), in 1584 owned twenty-five chácaras, scattered all over the region in clusters of three, four, five, and even six, many of which also included rancherías for his yanaconas. Nine of his chácaras were under coca cultivation. Most of the caciques owned at least one and usually more houses. Don Pedro Arapa, in 1574, not only claimed many chácaras, tierras, huertas, and *solares* (city lots) but also owned a house in La Plata with four *galpones* (barracks), no doubt to lodge his workers. Most of his houses came with orchards. Other caciques listed separate orchards. Most also claimed ownership of lands, the size usually stated in terms of how many *fanegas* (1.5 bushels) and how many *almudes* (half an acre using half a fanega of grain for sowing) of produce the property yielded.[45]

Cacique Arapa probably represents the wealthier of the caciques. He could count on producing thousands of bushels of corn, thousands of pounds of coca, and hundreds of bushels of potatoes per harvest. Like their European counterparts, these caciques produced all manner of goods, including, of course, coca and wine. It should be noted that some of their landholdings were inherited from their cacique fathers. These same caciques also raised livestock. Cacique Arapa's will declared ownership of thousands of sheep and goats (mixed together), more than a hundred mares, and many pigs and llamas, while Cacique Guaman also claimed impressive numbers of sheep, goats, pigs, and llamas and three yokes of oxen. Cacique Chirima, of the twenty-five chácaras, also raised a good number of sheep, goats, mares, cows, and oxen, but not to the same extent as his counterparts.[46]

A different set of documents, dated 1617, pertains to yet another cacique, Don Alonzo Guarayo, also known as "segunda persona del Pueblo de Mizque." Not to be confused with the Villa de Mizque, the Pueblo de Mizque refers to the Indian community, a legal indigenous entity that was completely separate from the township. Cacique Guarayo was known for his wealth, which included a considerable quantity of landholdings, one of which was a vineyard. He and his wife, Doña María Pacsima, in their last will and testament, bequeathed half of all their holdings, including half of the vineyard, to the *capillania* (chapel) for the Cofraternity of the Immaculate Conception of Our Lady. The other half of their properties, including the remaining half of the vineyard, they bequeathed to a boy named Alonso Anaba (he was identified no further). However, the town court, in accordance with the law, appointed town resident Don Juan de Saldana, lieutenant in the town government, as the boy's tutor y curador.[47] The subsequent battle over Alonso's welfare and rights reached an unprecedented pitch, the implications of which will receive further elaboration in chapter 7. For the purposes of the present discussion, Cacique Guarayo and his wife, like their counterparts, enjoyed considerable wealth, by any standards, European or ethnic, after the earliest years of settlement and colonization.[48] All of these examples involving caciques indicate that they, like their European counterparts, were actively involved in similar agricultural and livestock activities. Further, as in the case of Don Alonzo Guarayo and his wife, they could also, like some of their European neighbors, be quite generous with their worldly possessions and bequeath a good part of their wealth to their church and church-related activities.

A Broader Look at Landholding Patterns

Finally, one more chácara sample calls for examination. This case involved the chácara Cauta, owned by Rodrigo Hernández and his wife, María Trejo. Hernández apparently died sometime between 1596 and 1602, leaving the estate to his widow and their four minor daughters. These "Cuentas de Menores" (Accounts of orphaned children) provide a number of significant insights beyond the construct of units of production, the primary subject of discussion thus far. First, the children must have been quite young when their father died, because the accounts cover a considerable period of time—from 1602 through 1628. Pedro de Salazar served as the guardian and estate administrator for almost this entire period, keeping records of all production and financial matters pertaining to Cauta. Apparently he was also a son-in-law of the deceased, although which daughter he married cannot be ascertained. Captain Pedro Gaitan de Mendoza, *alguacil mayor* (chief constable) of the Villa de Salinas del Río Pisuerga, took responsibility for overseeing and supervising the final accountings and the partition of the estate among the five heirs and beneficiaries.[49]

Cauta primarily produced corn, wheat, and (for the first couple of accounting years) *ají* (a widely used Andean chili). Corn and wheat production increased over the years, as did the number of oxen needed for plowing (from six pairs in the 1602–3 accounts to ten by 1611). Guardian Salazar managed to sell all of Cauta's harvests over the years, keeping only enough to feed the family and hacienda personnel and service, including "a yanacona Indian, [who,] having fled for a long time, was given twelve cargas" of corn. The five heirs and "servants" consumed little more than the newly returned yanacona, their supply for the same time period coming to fifteen and one-half cargas.[50] Perhaps the former's twelve cargas were intended to sustain his family. Cauta production of corn and quite significantly wheat by the 1611–13 accounting had increased. Further, the chácara seems to have been breaking even all along. Apparently the family began renting out Cauta for 320 pesos a year around 1620. By 1626, the last year of the tutelage and prior to the partition of the property, chácara activities had obviously slacked off. This year's harvest yielded only 15 percent of its earlier harvests. Administrator Salazar complained, "there is no one around to harvest the crops." This may have been due to epidemics as well as flight. By then they were preparing to divide the properties.[51]

Apparently, all five parties involved—widow María Trejo and daughters Fernanda de Trejo, Juana Hernández, Ana de Trejo (now married to Pedro de Aquino), and Francisca Hernández—were satisfied with their shares of the repartition. Each heir received her respective *suerte* (parcel of land), carefully delineated by specific geographic boundaries and landmarks. Each also accepted her allotment of the existing tools, equipment, and livestock with adequate pasturage. The chácara yanaconas, in these accounts referred to as "indios" and "pieças," numbered seventeen. The executors distributed them among the five beneficiaries, and in one case this was done in accordance with the wishes of the yanacona family in question.[52]

Finally, the chácara Cauta itself, no doubt the casco, remained in the hands of Francisca Hernández, possibly the oldest daughter. The yanacona family mentioned above remained with her, to the obvious agreement of all concerned. Thus the documents once again provide more than a hint of mayorazgo, at least in a broader sense. Rodrigo Hernández provided as generously as he could for his heirs and dependents, at the same time keeping the parceled-out properties within the family. This does not appear to be the norm for the period covered in this work.[53]

The above has provided a fairly representative sampling of the many haciendas, chácaras, viñas, and estancias located in the Corregimiento de Mizque. Some of these holdings were situated in the Villa de Mizque (Salinas) proper, others nearby, and still others at varying and often considerable distances from the political center. Clearly, the region's multiple ecological niches played a major role in the diversity of agricultural activities in which property owners engaged. Inventories, last wills and testaments, and land disputes indicated not only who held the land but also the extent of those holdings. They also reveal the considerable presence of an imported slave population. Further, many of these extended holdings had considerable monetary value. Take, for example, Don Bernardo de la Fresnada y Zúñiga, 1624 owner of La Calleja, which we know had many owners. His properties in Mizque, Salta, and Tucumán (present-day Argentina), his houses in Lima and La Plata, his wife's dowry, debts owed him, and his African slaves easily surpassed 100 million pesos.[54] Others, some included in this study, could easily match if not surpass the wealth of the Fresnada y Zùñiga family.

One issue does require a bit of additional explanation at this point. Land values could be somewhat ephemeral and subject to different interpretations. If the properties were being assessed for tax purposes, the owners would no doubt wish to devalue their holdings. If, on the other hand, they were up for sale, there was a tendency to inflate the value. That said, there does appear to be a general consistency in property values at the time. The Paniagua, Carçola, and Encinas families, to name only a few, may have been the first to seize the opportunity to exploit the region's many resources. Others quickly joined the pursuit. In the process, a clearly defined propertied class rapidly emerged, with far-reaching sociopolitical implications. They established their political machine to serve their interests. They introduced African slavery. And, as we will see, they saw to the demise of the indigenous elite.

4. Harnessing the Resources

MIZQUE'S COLONIAL LANDSCAPE spread and layered itself over a vast territory of multiple ecological zones. Its upper reaches, temperate spheres, and lowland tropics overlapped and became intermediate terrains creating additional pockets for production activities. The same data that informed the region's settlement and landholding patterns lend support to a number of issues involving the nature of production itself. Within the context of agricultural activities we learn about planting and harvesting, the processing of goods for market, the transportation of those goods, and the trials and tribulations of the ubiquitous estate mayordomos and their respective administrative watches. Further, these documents offer rare "insider" views on area mining, an economic activity few scholars—with the exception of Eufronio Viscarra, who had access to most of the Mizque collection—attend to. Above all, the data underscore a diversity of production, in many cases yielding actual records of the quantities and market prices of goods produced, such as livestock, corn, wheat, ají, grape stalks, wine, sugar, syrup, and coca (see Table 1 for specific information).

Of equal importance, the documents also indicate the local, intraregional, and interregional markets for which these locally produced goods were destined. Here, the personal accounts of the mayordomos who actually supervised and participated in the day-to-day estate operations and production activities are particularly useful. The function of the mayordomo should not be confused with that of the estate administrator, guardian of minors, or the chácara curaca. The last was always listed in the padrones de chacara, along with the yanaconas whom he apparently represented while simultaneously serving as something akin to a foreman. Mining required an entirely different set of constructs and will be discussed separately below. Coca, because of its considerable pre-Columbian, historical, and present-day significance, will receive attention here and in appropriate discussions in subsequent chapters.

The Mayordomos

Needless to say, a good mayordomo was essential for efficient, profitable estate activities.[1] Without him, estates could, and often did, fail. The wise owner of a hacienda, chácara, or estancia paid his mayordomo well, by the standards in place at the time in Mizque and elsewhere. Such appears to be the case for the earlier-mentioned Don Bernardo de la Fresnada y Zúñiga, who, in 1610, took over ownership of the very productive hacienda and viña La Calleja, formerly owned by General Álvaro Abrego. In his will of 1624, Don Bernardo named the mayordomo of La Calleja, Joan Yrigo, to whom he paid a decent 600 pesos a year, 400 of which were to be paid in botijas of wine. He also declared his mayordomo "a good Christian," probably indicating a good measure of trust he felt toward his employee.[2] It is useful to recall that this is the same Don Bernardo who owned the extensive landholdings located throughout the viceroyalty and well into present-day Argentina.[3]

However, as the court records demonstrate, not everyone valued his mayordomo as did Don Bernardo. In 1608, mayordomo Captain Juan Trejo de la Cerda worked at La Calleja under General Álvaro Abrego, where he too earned 600 pesos a year. Upon the general's death, however, mayordomo de la Cerda met the opposite fate of his eventual successor Juan Yrigo. In a move that demonstrates just how intertwined Mizque socioeconomic relations would become, who should appear on the scene but Augustín Ferrufino, guardian of the earlier-discussed Encinas children's estate, Oloy, and now husband of Doña Ana. Since Abrego's estate had fallen into considerable debt (more than 3,000 pesos) to Captain Encinas (his father-in-law), Ferrufino decided to oversee the day-to-day management of the holdings himself. He reasoned:

> After all, Abrego has been in debt to us [Encinas estate] the longest. Now the Abrego estate is trying to keep on a mayordomo, which will cost a lot in terms of expenses, salaries and other *damages usually wrought by these hacienda administrators* [emphasis added]. Here I am, a virtual neighbor,

who has every interest in seeing La Calleja run well and expanding. I can see to her well-being very easily. Therefore, I offer my services in administering said estate, without any salary, being as I am such a trustworthy and reliable person, who can be depended upon, which is of much importance during these ongoing litigations. As one who has utmost interest in La Calleja's welfare, I beg Your Majesty to order the firing of the salaried mayordomo and allow me to take over without salary the administration of the estate, as the most interested party seeking justice.[4]

The authorities in La Plata granted Ferrufino his request in April 1608. True to his word, he ran the Abrego estate efficiently and profitably and began paying off Abrego's many debts. By July 1610 he had apparently accomplished his goals, maintaining that most of the debts had been paid off and that the hacienda had increased production under his direction. He again mentioned that this would not have occurred under the stewardship of just anyone. Such administrators would have caused more harm than not, because they did not take a personal interest in supervising properties that did not belong to them.[5] Soon thereafter La Calleja was in good running order, complete with a new owner and a new mayordomo, Don Bernardo and Joan Yrigo, respectively. At least for a while.

Regarding mayordomos, one thing becomes apparent. Mizque had an impressive record of hacienda ownership turnover, with the same yanaconas and purchased African slaves usually staying in place. It also appears that a number of individual haciendas experienced considerable mayordomo turnover. At La Calleja, estate guardian Don Juan Piñelo de Ayala noted in 1611 having paid hacienda mayordomo Francisco Sánchez 293 pesos 4 reales for the time he served on the chácara. No exact time period was mentioned, but the salary was paid sometime after August of that year, so it was probably based on a rate of 600 pesos per year. According to his accounts, between 1612 and 1614 Piñelo de Ayala hired at least three mayordomos for what appears to be specific short-term or seasonal assignments, such as grape harvest or grounds work.[6] However scant the information, some observations can be made. One of the mayordomos appeared to have been the more permanent of the group. Yet instead of the standard 600 pesos paid to full-time mayordomos at La Calleja, according to the available record, he eked out 319 pesos 5 reales in cash. There is no evidence that he was paid in wine, as were other parties to whom the hacienda owed money. Like the other three mayordomos, he still was not full time. Perhaps they made their living by hacienda hopping and taking on short-term assignments throughout the region.

Such was the case of Pedro López Tovar, mayordomo of La Calleja in 1633, now under the ownership of the estate of General Bartolomé Cortés. The general's widow, Doña Luisa, sent López Tovar off to Tomina on a matter of business. During his absence, the mayordomo appointed as his replacement "the Portuguese Cabral [possibly black] and a mulato Julio de Malaga." Doña Luisa paid Cabral 1 peso a day (a total of 40 pesos) for supervising the hacienda. There is no mention of pay for Julio de Malaga, which, along with his name, suggests that he was most likely an African slave.[7] Slaves, in numbers large and small, formed a common and identifiable component of the region's labor pool.

To help us understand the tenuous and seemingly erratic relationship between mayordomos and owners (or estate guardians), La Calleja's accounts again yield relevant information. One of the estate's many owners, General Bartolomé Cortés, died in June 1629. After his death, his estate executors saw to the usual run of wills, estate inventories (of which there were many), and, in this same case, the search for a "good" mayordomo to oversee La Calleja's many activities. They were willing to pay 500 pesos a year, not quite the 600-peso standard set for earlier mayordomos. However, the estate administrators added an additional perk of eight botijas of wine annually, bringing the salary up to about 550 pesos. In exchange, the mayordomo was expected to "run the hacienda, bring in the harvest, search for yanaconas [the constant runaways, discussed at length in chapter 6], feed and clothe them and the African slaves, and pay their tasas." To put this in perspective, successful wine producers in Arequipa in the late 1500s paid their trusted and therefore well-treated mayordomos 320 pesos annually, which was considered quite good.[8]

The estate's curador (probably Jacinto Villaroel) hired Rodrigo de Torres, touted as experienced, to serve as mayordomo. The curador indicated concern that Torres might not pay the 1630 tasas for the yanaconas and the slaves. This mayordomo lasted less than a year and was promptly replaced by Pedro López de Tovar, who agreed to stay on as mayordomo for two years at a salary of 450 pesos a year, plus rations that included twenty-four lambs and twenty-four cargas of flour, all of which could easily amount to 500 pesos a year.[9]

In 1632 mayordomo Tovar presented his 1631 accounts in a legal filing. In a litany of complaints, he described the mess he had inherited, mostly the result of the carelessness of others, including his predecessor Torres. He could not produce the three hundred botijas of wine expected of him from the last harvest, having barely reached two-thirds of the anticipated yield. The herd of sheep had dwindled to very few, most having died or strayed for lack of Indian shepherds—again, not his fault. The hacienda houses were falling apart, and it would cost at least 3,000 pesos to repair them. Worse, he was left with only two Indians and one negro, making it impossible to harvest the vineyards. He received no operating funds when he started the job and very little afterward; in fact, he had to dig into his own pocket and actually go into debt to bring in the *mingas de Indios* (supplementary outside paid labor) to work in the vineyards. He went on to complain that he also had to juggle accounts to meet payments on tools, tasa, church tithe, alcabala, food and clothing for the Indians, and other labor costs. None of this was of his doing or his fault, but nevertheless he had to meet these expenses in order to keep things running. He had done his best under the circumstances. Despite the obstacles, his harvest far surpassed that of his predecessor Torres, and his wine was vastly superior. In fact, the 401 botijas of wine Torres turned over to him were "pure vinegar" from which they could not earn "a single real."[10]

Continuing in detail, Tovar accounted for the cost and quantity of wine produced and sold and described the production process step by step. He also was very defensive about the time he spent away from the hacienda (absenteeism *was* a problem on the chacaras), arguing that his absences were never due to personal reasons. He left only on orders from the general's widow, who sent him to Tomina and La Plata (the latter more than once) on hacienda-related business and who also had him keep the Indians busy with repairs and such so that his absence would not cause any problems. Tovar, concurring with Doña Luisa's earlier comment, also mentioned that he had left "un fulano [deprecating, similar to saying "some so and so"] Cabral portugues"—a person well experienced in haciendas and vineyards—to serve as mayordomo during his absence. Cabral took good care of the haciendas and was paid accordingly. Tovar also noted, as had others at different times on other Mizque chácaras, that 1631–32 was a very "sterile" year for corn, which was consumed mostly by the Indians, and that neither corn nor Indians were available.[11] This sterility was in all likelihood due to a combination of circumstances—a damaging freeze and a dwindling labor force due to epidemic disease coupled with labor flight.

Tovar's final statements took an even more defensive and assertive tone as the mayordomo emphatically registered his complaints. Apparently, despite the problems and obstacles, not to mention the useless wine his predecessor left behind (which must have been a sore point, as he stated a second time that "my predecessor made vinegar, I make wine"), Tovar had come through for the estate, single-handedly salvaging at least 336 botijas for the 1631 harvest and apparently more than 675 botijas for 1632. His wine was selling at 6 pesos a botija, and at the time it was considered *añejo* (premium) and the best La Calleja had produced to date. Despite his efforts, he had not been paid. So he paid himself, in generous quantities of wine—200 botijas, in fact, amounting to 1,200 pesos. This unilateral move apparently did not please the estate, which accused him of theft.

In rebuttal, the mayordomo hurled forth numerous countercharges, including the sorry state of affairs with which he was left. He claimed that no one kept his promises and that even to get the salary owed him he had to present his case in court. All of this was the responsibility of one's *amo* (boss), as was the case with his former boss Don Gabriel Encinas (of the well-run Oloy), who took good care of salaries from the very first accounting period. Not yet finished with his accusations, Tovar plunged ahead:

> You won't find a single mayordomo willing to take on this burden even if you paid him 800 pesos, which still would not be enough because he would still have to spend 300 pesos in legal expense. And after all I have

done to get the hacienda back in working order, at my own expense, and I have brought in outside Indian labor all the way from La Plata at my own expense, I beg of you, please pay me for my personal service, sweat, and hard work, including the back pay owed me. It has cost me too much to pay out of my pocket without being reimbursed. I do not have enough money to run the hacienda.[12]

It is quite possible that Tovar was allowed to keep the wine. On August 1, 1633, his successor, Diego Phelipe García, reported having received twelve tinajas of wine from that season's crop, which in part should be attributed to Tovar's efforts. García wasted little time in echoing Tovar's now familiar complaints. He lacked money to bring in the required outside labor to finish the harvest. The yanaconas had yet to be given their usual ration of work clothing and were threatening to flee. Worse, not only had he not been paid his back salary, but he had not been reimbursed for the money he had drawn from his own funds to use on hacienda and vineyard upkeep. He urged the estate to sell some of its wine to pay what was owed him. One month later, estate guardian Jacinto Villaroel was also demanding *his* salary and expenses.[13]

One can only speculate as to why General Cortés's widow, Doña Luisa, was so reluctant to pay the salaries of these important administrators. Some possibilities come to mind. Perhaps, because her husband had died only recently, financial matters pertaining to the estate had not been fully resolved and thus she was reluctant to pay out any money at all. On the other hand, it is clear that Mizque agricultural properties—haciendas, chácaras, estancias, and viñas—collectively experienced a nearly dizzying rate of turnover. As observed earlier, anything even faintly resembling a mayorazgo was the exception, not the norm.

General Cortés's landholdings were numerous and extended throughout the entire region. Perhaps the estate turned its attention to its lowland sugar plantation, Turque, to focus on sugar production. Moving individuals or an entire workforce from one agricultural unit to another appears to be another Mizque tradition. Owners often moved their servants, slaves, and yanaconas from estancia to chácara to viña, and even to their town houses in Mizque or La Plata, depending on specific need or harvest season. General Cortés already had thirteen African slaves working at another of his holdings, Tiraque. Slaves were an extremely expensive source of labor, not to be left idle. Interestingly, by 1635 yet another set of new owners had taken over Turque. The inventories now included sixty-eight African slaves. Further, Turque's operation had expanded to include two working units: Turque Arriba and Turque Abajo (Upper Turque and Lower Turque, respectively).[14] In terms of interregional exports, sugar from these lowland reaches was a close second to the wine exports of the more temperate zones of the corregimiento.

As often as not, responsibility for overseeing transport of the finished product from hacienda to local and distant markets also fell upon the mayordomo. Wine and other products were sold locally all the time. These products were also used to pay hacienda debts or church tithes and in other transactions that involved mutual agreement that the goods could substitute for money. These local and intraregional purchases and barters contributed considerably to estate coffers. More important, however, were the interregional transactions to La Plata and Potosí for which large quantities of goods were transported over difficult and often treacherous terrain—lowlands and mountains alike. While the harvesting of coca occurred year round, grape and sugar harvest took place on a seasonal basis. As mentioned above, Mizque grape harvest occurred every April.

An Insider's View of Winemaking

The 1614 accounts of wine production at La Calleja, then still under the ownership of General Abrego, provide a day-by-day, insider view of the entire process. Diego Pérez, mayordomo in charge of the harvest, in a written report requested by Mizque cabildo officials (possibly for alcabala or sales tax purposes), noted that the first stage of the process took exactly fourteen days. Starting on Friday, April 18, the stompers began smashing grapes by foot and the *mosto* (juice) was immediately poured into botijas that were promptly stored in the *bodega* (wine cellar). The first day they filled 86 botijas, the second day 66, the third day 78, and so on, testimony to how hard and fast they needed to work so as to not lose the entire harvest. They apparently stopped stomping for a couple days to pick more grapes for further winemaking. In those almost two weeks they produced 907 botijas of mosto, which was then poured into the much larger tinaja containers.[15] Similar to sugar production, grape harvest and subsequent processing into wine required swift, almost nonstop labor-intensive work for a relatively short period of time. One error in judgment or timing could cost the entire harvest.

On September 30, 1614, yet another person, identified only as an "authorized" Bartolomé Carrasco, reported to municipal officials that he had completed the decanting of the wine, now a total of 633 botijas. These he had transferred (decanted and clean) into twenty-four tinajas of different sizes, each holding anywhere from seven to forty-two botijas. All of the tinajas of wine were now secure in the bodega of La Calleja, the key for which would remain in his possession.[16]

The harvest responsibilities of the mayordomo did not end with the storage of clean wine, however. He still had to deliver his product to near and distant markets. All of the larger, interregionally active haciendas possessed their own recuas. If the hacienda did not possess its own recua or if the hacienda recua was otherwise occupied, the mayordomo had to hire one, which was referred to in this context as a *flete* (recua for hire). *Flete* also refers to the actual fee charged for the transport of goods. For example, recua owner Sebastian López de Arora, who resided in the Villa de Salinas, authorized driver Antonio Luque from San Lorenzo de la Tierra to "fletar" López de Arora's recua to whomever was interested in renting it, to transport goods of up to 500 arrobas anywhere in the region—La Plata, La Villa Imperial de Potosí, or anywhere else in the viceroyalty of Peru. In another instance, sometime in 1624 the Paniagua estate hired *indio ladino* (Hispanicized Indian) Lorenzo Pacheco and his team of twenty-four and one-half (!) mules to carry ninety-four "signed and sealed" botijas of wine and nineteen wool blankets from the *obraje* (textile mill) located on their large Mizque hacienda Buena Vista. Pacheco was to deliver these goods to Miguel de Sepulveda in La Plata and was to be paid 8 pesos per mule upon delivery. In the meantime, the Paniagua estate loaned him money to cover his travel expenses and fees for crossing the Río Grande, still a very dangerous passage.[17] The bridge discussed in chapter 2 had not yet been built.

The 1604 Encinas accounts indicated that the hacienda-viña Oloy also had its own recua. In fact, estate guardian Francisco Encinas Saavedra noted that twelve of their recua mules had been stolen and he needed to replace them. Soon thereafter he bought sixteen mules. All the while, and no doubt with the assistance of his mayordomo, he had to arrange and prepare for several shipments of hacienda goods for local and distant distribution. One such transaction involved 620 botijas of wine and was apparently supervised personally by Encinas Saavedra. The estate recua carried the 620 botijas of wine up to La Plata. There the estate guardian repacked unsold wine and transported it to Potosí, where he sold the remainder. The trip and sales transactions took three months. During the same year, several more interregional transactions occurred involving flete transports between the Oloy, La Plata, and often Potosí. In one case, Encinas Saavedra paid recua driver Miguel de Ramón (the nomenclature suggesting African origins) almost a thousand pesos to carry 500 botijas of wine up to La Plata. Over the year he sent three other shipments on different recuas to La Plata and Potosí, amounting to 443 botijas at a total of nearly 900 pesos for delivery. Renting a recua was not inexpensive, but the returns made the outlay worth the effort.[18] Apropos of area wine production, two very popular misconceptions require attention. First, the decree of Philip II (1527–98) prohibiting wine production in the colonies was never enforced in Mizque. Further, I have yet to see documentary evidence that any Mizque official ordered the burning of vineyards, as is popularly alleged.

Apart from wine, Oloy also shipped livestock. In this case Encinas Saavedra paid to transport forty-four *novillos* (young bulls) up to La Plata. And finally, during one of those many trips to the highlands, the Encinas estate bought two hundred empty botijas in preparation for the year's wine harvest at Oloy. These must have been brought down the mountains in the estate recua because again, as in the shipment of 620 botijas, there is no mention of a flete.[19] Earlier discussions of Encinas operations established the presence of mayordomos at Oloy, some for apparently short periods. Regardless, all received their due salaries at the appropriate time. This brings to mind the wishful thinking of La Calleja's mayordomo Tovar in his legal filing against the estate of

General Cortés for back salary. How he longed for the good old days when he worked at Oloy for Don Gabriel Encinas, who always met his payrolls promptly!

The 1610 accounts for the estate of General Álvaro Abrego (which included La Calleja) indicate that the three-month recua trip from Mizque up to the highlands of La Plata and Potosí and back was a well-established routine. Abrego's records also reveal exactly how much it cost for the upkeep of the mules on these journeys. On one recua trip to La Plata and back, which took four months and ten days, the maintenance of the pack team totaled 266 pesos. Other trips involved shorter periods, one only two months. Average cost for recua upkeep on the road hovered abound 60 pesos a month, enough to discourage any dawdling along the way.[20] Estate guardians often traveled up to the highlands with the recuas in order to attend to a myriad of estate legal and commercial matters for which they were responsible. Estate administrators, mayordomos, and guardians in charge of commercially active chácaras and viñas kept well occupied.

However busy some Mizque mayordomos may have been, they also were not above getting themselves into trouble. Take, for example, the February 1603 criminal case filed by mulato (this ascription, like all the others pertaining to race and ethnicity in this work, is a direct transcription from the actual document and in the sequence in which it appeared) Juan Gutiérrez Altamirano. Basically, Gutiérrez accused Estevan Navarrete, mayordomo for the Gabriel Paniagua de Loaysa valley haciendas Coloy and Chimboata, of slaughtering his livestock, amounting to eleven oxen, two hundred pigs, and an unspecified number of cattle. Mayordomo Navarrete, in turn, filed a countersuit in which he claimed that Gutiérrez, whose properties lay adjacent to the Paniagua properties (as well as to community fields belonging to the *indios* from the pueblo of Pocona), had time and again allowed his livestock to stray onto Paniagua properties, where they caused major crop damage, particularly in 1602 and 1603. Claiming the animals had cost the Paniagua haciendas at least two hundred cargas of wheat intended for hacienda consumption, Navarrete demanded that Gutiérrez reimburse the haciendas the estimated 300 pesos in damage.

Apparently, some pigs belonging to local priest Juan Caño de Paredes (of the prominent Paredes family discussed elsewhere in this work) were also involved, but the mayordomo aimed his major thrust at Gutiérrez, giving possible credence to the defense of the latter's lawyer. The lawyer argued that the Paniagua mayordomo had no legal case against his client. Not only had his client done nothing wrong, but the mayordomo, neglecting to follow proper legal procedures, had taken the law into his own hands. Instead, the mayordomo should be "rigorously" punished for having himself committed a serious crime—among other things, for having killed the aforementioned livestock, which had not caused any real damage. He also claimed that his client had suffered a major loss and the Paniagua mayordomo owed Gutiérrez more than 2,000 pesos. The lawyer added that Navarrete's slaughter of his neighbor's livestock was an act of retribution for something that had occurred between the two litigants a long time ago. Worse, Navarrete, rather than face the punishment for his actions, had collected his belongings and "fled" the Oloy hacienda to avoid justice.[21]

This case abounds with revealing data pertaining to social relations, particularly in regard to race and ethnicity, which will be discussed in the following chapters. For the purpose of the present discussion, at first glance justice *seems* to have been served on both sides. The case did end up in La Plata, in the court of final appeals, where the presiding judge reviewed the arguments of both parties and decreed accordingly. He found Gutiérrez guilty of allowing his livestock to damage Paniagua property. He ordered him to pay Don Gabriel Paniagua eleven cargas of "top quality wheat" (worth 150 pesos) and one hundred lambs (worth 50 pesos). The judge also found mayordomo Navarrete guilty and ordered him to pay Gutiérrez two oxen (worth 30 pesos) and thirty pigs (worth 45 pesos). The judge considered this sufficient payment to cover some of the losses inflicted on Gutiérrez's property and his source of livelihood. The judge ordered both parties to pay the other within six days of the decree. He further admonished the two litigants not to assume that the punishment meted out to the one party in any way mitigated or lessened the punishment decreed upon the opposing complainant.[22] This was a curious admonition considering the fact that the decision unmistakably came down in favor of the powerful Paniagua estate. The judge awarded the estate more than twice as much money as the mulato landowner Gutiérrez, when the monetary loss in the latter's slaughtered livestock amounted to nearly twice as much as the Paniagua loss. And the monetary value of the Gutiérrez decision—75 pesos—came nowhere near the 2,000 pesos demanded by his lawyer.

Further, after having established that his decision was to be taken seriously by all concerned, the judge included in his writings a 1574 ordenanza issued by Viceroy Don Francisco Toledo pertaining to live-stock production and regulations:

Item: Whoever is raising up to 100 cows is obliged to have one person, negro, mulato, or indio to watch them, and up to 400 cows must have two, and 400 and above, just have three cowboys, and up to 1,000 cows, one additional person is required and so for each additional 1,000, an additional person is required, each with their own horse and lance to bet-ter round up on penalty of 50 pesos per person who neglects the stated requirements.

Item: Should said cows and calves be far away and their herders are sent to distant places after them, [if] the herders are not to be able to tend to [the animals] as they are supposed to, and take care of the roundup, then those who find animals who have wandered into their crops have the right to kill the animals and use the meat as compensation for crop damage.

Item: Since mares are the easiest livestock to control, they must be kept at least a league and a half from the crops of said pueblo, and their corrals must also be located at this distance and the same conditions ordered for cows also apply to the mares. There must be a herder for each 200 mares, and up to 600 mares requires 3 herders, and should any mare wander into the chácaras, for every ten found in the crops, two may be kept and after notifying the proper authorities, may be branded with the hacienda iron or taken possession of by other accepted means, unless the crops have already been harvested in which case [the livestock owner] must only pay for any damage done to the present crop before the harvest.

Item: Wild horses are prohibited from mixing with said mares because of the harm [they cause]. [This part of the document was damaged beyond legibility.]

Item: As for the smaller livestock, sheep, pigs, goats these do not require the same attention as the larger beasts because they do not stray as far afield, but they must be kept half a league away from the property of others, and there must be one shepherd for every 600 sheep and for each 200 goats another and for each 200 pigs another and the pigs must be kept 3/4 league away from the property of others.

Item: I command that this provision be announced by the town crier in the main square [illegible] in Spanish and in the language of the *indios* so that everyone is aware of this order, and it be included in the official records of this royal audiencia [La Plata] and cabildo, and in the royal books in Potosí, and that all chacara owners and their people be informed and accept this provision on penalty of 1,000 gold pesos for the Chamber.[23]

This court case offers additional insight into mayordomo activities and responsibilities. The extent and diversity of the Paniagua estate has been established. The holdings produced nearly every possible product and respective by-product—wool blankets from their obraje at the Buena Vista hacienda, for example—that the region's complex system of multiple ecological zones could yield. Yet mayordomo Navarrete had no business taking the law into his own hands (and there is no record that he consulted with a higher authority before he took action). Further, later discussion will reveal that the mayordomo did not have many friends among the neighboring landholders, indigenous and otherwise. Nevertheless, two hundred cargas of corn (the year's crop) came to a sizable amount and was intended to feed the entire hacienda population, possibly Paniagua family members and certainly the many hacienda staff workers, yanaconas, slaves, day laborers, and so on. His harvest destroyed, Navarrete would have to replace it, which at the going price would cost him (or the estate) an unanticipated 300 pesos and possibly his job. But to slaughter eleven oxen, two hundred pigs, and an "unspecified" number of cattle seems a bit extreme. As Gutiérrez's lawyer suggested, the massacre of the animals may have had less to do with immediate crop damage and more to do with an old grudge. Yet Navarrete did kill the livestock, the indispensable livelihood of his neighbor. However, that livestock should never have been allowed to stray and damage crops. The judge reprimanded and fined both parties, though whether he did so fairly is an issue for later. He also reactivated or at least reaffirmed the Toledano decree regarding livestock, originally issued thirty years earlier.[24]

This case was but one of many involving mayordomos. They played an important and oftentimes controversial role in the maintenance of the region's privately owned units of production. A good mayordomo, short or long term, had to be on his guard and work hard to earn his salary when healthy intra- and interregional markets fueled lively production activities.

The Indispensable Mule Team

In tandem with effective administration, and equally pivotal to an ongoing and successful exchange between hacienda and market, stood the recua. The pack team was far more than a mere delivery system. Until the advent of the railroad, it played a key role in the economic survival of Spain and its colonies. For many reasons, the modern rail system often failed to reach the more distant, "peripheral" zones of the colonies, and the recua system continued to function well into the nineteenth and twentieth centuries and still does today. In the colonial context, the entire region and considerably beyond teemed with transport activity. General Bartolomé Cortés again comes to mind. Upon his deathbed in San Lorenzo de la Frontera in 1629, he made note of having sent two of his African slaves all the way to Lima with his recua of twenty-eight mules. That was a very long trip.[25]

Whether owned or rented by the hacienda, these drivers with pack teams did much more than carry hacienda products from one destination to another. In all likelihood they served as an informal system of conveying communications of every kind. One of the prevalent themes upon which this work is based is a tradition of migration and mobility that predates the arrival of the Europeans. How many people, themselves heirs of this tradition, accompanied the recuas in exchange for money, work, or the driver's kindness, to try their luck elsewhere, to join displaced family, or to return home? The case of an African slave, Francisco, is probably typical. Francisco, already intent on fleeing his Mizque chacarero master, unhesitatingly accepted a recua driver's invitation to ride with him to Santa Cruz, where, the driver assured the slave, he would find plenty of work.[26] The driver was no doubt seeking hire for sugar transport. The documentation I have available directly and indirectly confirms the importance of sugar in the tropical zones "very distant from the Villa de Salinas." There, the sugar plantations Chuquioma, Turque, and Tucuma Baja and the Jesuit holdings Chalguani and La Havana, to name but a few, boasted annual production anywhere from 347 to 3,000 arrobas (8,675 to 75,000 pounds).

Although people in the wine-producing zones of Mizque paid their debts or purchased goods and services in botijas of wine, in the sugar regions planters paid for the same in arrobas of sugar. The earlier-mentioned recua owner Sebastian López de Arora, who lived in the town of Mizque, had authorized Antonio de Luque, a resident of San Lorenzo de la Frontera (sugar zone), to rent out the former's recua for transport anywhere in the viceroyalty. López de Arora specifically referred to sugar in loads of 500 arrobas (12,500 pounds). When Doña Elvira Suárez (sister of Antonio Suárez, another resident of San Lorenzo) married Don Álvaro de Mendoza de Altamirano, her dowry consisted of one mule and 1,250 arrobas (31,250 pounds) of sugar.[27] Looking again at the accounts of the estate of Bartolomé Cortés, the general too paid many debts in arrobas of sugar from his plantation, Turque. Further, the instructions in his last will and testament referred to his daughter, Doña Marcela, a nun, "who will enter the convent in Chuquisaca and whose expenses will be paid in [her dowry] of 7,500 lbs. of sugar." These figures compare favorably to late-1600s Jesuit operations in coastal Peru.[28]

The importance of regional sugar production is best illustrated in the impassioned pleas and arguments proffered by local and regional residents in support of the construction of a bridge. They knew it would facilitate the recua transport of products from Santa Cruz, San Lorenzo, and Mizque to the highland markets of La Plata and Potosí. They repeatedly stressed the importance of moving sugar from the tropical lowlands to the highlands without the risk of losing lives (hacendados, mayordomos, drivers, and slaves) and goods at the dangerous Río Grande crossing.[29]

The Ubiquitous Coca

Moving on to coca production, a few caveats are called for. First, coca is the leaf of a bushy plant that reminds one of holly without the sharp, prickly leaf edges. It has its own pre-Inca history of consumption as a mild stimulant. Most scholarship focuses on coca production in the yungas (hot lowlands) (see chapter 6) outside Cuzco and La Paz, and less is known about the coca-producing yungas of Chuquioma and Pocona in the Corregimiento de Mizque. When the Spaniards arrived, the Inca tradition of bringing in rotational labor from afar for coca production was firmly established. Coca grew all year long and required continual attention. The Inca project involved rotating work crews periodically throughout the entire year.

Coca's prehistory would take a harsher turn with the arrival of Europeans. Spanish entrepreneurs elbowed their way into coca production soon after conquest. As they did with many other autochthonous traditions and practices, the Europeans—with the assistance of local curacas—also redirected coca production. Spanish imperial goals far exceeded those of their predecessors.[30] The sale of coca benefited royal treasuries and private coffers. Further, with the unprecedented silver boom, round-the-clock mine workers consumed vast amounts of the energy-producing leaf. As the early demand increased, prices rose accordingly. Shortly after the conquest and the first big silver strike, Brooke Larson notes, in 1549 coca sold at 18 pesos a cesto. Ten years later it had dropped to 6 pesos. Thereafter the price fell to 4 or 5 pesos per cesto, which she attributed to an "economic slump."[31]

Economic fluctuations notwithstanding, data for the Mizque region show that in 1553 coca sold at $5^{1/2}$ to 6 pesos per cesto. However, reflecting a scarcity of labor and rising demand for the product, by 1596 the price had risen to $16^{1/2}$ pesos per cesto. Yet regardless of falling or rising market prices, Mizque suffered its own set of ongoing coca-related problems. This involved the abuse and exploitation of a dwindling indigenous population that was under pressure to produce greater amounts of coca to meet the increased highland demand. Despite the fact that by 1563 and 1564 Philip II of Spain had issued royal orders specifically addressing harsh treatment of coca workers and calling for its halt, this abuse (and abuse of Pocona Indians in general) continued throughout the remainder of the sixteenth century through the seventeenth and well into the eighteenth, and at least to 1769 as tax collectors continued to abuse Pocona Indians. Market demand outweighed any significant amelioration efforts.[32] Beyond any measure of doubt, coca had and continues to have its own prolonged and controversial history of fueling Andean economies.

In Mizque, the aggressive Paniagua clan quickly jumped on the bandwagon. At least three family members held coca-producing encomiendas in the region's yungas. Clan patriarch Pedro Hernández Paniagua received his encomienda early on, as did his daughter-in-law, Doña Mayor Verdugo. Pedro Hernández's firstborn son, Gabriel Paniagua de Loaysa, inherited his father's encomienda, but in the 1580s he purchased additional coca properties in the yungas of Chuquioma. As discussed earlier, by 1608, Gabriel, in seeking remuneration for services rendered to the crown during the earlier pacification period, swore that his yungas encomienda was worthless because it no longer yielded coca.[33] In all likelihood, however, it was his Indians who were wiped out, not the coca. He did, after all, buy the coca-producing property from Joan Álvarez Meléndez for 1,000 pesos. Records of the Álvarez Meléndez estate for 1624 indicate that *his* sugar plantations and coca chácaras in Chuquioma remained quite active, producing thousands of arrobas of sugar and hundreds of cestos of coca.[34] How Gabriel Paniagua (or the estate) worked the purchased coca property cannot be ascertained. The numerous padrones de chácara and other documents analyzed in this study indicate that Mizque chacareros continued to harvest coca throughout the seventeenth century.

The coca-producing activities of the local curacas provide an additional perspective into the regional history of this sought-after plant. Many regional indigenous leaders, like their European counterparts, were economically involved in area agricultural activities, and coca was no exception. The curacas possessed coca farms in the yungas, as they did before the arrival of the Inca and later the Spaniards. The 1557 Visita a Pocona lists five landholding curacas; all five had properties in the yungas. Don Pedro Arapa, although somewhat later, again comes to mind. In 1574, in his last will and testament, he acknowledges his many and far-reaching landholdings, including his coca-producing chácara, which was producing at least 106 cestos (2,120 pounds) of coca per year.[35]

As the padrones de chácara reveal, property owners up in the more temperate valley regions frequently dispatched their yanaconas from their valley units down into the tropical yungas to work the coca fields. Further, royal officials acknowledged and permitted these temporary transfers. Apparently, the chacareros and hacendados could determine the activities of their "perpetual tenants" at will as long as they were forthcoming in their annual tasa payments.[36] On the other hand, coca producers also relied on local residents of the yungas, blacks and Indians, to harvest coca crops. In the Andean world, then as now, yunga is almost always synonymous with coca.

The Enigma of Mining

Finally, some discussion of yet another regional industry—mining—is in order. Of the printed sources consulted, that of nineteenth-century historian Eufronio Viscarra provides the best description of this activity. Although he tends to eulogize Mizque's past glories, Viscarra does provide a solid depiction of the region's mining history. He discusses not only the industrial potential of these natural resources but also offers a historical perspective into their discovery and development. Apparently the Mizque public archives had not yet been redirected to the repositories discussed in the introduction. Viscarra must have used this invaluable collection of documents while they were still in town, as he claims that the evidence of Mizque's own silver boom "is still available today in Mizque's public archives." He suggests that the region's Quioma silver mines, located on the banks of the Río Grande, were probably discovered and first worked by the Jesuits. Viscarra further notes that the Quioma boom hit "colossal proportions" by the mid-1600s and reached maximum, extensive production activities toward the end of the seventeenth century. The impressive amount of silver extracted from Quioma's rich veins apparently supported generations of Mizque families and further established Mizque as a significant market for regional consumer products.[37] In addition to silver, Mizque's mines also produced quantities of gold, bronze (according to Viedma), and aluminum sulfate, the latter critical in the processing of silver.[38]

The earliest reference to Mizque mining I came across was dated 1586 and referred to a silver mine located in the Cerro de Uquima (Uquima Mountain) near the mining town of San Pedro de la Salina. In that year, Juan Gómez Leal laid claim to this new discovery, named

Allallona, which consisted of a number of veins. Other references to mining activities followed in 1588, 1590, and 1592 and involved queries from Spain directed to the audiencia in La Plata concerning the state of the mines "in Salinas."[39] Far more useful and relevant to the goal of this study were numerous legal filings and court cases, which provide a very different and revealing slant that sheer numbers or royal orders fail to yield.

Consider, for example, the 1619 litigation filed by Captain Joseph Cano de Manzano, vecino and hacendado from the Villa de Mizque, against Juan Santos Ugarte, mulato, over a mining claim.[40] This litigation is very similar to the earlier case involving mayordomo Estevan Navarrete and Juan Gutiérrez Altamirano, also mulato. This mining claim also involves significant data on race and ethnic relations, which will receive greater elaboration in subsequent chapters. The purpose of the following discussion is to reveal the nuts and bolts of how people actually staked claims on "their" mines, how contenders frequently challenged these claims, and how the law stepped in to mediate. The audiencia in La Plata was the last domestic court of appeal, so the cases that made their way there had exhausted all channels at the local or "district court" level. They must have been considered sufficiently important to make it to the highest court in the land. This in turn suggests that the significance of the Potosí silver production notwithstanding, other mining zones and attendant ore production also were taken very seriously.

Sometime around October 1619, Captain Cano filed against the mulato Juan Santos Ugarte over possession of the mine called Nuestra Señora de la Asunción. This particular mine was part of the extensive mining site discussed by Viscarra, which I refer to here as San Miguel de Quioma. The mine had been operated earlier by Don Bernardo de Cisneros, who had abandoned it years ago. Cano claimed he had worked the mines in the region, including la Asunción, before and after Cisneros's time, but as hard as he tried he was never able to make that big strike. The reason why he had failed thus far, despite all the time, effort, and money he had invested, was an "Indian named Blasquillo" (also called Blas or Blasillo in this litigation; the "illo" suffix on an adult's name was sometimes intended less as an affectionate diminutive one would use for a child and more an infantilizing, neutralizing ascription to keep indios, negros, and mulatos in their place, although some caution is urged in applying this interpretation). Apparently, Blasquillo had worked la Asunción some twenty-six to thirty years earlier when Cisneros ran the operations. For unknown reasons, Cisneros had abandoned the mine, which contained a major vein. After his departure, only Blasquillo, known as a *barretero* because of his skills at working the iron digging rod, knew the mine was still producing "metal" (obviously silver). He continued to work the mine illegally—he never staked a claim—and kept the matter hidden, extracting ores for himself over the years.[41]

Blasquillo suffered a fatal accident (some said illness), and upon his deathbed, allegedly filled with remorse over his ill-gotten gains, he prepared his will, in which he acknowledged his wrongdoings. According to Cano, Blasquillo not only personally confessed his secret to him but also gave Cano instructions on how to find the metal-rich vein. Cano promptly found the vein as indicated, extracted sufficient ore to prove his case, and appeared before the corregidor of the Villa de Salinas. Ore in hand, he argued:

> I wish to claim this mine, which has been abandoned almost 30 years, having been kept a secret. [The mines] should be worked for everyone's benefit, and for those who are specifically interested [in excavation] such as Mateo Cano de Manzano, Pedro Gutiérrez de Lizarraga, Geronimo Guillen, Don Joseph de Ulloa, and Nicolás Velarde de Herrera, without in any way placing the Salteada mine [apparently adjacent] in jeopardy. Please grant me permission to take possession of and work the mine and its *lavares* (washes). I will comply with all regulations and payments of the royal *quintos* (fifths).[42]

As observed above, more than one mine existed at the San Miguel de Quioma site, and equally obvious, the consensus held that La Asunción would yield sufficient ores to satisfy a number of interested parties.

The evidence appeared to be working in Cano's favor until case defendant mulato Juan Santos Ugarte, now working as an "assistant" at the Quioma site, appeared before the corregidor on October 31, 1619, to argue that *he* had the rights to the La Asunción mine. He stated that the "indio alcalde Blas" had told him about the mine and that they had worked it together until Blas's untimely illness and subsequent death. (It needs to be noted here that Juan Santos not only used Blas's name without the diminutive but also identified Blas as an indigenous alcalde.) Santos Ugarte further claimed that Blas's widow, Juana Barbara, would never have to worry about her future. Blas had seen to it that Juan would take care of everything. Apparently, Blas's widow shared this information with Cano, who told Santos Ugarte never to appear in the mine again because it was *his* (Cano's). But, continued Santos Ugarte, *he* had personally worked the mines and had just as much of a right as anyone else to possess them; therefore, he implored the corregidor to put the claim in his name. Corregidor General Don Joseph Antonio Ponce de León ordered "the mine to be embargoed and closed, and all materials accounted for until the case has been resolved and all sides heard." [43]

On November 7, 1619, Captain Cano presented his argument. He maintained that "Blasillo Indio Alcalde," now deceased, had been working the mine and lavar on the sly and had confessed as much on his deathbed, "candidly and simply." Without delay, Cano had the mine registered in his name so that no one could dispute his claim to possess and work it or accuse him of procrastination, "as often happens." "So please recognize the mine as belonging to me," he asked, "as it has been properly claimed and registered, and please continue with the process and ignore the mulato Santos opposition which has led to this embargo. Said indio and said mulato Santos never registered any claim. They worked the mine secretly and should be punished for so doing. I am the one whose claim should be protected against the lies of said mulato and inferred lies of others." [44]

Blas's widow, however, provided a somewhat different perspective on the proceedings. She claimed that her husband had extracted very little from the la Asunción mine and that shortly after her husband had taken ill, Santos Ugarte visited their house and remarked that he did not know where he could find some silver. Blas told him to go to la Asunción. There he would find silver, but in return Santos Ugarte would look after the deceased's wife and pay his debts. But apparently Cano had also agreed to look after Blas's widow with profits from the newly disclosed mine. She went on to explain that a number of indigenous people originally worked for Don Bernardo Cisneros, including her husband. After Cisneros "abandoned" the mine, they continued to work it, without bothering to register claims, for twenty-six years.[45]

Other witnesses appeared before the corregidor. Juan Mercado, corroborating the widow's testimony, also stated that Blas had extracted very little from the mine—maybe two or three *quintales* (a quintal equals 100 pounds) at best. The widow's son-in-law, Ignacio Pérez, "Indio with interpreter" (meaning he did not speak Spanish and required a translator), added further information. Apparently, at some earlier time Santos Ugarte told Juana Barbara that God had taken pity on them and that he, Santos Ugarte, would find a "peon" to work with him. According to Ignacio Pérez, they all worked the mine together, "en compania" (as in a company of business partners).[46]

The following day, November 8, a group of officials, accompanied by Santos Ugarte—there is no mention of Captain Cano—visited the mine, where Santos Ugarte explained its capacity in terms of yield and depth. He had worked perhaps about three *varas* (a vara is one yard) of this particular vein. Apparently, the officials regarded his excavations as "shallow," "disorganized," and "illegal." Further, these same officials noted, no one had the right to dig abandoned or virgin mines at will or clandestinely. Everyone had to abide by royal laws and regulations. In short, the officials denied Santos Ugarte's request and granted Captain Cano possession of Nuestra Señora de la Asunción, estimated to run eighty varas deep. This permit was given under the condition that Cano would actively work the mine and protect it, in accordance with the law. Santos Ugarte also benefited. The authorities assigned him a somewhat smaller vein (seventy varas deep), the Salteada mine (cited earlier), also within the parameters of the Nuestra Señora mine. The proceedings concluded with the firm admonition that the deceased "indio Basquillo" was never in a position to determine who could work those mines.[47] The racial and ethnic nuances of this decision will receive further elaboration in chapter 7.

The Mizque region was not lacking for rich, productive mines that reached their peak activity in the late seventeenth century. Judging from the above and following cases, the crown *appeared* to make every effort to encourage competent, law-abiding people to work Mizque's silver mines, seemingly regardless of economic status, race, or ethnicity. For example, the outstanding Spanish miners cited by Viscarra left many records in their wake. In 1688, Baltazár Rojas staked a claim for the San Bartolomé vein, located near an important gold mine named la Descubridora apparently once owned by the Rubio Betancourt also cited in Viscarra. In establishing his claim, Rojas swore to uphold all the rules and regulations, pay the required royal quintos, and work his mines diligently.[48]

Crown support notwithstanding, local officials did not necessarily heed government urgings to cooperate with all parties wishing to mine for silver and gold. For example, in 1691 the audiencia of Charcas ordered the corregidor of Mizque to desist from "obstructing and bothering" the indio miners hired by General Antonio Gutiérrez Caro. Apparently the general and his hired miners at the Quioma site had already provided, in Gutiérrez Caro's words, "muchos quintos for your magesty." Judging by what they were now extracting, the general anticipated considerable yields *if* he could find dependable "indio workers." He claimed he had to beg the few volunteers and forasteros to work for him, at an enormous expense, and they rarely lasted.[49] There may be a connection between the audiencia's ordering the Mizque corregidor to stop obstructing mine workers from their labors and the frustration of mine owner Gutiérrez Caro. He possessed the mines and the means by which to pay his mining crews, yet the few who signed on did not work for long, despite the fact that he paid them. The following may explain the problem.

In 1705, Bernardo Rubio Betancourt and Juan Mejía de Illescas, owners of various mines at the Quioma site, registered a vociferous complaint against Mizque corregidor Don Juan Justino de O'Campo regarding his abusive tactics. They claimed that they were poor, struggling miners and that O'Campo was taking unfair advantages by trying to force them to fork over 600 pesos in advance so that *he* could pay up his own overdue taxes. Orders from the audiencia came swiftly: the corregidor was to leave the two miners and the "Indians" who chose to work for them alone. Should the corregidor ignore this order, he would be fined 500 pesos. Captain Betancourt, Juan Mejía de Illescas, and anyone else who indicated interest in working the Quioma mines were to be allowed to act freely. The corregidor was not to charge them tribute fees, visita fees, or clearing fees; nor was he to impose any other hindrances as stipulated in the royal ordinances. The official was to follow these orders and keep the audiencia informed of same.[50]

By 1706–7 the royal government began appointing additional officials, *tenientes de corregidor* (lieutenants to the corregidor), to the region. The government established new posts for these functionaries in Aiquile, Omereque, and the Yutumi mines.[51] Its goal may well have been twofold. By now the corregimiento had matured in terms of settlement and economic viability and was now recognized as an established asset. As such, more administrators were required to serve regional needs *and* to keep a closer eye on the increasingly autocratic, corrupt corregidores.

Yet regardless of the crown's apparent encouragement to work these rich mines, it would seem that Mizque's mineral resources were never fully tapped. This remains a puzzle. While Viscarra offers some explanations, they are not entirely satisfactory. He argues, in part no doubt correctly, that the decline in mining activities coincided with the fading of the "ciudad" (city) Mizque as it lost its grasp on the "grandeur" and "prosperity" in which it had once basked. Surely the slow shrinking of the Potosí mining industry throughout the seventeenth century and beyond had repercussions in Mizque and elsewhere in the viceroyalty.[52] The following chapters will demonstrate that multiple, interconnected issues resulted in Mizque's decline.

III

The Human Face of Mizque

*The Actions and Interactions
of Africans, Indians,
and Spaniards*

5. The Africans and Their Descendants

CONTRARY TO PREVAILING WISDOM, Africans and their descendants played a significant role early on in the Corregimiento de Mizque. Here, I unequivocally establish an African presence in the region, which, I postulate, occurred in two waves. I then move on to explain why slaves were expensive regional commodities, why they were needed, and in which sectors. The latter discussion permits me to weave into the subtext key issues of ethnicity (and, where possible, the implications of this variable), slave treatment, and slave response to that treatment. Despite their efforts, royal authorities could not control the behavior of African slaves and their descendants any more than they could that of the indigenous populations. The African presence in colonial Mizque accounted for many socioeconomic and demographic transformations.

The legendary 1545 silver strike in Potosí determined the destinies of people near and far. Ignoring boundaries of race, class, or ethnicity, it set into motion swift action on the part of royal authorities, who were now faced with a dramatic, unprecedented drop in the indigenous labor market. Promptly, the crown turned elsewhere and authorized the exploitation of another, far more distant group of people. Like the Portuguese before them and the English after, the Spaniards reached into Africa, fueling the enslavement of hundreds of thousands of human beings. Slaves from Africa—as multiethnic as the indigenous populations they would soon join—became an ongoing source of much-needed labor in the Andes. The now-classic works of James Lockhart and Fredrick Bowser established a strong African presence in the conquest and early colonization of Peru and served as an incentive for this study. While these noted scholars looked to Lima and the Pacific coast-to-highland economic axis to examine African slavery and its many and complex ramifications, this work extends the examination far beyond the traditionally established regional parameters.[1] Instead, it will focus on the long-standing African presence in Mizque, a subject that has received at best passing recognition from a few scholars. Further, up until now the scholarship has focused on the overland passage from Buenos Aires to Potosí, where the slave unit value more than doubled. No one has yet studied what happened to those slaves who were transferred beyond Potosí and into the hinterlands of the eastern Andes.[2]

The Two Waves of the African Diaspora

My ongoing research in the region reveals that the African diaspora, propelled by internal and external economic forces, reached far deeper into the eastern slopes and hinterland of Charcas than has been previously recognized. For example, we know that the generation of conqueror-warriors searching for their gardens of Eden—or at least some earthly rewards for their participation in the conquest and its chaotic aftermath of civil wars—looked east. Like their counterparts throughout Spain's newly acquired colonies, they too were accompanied by their African slaves, or freedmen, who served as military personnel or servants in the many campaigns of discovery, pacification, and settlement.[3]

I refer to these very early exploits as the first wave of the African diaspora into this particular region of the eastern Andes. While men of African origins lost their lives in the campaigns, many also survived. Thus, the first wave had its own long-lasting historical, cultural, and economic impact. The African slaves and people of African descent were active participants—voluntary or otherwise—in a militaristic, conquering/pacifying, horse-and-gun culture here, as elsewhere in the Spanish Americas at that time. I am convinced that some of them remained in the Corregimiento de Mizque as, among other things, slave and free cowboys and ranch hands. Over time they formed unions with more recently arrived slaves (and soon those slaves' descendants) brought in to work other agricultural or service sectors. They also mixed with the indigenous peoples to form a fast-growing population of color. Others emerged as landholding (possibly having obtained land as reward of service to the crown) ranch owners themselves, assertively demanding their property rights.[4]

Meanwhile, the other wave of the African diaspora into the eastern Andes was already in progress. In the Andean world, European diseases preceded the arrival of the Spaniards. The death toll among the indigenous populations created a draconian loss in the labor pool now urgently needed for the unprecedented market boom sparked by the Potosí silver strike. The Corregimiento de Mizque, with its 87 percent population loss, reflected the colony-wide dilemma threatening Spain's political economy in the new viceroyalty of Peru, but with an additional caveat. In these lower altitudes, a culture of resistance, migration, and flight prevailed. These pre-Columbian components took form in collective and individual actions against the Spanish state, and soon against local landowners as well, primarily through flight. Indigenous people fled from the state-imposed and state-regulated Indian communities and attached themselves to area haciendas, chácaras, and the like, from which they would also flee at will. The reduced indigenous population became increasingly elusive, to the frustration of both the state and the entrepreneurial settlers. Spain turned quickly to Africa for additional labor to both complement *and* supplement the reduced Indian labor pool. Local settlers had already embarked on extensive, diversified production activities, for which they were now willing to purchase African slaves regardless of price.

Slave Prices, Sales, and Traffic

At this juncture of the narrative a discussion of slave prices becomes imperative, since a willingness to pay the high cost for labor underscores the determination of the region's now-established landed elite to pursue their economic goals, aided and abetted by the imperial state. The state *supposedly* had the final say on the importation of African slaves into its colonies. It stood to benefit from all economic activities, including the slave trade and agricultural production. Many of the African slaves destined for the Corregimiento de Mizque were part of the transatlantic Buenos Aires–Charcas trade system. In the port of Buenos Aires, for a good part of the time period this work examines, slaves were worth at very most 200 pesos, and usually much less. Those who survived the arduous overland trek to Potosí increased in value to as much as 500 pesos for an able-bodied adult slave.[5]

Further, the 500-peso value established for Potosí appears to have been the average price throughout the eastern highland-lowland region. Some slaves cost a bit less, others considerably more. The earliest slave transaction I have found was dated 1551. Two slaves named Diego and María, belonging to the old clan patriarch Don Pedro Hernando de Paniagua, were in the process of paying for their *rescate* (which in this context I would translate as manumission). Although Don Pedro was in Lima at the time, his two slaves processed their payments through legal channels in La Plata. Together they were worth 1,000 pesos *de buena moneda* (good money, possibly the peso ensayado of 12 reales, making the couple worth 1,200 in pesos corrientes), of which they had already paid 742 pesos. Once they had paid in full, according to Don Pedro, they were to receive their *cartas de libertad* (manumission papers).[6]

In 1586 a seller from Mizque put his slave Antonio negro esclavo (who apparently had first been in Santo Domingo but was purchased in La Paz) up for sale at 550 pesos ensayados (approximately 910 pesos corrientes). That same year, black slave Sebastian zambo, "more or less" forty years old, was sold to the wine-producing slaveholder Joan Álvarez Meléndez for 300 pesos 8 reales. Sebastian's age no doubt influenced the relatively low price he fetched. By the 1590s the asking price for mulato slave Diego de Sevilla, about twenty years old, was 821½ pesos, while Alonzo "criollo, negro esclavo" (a black slave born in the New World), from Panama and also about twenty years old, cost 826 pesos. By 1605 a twelve-year-old boy named Simón from Angola sold for 500 pesos. During the same year, a litigation occurred over an allegedly fraudulent slave sale/trade in which both parties appear guilty. A female household slave worth 700 pesos was "sickly," while Juan from Angola, for whom she was traded and who was purportedly worth 800 pesos, was actually "lazy and no good."[7]

As slaves bought and sold in the region became more expensive, a formulaic caveat appeared more frequently in the bills of sale in order to avoid such litigation. Kris Lane, discussing African slaves in Quito, interpreting the language used there in the sale of slaves, found it "detached and dehumanizing" and notes that "'blackness' was already deeply stigmatized" in the region at that time.[8] My data strongly support Lane's interpretations. For example, in 1610, one seller advertised his slave Juan, from Angola, more or less thirty years old, for 650 pesos. In the seller's words, clearly protecting himself against possible litigations, he wanted to sell Juan, "captured in a just war due to his drunken, thieving, runaway and all other bad habits and sicknesses that he had." Other sellers were equally descriptive. Juan, originally from Biafara, was for sale for 500 pesos, but his owner cautioned that Juan was not only a drunk but also a swindler and lame (from a broken leg that obviously had not been properly treated); he also had a finger that never healed, and he possessed "the usual maliciousness." On other occasions, slave owners sold their slaves with a blanket disclaimer such as "I sell this slave with all of his or her defects." Then we have the enigmatic owner who, in 1606, wished to sell his slave Francisco from Angola, about fourteen years of age, for whatever price he could get. The owner stated that he "promised nothing" concerning the slave, admitting only that Francisco was a *bozal* (a new arrival from Africa; "unseasoned").[9]

References to slave groups and their tabulated worth also appear in the documents. The two men (discussed in chapter 4) who formed a vineyard partnership pooled together 3,500 pesos for as many slaves as the money could buy (probably six or seven, given the going prices) either from the Mizque province or from Potosí. The slaves were destined to work in their vineyards and chácaras in Omereque. The vineyard La Calleja, discussed at length in chapter 4, emerges here again in a 1624 inventory in which the vineyard's wealthy owner, Don Bernardo de la Fresnada y Zúñiga, brother-in-law to another wealthy property owner, Don Gabriel de Encinas, claimed as his property thirty slaves worth 14,000 pesos. This in turn brings to mind slave owner Joan Álvarez Meléndez, who, during the 1598 assessment of his estate's incomes and debts, offered as a payment against pending debts two of his slaves— Francisco Macompabomba of the "Maconga" (Congo) nation, and twenty-four-year-old Luís of the "Lulof" (Jolof or Wolof) nation— along with eight mules and nine cestos of coca. The total collateral package could have easily come to around 1,250 pesos, the slaves' value no doubt ranging around 1,000 pesos, if not more.[10]

Over time, slave prices do not appear to have fallen in Mizque as they

did elsewhere. In a 1638 litigation in the Cazorla family, Mizque vineyard owner Urbino, husband of one of the Cazorla women, claimed
in 1633 to have purchased two slaves. One was a "negro" named
Domingo of the Angola "cast," about fourteen or fifteen years old,
and the other was a negra *muleyca* (originally a Cuban term assigned
to African slaves between seven and ten years of age) named Luisa,
about thirteen or fourteen years old. They had been transported from
Buenos Aires and "received" by merchant Mateo Saez Ortíz in Potosí.
Together they fetched the sum of 800 pesos 8 reales. Further, Urbino
paid 12 pesos for his newly acquired slaves' clothing, 12 pesos for their
food and passage to Lima, and bought a hat for "el negro" (this is the
second time the issuing of a hat for a black male slave appeared in the
documents, possibly indicating status). He also paid a 16-peso alcabala on the slaves, raising the purchase price to about 850 pesos for
young Domingo and Luisa, both probably unskilled and yet to reach
the prime of their work life. Five years later, Urbino again listed them
as his property, still referring to Domingo and Luisa by name and as
the "two muleques angolos" who now resided at his Mizque vineyard,
La Chimba.[11]

Later in this chapter I will elaborate on the significance of African
slaves in the Mizque vineyards. In the context of the present discussion, the case of twenty-five-year-old runaway slave Josep is relevant.
In 1650, Josep's owner demanded the return of his slave. He had purchased Josep several years earlier for 600 pesos, but since then he had
trained Josep in the skills of winemaking, and Josep was now worth
1,000 pesos.[12]

Two slave transactions from 1684 indicate, among other things, that
the price for African slaves and their slave descendants remained high
in Mizque. That year, two female slaves were offered for sale in order
to defray a debt of their owner, Don Francisco Álvares de Toledo y
Gatico, dean of the cathedral in San Lorenzo de la Barranca (halfway
between Mizque and Santa Cruz). The older woman, "negra Juana,"
was said to be around fifty years of age, which was quite old for an
African slave at that time, given both the general life expectancy and
that of slaves in particular. As Colin Palmer notes, if we take into account the short life span of slaves, "a slave in his thirties or forties

was practically unsalable." Juana had been purchased in the city of San Lorenzo from Don Juan de Molina. The younger slave woman was described merely as "una mulata" of about twenty years. The owner claimed the younger slave was his slave and his "own property" because she was born from another slave he owned, now deceased, named Beatríz. The dean was selling his two slaves for 1,100 pesos, as ordered by his superior, the bishop of Santa Cruz. The written offer to sell clearly indicated, as did other bills of sale I examined, the provenance of both the slaves. Further, typically in keeping with the language and intent of the transaction, the ecclesiastic professed the usual litany of their "defects" of drunkenness, thievery, and flight. However, in a more unusual move, he also promised to take full responsibility should matters not meet the buyer's satisfaction, offering in that case to return the full amount of the purchase price to the buyer.[13]

I find some compelling contradictions in the above transaction. The dean's sense of responsibility regarding the selling of his "properties" belies any sense of personal or (even less) ecclesiastic responsibility toward the younger, nameless mulata. The two other women, Juana (for sale) and Beatríz (deceased), were clearly older and no doubt came to the prelate's ownership already named. The younger, nameless mulata was born into this cleric's ownership. As a prominent actor in a church where the sacraments are the cement that bonds the flocks to their shepherds, and upon which much of the structure of the secular arm of the church is based, baptism is elemental. And upon baptism, one receives one's Christian name in the eyes of the church. That this particular mulata remained nameless in this detailed slave sale transaction underscores the issues of detachment and dehumanization toward those of African origins. Here we have a cleric so detached from his own slave that her name either did not matter or was nonexistent, suggesting she had not even been baptized.

The other 1684 record, which appeared in the same set of documents pertaining to the bishopric of Santa Cruz, further elucidates the price of slaves in general as well as the particularities of cleric Don Francisco's slave sale. This second transaction, somewhat more complicated, involved Isabel Malemba, a criolla slave about twenty-five years old, and her eighteen-month-old toddler, "el negrito Martín."

Apparently, owners Captain Domingo Martínez de Sandagarda and his wife, Doña Antonia de León y Terán, planned to sell the mother and child for 800 pesos. This was a hefty sum considering that the going prices in Buenos Aires remained in the same range that they had fifty years earlier, and would not vary markedly at the port some fifty years later.[14] The point here is that all parties acknowledged the young mother's name and, equally important, the name of her small child. In fact, the sale of the cathedral dean's slave was the only transaction of the thirty-five I reviewed dating between 1551 and 1685 in which the slave's name was never addressed.

Regarding the higher prices of slaves in Potosí (and consequently in Mizque), Palmer offers relevant information from British slave trade data. Apparently, slaves dispatched from Buenos Aires to "Chile, Bolivia or Peru averaged 100 to 400 in each group." Even as late as 1731, traders found the trip to Potosí, especially in the winter, to be devastating. One party destined for Potosí lost 17 percent of its "cargo," partly in transit and the rest upon arrival.[15] In the early days of Mizque's settlement, experienced travelers and merchants dreaded the overland passage, which was treacherous in the higher elevations for a good part of the year. Further, the altitude—thirteen thousand feet in Potosí proper and much higher in the surrounding mountains that had to be crossed—certainly took its toll on people accustomed to the increased oxygen found at lower altitudes.

Before moving on, however, we must briefly address the issue of contraband slave traffic, which we will later discuss in detail. One need only glance at the many imperial and civil documents relating to the smuggling of Indians and livestock from Tucumán and of African slaves from the port of Buenos Aires to know that this was an ongoing, very profitable practice (when is smuggling not profitable?) which, for considerably different reasons, continually concerned both royal authorities and merchants alike.[16] It is very possible that a number of Mizque slaves were obtained through contraband.

Slaves and the Workplace

Whether or not their sale was legal, life did not necessarily ease for the enslaved once the traders had delivered them to their appointed masters. In 1629, in a treatise written in the polemical style of the day, Catholic cleric Fray Benito de Peñalosa y Mondragon presented to King Philip III his case against Andean wine production, its destructive influence on the "Indio, Mestizo, Zambo, Mulato and Negro" population, and the related evils of African slavery. The friar noted that African slaves did not work the mines. It was too cold, and local Indians were much cheaper and better adapted to Potosí mining. He argued that the slaves also were not suitable for the sweatshops or for agricultural or livestock activities. Fray Benito claimed that while some African slaves may have been used in domestic service, the overwhelming majority were put to work in the vineyards of Mizque and elsewhere.[17]

What Fray Benito did not know or did not acknowledge was that, according to Alberto Crespo, local authorities had seriously considered using African slaves for mine labor in Potosí as early as 1554 and, as we now know, even earlier for Porco. They deemed that the Africans could withstand the rigors of mining far better than the more fragile Indians. However, an assessment of labor and labor-related costs involving African slaves in the mines conducted in 1548 by Jerónimo (Gerónimo) de Soría, one of the founders of La Paz and himself an encomendero and mine owner, discouraged the use of African slaves in Andean mines.[18] The argument had nothing to do with which group could better tolerate the excessive demands of mine labor; instead, it was merely a matter of cost-effectiveness. African slaves cost a lot of money in Charcas and even more in the eastern reaches of the region. Unlike elsewhere in the colony, in this area no one was willing to subject the costly investment in an African slave to harsh, life-threatening work conditions.

This is not to say that slave masters and supervisors avoided subjugating slaves to harsh conditions in the royal mint, known then as now as the Casa de la Moneda. Actually, two mints existed: Viceroy Toledo established the first one sometime around 1573, and the second was constructed in 1759. In both, African slaves were virtually imprisoned, prohibited from leaving for any reason, let alone on Sundays or holidays, on penalty of "200 lashes," because once outside "they have a tendency to rally with other negros and create scandals and riots."[19]

Labor in the dank, dungeon-like mint was little assuaged by the dark, cramped rafters that served as the slaves' sleeping quarters. Despite the vigilance and locked gates, the slaves did manage to steal from the mint, or even to escape, and they succeeded in "creat[ing] scandals and riots."[20]

And finally, notwithstanding the pervasive anti–wine production, anti–African slavery, anti–contraband slave trade polemic so heatedly argued by Fray Benito, the eastern Andean reality posits a stark contradiction. After the silver strike in Potosí, coca—the traditional crop grown in Mizque's tropical eastern reaches, such as Arepucho and Chuquioma (as well as in other yungas areas beyond the Lake Titicaca region of La Paz), as many as two thousand years ago—came into intense demand for reasons far removed from those of the pre-Columbian eras. Now, coca would fuel the silver miners to endure their demanding toil within the mines.

Thus, with a flourishing mining industry and a concurrent voracious highland market for goods produced only at the more temperate levels of the viceroyalty, Mizque's reduced native labor pool, like those throughout the entire colonial empire, was supplemented with African slaves. The latter group's proportionately smaller numbers—and I am convinced that the available numbers underrepresent the actual population and that many more Africans arrived in the region as contraband—in relation to the Indian population belie their importance in the region's economic development, demographic transformations, and sociocultural interactions. They would provide the human resources that the dwindling and increasingly unreliable (in the European construct) indigenous population could not and would not. African slaves and their descendants would work in the town houses, churches, chácaras, haciendas, and plantations not only as domestic servants but also as laborers, skilled and unskilled, particularly on the estancias and sugar plantations, and yes, African slaves were well represented in the vineyards. African slaves and their descendants would also emerge in non-agricultural sectors as town criers, municipal government officials, military personnel, mine owners, and overseers and owners on chácaras, haciendas, and estancias.

At the beginning of this work I established that the Villa de Mizque had acquired legal recognition by 1561, if not earlier, and that the prominent Paniagua de Loaysa family had obtained their Mizque holdings by 1548. The first documented record of an African presence in the region itself, however, does not appear until 1573, when cacique Don Pedro Arapa listed his extensive landholdings and personal properties as well as people in his debt. Here he noted one Cristobal Roldán, mulato, owing him 29 silver pesos for a colt and a stallion.[21] However, the discussion here is further informed by recalling earlier mention that African slaves actively participated in the expeditions of exploration and Indian campaigns led by those warrior-cum-encomenderos during their post-civil-war 1540s heydays. Surely, as was the case elsewhere in Spanish territorial possessions, the African participants and their descendants were rewarded with manumission, land grants, and monetary remuneration for their service to the crown. They could easily have settled in this attractive multi-ecological, still-untapped zone. This would explain why Cristobal Roldán purchased his own horses. Horses, of course, represented mobility and status.

By the 1580s some bills of sale begin to appear, which now seem suspiciously few in number when compared to all the other slave-related records.[22] By the 1590s the African presence, slave and free, is visible everywhere in a wide range of documents: parish reports, parish records (baptisms, marriages, funerals), dowries, last wills and testaments, bills of slave sales and business contracts, civil and ecclesiastic court cases, and estate records and papers. In fact, it is precisely through a variety of estate-related documents—padrones de chácara, inventories, last wills and testaments, tax appraisals, and guardianships—that the African presence on the chácaras and haciendas is clearly revealed. Take, for example, the padrones de chácara. These were conducted yearly by local government officials, who traveled from chácara to chácara with their scribes and their Indian interpreters, asking the same set of questions at each stop. The questions raised and the answers summarily encoded into each document comprised a surprising number of variables, including place of origin, race, gender, ethnicity, and more (further detailed in chapter 6). Due to their serial nature, these documents reveal both changes and continuity over time, serving as a window through which we can observe a number of characteristics of chácara labor, both indigenous and African. Not only do the padrones reveal an impressive diversity of distant origins for the yanaconas, but unexpectedly, negros and mulatos are listed along with the resident yanaconas, a nomenclature until now traditionally assumed to be synonymous with Indian labor.[23]

Further, and perhaps connected to the general pattern of diversity of origins, is an outmigration from the chácaras and haciendas that changed over time from predominantly able-bodied indigenous males, to native people of both genders and all ages, to workers of African origins, slave and free. People were constantly on the go. Not only were royal administrators unable to keep the Indians restricted to their communities or reducciones, but chacareros could not control either them or, soon, people of African descent on their private estates.[24] In the census records I examined, yanaconas of both population groups came to Mizque, directly or indirectly, from the farthest reaches of the viceroyalty. They also left in droves.[25]

The earliest Mizque padrón used in this work was dated 1597. It lists negros and mulatos in the same columns as the yanaconas. At least six chácaras—some in the lower sugar-producing areas, others centrally located in the temperate niches of the jurisdiction—claimed the presence of Africans and African descendants often living in family clusters with a mother and a father present and in some cases up to five children, such as one of Captain Gabriel Encinas's chácaras in the valley of Oloy. On the large Buena Vista chácara owned by the Paniagua de Loaysas, two padrón categories were created—one for the Indians and another for the chácara mulatos, referred to as the "visita de los mulatos," of which there were at least fifteen, two of them *horros* (former slaves, now free) and all but one male. They were not identified as slaves. Only years later would slaves be identified in a padrón.[26]

Significantly, the padrones also reveal that, similar to their Indian counterparts, the African-related groups also chose "flight." For example, on one of the Paniagua livestock estancias, El Novillero (which is also the term used for a holding corral for young cattle), "Anton negro" was recorded as present. But son Antón, age twenty-five, "went" to Cuzco, while Martín Chare, mulato *natural* (meaning he was born on the chácara), was listed as "huido" (a runaway) from the chácara one year, only to reappear on the list the following year, while mulato Domingo Garro and wife were recorded as present on the same chácara one year but were not listed the next year. We have Barbola mulata and her three children moving from El Novillero to Álvarez Meléndez's Copachuncho holdings within a two-year period. Further, I am convinced there are a number of "hidden" Africans in these padrones (and in other documents examined), not identified by ancestry, but who possess surnames that have neither a European nor a native resonance, such as Tongo, Llororo, and Gororo, to name a few.[27] Similarly, names such as Juan de Ramón, Diego Portugal, or Juan hospital usually indicate African origins, particularly in conjunction with occupational roles, as chapter 7 will discuss at length.

Fortunately, a number of cross-references on chácara labor add to the discussion at hand. Several hacendados and chacareros left last wills and testaments, many of which called for detailed inventories of all properties, including, of course, their haciendas, chácaras, and other production units. Here more data emerge on African and African descendant labor, slave and free. Joan Álvarez Meléndez left a will dated 1597 that reflected a successful chacarero who, like others of his status, owned properties throughout the entire corregimiento. He owned a twenty-two-mule recua and raised livestock on his estancia Episana, wheat near Buena Vista, coca in Chuquioma, and sugar, honey, and wine in the Copachuncho area. All of these were ongoing operations at the time of his death. Among his possessions he listed an unspecified number of Indian slaves (which were usually war captives), and in his Copachuncho inventories he listed the eight African slaves he owned— six men and two women, three of whom were identified as bozales. This listing suggests that at least some of the six were agricultural labor and that Álvarez Meléndez moved at least some of them from sugar to wine production upon seasonal need. The Copachuncho operations also supported up to seventy-two people, including the wives and children of his tribute-paying yanaconas.[28] We also know that he had at least one household slave—Sebastian sambo, about forty years old when he was sold to Álvarez Meléndez in 1586.

Upon the death of Álvarez Meléndez, the transfer of ownership of his estate varied little from the eastern Andean norm. Estate transactions were often tedious, protracted affairs, dividing large holdings into small parcels and dividing families and other self-interested parties into conflicting factions. Certainly the absence of a mayorazgo system in the region influenced these patterns.[29] It would appear that by 1603 the livestock estancia Episana had changed ownership at least once and was again up for sale. In this instance, Episana's two owners at the time, Bartolomé García and Francisco Macías Torrico, were attempting to sell the estancia to Francisco Corzo, *pardo* (of African mixed with indigenous or European parentage), and Gerónimo Bosa. Further details emerge pertaining to Episana. Along with boasting an extensive terrain and appropriate features and conditions for successful livestock production (it was still producing at least a thousand head of full-grown, branded cattle, not to mention horses), the estancia also came with the "usual array" of attached household and field labor as well as draft labor coming in on a regular basis from the nearby pueblo of Pocona. Special note was made of an estancia slave, "Francisco Angola, cowboy," identified as being associated with the estancia's yanaconas and their housing, suggesting a possible supervisory position.[30] Francisco Corzo would not be the only person of African descent interested in owning a livestock estancia during this time, as the litigation between the mulato Altamirano Gutiérrez, estancia owner, and the Paniagua mayordomo discussed below will further elaborate.

Other studies suggest that African participation—as slave or a free descendant—in livestock production was not uncommon throughout colonial Latin America and the Americas in general. Given the strong Nupe (Nigeria) tradition of horsemanship and the equally prevalent history of the Fulbe (Senegambia) as cattle herders, it is not surprising that elements of these long-held African traditions carried over to the Americas and first took root in the Spanish colonies.[31] In the Spanish colonial context, then, actual ownership of an estancia would be a logical further step in the progression from slave to slave cowboy, and then to free supervisor or overseer, and finally to ownership itself, particularly in the Mizque construct of rapid land turnover at negotiable prices and where livestock production was a pivotal economic activity. The asking price for Episana was 13,000 pesos with a down payment of 4,200 and yearly payments of 300 pesos, certainly not an intimidating financial commitment when absorbed, as was intended here, by two parties.[32]

The Episana transaction brings to mind the 1610 partnership (discussed earlier) between two men seeking to venture into wine production. Their landholdings included wheat fields as well as vineyards where each man had contributed his half of the 19,000 grape bushes planted that year. They also agreed that each would put up half of the 3,500 pesos toward the purchase of as many male and female African slaves as the money would buy. This would probably come to seven or eight slaves, since at the time African slaves were an extremely expensive source of labor—especially able-bodied, responsible adults. Their modest investments rendered considerable profit as their wine enterprise flourished. Yet, in what appears to be more typical than not of the region, at the very peak of production around 1617, when the partners were selling an impressive 2,650 botijas of wine annually and their lands had tripled in value, everything collapsed. Due to familial or entrepreneurial intrigue (or possibly both), lands were sold surreptitiously and the partnership soured and apparently dissolved. In the context of the larger discussion at hand, their slave investments also contributed to the enterprise's success and increased value. Again, as is typical, the litigation dragged on for years, at least through 1635, when they had yet to resolve the land issues as well as the cost of the slaves and their maintenance.[33]

The 1629 will of chacarero General Bartolomé Cortés further informs the discussion. Cortés's operations exceeded those discussed above in size but not in scope. Included among his many holdings was the vineyard Tuyota, half a league from the Villa de Mizque, and the "very distant" sugar plantation and mill Turque, where eighteen (or thirteen, depending on which document examined) of the possibly twenty-two to twenty-seven slaves worked along with ten yanaconas. Five slaves resided in Mizque with the general's second wife, Doña Luisa Ponce de León, and four more worked at Tuyota.

After Cortés's death, Doña María Durán and her husband, Juan de Rivero, purchased at least the Turque and Tuyota units of the estate. Not surprisingly, Turque and possibly Tuyota had deteriorated considerably in the interim between ownerships, and the executors were searching for a good mayordomo who could restore the chácara to its former condition and assume full responsibility over hacienda labor. This position included, among other things, searching for yanaconas— the issue of flight appears throughout this work—and feeding, clothing, and paying the taxes on both yanaconas and slaves.[34] Once Durán and Rivero gained ownership of the properties, a major change began taking place within the labor force at the Turque sugar mill, which obviously was going to require reliable custodianship. Apparently, Rivero died within five years of possessing the properties, soon to be followed by his wife. The multiple testaments, inventories, and tax appraisals on their landholdings and considerable material possessions, including sixty-eight slaves, reveal the significant role of slave labor in these regional enterprises.[35]

Table 2, which lists the tax appraisal for the Turque slaves, underscores several issues at hand. To keep matters in perspective, it is important to understand that these appraisals followed directly after the listings of thousands of heads of livestock and appeared immediately before the extensive records of agricultural and sugar-refining equipment and household belongings. The issue here is unequivocally that of chattel slavery. All but one of the slaves assessed came from the Turque sugar operations. "The black Manuel, slave shepherd" worked on the livestock estancia at the Tuyota holding and was appraised separately at 600 pesos.[36]

The most obvious purpose of the Turque slave roll is that of slave worth. Here we have an excellent example of a systematic calibration of slave prices in accordance with age, physical and mental condition, and skill. The record supports the earlier observation that the average cost of slaves in the region was higher than in Buenos Aires, for example. But even this generalization is further underscored by the fact that in Mizque small slave children were sold for the same price—200 to 300 pesos—as able-bodied slave adults elsewhere. Even newborns were assigned a value of 50 pesos, which increased as the baby survived infancy and reached the two-year mark, at which time the toddler was worth 150 pesos and remained so until the age of four. After that, the child's value increased in increments of 30 and then 50 pesos until able-bodied adolescence or young adulthood was reached.

Table 2. Tax Appraisal for Turque Slaves, 1635

Name	Occupation	Ethnicity	Age	Price
Manuel elderly		Congo		300 P
Cristina his criolla daughter				800
Maria his dead daughter				
Diego black ladino, sickly				400
Juana his black criolla wife				700
Catalina her daughter			4 yrs	200
Barbola her sister			3	150
Feliz her newborn brother				50
Francisco elderly black	irrigator	Angola		400
Maria hoga (?) his wife				500
Pascual criollo her son				600
Francisco Pacheco his younger brother				550
Bernauela (Bernave?)			6	230
Silvestre			2	100
Maria				??
plus 2 additional newborn children				??
Gonzalo elderly black		Angola	50+	250
Felipa his wife		Angola		350
Augustin the younger married to a free mulata		Angola		500
Augustin the elder	sugar processor	Angola		300
Juliana his wife				400
Manual black	carpenter	Angola		600
Maria Senja his wife				350
Mateo Garro elderly black				300
Catalina his wife		Anchica		400
Diego her single son	team driver	Bran		800
Domingo Garro his single brother	team driver		26	600
Lorenzo his brother	barber		21	1,000
Francisco Capagasa (Capasasa?)				600
Blas his son		Soxa (Xoxo?)	6	200
Ursula his sister			4	150
Pedro her brother who is sick			1	60
Isabel mother of the children And wife of Fr^{co}				600

continued

Table 2. Continued

Name	Occupation	Ethnicity	Age	Price
Simon elderly	team driver	Angola		500
Felipa his wife		Angola		500
Felipe his son			11	300
Feliciana his sister			4	150
Child, sent to owner's son				
Gabriel			13	??
Child, sent to owner's daughter				
doña Constanza			14	??
Sebastian, the elder				500
Lucrecia his wife		Angola		300
Inez very small, hunchbacked				
asthmatic daughter		Angola		100
Luis her half simple, torpid				
Brother		Angola		200
Diego Garimbola (Caraboli?)	sugar processor			650
Augustín his step-brother			12	300
Lazaro his brother sent to owners'				
son				??
Pedro his brother			8	250
Pedro Cayaya broken, elderly				
black married to an Indian woman				300
Juan his deaf son from a black woman			25	500
Andres (Pedro's son?)			25	350
Otro hermano given to owners'				
other son				??
Francisco Mosange (?) elderly single				400
Felipe Musinga (?) herniated black				300
Domingo crazy broken old black				300
Anton run away of 1 month		Bran		600
Miguel young married to		Angola		500
Maria his wife				550
Bartolome, crippled probably				
Long time		Angola		200
Anton	slave captain	Anchico		600
Isabel his wife				600
Isabel her daughter			2	150
Mariana another daughter				
newborn				50

continued

Table 2. Continued

Name	Occupation	Ethnicity	Age	Price
Lazaro black boy left to owners' son Xptoval			10+	300
Xtoval mulatto to son Xploval And not to be sold			5	200
Maria "negrita" to owners' daughter doña Isavel			10	300
Petronita "negrita" to daughter Isavel			8	250
Paula "negrita" to owners' Grandaughter Jusepita child of doña Ana wife of don Pedro de Monrroy			3	150

Source: AHMC-M, 1629–1676, Vol. 38, leg. 20.

At the other end of the age spectrum, a slave's value obviously declined over time.[37] While we know that longevity was somewhat unusual in colonial times, particularly among African slaves, some of the elderly on the Turque roll still commanded a peso value, no doubt because of the skill with which they continued to be identified, such as driver or irrigator. Physical condition also influenced value. For example, Bartolomé from Angola, crippled for some time, was worth 200 pesos, while the twenty-five-year-old deaf Juan was appraised at 500 pesos. And then there was poor old Pedro Cayaya, characterized as a "broken elderly black" worth 300 pesos, the same price as Domingo, also identified by the same attributes, but with the additional label of "crazy," itself fraught with many possible connotations (to be discussed in chapter 7). Missing from the roll is mention of infirm, elderly women. Possibly they died at an earlier age, but that is difficult to ascertain from this appraisal, where only the ages of children were systematically recorded, as the ages of all the women and even some of the men were systematically left out.[38]

Another less-than-methodical tendency was the assignation of place of origin. For example, the appraisers identified slave captain Antón's Anchico origin on one roll but excluded it on another. This raises the question of how much data on the African slaves remain hidden. Still, the samples of origins found in these slave lists are sufficient to inform the discussion. For example, 26.5 percent of the slaves were of African origin. The majority of those identified hailed from Angola, although three were from Congo and Anchico, all zones of central and southern Africa. Only two slaves were of west African origins, both Bran. However, Blas, son of Francisco Capagasa (alternately spelled Capasasa in this set of documents), was labeled Blas Soxa, which could refer to the Xoxo of west Africa or possibly the Zozo (or Xhosa) of southeastern Africa. Also, a number of unlikely surnames appear that could easily be half-invented, half-garbled versions of origins, such as Blas's father, Francisco Capagasa, or Francisco Mosanga, Felipe Musinga, and Diego Garimbola (Carimbola in another inventory).[39]

Another salient point gleaned from the tax appraisal concerns population. First, while the ratio of adult males to adult females was twenty-eight to thirteen, or 68 percent male, there were equal numbers of male and female children. By head count, there were about twice as many adults as children (forty-five to twenty-three). However, of this adult population, how many were able-bodied? Discounting the elderly and the mentally or physically incapacitated, the ratio changes. Fourteen of the adults are described as disabled, leaving as many as thirty-one as full-time, able-bodied workers. However, nine of the adult males, including two elderly, are identified according to their occupational skills, suggesting they all functioned in their occupational capacity, such that their being elderly did not necessarily connote inability. The few identifiable occupations assigned to slaves consisted of irrigator, *melero* (sugar processor), carpenter, recua driver (three), and a barber, the last being appraised at 1,000 pesos, "because the tools he uses for his trade, including instruments for pulling teeth, increase his value." It should be noted here that barbers often did more than pull teeth. They also tended to other minor and not-so-minor surgical emergencies, thus achieving higher value on the economic scale. Considering the seasonal nature of sugar production, undoubtedly every functioning child and adult slave was assigned to every perceivable cost-effective task when processing time occurred at Turque. Whatever skills they lacked upon purchase could easily have been acquired once they settled into the working operations of the mill. Women were not identified according to occupational skills, yet their appraised value—some at 700 or 800 pesos—clearly indicates their importance in the household and possibly in the refinery.[40]

Also related to the seasonal nature of sugar production is the classic *tiempo muerto* (dead time), the months of inactivity between harvests. Considering the cost of African slaves and their descendants in the Corregimiento de Mizque, owners moved their slaves, as they did their yanaconas, from one unit of production to another in response to seasonal or immediate need. Owners shifted slaves from their countryside units to their homes in the Villa de Mizque, La Plata, or, as was the case with General Cortés, even as far as his holdings in Lima. Also, slaves—usually children—were sent or left (not sold) to adult children, as occurred with the Durán and Rivero couple, who sent at least six of their slaves between the ages of three to ten years to their grown sons and daughters.[41]

The tax appraisers for the Durán and Rivero estate took lengthy measures to account for every slave's whereabouts, reflecting this involuntary work crew's considerable value. The very nature of tax appraisal calls for cold and cautious scrutiny. Not surprisingly, even the dead slaves had to be accounted for. They were listed in sequence, following the tally of dead livestock; much like livestock, they were explained as "the following slave units, *chicos y grandes* [small and large] male and female." They included black María from Angola and her son Juan; two-year-old Francisco, son of Diego "Carimbola"; and the elderly black María. Some telling items appear in the tax appraisals. The list of taxable movable goods (slaves, refinery equipment, household furnishings, livestock, and so forth) also included several pairs of leg irons, shackles, fetters, and handcuffs, a grim reminder of the reality of bondage.[42]

Sometime between the 1635 and 1637 estate appraisals and inventories, other changes occurred within the Turque slave population. In order to pay off Durán and Rivero's debts, estate executors sold six slaves: Felipa and her two children, eleven-year-old Felipe and four-year-old Feliciana (Felipa's husband and the father of the children, *harriero* (recua driver) Simón, was not included in the sale); old black Gonzalo and his wife, Felipa; and little eight-year-old "negrito muchacho" Pedro. They were all sold for the prices listed in the tax appraisal, which totaled 1,800 pesos. There is no indication to whom they were sold, nor did the estate records I worked with contain a single bill of sale regarding any of the sixty-eight slaves under discussion. By 1637 the Turque and Tuyota units listed only thirty-one slaves. The remaining thirty-seven were unaccounted for.[43] The issues of hidden data and contraband activity will be discussed at length in chapter 7.

Slaves and the Jesuits

Moving on to another time and a far more ambitious enterprise in the Mizque province, we turn to the Jesuits. Here, as elsewhere throughout colonial Latin America, the Jesuit order applied its organizational skills and expertise in profitable agricultural planning and production. By the 1540s the Jesuits were participating in the pacification and religious conversion of the indigenous peoples in the far-eastern stretches of the region that would become the Corregimiento de Mizque. They, like their astute lay entrepreneurial counterparts, saw the region's potential for diversification, and successfully exploited all possibilities to their advantage, establishing agricultural and mineral operations throughout the entire corregimiento. Wherever a commodity could be successfully produced, activities were launched and enterprises flourished. Such was certainly the case in the Jesuit wine and livestock operations in the warmer, more eastern zones of the province.[44]

The Jesuits' "copious" haciendas Chalguani and La Havana (they spelled it L'Abana) represent excellent cases in point. At the time of the Jesuit expulsion from Spain's colonies in 1767, Chalguani, itself a huge complex, was engaged primarily in wine production, whereas La Havana raised livestock. And here, as elsewhere, the Jesuits mirrored their lay counterparts and relied on African and *criollo* (New World born) slaves for an important component of their workforce. The slave crew, all housed in the Chalguani unit, totaled 134. They were organized into two distinct groups that the Jesuits regarded as separate entities. The brothers designated all married couples, with children and without, as well as one single woman, to the "ranchería de los negros" (the slaves' hamlet of huts). The ranchería consisted of 110 slaves who formed twenty-nine households, made up primarily of young families with growing children. A number of families had five children, while another produced four youngsters. The majority, however had two or three offspring each. Ten of the couples had no children. Interestingly, only five people in the entire group were designated as elderly, or elderly and crippled.[45] Obviously, they would be better cared for while living among families.

The slave living quarters, located on one of the hacienda streets, had thirty-three rooms with doors (the significance of doors will be discussed later). Another, unspecified space with two doors and entrances was apparently also designated for this group. A large "slave's kitchen" (as it was called in the document) with an array of cooking vessels and utensils served both slave groups. The other group, "los negros solteros" (single black men), was housed separately on another hacienda street, possibly adjacent to the married housing, as the kitchen arrangement would suggest. Twenty-four adult men of all ages were assigned to this group. Their quarters were more barracks-like, but they also had access to a patio with nine rooms, a corral, and the kitchen.[46]

Mirroring the earlier slave data from Durán and Rivero's Turque estate, the Jesuits provided almost no information on the age of their married slaves. They referred to the elderly as such, sometimes with additional descriptives of "shriveled," "broken," "unserviceable," and "ancient," except for one septuagenarian who was described as "viejisímo y tan anciano" (very old and very ancient). According to statistics, the age of seventy was quite ancient for anyone, let alone a slave. No doubt the others were fit and able bodied. Compared to Turque, remarkably few Jesuit slaves were identified as infirm or disabled. It may be that people in this category were no longer serviceable and therefore were manumitted to avoid paying property tax. Or, also very possibly, the Jesuits took better care of their slaves. Interestingly, only the single men were individually identified as able. Unlike the Turque lists, the fathers refrained from further identifying youngsters with the diminutive *negrito* or *mulatillo*. Instead, babies, toddlers, and young children were listed by age. Further, unlike the Turque data, the Jesuit records contained no information regarding slave occupation, but for one exception. The seventy-year-old was described as being "so old that he had no real occupation." He "only" helped out in the dispensary. No other slaves were listed by occupation.[47]

The Jesuit slave demographics differed from those of the earlier Turque group in other significant patterns as well. For example, only 26.5 percent of the slaves at Turque were declared to be of African ethnicities or origins, while 49.9 percent of the Chalguani slaves claimed African continental origins, but with notable geographic and ethnic variations. While the majority of Turque's slaves hailed from Angola, the bulk of Chalguani's slaves (67 percent) came from Sierra Leone, west Africa–Windward Coast, followed by 28 percent from the Congo and central-south Africa. Four slaves (7.4 percent) were Arara, from west Africa–Dahomey, and one was a Fula, of Senegambia. Two out of every three women were criollas, while in the male population 76 percent of the men were of African birth or ethnicity (compared with 45 percent African men and 42 percent African women at Turque). Finally, significant variations emerge within the children's population. Although in Turque the ratio between boys and girls was evenly balanced (twelve to twelve), the later Jesuit slave population registered nearly twice as many girls as boys (twenty-eight to fifteen). There may be two possible explanations for this gender imbalance. One is that stress can result in a naturally aborted male fetus. The other could be male infanticide. Mothers did not want their sons subjected to the harsh treatment that awaited them as adult male slaves. Certainly the following restraining devices itemized in the Jesuit inventories do not induce images of benign treatment: shackles with chains, two collars with chains, and four spiked collars with chains. The treacherous spiked collars were not in the earlier Turque inventory of restraining devices.[48]

Three slaves who are missing from the actual list but discussed at length in the documentary text require explanation. The commission of local officials established to oversee the embargo and inventories of all Jesuit properties was itself under rigorous orders from the viceroy to proceed with utmost care. Nothing was to be missing from the inventories. This order applied particularly to the African slaves and was repeated several times throughout this demanding expulsion and expropriation process that lasted from September through December. The slaves composed a single integral group, to be turned over to the commission as such. No slave was to be removed from the list or taken from

Table 3. Inventory of Hacienda Chalguani Slaves, 1767

Name	Origins or Ethnicity	Age
Rancheria de Los Negros		
Fermín, married to	criollo casta de Congo	
Ana	Arara	
Josepha [single]	criolla	
Andres, married to	Congo	
María, with daughters	criolla	
Juana Ventura and		4
María Forivia		6
Juan, married to	Congo	
Pascuala, with children	criolla	
Miguel and		15
Melchor and		4
Luisa and		11
Pituca and		6
Rosalia		2
Pedro, widower, with children	Congo	
Donassio and		14
Julio and		11
Ursula, crippled		7
Antonio, married to	Fula	
María, with daughter	criolla	
Francisca		6 mos.
Francisco, married to	criollo	
María Castillo		
Bernardo, married to	Congo	
Dominga, with children	criolla	
Pablo and		9
Agustín and		8
Andrés and		7
Bernardo and		5
Isidro, still nursing		??
Vicente, married to	Sierra Leone	
Silbestra	criolla	
Melchor, very old widower	Arara	
Balthasar, married to	Sierra Leone	
Luisa	criolla	
Domingo, married to	Sierra Leone	
Rosa, both elderly	Arara	

continued

Table 3. Continued

Name	Origins or Ethnicity	Age
Marcos, married to	Sierra Leone	
María Santos, with daughters		
Atanasia		2
Viviana de Jesus		1
Santiago, married to	Congo	
Alathea, with children	criolla	
Juan and		12
Geronimo and		5
Antonia, blind		7
Pascual, married to	Congo	
Josepha, with daughters	criolla	
Maria and		7
Bernardina		4
Geronimo, married to	Sierra Leone	
Margarita, with children	criolla	
Juan and		6
Antonia and		9
Melchora and		14
Antonia		2
Miguel, married to	Sierra Leone	
Gabriela	criolla	
Manuel, married to	Sierra Leone	
Sebastiana	criolla	
Pablo, old and broken, married to	Congo	
Ana	Sierra Leone	
Pedro, married to	Congo	
Teresa, old	Congo	
Salvador, married to	Sierra Leone	
Petrona, with children	criolla	
Nicolasa and		10
Magdalena and		6
Simona		4
Josseph, married to	Sierra Leone	
Barbara	criolla	
Clemente, married to	Sierra Leone	
Vernadina, with children	criolla	
Ignassio and		1
Juana		3

continued

Table 3. Continued

Name	Origins or Ethnicity	Age
Maurisio, married to	Sierra Leone	
Juana, with daughter	Sierra Leone	
Marissa		4
Dionissio, married to	Sierra Leone	
María	Sierra Leone	
Felissiano, married to	Congo	
María Jossepha, with daughter	Sierra Leone	
Maurissia		1
Miguel, married to	Sierra Leone	
Rosa, with children	criolla	
Manuel and		3
Juan Chrisostomo and		8 mos.
Lorenza		3
Isidro, married to	Sierra Leone	
Teresa, with daughters	Sierra Leone	
Faviana and		5
Marsela		2
Alvaro, married to	Sierra Leone	
Clara, with daughter	Sierra Leone	
Eulalia		5
Visente, married to	Sierra Leone	
Fulgencia	criolla	
Eugenio, married to	Sierra Leone	
Jossepha, with daughters	criolla	
María and		1
Jacoba		1 mo.
Juan, old, shriveled, widower	Arara	
Silverio, married to	criollo	
María Rossa, with daughter	de la Colonia	
Isavel		12
Inventory of the Solteros		
Exidio	criollo	28
Gregorio	criollo	18
Julian, widower	Congo	48
Miguel, very old	Congo	??
Alonzo	Sierra Leone	30
Miguel	criollo	15

continued

Table 3. Continued

Name	Origins or Ethnicity	Age
Blas	Sierra Leone	??
Esthevan	Sierra Leone	26
Mateo	Sierra Leone	27
Thomas	criollo	25
Francisco, old, unserviceable	Congo	??
Francisco, widower	Sierra Leone	40
Christobal, widower	Sierra Leone	27
Martín	Sierra Leone	40
Jauctin (?)	Sierra Leone	48
Alexandro	Sierra Leone	40
Guillermo	criollo	20
Vitorio	criollo	28
Jasinto	criollo	18
Sevastian	Sierra Leone	30
Diego	Sierra Leone	36
Lasaro	Sierra Leone	28
??benal	criollo	20
Enrique	Sierra Leone	22

Source: ANB-JMC, fs. 209–210v.

the hacienda. Thus Chalguani's mayordomo, Don Matheo Romero del Castillo, was held accountable for the whereabouts of three slaves: Martina del Castillo and her eighteen-year-old son, Juan del Castillo (referred to alternately as negrito, pardo, and mulatillo), and Agustina, apparently not related. While the surname del Castillo does raise some questions, the mayordomo professed to have no idea where the brothers had sent the three slaves. He thought they might have been sent off to the yungas.[49]

Those in charge swiftly located the mother and son. She was now in the town of Pocona, but her son had journeyed a more complicated path. First it was noted that he had been in Tarata, learning to play the organ. However, he would soon be reassigned. The order—all but a few now sequestered in the Franciscan monastery in La Plata awaiting passage overseas—requested and received a special permit from the viceroy. This permit allowed "mulato slave Juan Castillo" to accompany a disabled priest who had suffered a "violent accident" twenty-three years earlier. Apparently, the youth had already been in charge of the hapless priest—variously described as "idiota" or "el loco"—who was given to violent tantrums that only Juan knew how to subdue. Further, Juan knew how to feed him and monitor his medications in order to keep him alive. In the Jesuits' words, "No one else can do it. Juan needs to be with this priest. We beg of you that Juan be allowed to accompany said priest on this protracted journey, to be by his side, from La Plata to Arica to Callao."[50]

Curiously, at least in this set of documents, not a single monetary value was assigned to the Jesuits' copious properties and voluminous possessions, including their 134 slaves. On the other hand, the inventory commission noted that various important deeds and financial records had been accounted for, including bills of sale for eight slaves.[51] One can only speculate about the majority of the slaves. Were the bills of sale lost, or had the slaves been purchased illegally?

Finally, a current of concern over slave welfare appears throughout these detailed documents. Maintaining control remained the overriding objective and subsumed a correlated objective of keeping the slave groups intact, namely, that no slave was to be removed from his or her respective group. Apparently, two-year-old Agustina was accounted for somewhere along the way. The authorities wrote, "We want the truth. Everything must be in its proper place—inventories, slaves" in the embargo, and sequestration of all Jesuit properties. "We must avoid fraud at all costs. Everything must be accounted for. Silver, slaves, everything must be turned over to the *arrendatario* [renter]." The recuas, the instructions continued, and the convoy escorting the Jesuits and their personal belongings to the ports of departure required rations and other necessities for the trip. They were not to forget the mulatillo who was going with them. As for those who stayed behind, every effort must be made to take good care of all remaining slaves. They must not be overworked, and they should be given their day of rest and fed well, "just as the priests treated them." But they must neither flee nor steal from the haciendas. The harvests must be maintained to provide subsistence for the slaves.[52]

As the Jesuits' date of departure approached, the commission advised the president of the audiencia that the slaves were being treated in the same manner the Jesuits had followed and were "very content." Possibly in response to suggestions to the contrary, they informed the president that, as was customary, the slaves would be clothed and would receive a gift on the day of Saint Javier, adding, "you do not need to tell us how to proceed in these matters." Twice the officials reminded the president that the royal government was responsible for paying the "poor mule drivers" transporting goods back and forth to Santa Cruz. And finally, on December 9, 1767, the commission, near what appears to be the end of Mizque's designated role in the sequestration process, again referred to the slaves. The officials repeated that the slaves were to be cared for with "mercy" and with the "humanity their condition required." They needed a new set of clothing annually, as well as the appropriate meat rations—four slaughtered cows per week—all in keeping with the standards established by the Jesuits. The available documentation covering Mizque's participation ends shortly after these observations. In what appears to be a final exchange, the audiencia admonished the commission that it was not moving quickly enough (as usual, those in distant seats of power often have little notion of the local landscape, physical or cultural) and that some unfinished business remained regarding transfer of Jesuit properties and tax matters. "You are to get the papers to me with utmost speed," the audiencia president wrote. "Your carelessness has resulted in serious detriments to royal interests."[53] By now the Jesuits were surely seaborne. Under whose ownership the 134 slaves found themselves remains unclear. One of two possibilities, documented by Nicholas P. Cushner in his Peruvian study, could pertain. As part of the Chalguani hacienda complex, the slaves may have been rented to the highest bidder. Or, also under the supervision of royal government officials, they could have been sold on the auction block.[54]

Slaves and the Chacara Censuses
Turning to yet another source of slave-related data, we draw from the padrones de chácaras, which illustrate so well many of the issues raised in this work. While the purpose of the padrones was to maintain control over the yanacona tributaries and to monitor tribute payments destined for royal coffers, they also yield a surprising amount of in-

formation regarding slaves and slave descendants. Slavery and yana-conage were very different forms of labor. Slaves ostensibly were movable goods and the personal, inalienable property of their owners, who could do with them as they desired. Colonial yanaconas, on the other hand, were indigenous laborers who were supposedly no longer active participants in their original communities; instead, they were officially tied to the land and thus to the presiding landowner. Regardless of the rapid turnover of landholders, the yanaconas were to remain in place. They were neither to move on their own volition nor to be moved (except with special royal permission) by their landlord of the moment. In this context, as in others that will be elaborated upon in chapter 6, royal objectives did not always prevail.

Regardless of whether they were born in Africa or the New World, the slaves were not perceived as, nor confused with, yanaconas. Thus it comes as a surprise to have slaves appear in at least 50 of the 157 padrones consulted throughout this project. The first to catch my attention, Kaspar, emerged in 1630 as the lone worker at the time on the viña and chácara Chinguri. That same year, Hernando Berbesi appeared on the padrón of Captain Augustín Ferrufino's hacienda Oloy. On that padrón the census takers also noted a slave named Francisco married to a María india. Two of their four children were identified as çambiagos. This term (like its common variations *cambolo*, *zambo*, and *sambo* and their respective feminine spellings) was used interchangeably with *mulato* in the more than one hundred years of the serial chácara census and other records I examined. Both unequivocally referred to the offspring of a union between a person of African origins and one of indigenous roots. Similarly, on Antonio Calderón's estate Ypisana the census takers recorded "slave Manuel, married to Inéz india, with one child, mulato Juan." A "Pedro negro" was also listed. Here, as in Mexico during the same period, *negro* was synonymous with slave, as was usually but not always the case with ethnic labels. Hernando Berbesi was in all likelihood a slave. On the other hand, the padrón for Bernardo de Paniagua de Loaysa's chácara Chimboata listed María Orcoma, wife of Francisco Congo, and their child Juan Congo, mulato.[55] As will be discussed in chapter 6, ethnic identity was usually passed on to the children.

Some fifty years later, in 1683, the padrón for the hacienda Lower Oloy showed a Salvador Berbesi married to Josepha, slave mulata, with one child, two-year-old Pedro negro (obviously born a slave). That same year, the padrón for the heirs of Francisco Ovando's hacienda Matarani listed among the yanaconas Francisco Clemente, slave mulato. On Doña Juana Merubia's estancia Pograta, Pablo negro slave was married to Sebastiana mulata, their three children identified as Josep negro, fourteen, Vitoria negra, thirteen, and Thomas negro, eighteen. Then there was the padrón for the estancia Pizana (referred to alternately as Ypisana, Episana, or Episana-Callejas, depending on the attendant scribe) owned by Captain Don Juan Calderón.[56] This extensive padrón revealed a somewhat complicated but increasingly representative entry. It listed a deceased Paula Arias, daughter of a male slave (esclavo negro) and herself identified as a negra esclava, having been married to widower Juan Mauricio Chiminea (not your usual indigenous or European surname), a negro slave. Together they had four daughters, not identified as slaves. The family was again listed five years later in a 1688 padrón for the same chácara. Somehow Paula's husband was now listed as Juan Bentura Mauricio, but still a "negro esclabo [*sic*]." Recorded on the same padrón was one Bartola married to another hacienda mulato slave. They had a son, Isidrio. In 1694 the pattern of listing slaves on the padrones throughout the region persisted. On the chácara La Calleja, owned by Doña Otalla Cortés de Encinas, once dwelled a María Sisa who had married a mulato slave of the same hacienda. And finally, on the chácara Laibato, yanacona Dorotea was recorded as being married to a slave. They had one daughter.[57]

In addition to references to specific slaves on the chácaras visited by the census takers, a related and equally significant set of demographic data emerge. This information concerns the growing number of mixed unions between slaves (and their descendants) and hacienda yanaconas. These mixed marriages occurred within the chácaras or estancias and also, increasingly, between residents of one unit and residents of other units, some neighboring, others more distant. These latter marriages, which I refer to as cross-chácara unions, in turn, reflected other demographic changes. First, mixed families appear in the padrones under discussion from the outset. In a 1588 court case, chacarero Francisco de Macías claimed that Catalina Cota (indigenous) and her children Diego mulato and Cristoval, born in Pocona, were yanaconas on his chácara. He insisted that he fed them, clothed them, and paid their tribute, and they were listed on his padrón. Catalina rejected Macías's claim and declared that she, her son Cristoval, and his father were all from Pocona. Diego's father was clearly of African origins. So already we have a mixed family, some of whom resided on Macías's chácara as yanaconas, at least for a while, but now even challenging this residential status. The case dragged on for several years.[58]

Moving on to 1597 and Juan Álvarez Meléndez's chácara Copachuncho, aside from Meléndez's slaves who appeared in his wills and litigations, at least one individual mulata appeared in the padrón, along with a mulato family of several members. Similarly, in the nearby chácara of Julio de Aguilera, another entire family with several children of mulatos resided. While on another chácara belonging to the encomendero Captain Gabriel Encinas in the valley of Oloy, yet another large family of mulatos was recorded on the padrón. The family consisted of Pedro Cinche, born in New Spain; his wife, Ana Álvarez mulata; and their five children, who ranged in age from four to fifteen years. Over in the valley of Chinguri lay one of several holdings of Gabriel de Paniagua de Loaysa, Novillero, where at least five adult mulatos and several of their children resided. At the same time, his largest operation, Buena Vista, located near the Villa de Mizque, utilized sixteen mulatos, none of them slaves but many identified as children of slaves, now mostly grown. Buena Vista also yielded one hitherto unheard-of document (to be discussed at length below), referred to simply as the *visita de los mulatos* (census or registry of the mulatos). Mulatos were recorded on three other chácaras during this time as "four males," "two mulatos," and at least one "negro ladino" (Hispanicized black).[59]

By 1630, the earlier-mentioned Hernando Berbesi on Captain Agustín Ferrufino's chácara (referred to in the estate accounts as hacienda) Oloy was married to Isabel. They had five children and one grandchild, all referred to as mulatos. The next set of padrones I examined were dated 1683 and clearly indicated an additional phenomenon that the earlier records merely suggested, namely, that mobility and flight were no longer actions pertaining exclusively to the indigenous populations. For example, on the hacienda Condor Pata, operated by the Dominican brothers, Agustina mulata was listed on the padrón as married to a mulato slave belonging to Don Bernardo de Paniagua, owner of the chácara Chimboata. Further, Agustina was noted as "absent" from Condor Pata and now "resided" on yet another hacienda of Don Bernardo's, Puxioni, where she was listed as Agustina (and *not* identified as mulata), age twenty-nine, married to a negro slave belonging to Paniagua. It would appear from the wording of the entry that she and her slave husband were together. On another chácara, Las Tipas, Juan de Rosas, twenty-eight, was married to "a woman slave from another hacienda." In most likelihood, he had "fled" to join or be nearer to his wife.[60]

The profile of the Puxioni hacienda raises some questions. Its curaca, named Sebastian Ambrosio Virito, pardo age twenty-seven, was one of several adult children on the hacienda and the offspring of the deceased Jacinto Viriti and an unidentified "first wife." Jacinto had no children by his second wife, María india. Yet curaca Sebastian was the only one of seven Viriti brothers to be identified first as the "curaca pardo" and a second time as "de color pardo" (of the color of pardo), whereas none of the others were identified by race or color. Why was Sebastian doubly identified as pardo and the others not? They were all children of the same marriage, and Sebastian's racial status indicated that either his father, Jacinto, or the unidentified wife was of African origin. Very possibly Jacinto was further identified because of his status as curaca, a once-significant indigenous role, as will be discussed extensively in chapter 6.[61]

Further, we know that twelve of the forty-eight resident yanaconas had left or "fled" Puxioni. However, the evidence also suggests that there were many more unidentified pardos and mulatos intermarrying and producing children. The twenty-nine-year-old mulata Agustina, listed with the Dominican hacienda Condor Pata but now residing on Puxioni with her negro or mulato slave husband, also happened to be related to the Viriti family. She was identified as a "sister" to second-generation Viriti. As more cross-chácara unions occurred, resulting in further departures, the remaining yanaconas were quite literally "stepping in" (answering in their name) to fill the vacancies.[62]

Captain Don Gerónimo de Salazar Negrete's hacienda, Santa Ana de la Chimba, further informs the issue. This much larger operation listed 131 yanaconas, of which 44 had left—34 percent as opposed to Puxioni's 25 percent. The padrón also recorded 23 mulatos, of which at least 11 had slave fathers from other chácaras. Apparently five of the mulatos had left or fled. The padrón for the hacienda Upper Oloy, owned by Maese de Campo Don Juan de Mesa Zuñiga, further supports the theory of an ever-expanding mulato yanacona population that was forming cross-chácara unions and moving in and out of the region's chácaras. The census takers listed a total of 137 yanaconas, 31 of whom were mulatos and most of whom were interrelated. Ten had left the hacienda. Meanwhile, one small family on the hacienda Lower Oloy certainly represents a microcosm of the larger phenomenon. A Salvador Berbesi was married to Josepha mulata slave. Salvador's son (not Josepha's, or at least not declared to be hers) Thomas, age seventeen and identified as a tributary, was married to Ana, a *forastera* (outsider) from Cochabamba. The reasons why one might not wish to be identified as a slave are obvious. At least three other haciendas reporting cross-chácara unions listed small to large mixed family units. Further, two more curacas of African origins appear in this 1683 set. On the estancia Matarani, curaca Bernabe Clemente was described as a *ladino en lengua española* (a Hispanicized Spanish speaker), son of Francisco Clemente mulato slave. The other fifteen mulatos on the estancia were also related. On the estancia Pizana (actually Episana), the other curaca, Juan Calchari Alberca, color pardo, was married to Ana Sisa, now deceased, and their six children, including a daughter *bastarda* (the usual term is *hijo natural*) were all identified as pardos.[63]

The padrones studied for 1688 and 1695 more than reinforce these trends. Further, by comparing these two sets with the 1683 data I was able to compare specific chácaras at these three given times. The mulato families continued to expand and cross-chácara unions remained commonplace, as was the flight of non-slave workers to be with their slave spouses and the flight of slaves to join their non-slave mates. By now, generational factors begin to emerge more clearly. In 1630 only one family consisted of three generations. Hernando Berbesi, old and retired, was married to Isabel. They had five children and one grandchild, all of whom were labeled mulatos. By the 1680s, many slaves and non-slave people of African origins were now retired or deceased or into second marriages, with a good number of their children now able-bodied adult yanaconas, sometimes identified according to their African ancestry, but not always. For example, at the large Santa Ana de la Chimba hacienda, which had a yanacona population of 131, 23 were recorded as mulatos in the padrón, and at least 11 (two young adults, the remainder children between the ages of four and seventeen) were recorded as children of African slave fathers. Yet not a single one of them was ascribed any of the several racial labels (mulato, pardo, sambo, etc.) commonly used in reference to African origins throughout these padrones.[64]

Another variation of the above was the family on the chácara San Nicolás, where the only yanaconas listed were María and her three grown children: Ylario Angola, twenty-one; Juan Angola, nineteen; and María Angola, fourteen. Clearly. the unnamed father bore the ascribed descriptive Angola along with his first name. Yet as already mentioned, Salvador Berbesi's grown son Thomas (not born of his second wife, slave Josepha, or so it was claimed), like the above La Chimba youngsters, had no identifying label attached to his first name. And yet another variation, on the estancia Pograta, was that of Pablo negro slave, married to Sebastiana mulata. Their three children were recorded as Joseph negro, fourteen; Vitoria negra, thirteen; and Thomas negro, eighteen.[65]

To further underscore the issue of ambivalence in the racial ascriptives, in 1683 Juan García, twenty-six, son of negro esclavo, lived at Episana/Calleja with his wife, Juana. They had no children. At the same hacienda five years later, he was now referred to as Juan García Zambo, yanacona son of negro esclavo married to Pascuala, with children Juan, six; Simón, three; and Monica. Meanwhile, at the chácara Tucuma in 1683, Francisco Malaga was identified as the curaca, thirty-two, married to Josepha with several children; in 1688 he was described as Francisco Malaga, pardo color, yanacona, and curaca. His four children bore no identifying ascriptive labels.[66]

Finally, we return once more to the couple that represents several anomalies referred to throughout this work. In 1683, Juan Mauricio Chiminea (literally, "chimney") was listed on the Ipisana (Episana) padrón as having been married to the deceased slave Paula Arias. Contrary to the law—the children were supposed to acquire the legal status of the mother—none of their four children were identified as slaves. In 1688, movement, intermarriages, and cross-chacara unions continued to characterize this racially diverse chácara, where deceased Paula Arias was again accounted for. This entry reflects another difference, however. First, she was now referred to as a yanacona (instead of negra esclava), daughter of negro slave (father). However, her widowed husband remained identified as a negro slave. His original name in earlier censuses, Juan Mauricio Chiminea, apparently was permanently changed to Juan Bentura Mauricio (possibly indicating that he had been baptized). The year 1695 brought no major change in patterns, except that the older population was dying off and the padrones now cited more multigenerational families. Slaves, consistently more male than female, remained visible, and the slave/non-slave unions continued, as did the "flight" of slaves and non-slaves alike.[67]

The Ambiguities of Census Taking

While most of the recognized slave parents in these censuses appear to be male slaves, this issue, like others concerning mixed unions, mixed parentage, and other race-related matters in the eastern Andes, is extremely nuanced and requires multiple layers of explanations. One certainly comes immediately to mind: that the census-taking system was fraught with imprecision and inconsistencies. From the broadest perspective, these issues involve three diverse interest groups or agencies— the slaves and yanaconas, the census takers, and the curacas. These groups, overlapping physically and culturally in varying degrees yet often representing conflicting interests, served to fuel the census-taking system while simultaneously dismantling it.

The inconsistencies in records for the deceased Paula Árias and her widowed husband underscore the point well. The switch from slave status to free, and vice versa, for both of them, not to mention the husband's name change, all within a five-year period, is considerably frustrating for the investigator. I do know that different census-taking teams conducted the two conflicting inquiries. Mizque's corregidor Juan de Saldía y Espinosa and public scribe Mathias (surname illegible) officiated over the 1683 Ipisana (Episana) padrón, while the 1688 padrón was conducted by Captain Balthasar Cereso de Aponte, lieutenant general of the Mizque province, and one Joseph Manuel de Medina, acting as scribe, since neither public nor royal scribes were available for the recording. Two local witnesses accompanied this team, suggesting their approach was something out of the ordinary. The main purpose remained consistent, though: they were to collect "three pesos and one real per each yanacona, per each year."[68]

Ambiguities emerge in other applications of racially descriptive nomenclature and what might be construed as mislabeling or nonlabeling of individuals. This tendency appeared early on. In May 1597 the padrón for Gabriel Paniagua de Loaysa's chácara Novillero recorded Martín Chare, Domingo Garro, and Domingo's indigenous wife, Isabel, as mulatos residing on the premises. In November 1598, Martín Chare was no longer identified as a mulato, while Domingo and his wife were nowhere to be found or accounted for. Looking to the padrones of the 1680s and 1690s, the offspring of female Indians and male black slaves were alternately referred to as mulatos, pardos, or negros. The latter is all the more ambiguous because the label *negro*, without the qualifier *libre* or *horro* (free), was usually synonymous with slave. Also, evidence points to the custom of one's occupation being used as an identifying label in place of a surname. For example, on the chácara Chimboata, seven-year-old Pedro Congo was the child of Pascuala and Diego harriero. Most harrieros in this region were of African or mixed-African origins, easily identified because of the customary occupational labeling.[69]

The issue of labeling raises further questions. The ethnic surnames—Congo, Bran, Berbesi, Angola, and the like—were sometimes (but not always) passed down from one generation to another and did not necessarily imply a new arrival from Africa. Seven-year-old Pedro Congo was not a recent arrival. However, the term *criollo*, which was used in documents such as litigations, bills of sale, and the Jesuit inventories to distinguish those born in Africa from those born in the New

World, was not a part of the padrón lexicon. Therefore, while I am convinced that many of those identified as Hernando Berbesi or Juan Negro could easily be new arrivals or slaves, I take a more cautionary stance for now. The handful of identified slaves sprinkled throughout the padrones are specifically so labeled. Most of the slaves cited in the censuses were in reference to the many mixed unions of chácara Indian women with male African or African-descent slaves from other haciendas. The many children resulting from these first and second marriages remained with the mother on their respective chácaras and were usually (but not always) identified by the above racially ascriptive labels.[70] They would join the ever-growing pool of free mulatos residing on and (increasingly often) leaving the haciendas.

Finally, one more subtextual but relevant set of observations concerning the complexity of labeling calls for explanation. This involves the term *zambo*. Like the term *pardo*, *zambo* is used somewhat less frequently than *mulato* throughout the chácara censuses. In these Mizque chácara padrones, all three labels refer specifically to the offspring of unions between indigenous Andeans and Africans or African-descended individuals. Unlike the ascriptions of *mulato* and *pardo*, however, *zambo* acquired several variations. For example, in 1630 the often-cited estancia Ipisana (or Episana), on one padrón, listed Pedro Sánchez *cambiago*, Juan *çambahigo*, and Sebastian *çambo*. The latter two were usually penned with the cedilla (diacritical), making it a medieval form of the Spanish z, and used quite commonly in the earlier Mizque documents. However, the scribes often neglected to use the cedilla, and thus *cambo* and *camba* appear throughout the documents, throwing the uninitiated investigator off guard. *Camba* is the term currently used for residents of the Santa Cruz and contiguous lowland regions, once part of the Corregimiento de Mizque. The son of Pedro Sánchez cambiago from a mulata wife was named only Pedro Sánchez. He too married a mulata. Juan çambahigo and his brother, named only Diego, were the children of a negro slave and María india yanacona, both from Ipisana. Meanwhile, another male slave and Inéz india yanacona were parents of Sebastian çambo.[71]

Again, the census takers remained consistently inconsistent in their application of ascriptives to the children of mixed unions. At the vineyard Poco (Pojo), two of Francisco slave and María india's four children were called çambiagos. Yet on the same padrón the two children of an identical union were labeled Juan mulato and Pedro negro. By 1645, at the chácara Santa Ana en Zacasso, the ten people of mixed origins were not only recorded as mulatos, but for good measure the officials decided to affix the additional çambo onto it, thus Ana mulata çamba. By the 1680s the term *zambo* (with a z) surfaces, although both çambo and zambo along with pardo and mulato appeared through the 1690s.[72] Whatever the officials chose to label them, this demographic explosion continued unabated, far beyond the parameters of control so desperately sought by the Spanish state apparatus.

We noted above that at one point early on, the listing of the growing mulato population on a separate padrón had been implemented. In 1597, on Gabriel Paniagua de Loaysa's huge hacienda Buena Vista, all fourteen free mulatos were listed separately on what the officials referred to as the visita de los mulatos. Curiously, this Buena Vista mulato padrón was the only one to appear out of the 157 padrones I studied. More must have existed, because mulato yanaconas made reference to them on other occasions. For example, in 1635 a mulato family on the chácara of Juan de Valenzuela filed a complaint against the chacarero, claiming he had wrongfully listed them on the Indian yanacona padrón. The family argued that if they had to be on any padrón, they wanted to be registered in the "padrón de los mulatos."[73]

I have referred several times to the issue of children of yanacona or slave women inheriting the status of their mothers. The collective wisdom—dictionaries, textbooks, monographs—holds that *yanacona* was synonymous with *Indian*, but the following clearly rejects this assumption. In the estate papers of General Bartolomé Cortés, officials and accountants unhesitatingly defined the status of his Turque chácara mulatos: "The five children of María India shepherdess, wife of the negro Manuel, shepherd slave of said estancia, although they are the children of said black slave they are not slaves. Because their mother is a india yanacona as such they too will be recorded and taxed as yanacona of said estancia where they were born and raised and where they still reside with their parents."[74] In the 1579 Buena Vista padrón de los mulatos, chácara yanacona Antón negro ladino

(Hispanicized African) received a warning to mend his drinking habits. Further, he was to behave responsibly, as were all yanaconas, toward his *amo* (a term loaded with nuances, to mean anything from master, proprietor, overseer, or lord, to a person requiring submission). Antón's drinking habits notwithstanding, padrón data also suggest that this adult son of chácara slave Antón negro (listed with the mulatos but never identified specifically as such) enjoyed considerable mobility, whether of his own volition or through orders from his amo. The census takers note only that he "had gone to Cuzco." The following year, 1598, he appears on the regular padrón at the chácara La Calleja.[75]

Which brings this discussion full circle regarding the issue of the padrón de mulatos and the preference of free adult children of slave/non-slave unions to be on this particular padrón and not on the Indian records. As I have argued throughout this work, the padrones reflect the ceaseless efforts of the Spanish imperial state to maintain economic and political control of the nearly uncontrollable by keeping the rural population locked in place. Thus, as a member of an Indian community under the delegated authority of its respective curaca, each able-bodied indigenous tributary was obligated to pay his share in goods or specie. Like the chácara yanacona, the community population was also recorded in periodic padrones. On the chácaras, however, the *owner* paid the tribute for the yanaconas "attached" to his property. Or so it would appear. Apparently, however, this applied only to the Indian yanacona sector, for whom the chacarero or hacendado normally paid some three pesos a year per tributary.[76]

The mulato yanaconas, it appears, paid their own tribute, at two pesos per tributary.[77] It would stand to reason that this population group would wish to pay two instead of three pesos yearly, especially when they were required to pay for themselves. However, the question remains: Why did the mulato yanaconas have to pay their own tribute while the Indian yanaconas did not? Were their tributary rates reduced because they were paying their own way? Were they perceived by others and themselves as having somewhat preferred status over the indigenous groups and thus actively sought separate categorization? And conversely, did some mulatos prefer to remain unidentified as such, and remain on the Indian padrón with their tributary obligations taken care of by the chácara owners? And by doing so, was their status in any way lessened? Chapter 7 will address these and many other questions raised in this work concerning race, ethnicity, and how these intersect with identity, as well as values, mores, and other measurable, recognizable social behavior.

Occupational Patterns

Now that we have established the existence of a viable population of African slaves and their descendants in the eastern Andean Corregimiento de Mizque, it is time to look more closely at what they did. I have referred throughout this work to African slaves and free black and mulato roles and occupations. The following explores these key issues further, starting with Mizque's active, profitable wine industry. As noted earlier, Fray Benito Peñalosa's impassioned pleas in 1629 to end African slavery and ban wine production fell on deaf ears. Further, it cannot be emphasized enough that the popularly held local myths of royal prohibitions against the Andean wine industry and the burning of Mizque vineyards remain groundless. The decree of Philip II (1527–98) prohibiting wine production in the colonies was never enforced in Mizque. Further, I have yet to see documentary evidence that any Mizque official ordered the burning of vineyards. Wine production flourished throughout the seventeenth and eighteenth centuries. Earlier discussions of the Jesuit enterprises underscore a strong wine production and market system still in place in the 1760s.[78]

In terms of labor, Fray Benito was, in part, quite correct in identifying a strong African presence in the wine industry. Almost every document I encountered concerning viticulture and wine production bore references to African and African-descent slaves, in small and large numbers. The Laibato complex, which included vineyards in Omereque, experienced many litigations and slave transactions over the years, and every single reference to vineyards and related wine production referred to anywhere from five to fifteen slaves. In the 1624 last will and testament of an owner of the Callejas vineyard and wineworks, Don Bernardo de la Fresnada y Zúñiga claimed that his thirty slave "units" were worth 14,000 pesos. The 1651 case of the escaped

slave winemaking specialist at Callejas will receive full detail in chapter 7, as will the 1657 litigation concerning the untimely death of still
another valued slave skilled in winemaking. And finally, we know that
by the 1680s wine growers were using mulato offspring of slaves, as
was the case at the Lower Tucuma vineyard and others.

A closer look at the vineyards of the General Bartolomé Cortés readily serves the discussion. When he first launched his winemaking activities he did not have much money himself. What he did have, however,
was access to the bountiful dowry of his wife, Doña Luisa Ponce de
León, which he easily could have used as collateral. Throughout the
years, Cortés kept careful record of his investments, his debts (and payments of), and his wife's dowry. Upon his death, Doña Luisa's dowry
remained intact, including lavish ball gowns, jewelry, and 10,035 pesos.[79]

The general's wealth far surpassed that of his wife, and he was able
to leave her considerable land, including his vineyard in the Callejas
valley and its five slaves. In fact, in most of the vineyard transactions I
came across (buying, selling, and renting), African slaves, winemaking
equipment, and the like came with the vineyard as part of the package.
Then there were Cortés's three slaves who were in Lima with the recua
at the time of his death. Over his lifetime Don Bartolomé acquired at
least twenty-four slaves, some of whom he shifted from one production unit to another (he also ran a sugar plantation and mill in the San
Lorenzo area) according to seasonal need. At the time of his death in
1629, he was searching for a good mayordomo to oversee the Turque
vineyard, where thirteen of his slaves resided, and his other vineyard
in the valley of Calleja, where the mentioned five slaves were living
at the time. The general was adamant that he needed a good mayordomo, and he was willing to pay such a person a respectable salary
because it would be his responsibility to "bring in the harvest, search
for the yanacona, and feed and clothe them and the slaves, and pay
their [yanaconas' and slaves'] tasas."[80]

After Don Bartolomé's death the properties languished for a while,
but they quickly revived after Durán and Rivero's purchase. The latter
invested even more slaves in Turque's wine production, and by the time
of their deaths around 1635 they had increased the slave population in

Turque alone to sixty-nine adults and children. The inventories of the Jesuit properties Chalguani and La Havana reflect the same pattern, albeit on a much larger scale. The Jesuits' slaves were to be sold along with the related production equipment at each unit.[81]

Livestock was another significant Mizque industry. The well-intentioned treatise calling for the prohibition of wine production in order to reduce the importation of African slaves did not accurately portray the reality. Throughout much of the Spanish colonial New World, livestock production relied heavily on African slaves and their descendants, and Mizque was no exception. Chapter 2 included detailed accounts of the early campaigns of exploration and pacification led by the Spanish warriors who had survived conquest and years of internecine battles. Their visions turned east, to what would soon become the wide-reaching multi-ecologically enriched landscape, the Corregimiento de Mizque. Significantly, these warriors-cum-settlers— the Paniaguas, Cazorlas, Chavezes, and the like—equipped their large, diversely staffed expeditions entirely out of their own resources, including food supplies, livestock, African slaves, and Indians mostly from their Mizque holdings.

The earliest written records I found of livestock production per se come from the 1597–98 padrones. In 1597 alone the census officials recorded two Gabriel Paniagua y Loaysa operations: El Novillero, near the town of Totora; and Llallagua, also in the Totora area. El Novillero, like Episana, had its mulato cowboy population at least by 1597 and in all probability considerably earlier. At another holding, Cotoguaico, the officials noted that the tutor of the deceased owner's minor children apparently was doing a less-than-responsible job of taking care of the estate. "He has their yanaconas working on his properties, rounding up [his] cattle and he is not doing a good job [for the children]." During the same round of census taking, officials listed the estancia Potrero (meaning a farm for raising horses), owned by Pedro de Mesa, as well as the estancia Tarantara, belonging to Doña Leonarda de Avila, and the estancia Salanche, owned by Don Juan de Montenegro. While the 1597 census for El Novillero specifically listed mulatos among the yanaconas, the others were less concise.[82] Nevertheless, judging from the ever-growing African slave and mulato (slave and free) population on the chacaras and estancias, I would guess that these earlier livestock holdings had at least a sprinkling, if not more, of an African-related population, which we can document over time.

By 1603 slaves were already working at the estancia Episana, as they were by 1607 on the large viña/estancia operation at Laibato. At the same time, black cowboys—alone or with their Indian cohorts—were increasingly involved in court litigations concerning cattle rustling and slaughter. Also around this time, Juan Pinelo de Ayala, a native of Sevilla, was giving his attorney in La Plata a *poder* (power of attorney) to oversee his Mizque properties, which included livestock operations and slaves. Further, by 1624, La Calleja continued livestock activities supported by slave labor. And in 1630, Episana, despite several changes of ownership, was still going strong with an ever-growing free mulato cowboy/family population. As discussed earlier, this estancia continued to flourish throughout the late 1690s and most likely beyond, with a yet stronger mulato cowboy presence. And as we know, estancias Chalguani (not yet owned by the Jesuits), Matarani, Laibato, Pograta, and of course Episana remained active through the 1680s. The estancia Racaypampa appears in the 1713 litigations involving sambo yanacona cowboys and mulato cowboys from yet another hacienda, Chimboata. And finally, the flourishing Jesuit livestock operations remained active with their slave laborers up to the Jesuits' 1767 expulsion.[83]

Over time, individuals of African descent became highly skilled and sought-after livestock workers, as we see in the 1603 case of Gerónimo de Villapando, mulato official farrier (professional horse shoer), whose swashbuckling story unfolds in chapter 7. Others rose to the post of overseer at those very estancias where their forefathers had worked as slave cowboys. This is discussed at length in chapter 6, which traces the transition of the curaca role on the chácaras and estancias from the already-altered but still semitraditional post-conquest figure to that of purely overseer-quasi mayordomo with no claim to traditional elite-noble status. Thus by 1683 appears Bernabé Clemente, a Hispanicized mulato curaca of the estancia Matarani, whose father had been a mulato slave on the same estancia. Meanwhile, Episana, now owned by Captain Don Juan Calderón, was overseen by curaca Juan Canchari

Alberca "of the pardo color." And in 1688 the estancia at Upper Tucuma was run by Francisco Malaga of the pardo color, recorded as a
yanacona and a curaca.[84] Curiously, I have not come across a single
reference to a person "of a mulato color" or "of a moreno color,"
possibly suggesting that in this eastern Andean region pardo was more
closely associated with color as a distinguishing factor in conjunction
with racial categorization.

Further, individuals of African origins participated in livestock production in capacities other than ranch hand/cowboy or overseer. In the
1604 litigation between mulato estancia owner Gutiérrez Altamirano
and his neighboring Paniagua mayordomo, the latter accused the former of allowing his pigs and cattle to destroy Paniagua crops. Apparently, estancia ownership by a pardo or mulato was not that unusual.
By 1618, pardo Juan Ramírez owned the livestock estancia San Juan
de los Cedros in the Tiraque district (probably near Episana). And in
1645, census officials recorded the estancia San Cristobal owned by
pardo Pedro Hernández.[85]

Finally, mulato land ownership was not confined to livestock activities. Individuals of African origins owned and worked their own silver
mines, as we saw in chapter 4. Equally revealing from a number of perspectives is the 1645 case of the chácara Los Sauces. Census officials
registered the owner as "Captain Juan de Robles, of the pardo color,
captain of all of your majesty's soldiers." The only other information
added to the padrón was that the yanaconas serving the soldiers were
exempt from tribute. Nevertheless, the captain volunteered to pay their
tributes anyway. This chácara was located in the same vicinity as Pedro
Hernández's estancia. Also in the same area was the chácara of Barbola
de Uminchipa, widow of Captain Domingo Robles, pardo (discussed
below), no doubt related to Captain Juan de Robles. Throughout this
work I have frequently identified individuals by their given military
titles, in the contexts of landownership, active military duty, the bureaucracy, or in last wills and testaments. The only other person to use
and be addressed by his formal military title was the militarily active
Captain Juan Acevedo Godoy, appointed by royal authorities in the
1620s to lead the Indian campaigns in the Pocona region (see chapter
6).[86] Obviously, Captain Juan de Robles was, like Godoy, an active

commander of a local military unit, thus the reference to the yanaconas serving the soldiers. Further, judging from the growing body of literature on the subject, the group under his charge could have been of African origin.[87] This is another area that begs for additional regional research.

African slaves and their descendants quickly filled other roles and occupations as well. The harrieros were almost always slave or free negros and mulatos. The role of pregonero was almost exclusively occupied by individuals of African origins, possibly still slaves, particularly in the 1500s and 1600s. For example, in 1574 town crier "negro Francisco" publicly announced the sale of a mule belonging to the recently deceased, extremely wealthy cacique principal of Pocona, Don Pedro Arapa. Later in 1598, "through the voice of Manuel negro pregonero," Pocona community Indians announced the sale of one hundred cows and six hundred cheeses. References to black pregoneros (sometimes referred to as mozones) continued to appear throughout the seventeenth century, where at least in the early 1600s a pregonero was expected to cry out thirty pregones a year at a salary of 165 pesos. Local Mizque authorities in 1645 knew that they had a problem with Valle Grande and El Chilón and had a "pregonero negro" announce that owners of newly acquired chácaras in those areas should come forward and register their respective chácaras and yanaconas. In 1683 the "pregonero negro" announced that all forasteros had to pay a tasa of 6 pesos 2 reales—quite steep at the time. Lastly, in 1690, in a huge, convoluted estate litigation, it was recorded that the sale of specified estate products had been publicly announced by "pregonero Bartolomé Congo of the Chui Indians."[88] This lends a perfect touch to the ongoing discussion of race and ethnic mixture and identity that so engages much of this work. Also, one wonders about a possible cultural link between Africans in the colonial New World role of town crier and the west African oral tradition of the griot.

One more category joins the myriad roles and occupations that have thus far informed the discussion. In a 1650 litigation concerning a runaway slave, one of the officials overseeing and settling the dispute was "alférez Léiva, mulato alcalde público" (an alférez, as noted earlier, served as an ensign or standard-bearer; close to the rank of lieutenant). The closest I can define alcalde público is alcalde ordinario (magistrate), which, according to C. H. Haring, did lose its earlier luster of power over time.[89] Nevertheless, the fact that a person of African origins simultaneously filled these two posts is of considerable significance and raises provocative questions.

Population Figures for African Slaves and Their Descendants

At this juncture a closer examination of population figures is appropriate. For the most thorough assessment of the African slave population in Bolivia to date, Alberto Crespo's pioneering work *Esclavos negros en Bolivia* remains indispensable. Crespo explains that for a number of reasons, reliable population data for the colonial period are difficult to obtain and that past calculations are sketchy and incomplete at best. Nevertheless, comparing the data from the early seventeenth century to more precise information from the eighteenth and early nineteenth century, Crespo estimates that in the province of Potosí alone, by 1611, out of a total population of 160,000 inhabitants, people of African origins numbered 6,000 (3.74 percent).[90] A few years later, population data appeared relating to specific Mizque parishes—Mizque, Pocona, Pojo, Aiquile, and Totora. In his 1618 report to the viceroy, the bishop of the Mizque–Santa Cruz diocese (who spent most of his time in Mizque), Antonius de la Barranca, provided the following collective demographic information for baptismal records of six of the nine parishes under his jurisdiction.[91]

Spanish and Mestizo vecinos, encomenderos, chacareros, and merchants	600
Mulatos and Zambahigos	80
Negros esclavos	250

He added, however, that there was some "confusion" concerning numbers of men and women, and his revised calculations were as follows:

Spaniards, male and females	1,800
Community Indians	8,500
Male and female yanaconas	2,600
Mulatos y Zambaigos	150
Negros esclavos	250
Total	13,300

These figures are both intriguing and vexing, raising far more questions than they answer. For example, does the category "Spaniards, male and females" in Bishop de la Barranca's revised calculations include the earlier category of vecinos, encomenderos, and so forth? Does the "Male and female yanacona" category include the negro y mulato population discussed earlier in this chapter? Can we assume all slaves were baptized?

Crespo notes that in Potosí in 1719 the total population had dropped by more than one-half to 70,000 people, while the number of people of African origins had increased from 3.74 to 4.58 percent of the population.[92] However, moving along chronologically with this interregional comparison, some startling figures emerge regarding the Mizque region sixty-eight years later. In 1787 the highly respected Francisco Viedma, intendant of the province of Cochabamba, conducted a census of the Mizque province.[93] I have worked extensively with Viedma's published data and have managed to account for and make adjustments to a number of mathematical inconsistencies and inaccuracies. Taking the most conservative approach with his data, my own recalculations remain most telling, indeed.

First, the 1618 parish figures cited by Bishop Antonius reflected a still relatively small population, constricted to a smaller landscape. By 1787, Viedma's census activities covered a much wider swath of populated eastern regions that now included additional curacies and townships. By this time, Mizque's total population—despite the waves of epidemic disease and the economic decline—had more than doubled, from 13,300 to 33,499. In terms of the mulato population, Pocona had the fewest inhabitants (116, or 3.6 percent of the total population), which is interesting in the light of Viedma's observation that "the residential zone of this curate is composed of more cholos, mestizos, and zambos than Indians."[94] This, of course, adds further ballast to my argument concerning ongoing demographic transformations in the region.

Ciudad de Jesús del Valle Grande boasted the largest mulato sector, a hefty 38.2 percent (3,215). This should come as little surprise. Machicado cites a reference to Viceroy Marques de Montesclaros (1624?) giving Don Pedro de Escalante landholdings between Santa Cruz and

Mizque, in Indian warrior territory. Escalante died before developing these lands, which were inhabited by some "eight to ten poorly
inclined mulatos and mestizos." After his death, the audiencia sent
General Solís de Holguín to pacify the region. Viedma referred to the
"popular tradition that Valle Grande's first settlers were known by
the denomination *los Caballeros Pardos* [the gentlemen pardos]," and
Valle Grande may have been settled by slaves fleeing the many Spanish
haciendas of the old corregimiento. Hernando Sanabria F. wrote that
one of Escalante's many accomplishments in settling the Valle Grande
area was to immediately establish a fortress outside the city. Called
the "Fuerte de los pardos libres" (the fortress of the free pardos), it
was under the authority of Captain Domingo de Robles, the pardo
discussed above, who, along with other Robles pardo family members, owned estancias and chacaras recorded in the Mizque padrones.
This fortress may have come to be known as the town of Los Negros, located near Valle Grande on Bolivian maps (see Map 2 in this
work). Valle Grande's mulato population was followed by that of what
Viedma now called "the city of Mizque," whose mulato sector was 22
percent (632). Pasorapa followed with a population of 15.2 percent
(232), Samaipata with 14.5 percent (352), Totora with 13.3 percent
(488), Aiquile with 11.2 percent (341), and so on. The total mulato
population reached 6,128, or 18.3 percent of Mizque's total population. Unlike Viedma, I deliberately include Valle Grande (de los Caballeros Pardos) and Chilón within the political jurisdiction of the Corregimiento de Mizque, Chilón officially documented as such in 1630,
and Chilón, Valle Grande, and Ciudad de Jesús in 1645.[95]

Here again, the ambiguous issue of ascriptive labeling emerges. It is
known that slaves were present throughout the entire Charcas region,
including Mizque, from the earliest days of contact through the time of
Bolivia's independence from Spain and beyond. According to Crespo,
slavery was not officially, constitutionally abolished until 1868, yet
not once in the Viedma count does the term *slave* appear. In three locations he recorded the presence of "negros": .33 percent (28) in Valle
Grande, .25 percent (6) in Samaipata, and .2 percent (6) in Chilón.
And again we raise the question: In 1787, was *negro* synonymous
with "African slave"? Considering the region's history, forty negros

(slaves or not) is a puzzling number raising additional questions. Out of that 18.3 percent (6,128) mulato sector, were only forty identified (or identified themselves) as negro? Had all the Mizque slaves fled, or gained their freedom through birth or otherwise and assimilated into the larger mulato population? Crespo argued that despite a visible African and African-descent slave population nearly everywhere, Bolivia's independence from Spain did not bring freedom for the slaves. He adds that, liberal rhetoric notwithstanding, the abolition of slavery did not become a reality until the advent of Manuel Isidoro Belzu and the constitution of 1851.[96] Could it be that in 1787 slaves were still present in Mizque, much as they were in Potosí and La Paz, and that they were merely invisible to the Viedma census apparatus?

What we do know for certain is that Mizque had a much larger mulato population than was earlier thought and that this hefty mulato population (6,128), in turn, did not appear out of nowhere. The mulato men, women, and children were the direct descendants of African slaves and their slave offspring. Many of their ancestors were *legally* imported through the port of Buenos Aires, and many others were spirited through by illegal means. Buenos Aires served as the only transatlantic port of entry and licensing facility for goods and slaves destined for Charcas and ultimately (as held by the current wisdom) Potosí. However, early on the port became a hotbed of disorder, lawlessness, and corruption because of the growing number of undesirable outsiders and illegal trade. In particular, the growing trafficking in African slaves became an increasingly serious problem for government officials and private merchants alike. Slave trader Gabriel de Ojeda's angry grievance filed in 1614 with the audiencia of La Plata speaks volumes. Upon arriving in the port of Buenos Aires with his eight ships laden with two thousand African slaves, Ojeda was seized and locked up in a dungeon, where he was held incommunicado. He was then shipped off in the middle of the night to Santa Fe (upriver from Buenos Aires). He accused the port employees in charge of fraud and claimed they were in cahoots with smugglers and "their ways." They had "robbed him of more than 500,000 pesos of his income."[97]

However, once the imported African slaves were out of the port of disembarkation and in transit or in the hands of private owners, royal authorities could not keep record of them. Legal or illegal, they were, after all, only pieces of property. As long as their owners paid the government-assessed property taxes on them, the African slaves, unlike the yanaconas, were not even a passing concern of officialdom. Their care and welfare remained the sole responsibility or whim of the owner. Yet clearly the African slaves and their many descendants played a critical role in the development of the eastern Andes. The indigenous labor force could not and would not cooperate with the excessive demands of the Spanish imperial state or the private sector. Thus the Africans, representing a multitude of ethnicities, were imported into the region. Rather than merely replacing indigenous labor, they often added newly acquired special skills to those they brought from their lands of origin. Further, through various forms of adjustment, accommodation, and resistance to bondage, peoples of African origins not only played an important economic role in colonial Mizque but were also active agents in the sociopolitical and demographic transformations of this "forgotten" region.

6. Indian Affairs

OTHER WORKS HAVE EXAMINED highland indigenous groups per se and indigenous repartimiento communities. This project, instead, discusses the lowland ethnic warrior peoples as well as the migrating ethnic and non-ethnic individuals who served as yanaconas on the many haciendas, chácaras, and other units of production. The larger frame of reference is twofold, in which the issue of imperial (Inca and, soon, Spanish) political and economic control is juxtaposed against that of Indian accommodation and resistance to imperial hegemony. Here I analyze the repercussions of these conflicting forces within the context of coca production, land disputes, the transformation of the curaca leadership, ethnic identity, and the pandemic issue of flight.

The eastern Andean region's protracted prehistory of indigenous mobility and interregional trade, of ethnic diversity and interaction, and of ethnic aggression did not end with the arrival of the Europeans. Nor did the Inca propensity of moving clusters of *mitimaes* (Quechua term for colonists) from one location to another, often far from places of origin, end with the arrival of these same interlopers. On the contrary, throughout the Andean world Inca labor practices and other long-established cultural traditions were usurped and manipulated by the Spaniards, sometimes incorporated into Spanish systems imported from afar, all to serve the Spanish imperial vision of conquest, control, and exploitation.

Spanish Attempts to Control

Control is the key word here. The royal government implemented numerous means by which to maintain control of the indigenous population, economically and even physically. The creation of the idealized República de Indios and República de Españoles and the vast body of related laws is but one example. Tribute and tax collecting, census taking, the redefining of Indian communities into *repartimientos* and *reducciones* (resettlement groupings), and the arbitrary defining of "frontiers" also functioned as methods of control, not always—as the plethora of documents testifies—successful. As established earlier in this work, not all of the native peoples succumbed to imperialism, Inca-style or European. Those same groups who—as one or in alignment with former enemies—resisted the Inca expansion also resisted in various ways and sometimes with considerable vehemence the European onslaught. The scholarship on this subject has grown increasingly informed over the years. The more recent efforts deal extensively with indigenous movements, interchanges, and responses specifically related to the Mizque region, placing them in the context of prehistorical as well as historical time periods. The ongoing Yuracaré, Yumo, and "Chiriguano" attacks in the Mizque region against their ethnic "enemies" now under Spanish dominion and working the coca fields and salt flats (both coca and salt being in considerable demand in earlier times as well) are well documented.[1]

By the late 1500s and well into the 1600s the Yumo, Yuracaré, and Chiriguano had broadened their raids and massacres. These now included the Indian communities of Pocona and Mizque, the Spanish-owned chácaras, and Spanish merchants and hacendados or chacareros caught off guard while traveling between Mizque and Santa Cruz.[2] The myriad supporting evidence found in most of the regional collections studied in this project as well as the works of others makes it more than clear that Indian raids had been hampering regional activities for a prolonged period. By 1615, King Philip of Spain, the audiencia of La Plata, Mizque's cabildo, and the landowners themselves concurred that the atrocities must stop. Having acknowledged the ongoing Yuracaré attacks, murder, and plunder of the "defenseless, unarmed inhabitants" of the Chuquioma coca fields, on August 3, 1615, King Philip decreed the following:

> It is to be arranged that Don Pablo de Menesses, Corregidor de la Villa de Mizque may name an appropriate person from the valley of Chuquioma or wherever convenient, and with however many people necessary, to

guard and defend said valley, establishing sentinels and whatever else appropriate. And to do this and do it well, said corregidor will be issued two botijas of gunpowder [from the royal hacienda], for which the corregidor and the person he names shall be accountable, with no delay, to the royal audiencia, acknowledging receipt of said ammunition and of its distribution and [related] expenses . . . and that this decree be implemented, penalty of . . . and one thousand gold pesos for the chamber.[3]

A little over a month later, on September 2, 1615, in the *asiento* (seat; sometimes referred to as mining zone) of the valley of Tiraque (jurisdiction of the Villa de Salinas del Río Pisuerga), corregidor and justicia mayor Paulo de Menesses acknowledged the royal decree. In the tradition still in place today, having read the royal order, he "took it in his hands, kissed it, and placed it on his head, solemnly swearing to obey the King's command." He promptly named Joan Godoy Aguilera, vecino of Salinas (where he had earlier served as alférez real), to carry out the orders as "Captain of the Infantry of the yungas frontier."[4]

Seven years later, between November 24 and December 10, 1622, a series of writs, testimonials, and petitions appeared concerning Captain Godoy's tour of duty and his Indian campaigns. In his own statement defending his activities and explaining his successes, the captain noted that Yuma (his term) warriors had persisted in capturing, robbing, and murdering the Pocona Indians working the coca fields in the yungas of Chuquioma and Arepucho. Not only did these ongoing attacks prevent the Indians from paying the required tribute of coca to the king, but the Indians were also abandoning the coca fields and fleeing for fear of their lives. Godoy further explained that abandonment of the coca fields brought considerable loss and damage to the pueblo of Pocona as well.[5] Further elaboration on the social and economic issues pertaining to coca production will be provided later in this chapter. Suffice to say, the market for coca was huge and royal authorities met that demand at whatever cost to indigenous labor.[6]

Obviously, the ongoing Indian attacks threatened the imperial plan, and efforts to stifle the onslaughts often erupted in Spanish declarations of open warfare.[7] A closer look at Captain Godoy's experiences provides considerable insight into the complex relationships—far from one-sided—between the indigenous populations and the European in- terlopers. First, Godoy's tenure as "Captain of the Infantry in charge of frontier defense and Indian campaigns" lasted at least seven years. He also enjoyed the full support of two corregidores, Don Paulo de Menesses, in 1615, and an equally supportive Don Joan Paez de La- guna, in 1622. Corregidor Paez wrote an impassioned letter to the king explaining the difficulties in maintaining order in the Mizque and Pocona jurisdictions. He noted that this "frontier" zone had re- quired constant vigilance against the "warring Chiriguanos and other nations" since he had accepted the post of corregidor. Paez continued with the now-familiar litany of raids, assaults, kidnapping of Christian Indian women, robberies, and the equally familiar refrain lamenting the loss of revenues for the king.[8]

Paez made it clear that he could never have taken on the demand- ing task of frontier defense by himself. On the contrary, he had come to rely on Godoy's military discipline and his ability to form efficient squadrons at a moment's notice. The captain's many successful Indian campaigns testified to his abilities as a "great soldier who has demon- strated his utmost loyalty in service of Your Majesty." Paez concluded his petition by asking the king to reappoint Godoy to a permanent position as captain of the Spanish infantry, assigned to his home base, the valley and seat of Tiraque (strategically located near the yungas), to defend the embattled frontier as long as necessary.[9]

As for Captain Godoy, while he had little sympathy for the "thiev- ing" "delinquents" and "perpetual evil-doers" (his terms), he appar- ently remained law abiding in his military duty. He kept careful records of his expeditions and exploits, which in turn kept royal authorities informed and were (not surprisingly) soundly supported by his own infantrymen. His report of one campaign in particular merits further scrutiny. On November 24, 1622, the captain described one of his of- fensive drives against the "Yumo." (Yumo, Yuracaré, and Chiriguano are used interchangeably in this series of documents, leading one to wonder whether the Spaniards involved did not know the difference, refused to recognize the difference, or did not care.) He refers to the ongoing assaults against the Pocona Indians working the coca fields of Arepucho and Chuquioma and his most recent campaign to end these forays. At his own expense, he assembled a squadron of ten Spanish soldiers and—according to one of them who served later as a witness to this offensive—fourteen "friendly" Indians, all well-armed and experienced horsemen.[10]

Thus prepared, Godoy and his men descended into the lowlands and abruptly came upon a recently abandoned cluster of some six dwellings where the warriors had obviously set up camp. Alerted to the approaching troops, the warriors, numbering nineteen or so according to some witnesses, fled deeper into the forest. Before following in pursuit, Godoy and his men searched the camp, where they found discarded clothes. The Indian infantrymen in the unit recognized the garments as belonging to some Pocona Indians who had been massacred just a short while earlier in the Pocona valley. Further search yielded a store of machetes, knives, some broken swords, and other obvious weapons of aggression.[11]

They also found a hut that Godoy described as a "mochadero del demonio" (probably akin to "devil's lair"). It contained offerings, bows and arrows, flutes, *queros* (ceremonial drinking vessels; dates to pre-Inca) for drinking *chicha* (a beverage made from fermented corn), spears, and snake heads arranged on an altarlike structure of earth and painted stones where they apparently baptized their children. All of this, according to the captain, represented a way of life this group of "Chiriguano" had been pursuing for more than twenty years, despite the fact that some of them had been baptized as Christians. "They retreat in and out of the forest," Godoy said, "moving their camps closer to the Pocona valleys every day." The captain and his men persisted in tracking down some of the retreating warrior group and succeeded in capturing *nuebe piecas* (literally, nine pieces or units), mostly youngsters. Apparently, after the captives were brought into the Villa de Salinas and delivered to the local authorities, one Indian girl escaped and a small child died. Having deposited the new captives, Godoy had one request. Would it be possible for these captives to be distributed among his infantrymen in payment for their hard work? Perhaps in this way they could begin to put an end to "these thieves."[12]

As Captain Godoy made this request, he also made it clear that he was acting in the capacity of a military man appointed by the royal government and that he strictly abided by all orders. Thus he had done his utmost, at his own expense, to bring his young captives safely to the proper authorities. However, as far as he was concerned, all the other marauding warriors should be punished. He wrote, "I ask, beg your majesty, that you order that they be totally consumidos [obliterated] . . . and that as your appointed Captain of the Spanish Infantry, you grant me the power to execute said task." Children under the age of ten years, such as those he had just brought in, should be "exempted" from such a fate. Again, Godoy repeated his request that the seven children he brought into captivity be distributed among his soldiers in reward for their activities in the most recent campaign.[13]

While we do not know the fate of the captured children or how many warriors were obliterated, the strikes continued to terrorize the coca workers. According to Raimund Schramm, the warrior raids abated by the 1640s, but they certainly did not stop. In fact, a number of fierce Yuracaré attacks in the 1680s prompted local officials to request permission to launch further campaigns. The audiencia denied these requests, apparently because the local headhunters were now enslaving their captives against the will of the crown. Instead, the local clergy was to "gently coax the resisters into the Catholic faith to best resolve" the ongoing problems. Significantly, the authorities still worried about the effects of these raids on coca production.[14] Gentle coaxing notwithstanding, thirty years later, in 1728, royal authorities issued a general proclamation calling on all residents of the corregimiento to enlist against the warring Chiriguano, still on the attack in the coca fields. And still later, in 1777, General Antonio Aponte, corregidor of Mizque, issued an order calling for residents to enlist in a general offensive to combat the "kidnapping, murdering, plundering Chiriguano infidels."[15] The traditions of the lowland peoples had a long trajectory extending back thousands of years in time. These traditions—including control of the coca territories—were not easily extinguished, and their legacies are still in place today.

Coca: The Green Gold of the Andes
What was it about coca that led the lowland warriors to so boldly and unremittingly seek its access? And why did the Europeans—private

and government interests alike—fight with equal ferocity and determination to prevent a "Chiriguano" takeover of the fields? In fact, coca has its own protracted relevant history. Coca (*kuka* in Quechua) is a South American shrub that is the primary source of cocaine.[16] The coca leaf is not addictive; its nutritional, medicinal, and sociocultural characteristics are well established. Archaeologists can trace coca's use back to 2500 BC to pre-ceramic coastal Peruvian peoples.[17]

Further, scholars have established that the ambitious, complex, and far-reaching Inca imperial system included coca zones that predated the Inca invasions. However, most investigators have looked only to certain yungas (or *yunka* in Aymara); apparently, earlier peoples used the term to refer to the Andean eastern zones veering down into the subtropics of the Amazon basin). Investigations have focused almost entirely on the yungas of Cuzco or the much later yungas of La Paz. Until recently, few have explored the coca fields of Mizque's eastern frontier.[18] We now know that the coca fields in this region were probably taken over by the Inca ruler Huayna Capac in the early 1500s. In their reordering system of colonist labor and military forces in Totora and in the yungas of Chuquioma, the Inca shuffled together various ethnic groups—the Yampara, Charca, Cota, and Chuy, to name a few—for the purpose of defending against eastern lowland warriors and for sustaining production, thus creating an unparalleled mix of ethnic groups in this region.[19] Coca production was obviously of considerable importance to the Inca, as it would later become for the Spaniards. Schramm suggests that coca production in Mizque was more important than it was in Cuzco or La Paz.[20] My research supports this suggestion, at least for the earlier periods.

By the late 1540s and early 1550s the Spaniards would heed the call of a fast-growing highland market and set up their haciendas, chácaras, vineyards, farms, ranches, and plantations, often adjacent to curaca holdings of equal diversity and magnitude.[21] Not to lose the opportunity, these same encroachers would soon elbow their way into the Inca tradition of coca production as well. Europeans, like their curaca counterparts, found ample fertile fields nearby and far away in the eastern hot, seemingly impenetrable yungas.[22] To avoid confusion, it should be noted that in the Andean construct of archipelagos, place-names, and their map locations can be misleading. Places such as Pocona, Chimboata, Chilón, and the like, specifically designated on the map, can include numerous ecological niches not necessarily contiguous. For example, the "seat" of Pocona and the yungas of Pocona were located at a considerable distance from each other, with the yungas of Pocona actually situated in Chuquioma. As early as 1550, two encomenderos were awarded the repartimiento of Totora, from where twenty-five designated Indians were to go into the yungas of Chuquioma for abusive four-month-long *mitas* (work rotations) to harvest coca.[23] One encomendero was still collecting coca from his repartimiento in 1553, when he sold a neighbor 100 cestos of coca (at 20 pounds per cesto, about 2,000 pounds).[24] Yet by 1560 a sharp population decline was already under way, as seen by reduced tribute demands, and now twenty rather than twenty-five Indians per encomendero or curaca were being dispatched from Totora down into the yungas.[25] Disease, now accompanied by flight, had begun to wreak demographic havoc. Accordingly, the price of coca began to fluctuate.

Needless to say, the Potosí silver boom fed into price fluctuations. Working around the clock, mine workers consumed vast amounts of the energy-boosting leaf. As the early demand increased, prices rose. By 1529, shortly after the conquest and the first big silver strike, coca sold at 18 pesos a cesto. Ten years later it had dropped to 6 pesos. Thereafter the price dropped to a consistent 4–5 pesos per cesto, perhaps related to the "economic slump" discussed by Larson.[26] The data for the Mizque region indicate that in 1553, coca sold at 5½–6 pesos per cesto. Yet forty-six years later, in 1596, reflecting a labor scarcity coupled with a rising demand, coca prices rose to 16½ pesos per cesto, while one hundred years later it still sometimes sold for a hefty 15 pesos per cesto.[27]

Mizque provides an excellent microcosm in which to examine social, political, and economic issues connected to coca's price fluctuations. The ongoing coca-related problems suffered by the region's labor sector surely occurred in coca regions elsewhere. Basically, these involved the abuse and exploitation of a dwindling indigenous population that was pressured to produce greater amounts of coca to meet the increased highland demand. Despite the fact that by 1553 and 1564

Philip II of Spain had issued royal orders calling for the halt of harsh treatment of coca workers, this abuse continued throughout the remainder of the sixteenth and seventeenth centuries and beyond. Market demand outweighed any significant efforts at amelioration.[28] Thus we have an exposure of a fundamental flaw in the moral economy of Spain's colonial enterprise. This deep fissure pitched a complicated Catholic Counter-Reformation ethic of indigenous protection against a hard driven economic imperialism hitherto unknown in the New World. The issue was not Indian welfare. The issue involved thousands of cestos of coca that the crown had come to expect from these eastern yungas. As they did with many other autochthonous traditions and practices, the Europeans, often (though not always) with the cooperation of the local curacas, revamped the traditional rhythms of coca production. Spanish economic goals far exceeded those of their Inca predecessors. The sale of coca benefited royal treasuries as well as private coffers and had little to do with the well-being of the state and its peoples.[29]

Consider, for example, the Inca's rotational system of draft labor, where all married able-bodied adult males were drafted into three-month labor stints. While this practice applied to all labor and industries—agriculture, road building, and the like—the system provided a health safety valve for coca workers sent into the yungas, where the mitas lasted from two to twenty days. Geographer Daniel W. Gade, whose works in historical geography and disease in the pre-Columbian and post-conquest Andes inform this discussion, found that the Inca deliberately chose *not* to establish roots in the yungas regions. He argues that the Inca recognized the many threats facing the workers of the highlands when exposed to unfamiliar, antagonistic flora and fauna of the yungas. In particular, for highland Indians dispatched to the lowlands, they reduced the rotational draft labor routine to the briefest stretches of time. They did so in order to get the workers out before they lost their resistance to the dreaded leishmaniasis, a terrible, progressive disease for which there was no cure (even now it can be cured only if caught in its earliest stages). The infection is caused through the bite of a vector sandfly that dwells in the yungas. Its manifestations are as grotesque as they are terrifying. This disease dates back to at least 200 AD.[30]

While conventional wisdom holds that the Spaniards demonstrated little concern over protecting the Indian workers from coca-related hazards, my research reveals that even this issue is complicated and contradictory. We made note of the encomenderos who were faced with a reduced quota of Indians—from twenty-five in 1550 to twenty in 1560—for a four-month coca rotation.[31] Essentially, they were still deliberately sending their charges to a known death, extracting as much coca as humanly (or inhumanly) possible in the process. A look at the 1557 Visita a Pocona underscores the issue. Who participated in this official review is of key relevance. Three prominent curacas (called caciques in the visita)—Don Diego Xaraxuri, Don Pedro Chirima, and Don Hernando Turumaya—requested that they be represented in the inspection by a number of Franciscan friars. The government appointed Melchor Orozco as official visitador representing encomendero Francisco de Mendoza, who apparently recently had been awarded the large, coca-producing repartimiento of Pocona. At the outset of the inquiry, the three lead curacas were warned against lying or hiding evidence (livestock, tributaries, and the like) from the official review party, with whom they were to fully cooperate. Here we already have a flag. It was and still is commonly assumed that the caciques did not always behave themselves, often keeping their "subjects" and produce under wraps in order to evade tribute payments to the crown and benefit from the surplus.[32] Or so said the Spaniards. The following is the official visita summary for the repartimiento:

1,128	inhabited houses
183	uninhabited houses
582	male Indians, married with spouses
97	single males
230	single females
314	boys
332	girls
98	old men [over the age of 50]
373	old women [over the age of 50][33]

The working population consisted of able-bodied married men, able-bodied single men, and able-bodied single women and *mozas* (adolescent girls) no doubt assigned the traditional domestic tasks. The elderly and boys and girls under the age of ten were not to be put to work. The summary did not include the caciques and their families, the *llacta runas* (temporary migrants with close ties to their ayllus), or the *indios venedizos* (outsider, newcomer residents), who occupied 120 houses but refused to be included in the census, whether they had been there for two, three, or even five years. They claimed, according to the caciques, that they should not be counted because they were free to come and go at will.[34] This in itself is an interesting manifestation of resistance and quite counter to the interests of the Spaniards. The glaring drop in the adult male population becomes apparent when comparing the almost equal ratios of girls and boys to the disparity between single men and single women and between old men and old women. The mortality rate for adult males gives ample credence to the following observations.

After the head count, the visita quickly moved from one pivotal issue to the next. Encomendero Mendoza complained early on to the authorities that the Indians were fleeing his repartimiento, and he requested a permit to locate and return them. Further, he asked that "Spaniards" be limited to no more than three days among his repartimiento Indians. He claimed the Europeans exerted a bad influence, took unfair advantage of the Indians, and should dwell in the settled towns where they belonged. Elsewhere, the visita revealed that the repartimiento of Pocona consisted of many *parcialidades* and *ayllus* (moieties and clan groups) and that the caciques and secondary ethnic leadership figures all possessed coca fields where the repartimiento Indians worked, some on a draft rotational basis, others as *camayos* (permanent residents used specifically for all coca-related production activities, given subsistence plots but no salaries, still connected to their ethnic ayllus, date back to Inca practices). "Where once they harvested coca for the Inca, they now harvest for their encomendero, and now many individual Indians have [coca] farms there."[35]

The issue of leishmaniasis, known locally as *carache*, and the related issues of population loss due to flight and disease and decline in coca production quickly emerged. The curacas repeated the soon familiar refrain, "We used to get 100 cestos of coca per mita from this farm, now we get 10," "We should be getting 800 cestos per mita," and so on. Apparently the review party braved the difficult journey into the actual yungas, moving from one coca farm to the next. The following summarizes the Franciscans' findings. The Indians were overworked, and many had died, returned to their places of origin, or become yana-conas. If their replacements were not sent to "relieve them of their bur-dens," the remaining mitimaes would either die or flee, leaving perhaps only a hundred local permanent inhabitants, all of whom were of the Cota ethnicity. The repartimiento should be producing thousands of cestos of coca per mita, but the land was sick, the people were sick and dying everywhere, not just in the yungas. Too much burden had been imposed on the Indians. They were sick, had no food, and the trip in and out for them was unbearable. Further, landowners were bribing them to come and work on the haciendas.[36] The Franciscans repeat-edly prevailed upon God and the "consciences" of the tax collectors, reminding them that their demands were depleting the Indian popu-lation. They swore from firsthand knowledge that the Indians in the yungas were worked harder than anyone else in the entire province (of Mizque). Just getting the coca out was a twelve-mile uphill battle for the Indian cargo bearers, who carried heavy loads, sweating profusely in the sweltering heat (llamas did not survive the heat and hazards of these lowlands), only to arrive at the much higher, much colder alti-tudes poorly clothed and poorly nourished. "They died!" Now, those who had not died were giving up, and even the plants themselves were no longer producing as they had before. When production and popula-tion were at their peak and the entire population engaged in harvesting, the yungas produced at least 4,000–5,000 cestos per mita (16,000–20,000 per year). Production had been reduced to a mere fraction. In a desperate attempt to keep up with the tribute demands, some Indians tried renting other Indians. This, too, failed.[37]

The Franciscans also expressed concern over the many mitimaes from a multitude of diverse clans led by too many different curacas (the Franciscan term), all resulting in chaos and confusion. The priests urged that only one lead curaca, Don Hernando Turumaya, be recog-nized as the primary leader for the entire repartimiento. They saw him as quite capable, possessing a known ability to deal effectively with the

Spaniards. He also successfully led the Indians, the friars reasoned, because he was an outsider, not a local.[38] He was also very wealthy and owned, among other things, extensive coca fields. The friars decried the fact that replacement labor for these fatigued, confused workers had not been forthcoming. Further, someone had recently purchased a few cows, and 120 llamas had been provided to help transport coca out of the yungas (no doubt at the higher, cooler elevations). Now, complained one friar, the Spaniards think everything is fine and that it should not be so difficult to get the coca out. Another priest, who, like the others had lived and worked among the coca workers in the yungas, criticized encomendero Mendoza, claiming he ordered the Indians to work before sunrise and kept them in the fields until sunset, when they often got caught in the rain and had to return home wet with no clothes to change into, no one to cook for them, and no one to gather firewood or build a fire. They slept on the ground, consumptive and prone to disease. "This too, must be remedied," said the friar.[39]

To all the above testimonies, official visitador Orozco, representing encomendero Mendoza and himself a government attorney, cried "Fraud!" As he and his party moved throughout the yungas, Orozco found ample evidence of good housing, supplies, food, plenty of people to cook, and surplus workers to assist in all phases of coca production. The Indians had their own lands down there, their families were with them, all their needs were met. Moreover, they *were* being replaced—as soon as they died. "When one of them dies," claimed Orozco, "they are replaced by another who takes over the deceased's [coca] fields, house, and family. There is no shortage of labor." The visitador was convinced that more Indians existed than were declared by the caciques and that the repartimiento could easily produce at least 2,000 cestos each year. He swore they had plenty of llamas for coca transport, only the Indians did not take good care of them, "especially when they are sick with the carache and die, the llamas wander off." As to why the Indians were being worked too hard, Orozco claimed that the caciques were at fault. They forced the Indians into hard labor in the cornfields (corn was at a premium in the coca region, both for eating and for *chicha*) and then sold the corn to the Spaniards for profit. As for the caciques themselves, the visitador repeated several times throughout his testimony, "They lie!" Orozco also noted that some of the coca fields were so distant—particularly those in Arepucho—that no Spaniard had seen them, had any idea of their extent, or had any notion of the number of Indians involved. The visitador concluded the review with one recommendation: the distant Arepucho operations needed to be closed. Coca production there was too harsh on all counts: it was too far away; it had terrible, nearly impassable roads; there were no religious or health services; and the Indians were left to die, unattended.[40]

The imperial government moved slowly and claimed to close the Arepucho fields in 1582. They allegedly had the bushes uprooted and transplanted in the relatively closer, somewhat more accessible yungas of Chuquioma. The debate was far from over, however. Throughout the remainder of the 1500s and well into the 1600s the tug-of-war continued unabated. The crown, seemingly concerned over the plight of the Indians, issued a plethora of decrees that it could not or would not fully impose and which local coca farm owners and tradesmen, for all practical purposes, ignored. Paradoxically, all the while the government indicated "concern" over Indian abuse and called for the procurement of an appropriate magistrate to oversee local Indian affairs, it simultaneously made it clear that the colony's economic well-being depended, in large part, on coca production's meeting the market demand.[41]

All the while, those same curacas and their later replacements, whom government officials repeatedly accused of lying and malfeasance, told a very different story from that of the official visitador, one far more in keeping with the friars', which they repeated time and again. Their people, they said, were being abused in the yungas. They were ill and dying. They simply could not meet the grueling demand for Indian labor in the coca fields and elsewhere. "How can we possibly send workers up to La Plata? We don't have enough to work the coca in the yungas." Further, the "closing" of the Arepucho fields did not lessen the harsh treatment of the Indians, who were dying off just as rapidly in Chuquioma. In 1573 the curacas begged to have the coca tribute commuted to money. Their people did not want to go down to the yungas of Chuquioma, which threatened their health and caused many deaths. For their well-being, the curacas pleaded, "please commute the tribute." All of this fell upon deaf ears. The tribute abuses continued through the seventeenth and eighteenth centuries, and of course, beyond.[42]

The insatiable demand for coca—from the crown and from private entrepreneurs, European and indigenous—placed an additional burden on the already weakened, vulnerable, and increasingly resistant labor pool. Those who had not already died of diseases contracted from the Europeans were dying of forced, prolonged contact with the fatal leishmaniasis. Many of the survivors, Inca mitimaes plucked from other regions, returned to their original clans. Thus, as discussed earlier, the Spaniards turned to African slave labor. As explained in chapter 5, African bozal and criollo slaves served in all sectors of Mizque's economy. All, that is, but one—the production of coca.

Decisions concerning labor occurred at many levels, from the highest government strata down to the individual estate owner. The crown extracted coca, regardless of the human cost. Cheap Indian labor, despite the shrinking numbers, was still disposable. Just push them harder. The crown, now experienced in matters of African slavery, gave the official nod of approval. African slaves were brought into the corregimiento in an attempt to assuage the dwindling pool of Indian labor. Most of the Mizque estates—indigenous and Spanish owned—studied in this project possessed multiple holdings in the different ecological zones discussed earlier. Many of them had *at least* one or two chácaras in the coca fields, producing continually. Like the encomenderos of the Totora and Pocona repartimientos, the owners of private estates sent *their* people (referred to now as yanacona) down to *their* own coca fields in the yungas.

A number of significant issues emerge in the padrones de chácara relating specifically to coca production, race, and ethnicity. First, owners often moved their slaves from one production unit to another, from one region or ecological zone to another, or even from the countryside to their town houses in the Villa de Mizque, depending on current need. I have no evidence of owners sending their slaves down to the yungas.[43] Two possible explanations come to mind. The slaves were too costly to participate in activities reserved for Indians, who were still available, albeit in reduced numbers, and still dispensable. By the end of the 1590s, well-established encomenderos and hacendados were receiving citations for mistreating their yanaconas in the yungas: not providing their clothing rations and other needs for two or three years in succession. Worse, these highly placed gentlemen were further accused of not providing for their sick and dying coca workers. One of these elites, accused of all these infractions, went on the record as saying, "Que se mueran y que se les lleve el diablo" ("Let them die and go to the devil.")[44] Surely these astute businessmen were not about to subject their slaves to the lethal hazards of the yungas and lose their investments. Instead, the African male slaves could be more profitably occupied in sugar, wine, and livestock activities, the females in domestic service. Second, the Andean practice of flight was so pervasive and integrated into the culture that the African slaves were quickly acquiring their own skills in this tradition. Sending them off to the yungas would certainly create the risk of flight.

By the end of the 1590s and into the early 1600s, other patterns, very possibly interrelated, emerge. The Mizque landowners were shifting their yanaconas—now comprising ethnic and non-ethnic indigenous peoples *and* free negros/mulatos—from unit to unit, including down to the coca fields. The removal, without an official permit, of yanaconas from the property to which they were attached was illegal. These property owners were warned explicitly not to force their yanaconas to work on other chácaras against their will. It would appear, however, that some hacendados transferred their workers wherever and whenever they desired with no official reprimand. Others were served with hefty fines for the same infraction. Nevertheless, worker transfer commonly occurred. By now, not surprisingly, coca from private holdings enjoyed increased demand. People forced into bankruptcy sold all their properties except their coca farms. I suspect there were some shady dealings involved when, in 1599, a young son of a wealthy curaca, having squandered much of his inherited wealth and fallen into debt, was "persuaded" to sell his coca fields to a Spaniard. And in 1604, one Francisco Esteban was thrown into jail, where he remained indefinitely, for stealing the coca harvest of a Pocona Indian. The theft had "deprived said Indian of his means to provide for his family and to pay his tribute." Over time, other non-European peoples would join the surviving indigenous coca workers in Mizque's yungas, both involuntarily and of their own volition. Also, in 1604, corregidor/justicia mayor Captain Gonzalo Paredes de Hinojosa sent out a clear hint of things to come. He "could not find someone to conduct the padrones and collect tribute from the yanaconas residing on the chácaras between Totora and the Julpe River, nor from those living in the yungas of Chuquioma and Arepucho, as well as from indios, mulatos, and zambiagos *sueltos* [unattached]."[45] The entire coca region was quickly growing out of government control.

Indian Lands

Given the highly complex indigenous reality under colonial rule, it is not accurate, nor is it the intent of this work, to characterize all eastern Andean ethnic groups as either aggressive warriors or as exploited, dying coca workers. Take, for example, the issue of Indian landholding. This construct is nuanced with contradictions that have their origins in pre-Columbian traditions, both in the Andes and elsewhere in the New World. Obviously, indigenous populations held lands, lost lands, fought for lands, and died for lands long before the advent of the Europeans. And in the case of the eastern Andes and their adjacent lowlands and rain forests, archaeologists again provide sound evidence to underscore the pre-Columbian land tenure systems, as they have successfully established the prehistoric patterns of trade, movement, and migration.[46]

Thus, Indian land claims demanding the return of their territories now in possession of the Spaniards are of little surprise. The prominent Paniagua clan again serves to underscore the issue. Earlier chapters explained their presence in Mizque, particularly regarding pacification, early encomiendas, and land acquisitions. Although it has been established that in 1563 Gabriel Paniagua de Loaysa transferred his inherited encomienda of Chuy (or Chui; the spelling varies) Indians from Pojo to Mizque, Ana María Presta explains how his wide network of social, political, and economic connections greatly facilitated this maneuver. She also demonstrates that at the same time this indigenous group was resettled, they were also negotiating the sale of the lands they once inhabited and still possessed in the valleys of Cliza and

Punata. Of significance to the larger discussion here, however, is that their appointed guardian/defender *responsible* for the negotiations was Gabriel Paniagua's half brother Alonso Paniagua de Loaysa—a classic case of the fox guarding the henhouse.[47]

According to the 1575 source I consulted, several individuals, referred to as *tutor, curador,* or *protector de indios* (all officials appointed by the audiencia as guardians to defend the Indian population), were involved in this prolonged land dispute. In 1573, Gonzalo Min de Cetona, protector of these same Chuy who by now had been transferred to Mizque, accused Pedro Juárez Sermeño of usurping their lands in the Cliza valley region. Further, Juárez Sermeño had cultivated the lands and was now producing wheat, making the lands more valuable, thereby resulting in considerable loss to the Indians. Even though they were now in Mizque, the Indians still wanted their Cliza lands back. The lands belonged to them before and had been taken against their will.[48]

In response, Juárez Sermeño's lawyer repudiated the accusations, declaring that in 1563 the same pueblo, caciques, and guardian Alonso Paniagua had put the lands up for sale. The lawyer further insisted that his client purchased the lands legally and with full consent of the Indians' tutor and their caciques. He had all the appropriate papers to prove the legality of his purchases. He also pointed out that at least ten years had passed and no one had said a word or made any effort to contact anyone about the situation until the results of his client's efforts became apparent. The lands were now fully cultivated, irrigated, and productive, none of which pertained when the Indians held possession of the same properties. The holdings were now worth at least 4,000 pesos. The lawyer concluded that the Indians could not justify their demands.[49]

Late in December 1574, in the pueblo of Pocona, visitador/corregidor Pedro Quíroz de Ávila oversaw the proceedings in which the contending parties came to terms. The Indians, having been *reducidos* (forced to resettle) from Pojo to Mizque by Paniagua's skillful maneuvering, were now much too far away from their holdings—a distance of some thirty-six miles. In addition, Juárez Sermeño had already subdivided and sold parcels of the holdings. Even if the Indians could gain access to the remaining pieces, these lands were no longer contiguous and lacked water. Therefore, it was decided that Juárez Sermeno would retain possession but reimburse the Indians for the balance of their holdings at their original value—80 pesos.[50] The Indians agreed—or more accurately, their "witnesses" and "leaders" agreed for them, as they had throughout the many years of litigation. The most recent of these so-called representatives included Gabriel senior's son Don Pedro Paniagua and Chuy cacique Don Diego Layasa.[51]

The following protracted litigations further reveal how adeptly the Paniagua clan maintained its select status. Again, the people whom the Paniaguas came to conquer and exploit and whose lands they wanted to usurp raised their voices in collective protest. Here again the issues revolved around land ownership, this time in the valley of Mizque, where family members claimed multiple properties that they traded and bequeathed among themselves. This case also concerns the Pojo Indians; however, here the litigations begin much earlier, in 1558— five years before the clan manipulated the transfer of this group from Pojo to Mizque, thirty-nine miles away. The legal battles between the Indians and the Paniaguas continued at least through 1605, almost fifty years. While several curadores/tutores represented the Indians and their curacas throughout the litigations, often the caciques themselves also came forth to state their claims, revealing considerable ambivalence of their own.[52]

The arguments on both sides were consistent. The Indians insisted that the Mizque lands belonged to them. Gabriel and half brother Alonso—their amassed properties now including those of their father, Pedro Hernández, who died in 1554—swore to the contrary. They had witnesses, bills of sale, and land grants awarded them by the now-deceased Viceroy Mendoza to back their claims. Of the several parcels of land in dispute, one in particular merits closer scrutiny. This property consisted of forty fanegadas of prime wheat-producing turf "de cojer mucha comida" ("that would provide much sustenance"). In 1558 the Chuy, having been transferred from their previous terrains in the valley of Mizque and now residing in Pojo, officially reclaimed their lands. Specifically, on July 18 they demanded the return of the forty-fanegada estancia. This holding, called Laguaca, was strategically located at the mouth of the Loyochama River in the valley of Mizque. It was but one of their many properties in the region.[53]

Alonso Paniagua and his lawyers rejected the claim, insisting that the Loyochama properties as well as the others were legally his. For additional emphasis he further claimed that no one intervened when he went through the traditional rituals of taking possession of the holdings. Moreover, Alonso continued to defend his position with vague references to the land belonging to him even before the Indians were transferred to the Pojo repartimiento where they now (1558) resided. The Pojo Indians continued to press their demands. In September 1560, represented by their most recent guardian, Francisco Gallegos, they again called for the return of the properties in their original, prime condition or an equitable monetary restitution of same, as judged fair by the local authorities. The Paniaguas' defense maintained its position throughout the entire period in question. Unlike Juárez Sermeño in the Cliza litigation, the powerful Paniaguas yielded not one iota to the earlier inhabitants of Mizque.[54]

Yet the Chuy people persisted. In 1573 they mounted still other claims, this time in the Tin Tin region, nine miles southeast of the Mizque valley proper. The accused usurper, Juan Vargas de Toledo, vehemently denied the charges. His lawyer argued that neither the Chuy nor their ancestors ever inhabited these rugged, uncultivated, unappropriated "since time immemorial" hills. If anyone "occupied" the land, they would be the Sora, Cota, and Colla who, resisting European conquest after military defeat in Cochabamba, fled to this inaccessible region to hide out and heal their wounds. Once they were pacified, the lawyer continued, each returned to their respective caciques, who apparently turned them over to "some three or four" local encomenderos. This particular round of claims and counterclaims came to a halt in 1604.[55]

However, some of these Tin Tin claims must have been recognized, because in 1661 Francisco Amire, governor of the Chuy community, and other Chuy representative leaders raised a complaint concerning a former Chuy governor, Don Francisco Yarti. In essence they accused him of at least six years of misuse of their lucrative community livestock-raising and wheat-producing lands in the valley of Tin

Tin. Apparently, instead of delivering what he owed them, he withheld rental and other proceeds from the Indians. They had asked him repeatedly to hand over the money—at least 600 pesos—that was rightfully theirs. With the now-familiar refrain, voiced at least one hundred years earlier and still resonant, the Chuy argued that they needed the money "to help us pay the tasas to his Majesty, on all of our many runaway and dead Indians."[56] This certainly does not support the argument for reduced exploitation that some scholars propose.[57]

What the above discussion does reflect is that various Indian groups persistently claimed and reclaimed their earlier holdings. Thus the discussion requires a closer look at the indigenous leadership. Just how altruistically they represented their people remains uncertain. For example, I have evidence of curacas who were willing to go to jail rather than subject their tributaries to unattainable imperial coca quotas, but I have also shown that these same and other curacas had an interest in possessing large, productive landholdings (like their European counterparts) and were active participants in the Spanish imperial economic system. And of course, there was the former Chuy curaca accused of usurping community properties for personal gain. Such accusations were by no means uncommon.

The Curacas Take a Stand

Waldemar Espinoza, editor and transcriber of "El memorial de Charcas: 'Crónica' inédita de 1582," notes in his introduction that the Chuy were one of four very powerful Indian nations, the other three being the Charca, the Caracara, and the Chicha. He explains that even before the Inca conquest, all four enjoyed a privileged position as highly competent warrior nations. They maintained this status under Inca imperial rule as well. Upon the arrival of the Spaniards and their subsequent conquest of the eastern Andes, the curacas of these favored nations fully expected to maintain their elite status. Espinoza analyzed the 1582 memorial compiled and signed by the curacas of these respective nations, now united as the Provincia de Charcas. He noted that the curacas became very bitter over their rapid decline in status under the Spaniards, who—secular or ecclesiastic (with the exception of the Jesuits)—"treat us like slaves" (which in this context means African slaves).[58] The twenty-four curacas, representing lower and higher leadership status within their group, also voiced anger over the Toledano project of dividing the Charcas nation into twenty-five encomiendas or repartimientos. Further, they repeatedly referred back to the earlier times of glory, privilege, and ostentation with considerable nostalgia.[59]

Although Espinoza credits the Andean nations for their long tradition of military brilliance, he posits another dimension to the litany of grievances, reproaches, and petitions listed by the curacas to remedy their circumstances. He suggests that the curacas who compiled the 1582 memorial were so determined to "regain their ancestral preeminence, be it economic, political or social, that they did not hesitate, on many occasions, to betray their own culture."[60] After a careful reading of the transcribed documents, one might agree to some extent with Espinoza, but only to a degree. To be sure, perhaps two or three of the fifty-three *capítulos* (articles) sought respite for the overburdened Potosí miners, but overwhelmingly these articles represented the indigenous nobility in their demands for retribution, revalidation, and recognition of their noble, privileged status of the past. The curacas heaped the blame for their grievances on former viceroy Don Francisco de Toledo. They addressed their appeals directly to Philip II.[61]

At first glance it would appear that abuse of their people did concern the twenty-four curacas. In the opening capítulos they decry the tasa's being raised from 3 to $6^1/_2$ to 7 pesos per "indio" (their term). The Indians could not keep up with the earlier tribute demands, and with the imposed increase they were abandoning their repartimientos or reducciones to seek work elsewhere. "We are losing our labor supply because they are going to work on the [Spanish] chacaras," they wrote, "yet we are having to pay the tasas anyway. We want our runaway Indians returned to us. We are their leaders . . . we are supposed to pay for them but we can't. They are not even working for us. . . . Yet because of Toledo we now face the threat of losing our cacicazgos [chiefdoms—their term], and being replaced and sent into exile to Panama and Mexico. We cannot meet Toledo's demands."[62] Clearly, self-concern overruled concern for their "vassals."

As we move from one capítulo to the next, these articles take on a momentum and life of their own. The curacas beg "their" Spanish king to stop the audiencia and local cabildos from parceling out their prime lands in grants to the Spaniards. They fear their children will be uprooted and be left with no lands of their own. The Spaniards were taking the best, leaving them with that which was worthless. "They want to banish us from our country, our nation and our lands." The curacas complained about being forced to support the hospital in Potosí, which they said they did not need because "Our sick people do not go there. It is used by the Spaniards, mestizos, mulatos, negros, yanacona and servants of the Spaniards." They added that they did need a hospital closer to their repartimientos to tend to their sick and invalids. Further, they demanded more access to their mines, as well as a salary raise. What Toledo allotted them did not meet their needs. They required a salary befitting their superior position.[63]

One particular capítulo, titled "Social Discrimination," sums up the despair and resentment these displaced and dishonored indigenous elite suffered for having compromised with or sold out to the Spaniards:

[The royal officials] now subject us to corporal punishment at the slightest pretext. They beat us with sticks, lock us in pillories, tie us to stakes and whip us, confront us daily with violent cuffs and blows, throw us in jail [and treat us] worse than were we their slaves. And here we are being dragged along insulted, as if we were not the original nobility of this land, willing to compromise and come to terms [as] Christians . . . we beg of Your Majesty to decree . . . that we may enjoy our freedom like the Spanish nobility and order the officials of this reign to recognize and accept our privileges as they should in all civil and criminal causes that may arise, since we have such a fine and very Christian prince and king, as we are your vassals every bit as much as those in Spain.[64]

The curacas reminded the king that they had fought along with the Spaniards in the campaigns against the Chiriguano. They had contributed a thousand warriors and two thousand llamas in pack teams. Half of their people and all of their livestock perished in the expedition, yet the Spaniards never compensated them for their losses.

The curacas' list of demands called for the rescinding of the Toledano decree denying them horses, mules, and riding gear, which to them made no sense. They had been in alliance with the Spaniards since the latter's arrival. "How can we help to defend [the lands] as Your Majesty had ordered," they asked, "without horses, mules and gear?" They also wanted a university for the indigenous nobility to be located in Cuzco, which would be more convenient for the children of Charcas, Quito, and Lima than the present university, situated in Lima.[65]

The second, shorter memorial, identical in tone and tenor to the first, was written by Don Fernando Ayavire y Velasco. Long accustomed to positions of power, he presently acted as cacique principal of the Spanish-designated Provincia de Charcas. As such, his signature appeared first, followed by those of the other twenty-three curacas. He also enjoyed his hereditary position as cacique principal of his own people's nation of Charcas (from which the audiencia took its name). In his memorial he underscored his Charcas ethnicity, of which he was very proud, by identifying himself to a former *oidor* (audiencia judge) named Barros, now in Spain, as "one of the lead ruling gentlemen of this province of Charcas, and of the nation and dress of the Charcas people."[66] In this petition Don Fernando addressed earlier issues as well as additional questions regarding his own privileges and rights as the most important curaca of his people. Reminding Dr. Barros of his indigenous royal heritage, which predated the Inca, and the thousands of Indian vassals once under the authority of his prominent family, he begged that the former oidor plead his case.[67]

Further, Don Fernando demanded that royal authorities treat him and his family as they would treat the *hijosdalgo* (privileged gentlemen) in Spain. As such, the entire extended family should be exempt from *pechos y alcabalas* (commoner and sales taxes). In keeping with the logic fueling his petitions, in capítulo 3, titled "Arms and negros for the curacas," he made the following request:

> We beg of Your Majesty that you be willing, as our King and true lord, to grant me and my sons permission to bear both offensive and defensive arms such as swords, daggers, shields, coats of arms, arquebuses, spears, and partisans [a sixteenth- and seventeenth-century weapon with a long shaft and a broad blade] for our personal self-defense and that we may be allowed to ride horses and mules in dress harness as do the gentlemen in Spain, and that we be allowed to buy and own black slaves to serve us

and our households, mindful that we are gentlemen and hijosdalgo which is widely know.[68]

Loyalty to the king of Spain was raised repeatedly in these documents. The issue of vassals also resonated throughout—the curacas, as loyal vassals of the king, insisted that they too be recognized as lords and leaders over their own vassals. This, in turn, led to the oft-repeated "We too are lords, Christians, hijosdalgo just like the Spaniards" and "we want our rights and privileges returned to us. Toledo took away our yanacona. We had thousands, tens of thousands. We want them back. We need them to sustain ourselves and our families. They are now tributaries to the king and that is not fair. We are better than the [other nations]. We want justice."[69] The "justice" they called for, however, was essentially a justice for themselves and not for their own "vassals." They were not betraying their culture. They were reflecting it.

Whether or not their demands were fully met cannot be ascertained. Nor can it be determined which of the twenty-four signatures belonged specifically to the Chuy curacas. However, judging by the sampling of last wills and testaments drawn up by Mizque caciques discussed in chapter 3, these nobles possessed considerable material wealth. Their wills cover a span of almost fifty years, from 1573 to 1619. They had plenty of land worked by their yanaconas and enjoyed fruitful harvests of all manner of local products, including coca. They owned hundreds to thousands of head of livestock (including horses) and multiple houses, estancias, and chácaras throughout the region. Further, their luxury possessions included status symbols from both cultures— European and native.[70]

Interestingly, the indigenous elites, like their European counterparts, owed goods and money to other local curacas and Spaniards—as the latter two owed them—in local products and currency. Like the European entrepreneurs in the Corregimiento de Mizque, the indigenous entrepreneurs also bought from, loaned to, and borrowed from each other continually, all of them apparently working through informal systems of credit and loans not connected to the Roman Catholic Church. Further, the wealthy Mizque curacas and their families, like the signers of the memorial, had embraced Catholicism and, like all moneyed Catholics, bequeathed some of their wealth to their local church. Like the Europeans, they too lavished their money on church-related constructions and on masses sung to accompany their souls to heaven and to guarantee their souls a favored spot in the afterlife. Further, as noted in chapter 2, in 1630 one of the Mizque caciques, Don Francisco Turumaya, donated a hefty 100 pesos toward the construction of the much-needed bridge to facilitate trade and transportation to the highlands.[71] The post-conquest, early colonial wealthy indigenous elites of the eastern Andes did not *appear* to suffer the degree of indignities and deprivations so lamented in the 1582 memorial.

The Acculturation or Demise by Design of the Curacas

However, a number of works on Andean curacas provide a cautionary note that informs the larger discourse on the subject. James Lockhart, in a discussion of the Indian sector in general, notes a difference in acculturation rates between Indian nobles, servants, and laborers dwelling in the Spanish-dominated coastal Lima region and their counterparts living in the indigenous-dominated highland Cuzco area. He attributes the lesser acculturation of the latter to the fact that they were all a part of an "independent indigenous world" that fostered a resistance to European models. By contrast, the Limeño caciques emulated Spanish habits to the fullest, including the ownership of African slaves—which the signers of the 1582 memorial also coveted, along with the many other status symbols embraced by the Europeans.[72] This concept of acculturation could apply to the Mizque curacas as well. In their eastern hinterland valley and lowland frontier contexts, they too were further removed from the day-to-day influences of Spanish culture than many of the memorial's signers. They did not possess African slaves, but they did have yanaconas. They embraced Catholicism, but they also held onto their ethnic and indigenous costume, adornments, and utensils that represented native elite status. They owned European weapons. They not only raised horses but also rode them with full equestrian trappings. Thus, in this context they appeared a relatively independent wealthy curaca group, seeming to draw upon the best of both the Hispanicized and the indigenous world—at least for a while.

However, during the period under discussion some of the local curacas suffered repeated incarcerations for their inability to meet the tribute quotas (in coca or money) for their dead or runaway yanaconas, of which there were many. This aggravation continued at least through 1748.

But, as other historians demonstrate, the above was only one facet of the complex world of Andean caciques or curacas. The overriding theme regarding the post-conquest indigenous elites is that of inconsistency and contradiction. Further, as Kenneth Andrien has argued, the stage for ambiguity was set immediately after conquest, based on uneasy indigenous-European alliances and fueled by corruption and collusion. The local curacas participated in the power brokering that, together with other crucial factors, preordained the failure of the Toledano reforms.[73] And finally, Karen Viera Powers's insights into the complicated transitional roles of the cacique (she does not use the term *curaca*) in the northern Andes apply to the eastern Andean experience in a number of ways. For example, her explanation of demographic shifts resulting from migratory patterns suggests similar explanations for the Mizque province and curaca activities there. Powers examined the cacique penchant for hiding their subjects from colonial authorities in order to have ready access to this labor force for themselves—a tradition that may have been present in Mizque as well. There the curacas could easily have withheld the names of camayos, llacta runas, and laborers from what I have termed the "floating population," keeping them hidden from local officials. Powers also discusses the phenomenon of Indians hiring "foreign" workers (forasteros) to meet the excessive tribute payments they could not match on their own.[74] These and other northern Andean curaca-related activities found parallels in the Mizque model, as the following will soon demonstrate.

All of the more recent scholarship further illuminates the discussion on the indigenous elites in the Andes and elsewhere in the Americas. The native leadership and their respective peoples transformed—and were transformed by—access to power and material resources and the resulting dizzying shifts in the balance of this dynamic. Some of the shifts occurred unevenly and by increment. When, for example, did curacas stop owning African slaves, stop riding horses, and stop owning vast tracts of land? Other changes wrought by the now-familiar triad of disease, harsh treatment, and flight were more sweeping and thus more stunning in their ongoing reverberations. The terms used by the cited authors resonate even as they sometimes strike contradictory chords. Indeed, there is an overarching consistency in the seeming contradiction of terms that explain the indigenous response to Spain's drive to dominate, politically and economically, the New World and its peoples. The title of Ramírez's work—*The World Upside Down*—says it well.

Seen in this context, the 1582 memorial makes sense. The twenty-four curacas were furious, degraded, and offended over the loss of their territories and the multitude of insults inflicted upon them and their people. One could indeed say that they "betrayed" their own people, but then such betrayals, alignments, and realignments were not new to pre-Columbian peoples. This is neither to apologize for nor to cast judgment on the hereditary nobles/warriors for their actions; instead, the purpose here is to delve deeper into the issue and explore what happened to the curacas of that vast Mizque hinterland of which the Chuy people became a part. The Mizque lords were the very embodiment of the kaleidoscopic advances and reversals that left few untouched.

We know that enmity between local government officials and local curacas existed early on. This enmity was certainly formalized, as noted in the discussion on coca and the 1557 Visita a Pocona. Here and elsewhere, at every opportunity, local officials accused the curacas of lying, fraud, and cover-up. Yet the curacas had some powerful allies on their side—the Jesuits' support for the memorial curacas, for instance, and earlier the Franciscans speaking out in defense of the Pocona curacas and their respective subjects. The latter clergy emphatically placed the blame for the abysmal state of affairs in the coca fields and elsewhere squarely on the shoulders of the local tax collectors.

They did have a point, and a closer look at the tug-of-war between the curacas, government/civilian economic interests, and market forces provides some insight into this complex issue of moral economy. By 1563 the crown officially recognized that the Indians had suffered irreparable damage and needed legal protection. A year later the issue had not yet been resolved, and the king proclaimed another decree, ordering the audiencia to appoint a magistrate specifically to protect and defend the Indian coca workers. The king noted that although protective legislation existed, abusive landowners and tradesmen ignored the law. The timely procurement of an appropriate magistrate would remedy the situation. Here again, and repeatedly throughout the available documentation, the crown made it clear that the colony's economic well-being depended largely on coca production meeting market demands.[75]

While, as noted earlier, Indian-defense magistrates appear in the land-claim litigation, their overall effectiveness or even physical presence remains undetermined. The conflicts of interest continued unabated throughout the ensuing years. Local curacas petitioned continually to higher authorities to relinquish the increasingly excessive tribute demands for local products, particularly coca. Again and again, they pleaded their now-familiar case: they could not meet the demands; they could not place the tax burden of runaways and the deceased upon those few able-bodied tributaries who remained. Yet the authorities continued to pressure the curacas and their repartimientos, throwing Indian tribute debtors in jail and forcing minors and women down into the coca fields. Between 1582 and 1602 the lead curacas were jailed repeatedly for rejecting the unrealistic demands for coca or (now) cash tribute payments as well as wine and livestock. Throughout this period and beyond, the crown attempted several times to commute tribute in coca, wine, or livestock to cash payments. Typically, the so-called ameliorating policy to protect the Indians from the abuses involved in coca production turned out to be equally exploitative. Instead of the traditional 6 pesos per tributary, the crown demanded 8 pesos, still insisting on payments for the dead and runaways. However, the repartimiento Indians could not advance that kind of money, which Viceroy Velasco considered a "moderate" and "comfortable" demand, any more than they could have produced the required amounts of coca. Clearly, the viceroy was determined that the corregimiento's Indians remain a source of royal income, and he routinely punished the curacas for not guaranteeing the product and cash flow.[76]

It would appear that this round of litigations and punitive actions against curacas and Indians began around 1582. The incarcerations involved in the ongoing litigations no doubt represent the patterns of punishment so bitterly expressed in the memorial of 1582, "throwing us in jail and treating us like their slaves." Because indeed, Don Miguel Cevita and Don Alonzo Guarayo, lead curacas of the repartimiento of Mizque under the encomienda of Don Gabriel Paniagua, found themselves in jail time and again for noncompliance of tribute exactions, all accompanied by repeated royal orders demanding obedience and equally repeated supplications on the part of the curacas that they could not comply: "The Indians have died. . . . They are too old to pay tribute. . . . We cannot support ourselves and our families. . . . We are dying of hunger."

By January 1597, both curacas were back in jail for nonpayment of tribute quotas for 1595–96. Local authorities released them on a forty-day parole to collect the overdue quotas, but when more than forty days elapsed with no indication of tribute forthcoming, they were returned to jail and held in tight security. Jailkeeper Andrés Cabrera was instructed to keep a sharp eye on them to make sure that they neither escape nor "absent themselves." It appears that they remained in jail until August 29, 1601, when they obtained their release. Some of the back tribute quotas had been paid. Exactly how and why the debt was paid remains murky. It relates to the death of Rodrigo Muñoz Fausto and a possible lien against his estate, worth 1,599 pesos, to go toward the 4,000 pesos "owed" by the curacas. Muñoz Fausto's heirs deposited the money "in good faith" in the *caja de comunidad* (the repartimiento's communal treasury).[77]

All the while, a similar round of royal orders, pleas for exemptions, and imprisonment of curacas took place in Pocona. The issue here, of course, pertained to coca and, we now know, the meaningless tribute commutations from coca to currency, or more accurately, to part coca and part currency. Coca, as already noted, has its own lengthy legacy, its mode of production changing radically with the encroachment of the Europeans into this ancient tradition of cultivation. The visita of 1557 serves as a benchmark for the increased tensions and pressures concerning its production. Mutual distrust on all sides was firmly entrenched, and despite pleas from the curacas, viceregal orders persisted.[78]

Almost thirty years later, excessive labor demands remained unchanged. In 1586 a royal order came out of La Plata that called for the curacas to send up an additional thirty-five Indians with their wives and children to supplement the eighty-five Pocona families already there. The Indians were to reside in the city and comply with the requisite work obligations. Failure to meet the labor draft would result in the curacas' incarceration and fines. It is of little surprise that the curacas met with the same repercussions as their earlier counterparts. They, too, protested the impossible demands of the Toledano decrees. They, too, had suffered massive population declines. They could not spare the additional repartimiento Indians and their families to make the difficult ninety-mile trip up to the highlands when they were needed for local repartimiento labor on the community chácaras and participating in *tambo* (inn), bridge, and road construction, not to mention working their own lands. The coca issue was again raised. The curacas needed the Indians to meet the all-important quotas for coca, which, "as is known, is essential for the well being of the royal treasury."[79]

Like their Mizque counterparts, the Pocona curacas were held accountable for the tribute payments of elderly, dead, and absent tributaries. They complained that their tributaries, once numbering fifteen hundred, had been reduced since Toledo's time to five hundred. Their people had died from measles, smallpox, and, of course, harsh treatment. Again, they begged for their release from prison. Again, parish priests spoke out in their defense as did their (then) repartimiento mayordomos: Captain Percival Montesinos in 1593, and Pedro de Valdés in 1597. The Pocona litigations dragged on for at least thirteen years with no evidence of resolution. By 1602, calls for a reliable repartimiento mayordomo echoed repeatedly, bringing to mind the corregidor cited earlier in this chapter who complained about the general regional dearth of reliable administrators, particularly in the yungas. Now, according to Don Fernando Portocarrera, corregidor of both the Mizque and Pocona *partidos* (districts), abuse of Indians and outright theft of their hard-earned coca harvests came from all quarters. The acting (1602–4) mayordomo, as well as the curacas, indigenous accountants, camayos (yunga residents), and earlier mayordomos, all bore responsibility for stealing from the very people they were supposed to protect.[80] Or so claimed the corregidor, in the now-familiar pattern of accusation and counteraccusation. A different litigation in neighboring Aiquile further underscores the discussion. Here, in 1594, another official, Captain Juan Davalos de Zarate, defended himself against accusations of mishandling Indian repartimiento accounts. The false rumors, claimed the captain, came from his "enemies and the malicious caciques."[81] The available evidence suggests that depending on context and circumstances, both sides, to varying degrees, had some legitimate accusations, counteraccusations, explanations, and rebuttals. Given the flawed state of Spain's colonial moral economy, however, it can be safely said that the balance of social, political, and economic justice weighed heavily against the curacas and even more so against their people.

While the curacas of Mizque and other areas continued to protest abusive treatment and demand their rights throughout the seventeenth century, they also underwent transformations. The lavish last wills and testaments no longer appear in my investigations. This does not preclude their nonexistence. Larson discusses the "native landed oligarchy" in the neighboring Cochabamba valley system, who continued to exert their power well into the mid-eighteenth century.[82] The same could easily apply to Mizque. A more conclusive indication of changes in roles and occupations, however, appears in the padrones de chácara. Apparently, the haciendas retained curacas to oversee and represent the Indian yanaconas living on the property, either with or without a hacienda mayordomo present. The curacas answered directly to the census takers. The mayordomos did so infrequently.

Take, for example, the 1599 padrones, the earliest padrones studied in this project. Of the twenty-six padrones examined for this year, the majority of the haciendas retained curacas; however, four retained *indios principales* (lead Indians), considered subordinate to the curacas in the indigenous leadership hierarchy.[83] The fact that thirty-eight-year-old Lorenzo Ogate was actually born on the Paniagua Buena Vista properties already suggests a move away from the traditional curaca role, as does the presence of the secondary principales. Seniority apparently carried little weight for the role of the hacienda curaca. The youngest, twenty-three-year-old Don Juan Agicha, did have the honorific title of "Don" preceding his given name. The only other curaca afforded the titular "Don" was forty-five-year-old Diego Lucra. One curaca was recorded as huido (runaway), an issue that will receive further attention below. A number of the privately owned chácaras in the yungas areas recorded neither curacas nor mayordomos present and appeared to be off-season skeleton operations.[84]

In the small sample of ten chácaras visited in 1604, no principales were listed and only seven curacas were present on their respective chácaras. The year 1630 yielded a much larger padrón, totaling forty-five chácaras. Principales had disappeared, and fifteen chácaras had no curacas or at least did not note the presence of curacas. One was listed as huido. Of the thirty curacas listed, no one was addressed as "Don." By 1645 the sixteen chácaras yielded eleven with no curacas present or recorded. The one curaca listed bore no title. However, for the first time in the entire series studied, two non-indigenous mayordomos were recorded on the padrón, Juan Muñoz and Juan Fernández, with a good number of mulatos appearing under the latter's authority. But then, as also noted in chapter 5, mulatos appear in the earlier hacienda records as well. Further, this padrón lists Felipe Galarsa, "indio ladino que hace oficio de mayordomo" (an Hispanicized Indian acting as mayordomo), suggesting a blending of curaca/mayordomo roles into a lesser overseer position. Moreover, in this sample the two pardo chácara owners mentioned in chapter 5 appear. Neither one retained a curaca.[85]

In the thirty-four chácara padrones examined for 1683, twenty-six claimed curacas. These included one indio yanacona curaca natural de la Cordillera, three indios ladinos "acting as curacas," three more indios ladinos who spoke Spanish, one "mulato curaca whose father was a slave," and one ladino curaca "color pardo." Finally, one padrón deals with only one chácara, La Calleja/Ipisana, which we discussed at length in chapter 3 as a model hacienda dating back to at least the late 1500s, when it was named La Calleja without the Ipisana, a known place-name, helping now to locate more clearly the setting of the chácara. The census takers visited La Calleja sometime between 1694 and 1695. The hacienda still functioned as a large, probably still diversified, robust operation. It retained an ethnic curaca, Lorenzo

Guanca, who oversaw a sizable crew of 167 yanaconas (many of the Guanca ethnicity), African slaves, and free mulatos.[86]

This last finding probably raises more questions than it answers. Once again, a more traditional ethnic curaca appears, a figure increasingly diminished if not absent over the years, having been replaced on the haciendas by Hispanicized Indians, mulatos, and even an occasional yanacona. The transition and Hispanicization of the curaca's role is clearly defined in the one hundred years of serial documentation evidenced in the padrones de chácara. La Calleja may or may not have been an anomaly. It helps to remember that Francisco Viedma describes Mizque at the end of the seventeenth century as having reached the pinnacle of its glory. Possibly, curaca Lorenzo Guanca maintained some remnants of traditional authority because of his apparent ethnic ties. La Calleja, like other regional haciendas, experienced a major blow with the series of malaria epidemics and other natural disasters that swept through the region during the 1700s. The resulting population loss no doubt set hacienda production in considerable arrears.[87] The Bourbon reforms would seal the fate of the entire region.

Ethnicity and Ethnic Identity

At this juncture, the controversial issue of ethnicity and ethnic identity within the indigenous population must be addressed. Here the discussion can be best structured within the context of labor. We established at the outset that labor supplied the propelling force in Mizque's agricultural sector. Further, the demographic decline of roughly half of its repartimiento inhabitants between 1573 and 1684 had less to do with disease (as observed elsewhere in the Americas) than it did with demographic shifts within the region.[88] This was not a recent phenomenon. The archaeological investigations in the Cochabamba and Mizque regions reveal patterns of movement and migration dating as far back as 1200 BC. The data strongly suggest that between 600 BC and 200 AD these connections and movements of people in the eastern Andean valleys, the vast lowlands, and regions to the southeast and south (including northern Argentina in general), rather than events in the altiplano, set the basic pattern of state formation in the area. These configurations would be incorporated by the Tiahuanaco and ultimately by the Inca, who drew continually from earlier modalities.[89] The Inca, in implementing their colonizing policies, would add their own twist by shifting population groups from one region of their extensive empire to sometimes the most distant points. As already noted, highland mitimaes were relocated over much of the entire region. Thus a number of long-established traditions confronted and confounded Spanish authorities. Concerted efforts to control labor and enforce tribute payment by rearranging Indian communities, forced draft, and periodic census taking could not effectively quash deeply ingrained cultural traditions.

In a discussion of Indian responses to the forced Potosí mining draft in the non-exempt provinces, Jeffrey Cole notes that the Indians not only migrated at will but also "chose their patrons."[90] As noted above, this choice pertained to Indians elsewhere in the viceroyalty, draft-obligated or exempt. Here, draft-exempt Mizque provides an excellent microcosm of this Andean phenomenon. In terms of labor distribution, while Indian labor at first pertained exclusively to their tribute-paying communities or repartimientos, the restriction became difficult to maintain.[91] Similar to their Cochabamba counterparts, as early as 1556 Mizque Indians chose to leave their repartimientos and attach themselves to the privately owned chácaras established by the Spaniards throughout the jurisdiction. They would join with non-repartimiento workers—indigenous and, over time, free blacks and mulatos—all now identified as yanaconas, servants, or laborers detached from their respective communities and now under the authority of the European chacarero.

Again, the padrones de chácara continue to inform the discussion. As discussed earlier, census-taking officials and their attendants traveled periodically to take inventory of yanaconas residing in each chácara. These censuses are veritable windows through time from which a surprising number of variables emerge. Due to their serial nature, they reveal both changes and consistencies over time. The 151 padrones used in this project came from censuses of Mizque chácaras located throughout the entire corregimiento, including the coca-producing yungas of Pocona and elsewhere. These samples represent the *visitas* (reviews) of the census takers from six time periods: 1597–98, 1604, 1630, 1645 (very scant and incomplete), 1683, and the large but solitary padrón for a prominent chácara dated 1694. Needless to say, not all the padrones for the Mizque chácaras are accounted for, nor were all of the reviewed padrones complete. In addition, some were no longer legible. The following analyses are based only on 151 legible samples.

First, each chácara owner's name appears on the padrón, along with the name of the chácara and the name of the presiding curaca. Ten other significant variables appear on the padrones: the number of family members per family unit, the relationships within each family unit, and each member's age, gender, civil status (married, single, widowed), place or origin of birth, race (Indian, African, a trace of European, and variations thereof), fiscal status (tributary, forastero, slave, indigenous captive, etc.), residential status (*presente*, *ausente* or *huido*—explained below), and ethnicity.[92] Before proceeding, however, it should be noted that the following discussion is based on what the official census teams were told, what they were not told, and possibly what they assumed. The serial, temporally extended nature of the padrones serves the analysis well. They underscore certain patterns that corroborate or are corroborated by other findings in this work.

Preliminary examination of the padrones quickly revealed that some of the surnames listed were not surnames at all. Instead, they were names ascribed to ethnic groups who dwelled throughout the entire region—lowlands and highlands, former Inca-controlled territories and non-Inca territories alike. While the numbers may appear small, it helps to keep in mind that the focus is specifically on the yanacona population attached to a given chácara and pertaining only to the Corregimiento de Mizque. Further, to be on the safe side, an extremely conservative approach seemed preferable when discussing ethnic appellations. In the Andean world, ethnic designations, like place-names, can have multiple spellings, sometimes leading the unwary investigator astray. In addition, the children of ethnic yanaconas are only sporadically ascribed the ethnicity of the mother or father. Some anthropologists investigating the peoples and cultures of the eastern lowlands agree that the ethnicity of a parent is indeed passed on to the child. But in this instance again, the route of caution was followed. Similarly, the terms *indios de rescate*, *rescatado*, or *hurtado* appear in the documents, which refer to captive ethnic Indians sold into slavery by warring enemy tribes or given to military participants in the pacification campaigns. They are not always identified specifically by ethnicity. The total numbers presented here would be dramatically higher had I included all the unspecified but probable individuals of ethnic origins. I have merely opened the door for other interested scholars to further pursue the journey of inquiry.

Table 4, which treats more than twenty-eight ethnicities identified in the padrones, indicates that the most highly represented group in the first three time columns (1597–98, 1604, and 1630) are the Chané. As Thierry Saignes has demonstrated, this ethnic group did not originate in the highlands, nor were they involved in the Inca's colonizing projects. Quite to the contrary, he saw a connection with the montaña or valley and subvalley systems of the eastern Andes, much of which would become Mizque. They were longtime traders with the highlands and possibly with the Paraguayan peoples as well, trading in metals, shields, plants, animals, and slaves. Apparently, some mixed with the Chiriguano, and by the sixteenth century they were acknowledged as "guarani-ized" warriors. Together with the Chiriguano, now some one thousand to four thousand strong, they would attack the Inca "colonists" established in the area to defend the empire. The Chané would later join their former enemies to fight off the Spaniards with equal ferocity.[93]

The Chiriguano also figure relatively prominently in the padrones. The Chiriguano, like the Guarayo, Mojo, Moya, Yunga, Guaraní, Juri (Jari), Morocossi, and others more scantily represented, were all lowland peoples who not only resisted Inca control but as often as not attacked the defenders of the empire. The Chuy, according to Saignes, were part of the Inca's colonizing-defense plan, as were the Colla, Cota, Charca, Caranga, and others less represented in the padrones. They would become the Inca mitimaes referred to earlier, removed from their often distant homelands to populate and defend the montaña. The Guanca (or Huanca), not present in the early padrones but quite noticeable in the 1683 examples and in the lone 1694 padrón, have a somewhat different explanation than the Inca mitimaes cited above. Led by a strong warrior-leader, they finally suffered defeat under the Inca. Rather than remaining under Inca dominance and serving as mitimaes, the Guanca, led by their chieftain, fled into the Amazon region.[94]

Table 4. Ethnic Groups on Mizque Chácaras

Name	1597–98	1604	1630	1645	1683	Total
Chácaras Counted	38	12	45	16	37	
With Ethnics	24	9	28	4	17	
1. Cana	1	3				4
2. Caranga	2	2	1			5
3. Chachapoya			1			1
4. Chane	24	4	6	1		35
5. Charca	4		3		2	9
6. Chinca					2	2
7. Chiquito	1				2	3
8. Chiriguano	12	5	7	2	3	29
9. Chuncho		1				1
10. Churumata	2	1	1			4
11. Chuy	2	2	2		6	12
12. Colla	3	2	5			10
13. Cota	3	1				4
14. Guanca/Huanca			2		10	22*
15. Guarani		1	1		4	6
16. Guarayo	7		10		1	18
17. Inca	8	4	2			14
18. Itatine			1	1		2
19. Jari/Juri	2	1	1		1	3
20. Lupaca			2		1	3
21. Morocossi			4			4
22. Moxo/Moyo	2		3		7	12
23. Sirioni/Hirioni	1					1
24. Tupi			2			2
25. Uru	1				1	2
26. Yampara				2	2	4
27. Yunga	4		2			6
28. Yuracaré					1	1
Total	79	27	56	8	42	224

Sources: AHMC-M, Vol. 1591–98, Vol. 1597–1607, exp. 18. Vol. 1605–07, Vol. 1630–1730, 1694–95; and ANB-M, Vol. 1645, leg. 11, Vol. 1683.

*Includes 10 from the one 1694 padrón.

Before we proceed, another complicated issue concerning places of origin requires explanation. More pronounced than the ethnic presence on the Mizque chácaras was the presence of a population whose declared places of origin were as varied as they were numerous. They reached beyond immediate and nearby regions (Cochabamba, Tomina, Sipisipi, Cliza, to cite a few) and, in a number of examples, extended considerably further. The distant regions included Inca-controlled locations such as Cuzco, Arequipa, Quito, Santiago de Chile, Córdoba, Salta, and Tucumán. Places such as Santa Cruz, San Lorenzo, los Llanos, Paraguay, and Nueva España (Mexico!) composed the non-Inca distant reaches from where chácara yanaconas claimed their origins. Add to this another twist facing the researcher: place-names and ethnicities were often one and the same. Can we assume that a person identified in the padrón as Antonio yunga, for example, was both of the yungas location and of the Yunga ethnicity?

These questions aside, analysis of the padrones brings to light a number of fundamental issues. First, in terms of origins, the yanacona population on the Mizque chácaras fell into three basic categories: *natural de la chácara* (native to or born and raised on the chácara); born elsewhere—natural de Tucumán, for example; or born into a specific ethnic group or groups—Antonio Cota, for example. Also, a number of yanaconas were identified as having dual ethnicities, such as Bartolomé Guaraya-Itatine or Pedro Colla-Lupaca.[95] This ethnic category can be further subdivided into two basic groupings. On the one hand were the people of the highlands who remained in their place of origin at the time of Inca conquest in return for their allegiance to Inca rule. They would later flee the European-imposed reconfigurations—repartimiento, encomienda, and the new Europeanized form of draft labor, now intended for the silver mines in Potosí and elsewhere. They would reappear, sporadically, on the Mizque chácaras. This grouping would also include highland peoples whom the Inca transferred to the eastern regions of Mizque, Pocona, Cochabamba, and Samaipata. They would flee their mitimak conditions—some to become the "wanderers" and "vagabonds" in the "floating pool," others delegated to repartimientos and redefined as ethnic labor or Inca state labor, while still others became chácara labor.[96] Needless to say, within this grouping were many degrees of variation and crossovers.

The non-Inca-controlled lowland peoples of the montaña and Amazonic reaches made up the other basic ethnic category. They successfully and aggressively resisted Inca hegemony, just as they would resist later European attempts of conquest and pacification. They could not be sequestered into repartimientos—their turf, as Saignes vividly recounts, was all but impenetrable to the outsider. Nor could they be missionized. They took only what they wanted and accepted only what they wished from the missionaries. Mostly they used the European missions as they did the European entradas or explorations—to their advantage.[97] Yet as Table 4 indicates, the padrón sampling used here shows a chácara ratio of some 85 Inca-state-related ethnic yanaconas to 140 "independent" ethnic yanaconas (nearly twice as many) who claimed the lowlands as their place of origin. This raises the question of why far more Inca-free lowland ethnicities were present on the Mizque chácaras. They were not fleeing repartimientos or encomiendas as had their counterparts. Were they misfits in their own environment and attracted to a relatively "better" life on the chácaras tucked into Mizque's montes? Or were they merely heeding a far more archaic tradition of intra- and interregional exchange unfettered by the Inca's colonization project or Spanish visions of containment and exploitation? Had the Inca mitimaes also responded to their own earlier traditions and returned to their places of origin, thus in part explaining the lower numbers? This would make historical sense.

To move closer to the heart of this issue, and since the term is pervasive throughout the documents examined (see Table 5), a brief discussion on the Spanish term *huido* is called for. Loosely, it means "flight." Specifically, according to the *Velázquez Spanish-English Dictionary*, it connotes flight, escape, outleap, fugitive action, and fleeing. The *Diccionario de la real Academia Española* defines *huido* as, among other things, hiding out of fear of someone or something. The verb *huir* is so prevalent, the action so widely practiced, that the term and action, in my opinion, become the norm. As noted elsewhere, it was apparent early on that people were fleeing the Mizque repartimientos (and soon the chácaras) in very large numbers.[98] Since flight of the Inca mitimaes from their forced colonies was apparently more frequent than not, and flight from repartimientos and encomiendas was also a common action, perhaps flight from the chacaras simply represented a traditional, established practice, one having little to do with fear, danger, or risk.

Table 5.
Yanacona and Ethnic Count in the Padrones and Percentages of Huidos

	Total Count		Percentage of Huidos	
Chácara	*Yanacona*	*Ethnic*	*Yanacona*	*Ethnic*
1597–98				
1.	26	3	0	0
2.	54	3	21.56	?
3.	53	3	9.61	?
4.	35	2	3.13	?
5.	65	3	16.13	?
6.	19	4	6.70	50.00
7.	3	0	0	—
8.	21	3	5.56	33.33
9.	31	11	25.00	0
10.	17	2	6.67	0
11.	4	0	25.00	—
12.	30	1	3.50	0
13.	8	0	12.50	—
14.	27	0	0	—
15.	4	0	0	—
16.	5	0	0	—
17.	5	0	20.00	—
18.	2	0	0	—
19.	5	0	0	—
20.	8	3	20.00	33.33
21.	14	4	0	0
22.	179	7	7.00	0
23.	61	3	4.91	0
24.	51	4	14.90	0
25.	75	1	12.50	0
26.	17	1	18.75	0
27.	93	1	6.52	0
28.	51	13	13.16	0
29.	38	2	5.56	0
30.	20	0	0	—
31.	31	2	0	0
32.	7	0	0	—
33.	6	0	0	—
34.	29	1	0	—

continued

Table 5. Continued

Chácara	Total Count		Percentage of Huidos	
	Yanacona	Ethnic	Yanacona	Ethnic
35.	34	3	3.23	0
36.	166	3	6.75	0
37.	136	0	0	0
72.	83	0	10.84	—
1604				
1.	27	10	47.00	20.00
2.	4	3	100.00	33.33
3.	20	4	11.11	25.00
4.	4	1	33.33	0
5.	17	0	0	—
6.	36	3	9.09	0
7.	9	0	0	—
8.	7	4	0	0
9.	40	2	13.16	0
10.	19	0	15.79	—
11.	18	1	17.65	0
12.	8	1	14.29	0
1630				
1.	36	4	25.00	75.00
2.	5	0	40.00	—
3.	38	0	15.79	—
4.	11	0	9.09	—
5.	37	1	5.56	0
6.	47	5	30.95	40.00
7.	16	0	25.00	—
8.	10	0	10.00	—
9.	27	5	4.55	20.00
10.	11	0	9.09	—
11.	4	1	0	0
12.	114	3	22.22	0
13.	62	0	8.06	—
14.	20	1	15.79	0
14A.	8	1	0	0
15.	18	0	22.22	—
16.	15	0	6.67	—

continued

Table 5. Continued

Chácara	Total Count		Percentage of Huidos	
	Yanacona	Ethnic	Yanacona	Ethnic
17.	52	1	15.69	0
18.	20	0	25.00	—
19.	15	0	13.33	—
20.	11	3	0	0
21.	29	0	31.03	—
22.	26	0	53.85	—
23.	95	5	24.44	40.00
24.	54	3	23.53	66.67
25.	40	0	27.50	0
26.	21	1	35.00	0
27.	78	2	7.89	100.00
28.	42	3	23.08	66.67
29.	14	2	25.00	50.00
30.	28	3	28.00	66.67
31.	28	1	29.63	100.00
32.	13	4	0	0
33.	18	4	14.28	50.00
34.	11	0	0	—
35.	12	3	11.11	33.33
36.	22	4	33.33	0
37.	16	1	33.33	100.00
38.	15	1	21.43	100.00
39.	35	0	0	—
40.	28	1	25.92	100.00
41.	13	1	25.00	0
42.	21	1	15.00	0
43.	37	0	10.81	—
44.	23	1	0	0
45.	34	0	26.47	—
1645				
1.	3	2	0	0
2.	none here		—	—
3.	2	0	0	—
4.	14	0	0	—
5.	24	1	4.35	0
6.	3	0	0	—

continued

Table 5. Continued

Chácara	Total Count		Percentage of Huidos	
	Yanacona	*Ethnic*	*Yanacona*	*Ethnic*
7.	6	0	0	—
8.	17	0	0	—
9.	6	1	80.00	0
10.	2	0	0	—
11.	6	0	—	—
12.	3	0	0	—
13.	2	0	0	—
14.	6	0	0	—
15.	2	0	0	—
16.	4	0	0	—
17.	30	5	0	20.03
1683				
1.	28	3	0	33.33
2.	18	2	0	100.00
3.	39	0	69.23	—
4.	131	15	30.17	60.00
5.	10	1	44.44	0
6.	15	0	26.67	—
7.	45	1	15.91	0
8.	48	1	25.53	0
9.	46	0	71.74	—
10.	29	0	72.41	—
11.	6	0	0	—
12.	31	1	63.33	0
13.	16	0	25.00	—
14.	4	0	0	—
15.	13	1	50.00	100.00
16.	35	2	45.71	100.00
17.	94	0	24.72	—
18.	11	0	0	—
19.	71	3	33.82	66.67
20.	137	6	19.85	16.67
21.	69	0	27.53	—
22.	14	0	0	—
23.	16	0	81.25	—
24.	21	0	42.86	—

continued

Table 5. Continued

Chácara	Total Count		Percentage of Huidos	
	Yanacona	Ethnic	Yanacona	Ethnic
25.	23	0	21.74	—
26.	33	0	51.51	—
27.	29	0	24.14	—
28.	16	1	0	0
29.	39	0	7.69	—
30.	19	1	27.78	100.00
31.	25	1	52.17	0
32.	8	0	25.00	—
33.	2	0	0	—
34.	20	0	20.00	—
35.	154	3	13.24	0
36.	7	0	14.23	—
37.	26	2	12.50	0
38.	Exempt			
39.	11	1	90.00	0
1694				
1.	167	12	12.26	0

Flight represented an ongoing Andean cultural legacy of movement and migration, be it pre-Columbian ethnicities or whole villages, or the individuals and families in the discussion at hand.

Looking again at Table 5, which includes the total count of yanaconas and specific ethnicities as well as the percentages of huidos of both groups per given year of chácaras sampled, a number of observations can be made. First and foremost, even a quick glance at the huido percentages provides an impressive scenario, particularly in relation to the total yanacona count. In particular, the counts for 1630 show a marked increase, only to be dramatically overshadowed by the 1683 figures. And these numbers do not include the high mortality figures as a result of disease and other factors. Second, according to the 1597–98 and 1604 padrones, many more non-ethnic (by which is meant they neither claimed nor were ascribed an ethnicity) than ethnic yanaconas left the Mizque chácaras. The ethnic yanaconas remained on the rolls. By 1630, on the other hand, the padrones reveal that 85 percent of the chácaras experienced much higher numbers and percentages of total huidos—ethnic and non-ethnic—than the earlier counts. The ethnic flight numbers, while increased, still did not match their "independent" counterparts' numbers.

Advancing to the comparatively small sample for 1645, where figures are low and few across the board, especially for the ethnic population, there appears to be some increase in ethnic huidos. By 1683 the count is again much higher, with thirty-seven padrones indicating that non-ethnic yanaconas left 81 percent of the chácaras during that census period, while ethnic residents abandoned only 22 percent of the cited chácaras. Also, the non-ethnic yanaconas continued to leave at notably higher rates—a pattern already discernible in the 1630 documents.

And finally there is the 1694 anomaly, of the single padrón of one of the larger, more active chácaras, with a telling total yanacona population of 167, of which 12 were ethnic. What Table 4 does not reveal is that 11 of the ethnic yanaconas were Guanca peoples of the lowlands. The lone non-Guanca on this chácara was a Chuy. The Guanca seem to have remained off the chácaras in the earlier years, but 10 of them emerge in the 1683 count and the above 12 on the 1694 chácara. It is worth noting that in this later padrón, Alonzo Guanca was the curaca of the chácara, who with his wife, Antonia Sisa (a prominent local non-ethnic surname found early on throughout all the Mizque documents: padrones, baptisms, burials, etc.), produced four children. Three of the progeny—Mateo Guanca, fifteen; Mabar (?) Guanca, eleven; and Lucia Guanca, eight—were accorded the ethnic identity of their father. No ethnicity was acknowledged, however, for the fourth child, six-year-old Andrea. None of the ethnic yanaconas had abandoned this chácara.[99]

Two other interconnected lowland peoples require further explanation. The first group, the Raché, have not been included in the discussion thus far because, rather than participate in the European system, they resisted and attacked it. (Like the earlier-mentioned Yuma and Yuracaré, they were no doubt lumped into the nearly generic category designated by the Europeans as "Chiriguano.") Apparently part of the preceding Inca mitimak system imposed in the eastern valleys and lowland fringes, they began fleeing even before the arrival of the

Spaniards, making their way deeper into the Amazonic basins. From there they regrouped themselves and reemerged as the fierce Raché, who not only resisted Spanish control but terrorized much of the region for years to come, attacking, massacring, and plundering repartimiento and chácara alike. The Raché included among their targets the subvalley and lowland yungas area of Pocona, homeland also to the autochthonous Yunga people. The Yunga people, according to Saignes, of possible Arawak connection, would later be joined by Inca mitimaes who themselves barely withstood the hot, unhealthy environment.[100] The Yunga people listed in Table 4 were only those clearly identified according to their specific Yunga ethnicity. Those very few identified as "of" the yungas were not included (they may not have been of the ethnicity), again very likely shortchanging the total count of ethnicities present on the chácaras. Each ethnicity identified in the padrones had its respective history of origins, interrelations, conflicts, and congruencies. Not all of them came from local ethnicities or ayllus. In fact, the majority consisted of lowland independent or autochthonous groups unbeholden to any highland powers—Inca, pre-Inca, or post-Inca.

As a group, the ethnic yanaconas also appear to have been less likely than their non-ethnic counterparts to leave the chácaras once they arrived, particularly in the 1597–98 census taking. This earlier sample indicates that more independent ethnic peoples than Inca state ethnicities resided on the chácaras. This could have two explanations. First, as stated earlier, the former group was controlled by no one. The individuals came in from the lowlands presumably under their own volition, possibly seeking a (relatively) better life for themselves as yanaconas on the chácaras. Here, according to Spanish policy, they supposedly would be fed, clothed, evangelized, and provided a small plot of land for subsistence purposes. Further, in all likelihood, many of them or their forebears were already familiar with the region. The ethnic mitimaes, on the other hand, merely shifted from Inca oppressors to European oppressors who would do their own share of reconfiguring the former Inca "colonists" into combined ayllus and repartimientos. Very possibly, many chose to return to their own distant places of origin.

The 1630 middle period series suggest an increase in chácara abandonment by mostly non-ethnic yanaconas and even some ethnic ones.

By now Mizque was thriving, as the local power brokers had succeeded in having the bridge built to better connect the eastern lowlands to the highlands of La Plata and Potosí via Mizque in order to facilitate trade and transport.[101] More economic activity translated into more job opportunities, which resulted in more movement. Yanaconas were not fleeing their patrons and chácaras. As often as not—ethnic and non-ethnic alike—they were merely moving from one chácara to another, often to follow, join, or rejoin a spouse or family. Also, they no doubt joined the ever-growing "transient" or "forastero" population (discussed at length below).

The padrones for the later period of 1683 (and the single padrón for 1694) indicate a slight decrease in ethnic yanaconas. However, of possible significance in these later padrones is the appearance of two ethnicities not present earlier: the Guanca and the Moyo. Both were independent lowland (and possibly related) groups.[102] Perhaps they represented a new onset of migrations out of the lowlands.

In all, the padrones de chácaras for the eastern Andean subpuna valleys and montañas of Mizque serve to reclaim some of Saignes's "history of the forgotten." Further, they open windows to a tantalizing historical panorama. Not all can be seen, let alone absorbed in one glance, but the evidence is there. As has been repeatedly postulated, the figures provided here are extremely cautious and therefore conservative. Further studies will surely uncover an even stronger multiethnic visibility in the region, off and on the chácaras.

The Outsiders

Turning to still another nuanced and complicated subtheme within the construct of Indian affairs, the issue of the outsiders, or *forasteros* (very loosely, Indians who had left their community of origins), requires attention. The scholarship on the subject has expanded considerably, as exemplified in recent studies on Cochabamba, Cuzco, and Quito that finely hone the multiple definitions affixed to this mobile, quintessentially Andean sector. These studies shed compelling new light on the dominant indigenous phenomenon of migrants and migration, individually or in groups. Larson, for example, has reminded her readers of compelling arguments pertaining to the complexity of migrant issues and the labeling of "forasteros"—namely, that often the old ties to their original communities could be rekindled in ways not easily discernible to the investigator, much in the same manner that ethnic identity remains a difficult subject for investigation. Ann Wightman furthers the discourse by examining how the forasteros, in their diverse roles and identities, reflected the fundamental contradictions involved in the Toledano reforms. Karen Powers, like Wightman, has looked critically at the extended history of migration and its expanding historiography. Scholars, attests Powers, now see migration vis-à-vis *forasterismo* as instrumental in explaining the fundamental social and economic changes that would affect both the indigenous and European post-conquest populations in the northern Andes.[103]

Thus informed, we can return to the Mizque experience with clearer optics. Except for a very few, forasteros per se did not reside on the haciendas. Instead, the census takers insisted, for obvious tribute purposes, on entering the specific birthplace of all the yanaconas, vis-à-vis the term "native of." Further, the padrones yielded a huge array of outsiders, some having been born as nearby as a few chácaras downriver, others as far away as Nueva España, Salta, Córdoba, and Tucumán (many) in present-day Argentina, and Santiago in the gobernación de Chile. They came from Paraguay, Arequipa, Santa Cruz (many), La Plata, La Paz. They came from the yungas, Cochabamba, Arica, Cuzco, los Llanos, la Cordillera. In short, they came from all over and did so for the extended time period covered in my sample. They were rarely referred to as forasteros. The few forasteros to be labeled as such did not appear until 1630, when four were counted. None appeared in the 1645 padrón, but in the much larger (thirty-four chácaras) 1683 census, thirteen forasteros were identified as well as African slaves and many free mulatos. Rarely did the census takers enter into their records the forasteros' place of origin. Concluding this 1683 padrón, one official noted that two of the listed forasteros owed 6 pesos 2 reales in their annual tribute payments (yanaconas did not pay their own tribute).[104] Based on these data, it is safe to assume that the many non-chácara-born workers represented informal transient labor rather than forastero labor. This may have been a way of avoiding the financial responsibility of paying their own tribute quotas; in my opinion, however,

on the chácaras the line was exceedingly thin and ambiguous between
these two sectors, an issue that surely frustrated and angered the tax
collectors as it certainly befuddles the investigator. Add the camayos
and llacta runas to the mix, and the kaleidoscopic nature of Andean
migration and survival becomes even more apparent.

Consistent with the findings of others, forasteros did appear in growing predominance in the Indian communities of Mizque, as they did in
Quito and elsewhere. Rossana Barragán's study of Indian communities
and ayllus demonstrates that this eastern region experienced similar
population shifts. She notes that the Indian communities recorded a
predominance of *originario ayllu* inhabitants (Indians still living with
their original clans) in 1573, with almost 72 percent residing in Pocona,
nearly 21.5 percent in Mizque, and a mere 6.64 percent in Totora and
Aiquile (some 6,250 people all told). By 110 years later, in 1683, the
population had experienced a major demographic shift. First, the total
population suffered a 50 percent drop. Second, 72 percent of this reduced population now found itself in Mizque. Further, Barragán found
a marked surge, starting in the 1640s, of forasteros throughout the
area—80 percent regionwide, with a hefty 87.11 percent now residing
in Mizque, where in 1573 there were none. Further, by 1683 in Mizque
the originarios had all but disappeared.[105]

Based on her analysis of the corregimiento's communities, Barragán
suggests that the absence of tributaries from their communities was
temporary. They probably left to go work on the chácaras located usually in the same jurisdiction, and the two worlds—ayllu/community
and chácara—were not disconnected but rather part of one, interrelated economic system. Working on the chácaras, they still identified
with their ayllus.[106] I would add, however, that they fled the chácaras
in droves, moving from one chácara to another or returning to their
clans. Migration was (and is) one of the fundamental characteristics of
Andean tradition. The apparent increase of forasteros on the Mizque
chácaras from the 1640s on could reflect Barragán's community findings, particularly when it is recalled that no forasteros appeared in the
hacienda records earlier than 1630. But even this information contains
its own caveat—they were mostly women. This, too, could well have
been the precedent for another present-day Andean phenomenon, that

of women migrating by themselves or with their children, often into the cities, and often reduced to begging.

Further, in my research I happened across a 1645 census of Mizque community forasteros. Like the chácara "transients," these forasteros hailed from locations as near as Pocona and Cochabamba and as distant as La Plata, Chuquiabo (La Paz), Tarija, Cuzco, Lima, and Huamanga. Also, mirroring their chácara counterparts, of the thirty-nine tasa-paying workers listed (each paid 3 pesos), almost half—41 percent—had "fled" the community. Don Pedro Champi, "governor of the Indians" (not curaca), made careful note of the Mizque community forasteros under his charge. He recorded in his *padroncillo* (little padrón) such characteristics as race (including mestizos and mulatos), ethnicity (Cana, Chachapoya, Tarabuco, Yuma), physical condition (one adult and two young sisters, all mute), and occupation. Almost 40 percent of the forasteros in this census filled jobs in the service sector—tailor, cobbler, silversmith, carpenter, sacristan, courier, and driver.[107]

Except for the occupations and tribute obligations, the patterns of the community forasteros closely followed those of the chácara "transients." Specifically, while the transients did not have to pay their own tribute (because they were yanaconas, for whom the chácara owner was responsible), note was made of the two chácara forasteros who in 1683 were required to pay 6 pesos 2 reales toward their tributes. That this observation was included at the conclusion of the head count (much like the note referring to the mulatos who requested that they be placed on the negros y mulatos list and *not* the Indian list) indicates to me that both issues were viewed as extraordinary and were taken into account as such. This in turn raises additional questions. Were the two tribute-owing forasteros the only ones to owe money? Or were they the only ones under tributary obligation? Were they paid for their work on the chácaras? Did they provide their own rations, clothing, and gear? Were they free to come and go at will? These and other questions beg further research.

Further, this 1645 padroncillo concluded with some interesting observations. Don Pedro noted that he had three *indios manifestados* (Indians "voluntarily" manifesting their wish to be placed on the Mizque community census and be taxed accordingly). One claimed he was originally from Chuquiabo and had married in Pocona, but his sons were on the Mizque padrón and he wished to be on it as well. He had already obtained the official permission of the corregidor. The other two indicated the same sentiments. They had their permissions, and they wanted to be signed up and "pay their tasas like the other forasteros."[108] This is similar to the mulato request and does not hint at all of coercion. On the contrary, these requests to be on very specific padrones resonate with agency, which reinforces my earlier observation concerning the chácara demographics. Based on the data I have studied, I found that in the Corregimiento de Mizque, chácara and community alike, looms a persistent and nagging ambiguity between "native of" and "forastero" that has no facile answer. Nevertheless, this very ambiguity does raise some provocative questions.

Perhaps they were all forasteros or all transients, but the term *forastero* was not fully encoded until after the 1630s, and then it was used more in the Indian community context rather than in the chácara censuses. Also, the chácara owners easily could have played into the "hidden" or "unofficial" population phenomenon described by Powers by not listing them at all or by not calling them forasteros, thus unburdening these laborers of their onerous tribute obligations and simultaneously maintaining their "private" or secret labor force.[109] A third explanation could be that the forasteros retained the "native of" label with concurring hacienda owners willing to pay the 2 pesos tasa for each and thus assure themselves some degree of access to a very elusive and mobile labor force. And finally, the manifestados could represent another phenomenon Powers placed in the northern Andean context: they migrated from areas that imposed harsh tax and labor obligations to places less onerous, and bribed their way onto the censuses.[110]

This leads me to a more general observation resulting from the analysis of the data presented here. Clearly, in the eastern Andes, and specifically in the Corregimiento de Mizque, the indigenous majority—despite being shamelessly exploited by native elites, who were soon joined by the Spaniards—withstood and resisted, whenever and wherever possible, aggressively or indirectly, the perpetual attempt of economic and social subjugation from above. And while this study strongly advocates the idea that colonial migration was and is synonymous with Andean migration, I would add that in the Mizque model, migration and territoriality received further reinforcement through prehistoric and colonial ethnic warfare and aggressive raids. Couple these characteristics with a brillant capacity—aided in no small way by the physical landscape and the cooperation of some curacas and chacareros—to become invisible populations, and you have the basic formula for Andean survival. The legacies and traditions of this individual and collective determination, this cultural force, have evolved and restructured for thousands of years. They are an ongoing phenomenon today.

7. Town, Countryside, and the Social Construct

THUS FAR THIS WORK has examined the eastern Andean demographic histories of three peoples—African, Indian, and European. It has sought to place them, over time, into two evolving political economies, the pre-Columbian indigenous system and the later Spanish imperial plan. It placed them in their respective systemic contexts and explained how these constructs intersected with each other over time, reflecting in the process a moral economy to which the imposed-upon, in groups or as individuals, responded. While the previous chapters posited patterns of social, economic, and political change over time, they offered only glimpses and sketches of the human profile. The purpose of this final chapter is to examine, as much as the documents permit, the actual lives and quotidian activities of the above groups. However, the focus will be primarily on the African slaves and their descendants, whose history has been glaringly unwritten. Within the parameters of the demographic transformations that ensued and the overriding issues of control and resistance, as well as of paradox and contradiction, the narrative looks at the impact of disease and how this too interfaced with the long-established tradition of flight. It also explores how people—slave and free—lived, worked, and interacted with each other in day-to-day as well as life-and-death transactions that formed the realities of their colonial eastern Andean world.

It was not only the regional economy and demography that changed over time; the environment also experienced transformations. The Inca were not alone in coveting the region's temperate climate and fertile valleys; indeed, they faced fierce competition from the aggressive lowland groups who sought access to the same. As the noted Andean chronicler Felipe Guaman Poma de Ayala (see frontispiece) wrote in the late 1500s, "It is a villa of the most beautiful climate of all Castile.

It has many groves of trees, including fruit trees. It is a home for saints, with very good people, in awe of God, justice and your Magesty."[1] According to Viscarra, in their conquest of the empire's eastern slopes and valleys, Inca Capac Yupanqui's troops advanced to the valley of Mizque and, quite impressed with this "privileged" region's "singular beauty" and natural resources, promptly named it *Mizk'i*, referring to the region's production of honey. Viscarra continued his rapt description of the region in glowing terms—its picturesque beauty, its fertile fields, its abundant resources—not unexpected from a native son, but apparently fairly accurate. He also pointed out that Philip IV (1621–65) recognized Mizque's expanding prosperity and encouraged further growth.[2]

The Ravages of Disease and Environmental Changes

Yet even in its developing prosperity phase, Mizque was not without its environmental setbacks, underscored by references throughout the earlier estate documents examined for this project. For example, in 1597, apparently one of the Paniagua de Loaysa administrators complained of weather so severe in the wheat-producing niches of this eastern Andean ecological system that the wheat harvest froze. On the busy La Calleja complex, another administrator indicated that in 1611–12 production suffered because the Indians were too sick to plant or harvest. The whole yanacona crew had been felled by *chuc'cho* (the local term for malaria). And in 1631–32 one curaca/mayordomo complained that it had been a "sterile" year with no Indians and no corn to harvest.[3]

Daniel Gade has suggested that malaria in all probability struck the Mizque lower valley regions by the 1550s if not earlier. There exists in his data a curious lacuna for almost the entire seventeenth century, with only one reference, to a fierce 1611 *peste* (pestilence), no doubt the chuc'cho that paralyzed La Calleja operations. Disease apparently remained dormant for most of the seventeenth century but returned with a deadly impact throughout the entire eighteenth century and beyond—usually in the form of malaria, often accompanied by typhus. Viedma's much earlier description of the region certainly supports Gade's "historical ecology/ethnobiology" approach. Very clearly, centuries of disease took a drastic toll on the region and its populations.[4]

My brief, time-restricted foray into parochial data was limited to records for 1648 to 1738. Yet I found sufficient information to provide some insight into how the above and other epidemic diseases may have directly and indirectly affected one specific population group—the African slaves and their descendants. The ninety years of parish records I examined appear to follow the pattern of epidemic disease established by Gade. To begin with, between 1662 and 1669, ten slaves died, including one pardo, one child, a twenty-year-old, and the remainder poor and/or elderly. From 1672 to 1683, nineteen slaves and one free mulato died. However, by 1720, between July and December alone, nine slaves died. Between January and December 1721, thirty-three people died (twenty-eight slaves, one pardo, one mulato, and three libres), including infants and children, often two or three deaths on the same day. From 1722 through August 1738 the yearly mortality rates declined markedly to at most eight deaths (March–December 1737) and at least one (between October 1727 and May 1729).[5]

While these parish records give gender and legal status (slave or free) and sometimes age, cause of death was never mentioned or even hinted at for the entire ninety years of documents examined. Nevertheless, some conservative speculation is warranted. First, a spike in the African and mixed-African mortality rate obviously occurred during the fateful year of 1721. While the cause of death is uncertain, it is possible that malaria or typhus was not always the culprit—the complex issue of the sickle-cell factor afforded some members of this particular sector of the population almost total immunity from the ravages of various forms of malaria. Several specific and nonspecific diseases flourished in the Andes at this time, as often as not reaching epidemic levels, most of them life-threatening or potentially life-threatening. Gade discusses typhus as well as malaria in Mizque, but certainly measles, smallpox, diphtheria, various dysenteries, and the many generic "fevers" and other unidentified diseases and pestilences cut their swath through the eastern Andes, as they did at that time in Quito, Peru, and elsewhere.[6] Moreover, with the Andean cultural tradition of constant mobility and migration, disease would have many unwitting human and animal carriers to further its spread throughout the Andean world and beyond.

Other health-related issues in the region also require further comment. Viedma (and later Gade) refers to the demographic changes wrought by the epidemics. Where once the valley of Mizque and its political center, the Villa de Mizque, were immensely productive, temperate, healthy zones, with the advent of the seasonal malaria and typhus epidemics, places like Pocona, Totora, Cliza, and even the distant Santa Cruz siphoned off the Mizque population as people fled its disease-infected areas for healthier locations. Viedma describes the people who remained in the district in lackluster, dismissive, even pejorative terms. There is more than just a touch of ambivalence in his descriptions. On one page he laments the sorry plight of those who could not escape the malaria and typhus epidemics in the unhealthy areas, and the debilitating fevers they suffered once infected. Yet on the following page he lambastes those same suffering people—particularly the mestizos and mulatos—for being lazy, useless, unwilling to till the fertile land, and prone to excessive imbibing of chicha.[7] Viedma's *Descripción* does not dwell on the obvious link between these two sets of characteristics.

It would appear also that the region's populace had more than their share of physical abnormalities and disfigurements, which included the deaf, the mute, and widespread goiter, hunchbacks, and dwarfs. They were referred to as *opas*, from the Quechua *upa*, or idiot. Given the context, it can be assumed that this particular classification signified substantial mental retardation. Viedma notes that they were not able to receive the sacraments.[8] I can add that some of these abnormal conditions probably resulted from diseases other than typhus and malaria. Untreated measles, smallpox, or chicken pox can cause deafness and blindness. Lack of iodine results in goiter. Highland salt was (and remains) cheaper and was widely used throughout the region; it is freshwater lake salt and therefore contains no iodine. Clearly, the entire subject of disease and population defects in Mizque begs for further study.

The Survival and the Lifestyles of the Elite
However, for now let us return to the earlier, healthier Mizque that attracted warring indigenous groups and European explorers-cum en-

comenderos alike. Obviously, at one time the place flourished, life went on, and people adapted and adjusted to the short- and long-term demands that life in the eastern Andes made upon them. While many of the indigenous population did not survive the early ravages of disease and harsh labor, others—the indigenous and European elites—in particular, survived quite handily, amassing considerable wealth and living in relative luxury. Take, for example, the Encinas family, whose 1605 accounts and records (see chapters 3 and 4) reveal extensive holdings and production operations throughout the area. Their estate mirrored those of their elite indigenous and European counterparts regionwide. Because of the exhaustive bookkeeping that successful agricultural operations required, as in the Encinas case, the investigator can obtain insightful bits and pieces of data that give flesh and blood to the family of the economically and politically powerful first settler Captain Gabriel de Encinas. The core family that apparently resided full time on their hacienda, Oloy, consisted of the captain and his three children, Doña Ana, Don Marcos, and Don Diego. Any mention of a mother was noticeably absent. The boys were sent off to school, first to Cochabamba, ostensibly "to learn to read and write." Cochabamba may have been the practical choice for younger members of well-off Mizque families. Because it was considerably closer and the journey there was less dangerous than the one to La Plata—they had not yet built the bridge—it made sense to keep the youngsters somewhat closer to home. Marcos, no doubt the older of the two boys, was eventually sent off to the far more distant Lima, where he entered the Colegio de San Martín in 1604. His matriculation fee alone came to 560 pesos, four times the allotment for his wardrobe for that year.[9]

There is no reference to Ana's education. Possibly, and only possibly, by this time she had completed her education, and if so in all likelihood it would have been in a convent some distance from Mizque, in La Plata or even Cuzco.[10] The flurry of activity concerning Ana was not about schooling but about her pending 1603 marriage to Augustín Ferrufino. This prominent Mizqueño (he would become corregidor and justicia mayor in 1620) was already a respected man of action and, one suspects, considerably older than Ana. Upon marriage he was promptly made the children's guardian and entrusted to handle their estate finances.[11] Age disparities were not that unusual in the unions of prominent colonial families. In earlier chapters we noted that in the Paniagua clan, Doña Mayor Verdugo de Ángulo was probably about thirteen years old when she married Antonio Álvarez, who apparently was in his declining years and suffered from poor health. Several last wills and testaments further confirm this age gap, the husbands specifying that their young wives must be provided for upon said husband's death.

From the descriptions gleaned from the records, Ana's wedding trousseau for her 1603 wedding easily matched the lavish wardrobe of General Bartolomé Cortés's wealthy Limeña wife, Doña Luisa de Ponce de León. The bride-to-be made several trips to La Plata to select fabrics and accessories. Her wardrobe alone—dresses of silk, velvet, and taffeta, many pairs of shoes, and jewelry and accessories—came to almost 2,000 pesos. Don Gabriel, in keeping with the celebration, drawing from the children's account, had a fine velvet suit tailored for himself.[12] There is no mention of wedding ceremony costs, no doubt because, as in the present day, the groom's family paid the wedding expenses.

In general, Captain Encinas and his children, and undoubtedly many retainers, lived quite comfortably at Oloy. Ample furnishings, rugs, and cushions filled the house, along with silver platters and adornments, gold jewelry, and rosaries. They bought four arrobas (one hundred pounds) of fish for one year's forty-day pre-Easter Lenten period. Noteworthy in these inventories of household items was the recording of half a pound of saffron, which is very light and would thus involve quite a bit of the product (today, half a pound of saffron would cost about $2,000). The Encinas clan must have enjoyed their share of culinary delights that called for these savory little tendrils.[13]

The Oloy complex was quite large, with two houses, two vineyards, fruit-bearing orchards, wine cellars, a mill, a forge, and all the necessary equipment for wine production. It supported a large crew of yanaconas—179 all told, 49 of them working adults, including several mulatos. It would appear that Captain Encinas was a relatively conscientious chacarero. Throughout the records examined, only one citation of misconduct concerning his yanaconas appeared. It was issued in the census of 1598 for not providing clothing rations to twelve yanaconas. This might be considered a minor infraction when one reads the more nefarious records of his Mizque contemporaries. The likes of Julio Álvarez Meléndez (in this context acting as tutor for the Baez estate in Tiraque [Chico]), Gabriel Paniagua, Captain Juan de Paredes, and Juan Valenzuela, to name just a few, were routinely cited in the 1597–98 padrones for abusing one or more of the established Toledano codes concerning the minimal well-being of the yanaconas working on the chacaras. These included guarantees of one day a week (usually Saturday) for their own planting and harvesting, a yearly ration of clothing, care during illness, and religious indoctrination. These and other chacareros routinely disregarded one or two and in some cases almost all of the labor codes. In fact, acting tutor Álvarez Meléndez was incarcerated for his ongoing abuses against his charges' yanaconas. Authorities confiscated and sold some of his belongings in order to pay for the yanaconas' clothing.[14]

By contrast, there is no indication that Gabriel de Encinas ever allowed his yanaconas to run around naked, an offense of which at least two other owners in the 1597–99 padrones were accused. Rather, Encinas's administrators kept careful record of the annual purchase and issuing of clothing for the yanaconas. One other touch, as contradictory as it is captivating, concerns the following. Encinas's accounts refer more than once to Pedro negro. He was inventoried along with the household possessions, underscoring my postulation that at least through the first half of the colonial period, "negro" was synonymous with "slave," and "slave" was synonymous with "property." However, Pedro negro was again recorded, this time in clothing allotments/rations for the work crew. While all were issued their outfits, Pedro, unlike the yanaconas, also received a hat. In short, he was issued a status symbol in recognition of his station in the labor hierarchy, and, I suggest, within the Encinas family structure as well. He was possibly the same Pedro, identified as Pedro de Çarate, negro ladino esclavo, who served as a key witness for the captain in a 1633 land dispute. Significantly, there is no evidence that Encinas did not tend properly to the infirm. The many complaints entered into the padrones concerning such neglect were made unanimously by yanaconas working in the coca zones.[15]

Both the captain and his son-in-law, Agustín Ferrufino, would become increasingly active in Mizque's political life, each serving as corregidor, a position that, when taken seriously, involved considerable responsibility. Also, looking back to chapter 2's list of 1630 bridge construction contributors—a veritable who's who of Mizque elite and not-quite-elite whose names have appeared on many pages of this work— Encinas is right there at the top of the list along with the other Gabriel. They all wanted their town to work. They wanted better trade and transport systems. They wanted their products to reach distant and not-so-distant markets safely. They wanted to be part of the larger political economy and still be Mizqueños.

A Microview of Developing a Villa

Let us take another look at the bridge. It took a lot of planning, pleading, and money to get it approved and built. In their enthusiasm, the bridge advocates succumbed, not surprisingly, to the lowest bidder, Andrés de Melo, whose full story is yet to be told. But because those who were involved were determined to carry the project to fruition and see the bridge built according to correct specifications, a major disaster was averted. The inspection team, made up of engineers and other citizens and ultimately led by a master carpenter, heeded the call of duty to their "republic" and voluntarily participated in the inspection process. Indeed, the bridge was flawed and required considerable additional work.

All the while, town officials made concerted efforts to encourage settlement and growth, urging people to buy still-available city lots— more than ample in size, as noted in chapter 3—even if they already had haciendas in the countryside. While staunch bridge advocate Captain Encinas was testifying before the cabildo on the need for a bridge to more efficiently link Mizque to its highland markets and to prevent further loss of goods and lives of slaves, other officials before him called attention to town needs years earlier, such as public city fountains and improved public irrigation systems. Years earlier, the lack of accessible water for public use had become apparent in a seemingly unrelated legal case over land use. In 1619, prominent Mizque cacique Alonzo Guarayo and his wife, María Pacsima, in their last will and testament, bequeathed some land to an indigenous youth of undeclared parentage named Alonso Anaba. By 1617 the couple apparently had died, and their land bequest was now in litigation. One of the litigants just happened to be the lad's court-appointed guardian, Don Juan de Saldaña, who swore that the land was now his and that he had purchased it legally. He recited the familiar litany that the land was useless but that with his time, perseverance, and money it now boasted flourishing vineyards and orchards. The issue actually was as much about water rights as land rights.[16]

While Mizque abounded with rivers on all sides, access to this essential resource had not then been fully resolved. Saldaña claimed he had purchased the land—neglected and in terrible condition—two years before he even became the youngster's tutor. No one questioned his purchase or his tapping into a water supply whose source would later become the supply for the Villa de Mizque and its environs, including Indian communities.[17] Yet this particular aspect of the case (others will be examined below) informs the discussion on political economies and attendant conflicts, contradictions, and ambiguities.

According to town attorney Pedro de Torres de la Calancha, the case was not merely about an Indian youth's inheritance. The official noted that Saldaña was not only the appointed tutor for the indigenous minor and his respective properties but also that Saldaña served as lieutenant to the corregidor Don Juan Cazorla de Guevara, "a very powerful person." Torres de la Calancha swore the two were in cahoots to defraud Indians of their lands. He accused them of "fraud and deceit," stating that they had already sold a good portion of the properties that should have gone to the youngster and that the swindling involved far more than the youth's inheritance. Indeed, it also usurped water rights of both the Spanish villa and the pueblo of Mizque, to the great "detriment" and "notable harm" of all concerned. Furthermore, the town attorney argued that Saldaña and Cazorla de Guevara had flagrantly broken the law, which prohibited the sale of Indian properties, especially without a written permit or license from the indigenous party involved. The "boy" and no one else should have benefited from any sale of his inherited properties.[18] Ethics and lawbreaking notwithstanding, Saldaña did get his water and the consequent flourishing vineyards and orchards. Obviously, the case was resolved in his favor.

Thirteen years later, access to water remained a problem. Encouraged by the support the bridge advocates had garnered, town authorities took advantage of the momentum and called for an additional budget to carry out much-needed repairs on public works. Specifically, they argued, the town's major irrigation ditch was in almost total ruin. Furthermore, with the advent of a new bridge, the town needed, now more than ever, a fountain in the main plaza, not just for "appearances" but also in terms of town growth. Because the bridge would bring more activity to the town, it was imperative that there be a fountain and a working irrigation ditch to convey river water into the system. Supporters of waterwork improvements bolstered their arguments with references to the severity of problems resulting from the annual flooding as well as the seasonal droughts. Both of these seasonal crises wrought havoc, including loss of life among the poor.[19]

All of these projects, according to town officials, were of the utmost importance for the public good—not only for the rich but also, and especially, for the poor. The latter had not benefited from Mizque's growth thus far and did not have sufficient access to the water they needed for their households and subsistence gardens. Lima approved the bridge project, while the waterworks budget required only the nod of approval from the audiencia in La Plata, its budget supported by local monies only. Apparently, the entire cabildo approved the projects from the outset, including corregidor Cazorla de Guevara's replacement, Don Cristoval de Sandoval y Rojas, and his lieutenant, none other than Don Juan de Saldaña.[20]

Matters of Life and Death, and of the Heart

Then there were the people who were not public figures who tried to live their lives quietly and unobtrusively, taking care of their needs and those of their families, retainers, and workers, slave and free. Although they were not the "headline" makers (we have many of those who for a number of reasons appear and reappear in various documents), they were the ones for whom life's demands were no doubt buffered by some degree of material comfort, reflected in the very action of having someone prepare their last wills and testaments. These documents, however, often tell stories beyond the listings of properties and possessions, debts in currency or goods owed to others or owed by others, and about to whom the money will go. Take, for example, the 1597 testament of Alonzo de Nodar, a native son of Sevilla, now a very long way away from his birthplace. His will was drawn up in the "Valley of the Yungas of Chuquioma" (the very heart of coca country), where he emphatically declared he wished to be buried.[21]

Nodar wanted a prescribed (impressive) set of masses, prayers, and hymns recited and sung in his name in the cathedral of San Francisco up in Mizque upon his death. Apparently, he was at the time the mayordomo for Captain Juan Picón's coca chácaras in the yungas. He had a few debts that required payment, but more interestingly, several well-established regional figures owed him substantial sums. His boss, Picón, still owed him eight months of his annual 400-peso salary. Captain Juan de Paredes (of another prominent family) owed him 400 pesos, which suggests a mayordomo's salary. Another person owed him over 500 pesos, and even Gonzalo de Solís, governor of Santa Cruz, owed him 350 pesos. Two of Nodar's horses were somewhere in Mizque (he had sent them to the blacksmith there), while his "dappled steed" was at Picón's house in Copachuncho (coca territory). He even had some financial dealings with Joan Álvarez Meléndez, the papers for which Juan Cano de Paredes held a power of attorney. Cano de Paredes was directed to turn these and other papers over to the executor of Nodar's estate and to his heirs so that his obligations could be met.[22]

Nodar also participated in business and trade transactions at the local level, trading leather goods for coca with a Cata yanacona, with Catalina mulata, with Juan Álvarez's curaca, Domingo, and with various other yanaconas in the valley. He also left a donation "for the hospital in the valley." Judging from the various transactions, he seems to have had quite a busy network of contacts across the social spectrum and across a good part of the region.[23] What made him somewhat unusual was that, unlike many of his Spain-born contemporaries, he chose not to return to Spain. And he chose not to be buried in La Plata, or even Mizque for that matter, where he nonetheless wanted many masses said and prayed for him in the villa's cathedral. Yet, in a seeming paradox he made it absolutely clear that he wished to be buried in no other place but Chuquioma, a rather miserable zone if we are to believe the majority of accounts. Perhaps the passage of his soul was more important to this native-born Spaniard than the resting place of his bones, particularly in the light of the effort required to transport a coffin from Chuquioma all the way up to the Villa de Mizque.

The analysis of dozens of last wills and testaments revealed other elements of human nature. All made specific arrangements for guaranteed safekeeping of their respective souls to heaven, not only via the above-cited ecclesiastic rites of passage but also through various donations to the secular arm of the church. This included gifts for chapels, renovations, and such; contributions to existing or proposed convents and monasteries; and donations to local (church-administered) hospitals for medicines, supplies, and maintenance. Apart from these pious deeds stood yet another element in coming to terms with unfinished matters before one's death. Both men and women made specific provisions for their successors and heirs, usually as generously as possible, sometimes in strikingly tender, caring terms not usually voiced in these dry, formulaic legal treatises. Take, for example, the 1624 will of Don Bernardo de la Fresnada y Zúñiga, arguably one of the wealthiest men in the region: "Item. As I am married to doña Bernarda Miro, foremost person who I love, and care for, and esteem and since she has no known dowry, nor source of income during our marriage . . . better than any fixed sum, . . . it is my wish and *voluntad* [choice] that all of my properties be turned over to her, the best possible recipient, as my companion and consort, and the mother of my children." She indeed inherited the huge estate, which ultimately was appraised at 100 million pesos.[24]

In her 1598 last will and testament, Julia Medellín, widow of Juan Corzo, declared that although she brought a dowry of 1,500 pesos into the marriage, her husband had amassed considerable holdings that he left her, and therefore she felt justified in establishing a dowry of 5,000 pesos for her daughter. Further, widow Julia noted that she had a Chiriguana female servant who had been with her for a long time and was now quite ill. Should she (the widow) die before the servant, the servant was to be provided for.[25] In 1601, a well-to-do widow who had been married for twenty-four years wished to be buried in the monastery of the Convento de San Francisco in Pocona. She bequeathed sums of 70 to 100 pesos to a number of causes: books for the Santa Monica's choir in La Plata, and money to help release debtors in Mizque's jail and Indian captives. She also bequeathed 150 pesos to the dowry of her natural (born out of wedlock) granddaughter and another 100 pesos to the dowry of an orphaned girl. In both instances, the widow noted that these dowry contributions should make both recipients more marriageable. She made these bequests "so that God may take mercy on my soul and free it from purgatory as quickly as possible."[26]

In yet another example of a widowed woman desiring the best advantages for her close kin, Señora Ana in 1598 wrote into her will that she bequeathed her two chácaras in the valley of Sacaba (although she was a resident of Mizque) to her daughter. This may strike one as rather ordinary. However, written right into the testament was the fact that this daughter was her "natural child," the result of an affair she had with "a man from Toledo, who died in Chuquiago [La Paz]." Señora Ana wanted her daughter to marry honorably and thus bequeathed the holdings to the young woman. These were productive units at the time, the widow claimed, only because of the hard work she and her daughter had invested in them, particularly the daughter.[27]

Men also recognized their natural-born progeny, as in the 1582 will of a wealthy man whose parents were born in Spain. He ask for the usual round of masses not only for his own soul but also for the souls of everyone for whom he bore some responsibility, dead or alive. He also spread his generosity over a wider swath than the others—hospitals being his charities of choice. He donated a total of more than 200 pesos total to hospitals in Huamanga (80 pesos), Cuzco, La Plata, the pueblo of Pocona, the yungas of Pocona, and the pueblo of Mizque. He also left a house to a yanacona who had "served" him. Finally, he recognized his out-of-wedlock son, for whom he provided with 1,000 pesos. To the mother of his child and to her husband he designated one alpaca each. Alpacas were highly valued industrial animals whose hair could be spun into yarns finer than merino wool and used in clothing, blankets, and the like.[28]

A set of inventories (discussed earlier in an unrelated context) reveals still another aspect of inheritance and natural children. In this case, a prominent vecino with landholdings throughout town of Mizque and countryside met an untimely death and left no will. His next of kin, lawyers, and town officials joined forces to conduct painstaking inventories of this man's large, complex estate. Apparently he also left four under-age, natural children—two girls and two boys. One of the reasons given for the necessity of a thorough and accurate inventory of all his possessions was so that "his four heirs could receive as much as they were legally entitled to from his estate, once his debts and funeral expenses were paid."[29] Upon closer scrutiny, this statement hints at some possible ambiguities, given its context.

First, exactly what were the legal rights of his or anyone's natural or illegitimate children? In the many documents I examined, I noticed that the term *legitimate* (as in legitimate husband, wife, or child) was used as consistently as the term *hijo natural* or *hija natural*, whereas no one used the term *ilegítimo* (illegitimate). As the prevailing scholarship explains, the terms *illegitimate* and *natural* are themselves nuanced according to class, status, ethnicity, and access to documents of legitimacy.[30] To this investigator, although the children were referred to as his "heirs," something in the phrasing of "as much as they were legally entitled to" struck a wary chord. Even if orphaned natural children did have some legal rights, given the well-intended but ambivalence-laden nature of the Spanish written codes, not to mention their practical application, one wonders how these four orphaned natural children actually fared? They could become prey to avaricious, predatory lawyers and corrupt local officials. On the other hand, the powerful family name and lineage might have assuaged their precarious circumstances. Significantly, while references to the brothers, sister, nephew, and the natural children appear in the documents, reference to a mother (mothers?) is markedly absent.

The fragility of legal inheritance rights of orphaned natural children finds a parallel in the legal inheritance rights of the indigenous population. We turn again to the 1616 last will and testament of Mizque cacique Don Alonzo Guarayo and his wife, Doña María Pacsima. Here the last wishes of a wealthy cacique directly and indirectly reveal far more than the indigenous leader intended. His testament and the response to it underscore again the interconnectedness of the complex forces that fueled this multiethnic, multiracial society. As noted earlier, the cacique and his wife bequeathed some valuable properties to a young boy of no apparent relation. Upon their death, the youth was promptly swindled out of his inheritance by powerful local elites, including his appointed tutor, the aforementioned Saldaña.[31] The outcome of this filing is not entirely conclusive. Apparently, the boy's tutor ended up with prime properties intended for the youngster; however, there is no indication of what became of the lad himself, or if he even received a token of his inheritance. Whether the land "purchase" occurred before Saldaña assumed the tutelage of the youth begs the question. The land was not supposed to be sold, and self-serving interests remained an overriding issue. Given the history of European land acquisitions in Mizque, the will of a dead cacique apparently carried little weight, regardless of the status he was afforded while alive. The legal rights of an indigenous youth named Alonso Anaba carried notably less. Also, there is the puzzling element of exactly who was this young Alonso? I could find no reference to his parentage, yet he stood to inherit, if we are to trust the town attorney, valuable land in prime locations with access to water. The corregidor and his lieutenant made pretty powerful adversaries against a nearly anonymous Indian youngster.

A Rogue's Gallery

As I combed through the myriad documents concerning Mizque, certain people appeared more than once, as in the case of the prominent elites. However, one name appeared again and again in very different contexts that had a common denominator. This person could not stay out of trouble. Such was the case of Juan or Joan (as he was frequently cited) de Valenzuela, possibly a Spaniard but not of the elite. He first appeared in a 1580 document regarding a land dispute with the Indians of the pueblo of Mizque that involved misuse of their lands and his failure to pay land-use taxes. For his part, Valenzuela denied working Mizque community lands; he claimed that he had been working and paying rent for some Pocona community lands. The case went on for at least six years, and its resolution is unknown.[32]

Sometime in the late 1590s, in another unnumbered, barely legible set of documents, Valenzuela again appeared, this time in a dispute with a priest over the purchase of a slave. Valenzuela bought the twenty-year-old Gracía de Panama from the priest for 700 pesos. It turned out she not only suffered from a heart disorder but also had gout. Her health had not improved, and he had not gotten any work out of her. Apparently, Valenzuela's reputation for worker treatment was hardly impeccable. This was the same Valenzuela who was cited in a March 1, 1597, padrón on several counts of yanacona abuse on his coca chácara, to which he was said to have retorted, "Let them die and go to the devil." Valenzuela was ordered to make immediate reparations or face the penalty of having all of his yanaconas physically removed and placed under the custody of a neighboring chácara owner, Captain Juan Bidal Pericón. The yanaconas would remain under the protection of the captain and an appointed constable, at Valenzuela's expense, until the situation was remedied.[33]

While the likes of the Paniaguas and other elites got by with mild reprimands for their registered labor abuses, not so Valenzuela. The corregidor moved quickly and was in Tiraque (the regional seat for the yungas' coca trade and transport) the next day, March 2, with written orders in hand. From this day on, Valenzuela had to give his yanaconas their due Saturdays off to tend to their crops, and he had exactly one month to outfit all of them with their required annual clothing. Further, he was to see to their religious indoctrination and ensure that they attend mass on holy days and Sundays and not be forced to work on those days. He was fined 100 pesos (to be paid immediately) and warned that failing to abide by these terms would result in removal of his yanaconas. Valenzuela paid the fine and signed the warrant, as witnessed by the corregidor, the priest from Totora, and an official oath observer.[34]

This was, however, by no means the end of Valenzuela's story. The presence of another chácara in the yungas of Chuquioma owned by an Elvira de Valenzuela in the same 1597 padrón series where Valenzuela's chácara appeared was not coincidental, as the following will indicate. I share this account of a local murder for two reasons. First, the actors in this drama represent a nearly perfect cross-section of the

Mizque demographic profile. All sectors in the race, class, and ethnicity equation appear, directly or indirectly, in the detailed documents pertaining to the case. These include, among the witnesses, a yanacona (non-ethnic), a Chuy Indian, a mestizo, two Indian women, one mulata woman, and Valenzuela, who was of European origins and born in Oropesa (Cochabamba). Second, the testimonies reveal far more than a murder. Through their own accounts and thus through their own eyes, these descendants of Spaniards, Africans, and Indians show us how the intersection and cross-fertilization of values, mores, and other sociocultural measurements actually worked. They were identifiable, they were interrelated, and they reflected some deeply conflicting notions. In this one case appear patterns of interracial unions (informal and church sanctioned) between blacks, Indians, mulatos, and Spaniards. Issues of mistrust and stereotyping seep through the testimonies, as do images of swaggering figures who border on caricature or self-fulfilling prophecies, or perhaps accurately reflect the reality of a subculture.

On January 15, 1617, Don Gabriel de Encinas, by now alcalde de la Santa Hermandad and lieutenant general of the entire corregimiento, appeared on Valenzuela's chácara Tuyron in the yungas of Chuquioma with a warrant. It seems that on New Year's Day on chacara premises Valenzuela's brother-in-law Hernando Martín, mulato, killed an Indian named Cristoval. Valenzuela, who neglected to report the murder immediately, was accused of harboring a murderer and was suspected of being involved in the crime. The trial lasted two years almost to the day.[35]

To begin with, all nine witnesses concur that Valenzuela, his wife, all but one of his children, and several yanaconas spent New Year's Day attending mass in Totora and did not return to Tuyron until sometime the following Monday. In their absence, all bedlam broke loose. The Indian Cristoval (having been called upon by his curaca) had just returned from fulfilling a mita obligation for his ayllu. He and his wife, Joana, had been working for Valenzuela for only a few months. Apparently against the advice of one of his indigenous peers, Cristoval decided to join mulato Hernando and possibly some cohorts, including "two negros," in playing cards. Testimonies hinted of a possible amorous liaison between Joana and Hernando (himself legally married to an Indian named Isabel. She displayed her gold ring as proof, as was duly noted, suggesting that the symbolic power of the ring indeed carried weight).[36]

The evening wore on, now with only Hernando and Cristoval in the card game. Hernando wagered a 15-peso colt. He lost the bet. A man of some means, Hernando bet once more, this time a 9-peso mare. Cristoval won again. This was apparently his undoing. Declaring the game over and saying that he owed Cristoval nothing, Hernando by all accounts then lunged at Cristoval with a butcher knife, wounding him fatally. Cristoval never regained full consciousness. When Valenzuela returned home and learned of the stabbing, he promptly sent for the priest in Totora, sent word of the calamity to the corregidor in Mizque, and brought in someone to tend to "his worker" Cristoval's wounds. Cristoval died four days later.[37]

Juan de Valenzuela was exonerated of any complicity, yet a familiar theme emerges from his own testimony. The senseless, untimely loss of life was not the issue. Rather, the loss of Cristoval as semi-property/labor, and the 30 pesos he had advanced him, concerned Valenzuela. His own daughter testified that her father was very angry with Hernando for having murdered an Indian who was "in his service." In his testimony Valenzuela swore that his brother-in-law was not supposed to be on his property without his permission, yet Hernando had appeared soon after the family departed for Totora. The mulato, it would appear, had something of an aura about him. The yanacona who warned Cristoval not to carouse with Martín and his cohorts obviously knew something about him. Hernando was the legitimate son of Hernando Martín senior. Upon his death, the father left his livestock estancia (cattle, sheep, and no doubt some horses) to his four children, including son Hernando and daughter "Gerónima mulata," who would become Juan de Valenzuela's wife. The father's racial background is not known, and no reference to a mother appears in the documents. Earlier chapters demonstrated the strong association of Africans and their New World–born descendants and cattle ranching. The horses Hernando wagered were in all likelihood part of his inheritance. Hernando was convicted of murder, and his properties were placed in *depósito* (a state of custody or protection). I do not know his punishment. However, the fact that his belongings were put in depósito for safekeeping suggests that he was not condemned to life imprisonment or capital punishment.[38]

The documents also reveal that Juan de Valenzuela and his wife, Gerónima, produced several offspring over the years, including a daughter, Isabel mulata. She too was called upon to testify. She had remained on the chacara that New Year's Day to look after her baby brother. Like some of the Indian witnesses, Isabel also required an interpreter, "since she was a mulata and did not understand Castilian very well." This would suggest a possible linguistic subculture, since Isabel was now at least a second-generation Valenzuela. Also, the presence of an interpreter meant that Isabel's voice (and that of others dependent upon an interpreter) was subjected to possibly three sifting mechanisms—her interrogator, her interpreter, and the scribe. Nevertheless, her observations were consistent with the others', even when she unwittingly passed on misinformation. For instance, Hernando's wife, Joana, told Isabel that "a negro" had murdered Cristoval. Yet Joana also admitted to other witnesses that she was lying because Hernando had threatened to kill her, too, if she told the truth.[39] This, in turn, raises another relevant question. Why did Joana (and Hernando) choose to label the fictitious assailant a "negro"? Was a negro murderer more believable than a mulato murderer, easier to shift the blame to, less able to defend him- or herself? The indigenous population had their court defenders. The free black and mulato population did not. Or was conscious stereotyping and vilifying already in place?

Elvira de Valenzuela reemerged sixteen years later, this time in a land fight over choice holdings about twelve miles from the Villa de Mizque, somewhere between Pocona, Totora, and the Julpe River. In 1633, Andrés de Melo, the trouble-prone engineer whose bridge did not meet standard requisites, filed a lawsuit. He argued that he had legally purchased extensive agricultural and grazing lands and a livestock estancia at a public auction for 1,200 pesos. He claimed to have followed all the proper land-acquisition procedures and rituals, only to learn, after spending a year living at the estancia and working on improvements, that the lands were not for purchase. The lands belonged to others, including the mulata Elvira de Valenzuela.[40]

Unfortunately, the fate of Elvira's land (not be confused with her coca chácara in the yungas of Chuquioma) is not known. Elvira would probably need whatever property she could hold onto, because the lives of at least one branch of the Valenzuela progeny soon took a tailspin. In 1635, Juan de Valenzuela (Elvira's son) appeared before the cabildo on his family's behalf and presented a petition against his grandfather Valenzuela senior. It is from this petition that we learn that Elvira was indeed Valenzuela senior's daughter, although I am not convinced that she and Isabel (witness in the murder investigation) are not one and the same. She (Elvira) had been widowed and left with a child, referred to as Juan de Valenzuela, grandchild. She had remarried a man from Santa Cruz with whom she now had a second son. According to the filing, "our father and grandfather, who resides in the chácara Tuyron has registered all four of us as yanaconas of said chácara which we are not. He has sold the chácara to don Pedro de Monroy . . . we wish to put a halt to these actions and [request] legal intervention to prevent said Juan de Valenzuela our father from treating us like yanaconas and to impose serious punishment on him."[41]

Apparently, they already had a court order against Valenzuela senior. When they appeared at the chácara during census time, he snatched the document away from them and refused to return it. They demanded that Valenzuela obey the law, repeating they must not be treated as yanaconas, because they were *hijos rectos* (direct offspring), close blood relatives, and his underhanded deceit called for serious punishment. However, if they had to be registered and pay tribute, they demanded to be placed "on the padrón for the mulatos," where they would pay their due tribute to the king. To be treated so unfairly with neither their knowledge nor their consent was unjust and unacceptable. The authorities took their complaints seriously. Valenzuela senior was called before the authorities, and witnesses testified favorably on behalf of his daughter and grandson.[42]

Still acting as lieutenant to the corregidor, Captain Encinas prepared a decree for the beleaguered family. He wrote that he had reviewed all of the papers filed by Juan de Valenzuela, son of Elvira Valenzuela "bastard" (very strong term; no soft "natural child" here), daughter of Juan de Valenzuela the elder, and present wife of Andrés Choque,

Indian from Santa Cruz. Essentially, Encinas declared their registration as yanaconas null and void. Valenzuela had no right to force any of them to be yanaconas against their will. If they did not wish to be at Tuyron, they could reside with the forastero community in town and pay their tasas from there. Above all, no one—Juan de Valenzuela or anyone else—was to further harass this family, on penalty of punishment. They were to be given proof of his decree for their protection.[43]

Another individual, perhaps even more notorious than Valenzuela, was Andrés de Melo, who first appeared in the earlier discussion of Mizque's bridge. Like his counterpart Valenzuela, Melo could not stay away from litigation. We discussed the dismay of the bridge-inspection team when they realized that Melo had cheated the town with flawed construction and inappropriate, poor-quality materials. The lawsuits dragged on for at least six years, with the Villa de Mizque claiming Melo owed the town for not fulfilling the contract and for additional expenses required to correct his errors and to replace his poor choice of cementing materials.[44] All the while, Melo was suing another party for a lumber deal that went sour. How the bridge case was finally resolved is not known. What is known, however, is that Melo's troubles with the law predated his bridge problems.

Andrés de Melo was born in Tenerife, Canary Islands. By 1609 he was a resident of Mizque and worked as a professional (master) smith out of his own forge in town. He had taken an apprentice, Sebastian Casira, an Indian, who, in exchange for clothing, room, and board (no pay), was to learn the trade. Sebastian filed a suit against Melo, claiming Melo had not fulfilled his part of the agreement. Among other things, Melo would not relinquish Sebastian's tools and forge, for which the Indian had paid in advance. Melo countered by accusing Sebastian of absenteeism (five and one-half months), drinking and gambling, not tending to the business of the forge, and causing him financial loss, for which Melo demanded compensation before he returned anything to the Indian.[45] While the resolution of the case is not known, it represents a consistent pattern of behavior on Melo's part, as indicated in the following entanglement.

In 1628, two years before the townsmen contracted with him for the bridge, Melo faced criminal charges. Juan Cusihualpa, an Indian, accused Melo of beating him, hanging him by his hands and feet from the rafters, and "extreme mistreatment." According to Juan, who was Melo's employee, the horse Melo had given him as part of his job had strayed and gotten lost, as did he in attempting to track it down. Thus Juan explained his two-day disappearance from his place of employment. Apparently, Melo did not believe Juan and accused him of drinking and "fooling around." He then proceeded to abuse the Indian, first by putting him in leg irons "so that he could not escape," saying this was to "show you your place as a negro [slave]." Melo then tied Juan's hands and feet, strung him up to one of the beams in the rafters, and had already delivered ten lashes when he was interrupted by the *alguacil* (constable). Apparently a number of smiths had witnessed the abuse and summoned the alguacil. Chief magistrate Don Gómez de Figura ordered Melo's arrest and imprisonment.[46]

On June 27, 1628, Melo demanded his release from jail. He denied having mistreated Juan. The same day, Melo received tentative release from prison pending his payment of fines. On July 30, Juan vehemently protested Melo's release, again declaring that "he hung me, he whipped me, he put me in leg irons as though I were a slave . . . he should stay in jail." Finally, after a five-month lapse, Juan's father, Francisco Cusihualpa, appeared before the authorities. He stated that their cacique, Don Francisco Turumaya of the Pocona community, gave his son Juan to Melo to serve as an apprentice to learn the smith trade. Instead of teaching Juan, Melo nearly whipped him to death. Had the alguacil not appeared, he would have killed him. Apparently, by now Melo had been released and was on his way out of town. Said Francisco, "Before Melo leaves town, I ask Your Honor that he pay my son 50 pesos, for assault and maltreatment, and having put him in irons. That is the least that can be done, since he has been released from jail." Melo paid.[47]

The Common People and the Legal System

These examples of justice being moderately served are somewhat encouraging, especially if they are viewed within the constructs of race, class, and ethnic interrelations within the larger Andean social, political, and economic configurations. They are certainly revealing in terms of how these complicated and contradictory interrelationships actually worked in the real world. In the case of Juan de Valenzuela, the legal decision in favor of his illegitimate children was actually quite limited. Granted, Valenzuela could no longer register them as his yanaconas. Further, they were offered the option to move into town and be registered as forasteros, paying their taxes accordingly. But that was it. Freedom of choice and mobility, so deeply entrenched in Andean culture, were not legally mentioned. Similarly, Melo's brief jail stay obviously was incommensurate with the crime he inflicted, in which the victim, Juan, and his family considered his being clamped into leg irons like a slave as egregious as Melo's other heinous abuses. His father had to push for the 50-peso monetary compensation.

These and other cases demonstrate that if people plied the legal system with energy and determination, they might hope for some measure of success. But many variables were at play in the legal system that determined individuals' degree of power and thus the success or failure in any given case. What is known for certain is that people, including the poor and underprivileged, did, in desperation, turn to the legal system for succor. Thorough investigations of colonial court cases at the local level, reinforced with similar surveys at the audiencia level, would provide immense insight into the subject. But what about the vast multitude who could not seek legal refuge?

One of the prevailing themes throughout this work is that regardless of various approaches at different government levels to impose control over the labor and tribute-paying forces, people resisted those efforts and associated abuses as best they could. Chapter 6 explained at length the long-term Andean tradition of movement and migration that would translate into the colonial experience, now including the issue of agency or assertion. While the census takers continually admonished the yanaconas they were registering "not to leave the chácara on penalty of being punished," as we now know, the threat went largely unheeded. Some, however, actually sought legal means by which to extricate themselves from yanacona status.

Take, for example, the 1595 case of Catalina Cota, born in Pocona, the widowed indigenous ethnic mother of three young sons, "one a mestizo, the other indio, and the other a mulato." This nuclear family again reflects the essential themes of race, class, and ethnicity, and the intersection of each, with all the attendant variables. Speaking on behalf of Catalina and her sons, the protector of the Indians declared that they were being held illegally and against their will as yanaconas in a Mizque chácara. They were not yanaconas. They were all from (naturales de) Pocona, where they had family and ayllu. The chácara owner refused to release them, saying they had served as, and he had treated them as, yanaconas for years. He had fed and clothed them, paid their tasas, and registered them every year in the padrón. Despite the fact that he now faced a 500-peso fine, the chácara owner refused to hand the family over to authorities in Pocona. By 1605, not only was the case not resolved, but it was now clear that it had become a two-way legal battle between, on the one side, Catalina, her curaca, and her protector, and on the other side, the "judge" who recorded the chácara census and the chacara owner.[48] How it was resolved remains, as with so many of these cases, a mystery. My informed guess, given the region's history, is that Catalina and her now-grown children did what they pleased, as many did. There was always work available.

Then there were the Indian men, fed up with poor treatment on the chácaras, who came into town seeking individual attention from the magistrates. Such was the case of Salvador Quispe, who, in 1681, of his own volition and apparently unaccompanied by a court-ordered defender, petitioned to be removed from the yanacona status that chácara owner Don Juan de Encinas had imposed upon him. Salvador argued that he was born in the town of Copabilque and was thus a free man. Hence he could not be forced to endure the extensive abuse inflicted by his boss. According to Salvador, the mistreatment included years of failure to provide food and clothing rations as well as failure to allow holy days off and time for planting. All of this ongoing abuse culminated, apparently, when Salvador and chácara cohorts took matters into their own hands and came into town in search of food. Encinas "punished them" for their actions in an "atrocious" manner, and now he had Salvador's son "imprisoned" in another hacienda in Omereque.[49]

In a distinct tenor atypical of most of these petitions, Salvador, in his *demanda* (demand, a more-than-assertive touch; less a supplication for help than a demand for reparation), claims that he was seeking justice not only for himself but also for "all the poor indigenous people of this province." He requests that he and those with him be placed in depósito in town until the matter is resolved. He insists that the demanda be followed through, that "all we fathers have children and that Encinas must be made to release my son. We must see justice." The corregidor indeed acted swiftly, ordering the immediate release of Salvador's son (who apparently, like his father and of course his mother, who was not mentioned in the proceeding, was not legally a yanacona), on penalty of 100 pesos should Encinas fail to obey.[50] I suspect the lad was released and that Salvador's legal status gained official recognition. The fact that Salvador and his cohorts came into town with the sole purpose of filing a demanda against their boss and insisting they be placed in depósito until the problems were resolved bespeaks an energy and agency rarely seen in earlier documents.

Within these ongoing demographic dynamics that influenced and were influenced by the interchanging and borrowing of values, mores, and other sociocultural elements, we turn again to the African root of the New World tree of life. Chapter 5 established that Mizque benefited from the African component in its labor activities and more. In his report to the viceroy in 1618, the bishop of the Mizque–Santa Cruz diocese, Antonius de la Barranca, measured the material condition of the nine parishes under his jurisdiction according to whether or not they could afford African slaves for church-related activities. He noted that Mizque's parish not only had African slaves but also enjoyed sound economic support from its parishioners. Further, the parish also had *cofradías* (lay brotherhoods) in which everyone participated, "Spaniards as well as Indians and Blacks."[51] The African presence—slave and free—had become an irrefutable fact.

Slaves, Their Descendants, and the Many Forms of Resistance

Just as African participation was the historical reality in the Corregimiento de Mizque as in the colony at large, a parallel reality also emerged. African slaves and their descendants in the eastern Andes, like their counterparts elsewhere, resisted enslavement. Whatever slave codes, decrees, and ordinances applied to New Spain pertained equally to the viceroyalty of Peru. Certainly viceroys Mendoza and Toledo brought to Peru their many years of experience dealing with African resistance in Mexico. Not surprisingly, we hear a familiar refrain in the royal decree issued out of Valencia, Spain, on January 6, 1586, by King Philip II to

> the President and Magistrates of My Royal Audiencia [of La Plata] in the Province of Charcas. . . . I have been informed that in those provinces there are many negros, mulatos and mestizos and people of mixture and every day their numbers continue to grow, and many of them are hui-dos, have no idea who their fathers are . . . growing up with great vices and liberty, out of work . . . eating and drinking beyond control, mixing with the Indians, indulging in drink and witchcraft, not attending mass nor hearing sermons they know nothing of the holy Catholic faith, and if things continue this way great harm and inconvenience will arise . . . look into this matter and see that these damages be avoided and that these peoples be christianized and taught skills and do not mingle with the Indians, as I have ordered in earlier rulings.[52]

Resistance to this and similar rulings, to the many ordinances and codes implemented to control the *castas* (people of biologically mixed ancestry) and the slaves, persisted throughout the viceroyalty of Peru. Indeed, defiance endured the entire three hundred years of colonial rule and after. Earlier studies underscore *cimarrón* (runaway slave) activities in the Lima region very early on.[53] We now know that the tradition of active resistance continued into the republic of Peru.[54]

In the highland audiencia of Charcas, local authorities in the city of La Paz had implemented slave ordinances as early as 1548. One in particular forbade "negros, slave or free, to sell any meat whatever on penalty of 100 lashes and loss of said meat. Or in place of lashes, a payment of 10 pesos as punishment, two-thirds of which was to go to public works, one-third to the informer." This same ordinance also declared it illegal for black women to hoard bread.[55] By the 1560s, La Plata, the seat of the audiencia, also had strict codes in place. Authorities there, too, were fearful of the "free negros and mulatos, so many of them and their kind increasing by the day that soon they will be roving bands, assaulting and robbing or they will join with the Indians and cause them to rise up." By 1573 they were "prohibited from carrying arms, having horses, congregating in groups, or mixing with the Indians." All of this adds a bit of contradictory flair to an event that occurred in 1629 during the July 24 uprising in Potosí. A local magistrate, new to the area and still unfamiliar with the powers that be, saw a black slave with an open sword and promptly disarmed him. Unknown to the official was that the slave belonged to the prominent citizen Don Fernando Cabeza de Vaca. The magistrate was taken to court, no doubt by Don Fernando, for his indiscretion.[56]

Complaints of cimarrones emerged not only in La Paz and La Plata but also in Oruro and in the silver-mining center of Potosí, 13,253 feet above sea level. As noted earlier, the royal mint in Potosí, known as the Casa de la Moneda, also used slave labor. The mint also bore witness to a number of violent tumults and frays among the slaves held captive there, resulting in serious injuries among the slave population.[57]

The problem of runaways continued unabated in the highlands. In 1601, after receiving his orders from Spain, Viceroy Mendoza directed another proviso to the audiencia of La Plata. In it he focused on the need to deal with that region's cimarrones, who "live in the mountains and along the roads . . . attacking merchants and travelers, stealing all of their possessions, and killing many."[58] The viceroy considered this an acute problem and ordered travelers not to set forth unless they traveled in groups of twenty or more.[59] Stringent laws were enacted to underscore how seriously royal authorities took the problem: "The absence of a slave from his master's house for more than four days will result in a punishment of 50 lashes, after which the captive will be placed in stocks for public exhibition . . . if absent for more than eight days he will receive 100 lashes and wear a 12 lb. leg iron."[60] An absence of more than two months was punishable by hanging.[61]

These harsh laws notwithstanding, slaves continually ran away and defied the social order. Not surprisingly, women also participated in fugitive actions, either independently or in groups, and as often as not they suffered the consequences when caught. Other investigations demonstrate actual application of even harsher slave codes than those cited here, such as in early colonial Quito, Guatemala, Mexico, and Spanish Florida. My evidence strongly suggests harsh treatment (not necessarily legally sanctioned), such as the many restraining devices mentioned earlier, and the local sales of maimed and crippled slaves. Further, there was one case in which a slave woman, Francisca, accused her owners of physical abuse; her case actually made it all the way to the audiencia.[62]

Yet despite legally sanctioned or "informal" punishments, the following discussion will demonstrate that in the Mizque region, as elsewhere throughout the New World, resistance was a viable option for slaves. Even from this remote jurisdiction, solid documentation emerges to underscore agency on the part of the slaves and even their free descendants. In 1604, criminal charges were made against Diego Moroco (or Moroso), a mulato, and several other "guilty parties" for "setting on fire and burning down" the houses of Don Luís Zaragún and others in the pueblo of Pocona. Diego was accused of being the primary instigator and of acting on his own volition. Therefore, in order for "royal justice to be served," Diego was to be apprehended and imprisoned, deprived of his belongings, and punished in accordance with the severity of his crime. A search warrant for him was promptly issued. Arson is not uncommon in slave societies and is recognized as a draconian measure of resistance and rage. In other Mizque documents, two orders dated July 5 and July 15, 1605, refer to the Indian community of Pocona. The caciques were to take inventory within eight days of all the "negros, mulatos y mestizos" living among and fraternizing with the Indians. The inventories were to state cases of "maltreatment." All of the above non-Indians were to be expelled in accordance with royal decree.[63] This legally sanctioned segregationist thinking, allegedly established to prevent abuse of Indians, of course ignores the ongoing abuse of the tax collectors and the like.

Others have established a tangible fear among royal officials and private parties over the roving bands of cimarrones in the Lima, La Paz, La Plata, and other highland regions. We now know that cimarrones also roamed the Mizque province. In 1633 the municipal government of Mizque appealed to the higher courts that a negro named Amador, head of a small band of cimarrones operating in the valley of Mizque, not be pardoned for his crimes. The local officials, backed by local clergy, claimed the cimarrón leader did not deserve to be pardoned, since he and his followers continued to cause very serious problems ("to the excess") and had been doing so for a prolonged period of time. For the safety of all local residents, the appeal continued, every attempt should be made to capture Amador and his followers. If they could not be immediately apprehended, then their food and supply lines should be cut. If this action did not force them into submission, it would at least cause them to disband. The intent was for Amador to turn himself in, serve time in the local jail, and perform the obligatory work-related prison chores. There would be no pre-agreed settlements. The municipal government of Mizque requested sole authority over Amador's imprisonment as well as the terms of his release.[64]

Cases of individual *cimarrones* figure far more prominently in the Mizque court documents than those involving roving bands.[65] Looking first to litigations over runaways at the local level, one particular lawsuit merits closer scrutiny. It is somewhat complicated, but only in that the many twists and turns the case takes expose the vested interests of several parties and reveal how these played out in the moral economy in which slavery was a major component, not to mention the destiny of the *cimarrón* himself. The case of Don Diego de Venegas versus Sebastian de la Vega opened on November 24, 1650, and lasted until August 1, 1651. Don Diego de Venegas, a nobleman living in the city of La Plata, sued Sebastian de la Vega, a rancher and wine producer in the province of Mizque, for the return of his slave Josep, who had fled the Venegas household seven years earlier (Josep was now twenty-five years old). Only recently had Don Diego located his runaway, who was now working in de la Vega's vineyards as captain and overseer. Don Diego demanded that the slave, rightfully his, be returned immediately. He had the necessary papers to prove that Josep was born to his slaves Magdalena and Francisco, under his roof.[66]

In Mizque, however, de la Vega had another story. He claimed that Josep was one of five slaves included in the ranch and vineyards he purchased two years earlier. Since then he had trained Josep in the techniques of wine production, and now Josep was known for his skills and supervisory abilities. The slave was indispensable in vineyard operations and was responsible for its successful harvests. This highly valued slave would be very difficult to replace.[67]

The truth, not surprisingly, lay somewhere in between the arguments of both camps, and on occasion it even overlapped. Don Diego, it seems, had included Josep and some landed properties in the dowry he drew up for his daughter, who married one Bartolomé de la Fresnada, from Mizque. Apparently, de la Fresnada was something of a no-account. He squandered the daughter's dowry by selling off much of her properties and then abandoned her and their child. One of the sales included a vineyard and the slave Josep to Alonso Gonzáles Camorano. Gonzáles Camorano, in turn, sold the vineyard and slave in 1649 to de la Vega, who was now being challenged by Don Diego.[68]

In the meantime, what about Josep? His owner, Don Diego, claimed the slave had been huido for seven years. Obviously, he was not aware that Josep had been sold in a transaction over which the slave either had no control or desire to control. There are, after all, a number of time gaps in the court statements in which Josep is not accounted for, when he could have easily been fugitive. Once he was relocated by Don Diego's family and the litigation over ownership commenced, Josep did indeed flee de la Vega's properties. Under de la Vega's "ownership," Josep had fared reasonably well in a position of considerable authority. We also know that he had married a mestiza and thus probably had local ties (he was an unmarried youth when he "fled" Don Diego's house in La Plata). Don Diego now wanted Josep returned to La Plata, where he would serve out his days as the owner originally intended when he included the slave in his daughter's dowry as an economic buffer in time of need. The time had come. Josep was to be brought back to La Plata (no mention of the mestiza wife), and Don Diego would pay the required 25 pesos for someone to accompany him on the return journey. Installed again in La Plata, Josep would be hired out for the usual 4 reales (half a peso) a day paid to day labor (slave or free) in order to support Don Diego's deserted daughter and her child.[69] Little wonder that Josep took off as soon as the proceedings got under way.

The slave's taste of freedom (at least for now) was short-lived. De la Vega was not about to lose this one, whose value he now placed at 1,000 pesos—a very hefty sum when the going price for able-bodied African slaves ranged from 500 to 800 pesos depending on skills. He began a search immediately upon learning that Josep had fled, eventually tracking the slave down in the Villa de Mizque several days later and returning him to the hacienda. At this juncture the accounts diverge. De la Vega claimed that Venegas's people forced their way onto his property and illegally removed the slave, while the other side claimed that Josep was removed by mutual agreement. Either way, Josep ended up in depósito and remained there until the case was resolved.

Meanwhile, as the litigation drew to a close and Venegas's ownership was established, de la Vega entered his own demands. He insisted on reimbursement on two counts. First he wanted 1,000 pesos from Venegas in "reparation," since he had in good faith purchased the slave under false conditions. Although he had paid only 600 pesos for Josep, under his guidance the slave had developed highly marketable skills and was easily worth the additional 400 pesos. Further, because of Josep's depósito status, de la Vega also demanded compensation in the standard 4 reales a day for the two hundred days Josep could not be on the job. On August 1, 1651, the court handed down its decision: Joseph was to be returned to Venegas in La Plata. Venegas, in turn, was to pay de la Vega 600 pesos in reimbursement for purchase of a slave under false pretenses.[70] The is no further mention of the mestiza wife. She was not the issue. Given the economic incentives fueling the energy and determination of owners to recapture their runaways, those same runaways call for recognition for *their* energy and determination to resist and reject their involuntary condition of enslavement.

In keeping with owners' determination to return their expensive investments, I found still another dimension to the theme. In 1657, Diego de Cosio filed a claim against his hacienda and vineyard mayordomo, Don Antonio Cerrato, in which he accused the steward of having caused the negligent death of his valuable, highly skilled vineyard slave, twenty-four-year-old Simón. Allegedly, in the middle of wine harvest the mayordomo (without consulting with owner Cosio) decided to send Simón out of the vineyard for two days, on tasks in the Villa de Mizque relating to the mayordomo's interests, not Cosio's or his vineyard. Apparently caught in harsh weather, including overnight exposure to torrential rains, Simón took seriously ill, which Cerrato ignored. He continued to push the slave into running errands back and forth from the vineyard to the villa until the slave collapsed and died of fever and chills (this could have been malaria). The owner was suing for the loss of his property, which he valued at 1,000 pesos. This case was one of several of this nature which I came across.[71]

Later, in an incomplete and less-detailed local case, the economic significance of slaves emerges from yet another perspective. In the Villa de Mizque on December 5, 1671, Don Matías Saenz de Soto took Alfonso Cabrillo to court. Apparently, eleven years earlier, three of Don Matías's slaves fled his "house and hacienda." One slave, Salvador de la Cruz, got as far as the Tomina frontier, a considerable distance away. In Tomina he was taken in and kept hidden by Cabrillo for "a long time." Don Matías eventually learned of his slave's whereabouts and set in motion procedures for his recapture. When Cabrillo learned that the slave was being sought, he "maliciously and knowingly" sold the slave to a traveling merchant from Lima. While the search to track down Salvador continued, the court ordered Cabrillo to pay Don Matías the slave's ascribed working value of 4 reales a day for the entire time spent in hiding. Should Cabrillo not have the cash to meet this order, his goods and properties would be confiscated and used to reimburse Don Matías.[72] If Cabrillo had kept the runaway Salvador the entire eleven years, his fines could have amounted to about 8,000 pesos. Given the higher cost of African slaves in the Mizque region, this sum was equivalent to the cost of eight to twelve slaves. Also, nowhere in the above and other court cases I have examined was there any mention of the harsh punishments stated so emphatically in the slave codes, neither for the cited runaways nor for the people who harbored them. Again, this may not indicate that such punishments did not exist. However, I doubt that any of the litigants would want to cause bodily harm to such an economic asset as a very expensive, highly skilled slave. Perhaps the less-valuable slaves, sold with all of their alleged "negative traits" clearly spelled out for the buyer, were the ones who received the harsher punishments in order to set examples and intimidate others. Sebastian's accusation that Melo treated him "like a slave" continues to resonate.

Still another earlier perspective on cimarrones surfaces in the Mizque documents. On April 30, 1619, Antonio Corso went to court and accused Francisco de Tordoya, muleteer, of stealing his slave Francisco. As the story unfolds and several testimonies are taken into account (witnesses included several African slaves, Indian workers, and even some landowners), the case becomes more complicated than would first appear. Apparently, two slaves (one of them further identified as Congolese) belonging to muleteer Tordoya approached Corso's slave Francisco (also identified as Congolese) and began persuading him to join them and their owner Tordoya. They were driving a recua (which included horses, freight, and supplies) down to Santa Cruz. They told Francisco that he would find Tordoya a decent chap to work for and that he would surely find a much better life for himself in that distant, burgeoning frontier. It should be noted that the journey to Santa Cruz was a major undertaking; travelers moved through a number of ecological zones, including some rather treacherous mountainous curves and drops, cloud forests, and tropical rain forests. Few bridges existed, and fording the many rivers posed considerable danger. The trip took several weeks.[73]

Tordoya's men returned for Francisco the following day and took him to Tordoya, who was gearing up for the trek. According to witnesses, Tordoya found a place in the recua for the slave and told Francisco not to worry and to "just say I bought you for 600 pesos," which is exactly what they did as they made their slow journey out of the valley of Mizque and up through the mountains. Corso, upon taking his case to court, did not lack witnesses. These recuas were not only highly visible but also dependent on the local population for subsistence, supplies, and the like. Further, Francisco was known and apparently well liked. A number of witnesses recalled their astonishment at the time that Corso would even consider selling such a valuable slave for a mere 600 pesos.[74]

We do not know how the case was resolved. By the time it came to court, Francisco was long gone, and considering the territory, the possibility of recapture was growing increasingly remote. Corso accused Tordoya of stealing, but the witnesses were unanimous in claiming that Francisco clearly joined the recua of his own will. And the obvious ease with which Francisco rode away from one master suggests he might easily leave the next. This also underscores the possibility raised earlier that the recuas that traversed the viceroyalty from one end to the other served as convenient vehicles of escape for the cimarrones.

But another, more decisive means of making the final break from enslavement is reflected, again, in court litigations. These cases are referred to as *reclamaciones*, which translates easily into its legal meaning in English: "Reclaim: to claim or demand back."[75] They involve slaves going to court to establish and maintain their freedom, or former slaves suing to end illegal reenslavement. The audiencia of Charcas heard dozens of reclamaciones from all over the region. Although the slave plaintiff was usually placed in depósito during the hearings, some were willing to endure actual incarceration if necessary to fight for what they believed was rightfully theirs. Thus, while this type of action may not fall entirely within the traditional category of "fugitive," it was, in Peter Blanchard's words, "openly confrontational."[76] I would add that the reclamación action did indeed possess some fugitive overtones in that the slave, in many cases, had to muster up the courage to walk away from his or her place of servitude and go through the demanding motions of court action.

In the Charcas region, reclamaciones appear long before the concepts of abolition and independence were articulated. References to these cases emerge as early as the 1580s. For example, in 1584 there appeared a "reclamo de una negra," followed in 1592 by a "reclamación de una negra contra Pedro Martínez." And later, more specifically, a slave woman Juana Prieto reclaimed her freedom, and a mulato named Jerónimo demanded his rights. These continue throughout the 1600s through at least the early 1700s.[77] Further, these reclamaciones represent those cases *not* resolved at the local level or in district courts. How many cases were resolved at the local level throughout the viceroyalty of Peru about which we know virtually nothing? It can be argued that the reclamaciones, appearing earlier than expected, harkened back to something far more deeply ingrained than political independence from colonial rule.

In the Andean world, migration was a recognized cultural characteristic before the arrival of the Europeans. The Inca borrowed this tradition from their ancestors, who in turn adopted it from other cultures long before their time. The Inca, in fact, gave it a new twist by forcing people to migrate and colonize newly conquered regions, the consequences of which remain evident even today. With the arrival of the Europeans, this tradition of movement took on yet another dimension: the Indians quickly learned to use it as a means of rejecting European control. Thus migration—the act of a people moving from one place to another—adjusted to changing conditions and came to include the movement of small family clusters or even single individuals. While on the one hand it could now be seen as an effective means of resistance, that very act of resistance was also one of assertion. No one, as has been commonly speculated, was hindered by the terrain. In this context, the term *huido*, which so tenaciously haunts the documents, must take on a far more complex meaning than that of simple flight.

Thus the enslaved African was brought into a system in which the origins of resistance to subjugation dated back thousands of years. As Blanchard notes, courageous slaves who made the decision to become fugitives did so by taking risks their Indian brothers and sisters did not face. The slave, if caught, could be subject to severe corporal and possibly even capital punishment.[78] But as the above cases demonstrate, in Charcas by the early 1600s, employers did not look too closely at one's legal status. In this particular Andean region, there was *always* a shortage of Indian labor.[79] Further, there was always a shortage of skilled labor as well.

In the Spanish American experience, from the viceroyalty of New Spain to the viceroyalty of Peru, African slavery was synonymous with fugitive action. In roving bands of all sizes, cimarrones plagued city and countryside alike throughout the colonial period. In Charcas neither the Indian presence nor the terrain hindered the fugitive bands or lone escapees. Much to the contrary, long-established traditions played into slave resistance. Further, the patterns of legislation and defiance, participation in tumults, the replenishment of a diminishing indigenous labor pool, and the use of acquired skills as a negotiating tool all reflect the dynamics of slave resistance. In addition, the fact that slaves learned to use the court system to serve their own needs and take control of their own lives indicates not only resistance but also another, equally dynamic factor—that of agency.

Moreover, there exists one more long-term means of resistance to bondage, profound in its many implications. Through the myriad mixed racial-ethnic unions—Indian, European, and African—the resulting progeny (more often than not born of legally free Indian women, soon followed by mestiza and mulata women, and thus free themselves) appeared soon after the conquest. Their numbers grew exponentially over time, as their presence, reflected in their ascribed labels—mestizo, mulato, pardo, sambo, prieto, and moreno—and their alleged and actual activities, was recorded in countless historical documents still preserved today. Again, the numbers of those who for any variety of reasons were not recorded in the documents or may today be missing from document collections—silenced, either way—must be considered.

The World of the Cowboys

The following discussion on cowboys, ranch hands, and estancias underscores almost all of the above premises of resistance, agency, and assertion. It does so within the context of a population boom of unexpected proportions that, despite all of their efforts, royal authorities could not control. Further, the cowboys, almost caste-like in their subculture, provide yet another example of the intersecting and cross-fertilization discussed through much of this work.

I have established the importance of livestock production and the raising of cattle in Mizque. With settlement, African slaves began working as cowboys on the European estancias. A generation later, the children of these cowboy slaves themselves became estancia owners. Whether related to possible African cultural traditions or to inherent individual ability to adapt and acquire challenging skills or both, the cattle ranches and related activities became the predominant domain of African slaves and their descendants in the Spanish colonies.

Early on, African slaves were included in the campaigns of pacification. By the 1550s the leaders of expeditions were acquiring area landholdings. Their chácaras and estancias provided the necessary provisions of food, gear, and horses. The African slaves who accompanied the campaigns received firsthand exposure to New World livestock practices. By the 1570s free mulatos were buying their own horses. In

1595, Domingo Gerónimo, a free mulato, appeared before the authorities in the town of Mizque and demanded that cacique Don Miguel Cibita return his saddle and riding gear. By 1600 the estancia Episana was already in full operation, with the black slave Francisco Angola overseeing activities. In 1605, Miguel *vaquero* (cowboy, probably of African descent; African slaves did not arrive in the New World with last names, as explained in chapter 5), had garnered sufficient money to petition the cabildo for a town lot he wished to purchase.[80]

And then there were the cattle rustlers and mule thieves. If the proliferation of cases that were filed is any indication, cattle rustling for illicit meat sales must have been a fairly lucrative enterprise. The following are a sampling. In 1605 a negro named Rafael and an indio yanacona were found guilty of slaughtering more than twenty cows in order to sell meat illegally. Both were sent to jail. In a 1618 criminal case, authorities of the Santa Hermandad accused a pardo, Juan Ramírez de Romagera (whose name during the interrogation became Juan Ramírez Quiñoes), of mixing cattle from his estancia with cattle (including calves) belonging to neighboring estancias, tinkering with their brands to make them appear to be his, and slaughtering them for *charque* (in this case, beef jerky) to sell in the yungas. This "man of evil ways and of color" also used his own brand on unbranded cattle and horses belonging to others. According to witnesses, he had been conducting this rustling and branding for quite some time to supply his trade in charque. Apparently, he fled and attempted to sell off the evidence, but eventually he was caught, fined, and imprisoned.[81]

A court case from 1639 provides additional insight into how these operations were carried out. First, all the people involved in the proceedings had estancia connections and knew each other by name. For example, key witness "mulato Antón Cassanga" (and by association his "mulatillo" sons) was an estancia owner. Accused rustler Indian Agustín de Narvaez, muleteer assistant, worked on an estancia, as did the two cowboys not identified by race. Apparently, they had been rustling cattle from area estancias for quite a while and had by some accounts absconded with perhaps two hundred head of cattle. They finally did get caught (quite literally red-handed) in the act of slaughtering their most recent plunder. Agustín was released from jail when his boss, estancia owner Melchor Torricos (who had lost several head of cattle to the rustlers), posted his bond. The fate of the others remains unknown.[82]

Rustling continued throughout the seventeenth century and into the eighteenth. In a particularly noteworthy case from 1713, estancia owner Maese de Campo Isidoro Veraga Cabeza de Vaca brought charges of mule theft and assault on his yanacona cowboys against Captain Felix de Salazar. According to the cowboy witnesses, Salazar, "armed with a sword, dagger and gun," went straight for the heavily guarded mule pen, rounded up six mules, and in the process wounded the people trying to stop him, one severely. Pascual Romero, sambo yanacona cowboy, was the key witness in the case.[83] First, from the above cases and the many more that I have scanned, criminal assault is not the norm. Also, it was pointedly established that the mule pen was under heavy guard (hence the armed assault). This suggests that mules indeed were prime targets, and, I would add, rustling had taken on a more aggressive mode.

Using a wider lens to observe the inner workings and interconnectedness of ranches, cowboys, ranch hands, and ranch owners, one more look at an even earlier litigation is called for. We return to the 1604 lawsuit and countersuit between mulato estancia owner Juan Gutiérrez Altamirano and Paniagua mayordomo Estevan Navarrete concerning the former's livestock and the latter's crops. Here, for unstated reasons, ill feeling already existed between the two litigants, and they had been at each other for some time. Once the authorities actually viewed the massive slaughter of Gutiérrez's livestock and the proceedings got under way, immediate disclaimers and discrediting of the opposing party's witnesses began.[84]

Gutiérrez's Indian witnesses were discredited, as were Juan de Valenzuela mulato (son of Juan senior?) and Miguel Arias negro, for being "such good friends and relatives" of Gutiérrez as to make them unreliable and *trachados* (most likely intended to be *tachados*: censured, objected to, or challenged as a witness). Another witness, Francisco Pérez Verdugo, "was and still is a declared enemy of don Gabriel Paniagua's mayordomos." Navarrete's witnesses received equal mistrust and skepticism from the opposition. For example, a prominent curaca,

Don Gerónimo Chan, owned land adjacent to the Paniagua properties. The Gutiérrez side found him unacceptable as a witness because "he is afraid of them [the Paniaguas]." As for Baltesar Chuquiando, "he is a facile Indian, good pals with Paniagua yanacona. He eats and drinks with them. He will say whatever the mayordomo tells him."[85] Significantly, the authorities sided with the Paniagua forces, even though the mayordomo skipped town!

Gerónimo and Clara

A final vignette is the story of Gerónimo and Clara. This tale illumines the underpinnings and interworkings of Mizque's multiracial, socioeconomic construct, this time under the guise of religion. On May 5, 1603, Gerónimo de Villapando (originally from La Plata), and Clara Morena (origins not given) appeared before Bachiller Juan Cano de Paredes (of the prominent family cited elsewhere in this work), vicar and ecclesiastic judge for the Mizque district. They stood accused of concubinage—living as man and wife without the sacrament of holy matrimony. They were also "setting a very bad example for the people of Aiquile," where they lived openly together in Gerónimo's house with a *puerta adentro* (possibly referring to a house in town with a street door as well as an interior door for carriage access and security, which in turn indicates some degree of socioeconomic status; the two doors are repeatedly mentioned). At least twice it is noted that Clara's house has no door. To make matters worse (for them), they had been "living together publicly" for a number of years, and "everyone in town knew about their evil ways."[86]

Apparently, Gerónimo and Clara had been reprimanded a number of times. Gerónimo, a master *herrador* (farrier), was jailed twice, but on both occasions his boss, former corregidor Don Fernando Carrero, posted bond for his release because Gerónimo's skills at shoeing horses were greatly needed at Carrero's chácara. Each time Gerónimo was arrested by an officer of the ecclesiastic court and jailed, Clara was placed in depósito, from which she managed to escape on both occasions. The first time, the family in charge expressed bewildered surprise. Clara had been with them only a few days and then slipped through their fingers, as it were, to end up right back in Aiquile, in Gerónimo's house with the inside door! Her second escape (from another family), aided by Gerónimo, was considerably more flamboyant. By all accounts, he came dashing up to the depósito house on his steed, brandishing his sword, grabbed the awaiting Clara by the waist, and swept her up on his horse. With him still brandishing his sword, they rode off together back to his house in Aiquile. She later "boasted" of the incident (which must have really rankled the authorities).[87]

Only toward the end of this progressively nastier proceeding, which lasted from May 1604 to June 1605, and during which "witnesses" seeming more akin to spies reported acts they allegedly saw while peering through Gerónimo's windows, did two matters emerge. For the first time, Gerónimo was identified as a mulato, and he remained so labeled throughout these and the later (1608–10) proceedings. Simultaneously, when Clara Morena was asked to confirm her identity, she responded that her last name was not Morena at all but rather López. From then on she was labeled "the morena Clara López," or "Clara López morena," or "Clara López mulata," or "Clara negra." Finally, Gerónimo and Clara were apparently apprehended in a compromising situation in his house and were again jailed and placed in depósito. In 1608 the case was reopened, this time in La Plata. Sometime during the interim they had actually married, and now they were referred to as husband and wife. The authorities were suing them for 50 pesos each to cover the litigation fees and subsequent fines of 167 pesos that their proceeding had accrued. They threatened to confiscate Gerónimo's possessions if he did not pay.[88]

The litigation dragged on for two more years. It seems that one of the people who had promised to help pay the legal fees either died intestate, or for some reason his wishes had not been carried out or were deemed unacceptable. Further, Gerónimo, speaking on his own behalf (he was now in his forties), declared he would not pay all of those fees and fines. The local authorities insisted on pursuing the case long after he and Clara had married—which, Gerónimo claimed, they had no right to do. On July 17, 1612, Gerónimo de Villapando declared that as far as he was concerned, it was all null and void. As an extra measure, he had all of his possessions and properties, including his chácara in Chinguri, placed in his wife's name.[89]

My opinion is that there was a whole lot more going on in this case than meets the eye. Why did Gerónimo and Clara not just go ahead and get married? Both were single with no apparent debts or other legal responsibilities or obstacles to impede their union. People lived "in concubinage" more frequently than not, as we have seen. Were Gerónimo and Clara so bold and brash as the documents portray, publicly defying civic and ecclesiastic authority? Did someone have a grudge against Gerónimo? He seems to have been a self-made man of acclaimed skills. He had a modest house (with an interior door!) in town. He also owned (and this information is not revealed until the very last page of the litigation) a chácara in Chinguri, probably one where coca was cultivated. Did someone want his valuable land? Land grabbing in Mizque in the early 1600s was still the norm. At best, we can only speculate over the forces at play that drove the authorities to pursue (persecute) Gerónimo de Villapando, mulato, and Clara López, morena/mulata/negra. They were certainly determined to label her, even if they could not come up with her place of origin. On the other hand, what forces drove Clara and Gerónimo to such determined show of resistance?

Thus life in Mizque went on, people lived and died, made conscious and unconscious choices, adapted and adjusted, resisted passively and actively. This chapter belongs less to the encomenderos, chacareros, hacendados, and high-ranking church and government officials than it does to the "marginalized," "floating population" of indios, negros, mulatos, mestizos, and castas who made their way into the documents for speaking out, demanding their rights, taking the law into their own hands, and even ignoring the law. It belongs, equally, to the many who were not recorded in the documents. They are the ones whose history in the eastern Andes for the most part remained, and remains, silenced, ignored, or forgotten. A second look at Viedma's 1782 population figures for the corregimiento serves as a helpful reminder, as it underscores the matter of survival. The New World colonial reality is one of population mixture, in the Corregimiento de Mizque and elsewhere throughout the colonies. The population was the result of the coming together, voluntarily and otherwise, of three groups—African, Indian, and European. This mixed population shared its roots, its history, and its contemporary space with the above primary peoples. This in turn resulted in a myriad of racial, ethnic, color, and class combinations. It is the historical reality.

Conclusions

THE LITTLE-KNOWN AND even less systematically studied eastern
reaches of the Andes—referred to in colonial times as the Corregimiento de Mizque—possessed its own prehistorical and historical landscape and narrative. It encompassed multiple ecological niches that
permitted the production of many indigenous foods and goods long
before the arrival of Europeans. The region's native inhabitants had
formed into identifiable ethnic groups. They coexisted or fought with
each other, as they also formed and shifted alliances. They traded with
peoples across the entire area, often traversing the Amazonian lowlands to the Andean subpuna valleys in group migrations. The subpuna
valleys, particularly the temperate Mizque valley and its environs and
respective natural resources, appealed to the lowland dwellers as they
later attracted the Inca, and finally the Spaniards.

Several of the lowland groups resisted the Inca aggressors, just as
they later repelled the early attempts of Jesuit missionaries. Soon they
posed impressive opposition to the Spanish campaigns of Indian pacification that continued through the 1770s. The lowland warriors were
neither hindered nor intimidated by the so-called lines of demarcation
and territorial limits that came to be known as frontiers, as these lines
did not exist until they were arbitrarily imposed much later by the
Spaniards.

It did not take the Spaniards long to learn what the indigenous
peoples of the lowlands, the montaña, and the highlands had known
from much earlier times, namely, that the vast eastern region with its
ecological archipelagoes and fertile valleys would be ideal for many
lucrative European economic enterprises in agriculture, livestock production, and even mining. Thus began the European reconfiguration
of the region for local, intraregional, and interregional markets and

the creation of a new axis to compete with the more convention-
ally perceived (Pacific) coast-to-highland trade-and-transport system.
Instead, the new axis consisted of an eastern hinterland-to-highland
route: Santa Cruz–Mizque–La Plata–Potosí. In the process, encomiendas awarded to the men who fought in the conquest and civil wars and
who led subsequent eastern Andean campaigns of discovery and pacification were activated. They now had access to local labor. Soon, all
manner and sizes of haciendas, chacaras, estancias, and viñas sprinkled
the eastern landscape.

Meanwhile, the Spanish imperial machine moved swiftly to tighten
its reins on non-encomienda labor and forge ahead with one of the
most ambitious New World political-economic plans of the time. This
plan was miscalculated and assumed the acquiescence and cooperation of the traditional indigenous leaders and a total subjugation of
the hundreds of thousands of people who already formed the labor
and service population beholden, voluntarily or otherwise, to their respective indigenous curacas or caciques. In Spain's plan, the indigenous political economy, already long in place, would now serve royal
interests. The imperial plan did not anticipate the associated sets of issues that loomed almost immediately. First, despite the toppling of the
Inca leadership, the conquest of the vast Inca "empire" was far from
complete. The indigenous leaders did not unanimously capitulate to
Spain's demands, and the indigenous masses remained less than mal-
leable. Old World disease and Andean cultural traditions of mobility
and migration contributed to a hybrid set of colonial characteristics in
the eastern Andes.

Just as much of the Andean colonial scholarship has been centered
on the coast-to-highland trade-and-transport axis, a good portion of
the research has looked to what I call the now-classic Andean regions
of Potosí and Cuzco. However, much has yet to be learned about the
less-analyzed centers of economic activity. This is in no way intended
to diminish the immense prehistorical and historical weight the former
carry. The economic impact of Potosí alone, for better or worse, was
an overwhelming driving force that influenced, one way or another,
much of the Andean world and beyond.

However, to focus on a lesser-known regional center such as the

Corregimiento de Mizque and to examine at close range how economic, political, and social forces influenced and were influenced by
the Africans, Indians, and Spaniards who lived and worked in the region informs the wider historical panorama as well. A micro-historic
approach, drawing from as many varied documentary sources as possible, allows for an analysis of details not possible at the broader, macro-
historical level. Certain information vital to the comprehension of the
wider picture can be found only at the local level.

By centering on this seemingly "remote" Corregimiento de Mizque, I
was able to identify several sets of characteristics and processes. First,
the regional differences determined by climatic, geographic, and demographic factors were indeed very important. Such differences, in
turn, determined the nature of production and of demographic transformations. They also influenced a moral economy whereby economic
forces created seemingly conflicting sets of resistance/subjugation, vic-
tims/exploiters, and victims/protectors, and the resulting myriad jux-
tapositions, ambiguities, and contradictions that became the colonial
reality. Mizque's societal construct was tripartite, the unexpected third
element of which was the African presence. Although Africans were
not a majority by any means, their relatively smaller numbers belie
their importance in the region's economic, political, and sociocultural
structures.

Thus, in Mizque there existed an intersection and cross-fertilization
of values, mores, and other sociocultural measurements that were present and identifiable in the workplace, in the legal processes and the
courts of law, in the church, and in private lives. This phenomenon
directly and indirectly influenced interrelations and identity in terms
of race, ethnicity, and class. It was a combination of forces that in turn
interfaced with deeply conflicting notions of territoriality and power.
The results manifested themselves in a colonial world in which, in order
to survive—and many did not—people reclaimed or reinvented themselves and prevailing institutions.

The Spaniards' political-economic project encountered resistance at
many levels. First, there were the aggressive lowland ethnic warriors
who could retreat into tropical lowland, Amazonian forests at will,
only to reemerge when least expected. Some of them mixed with other

ethnic and non-ethnic groups or were captured. Voluntarily or involuntarily, some—such as the Chané, Chiriguano, and Yuracaré—ended
up working on the local chácaras. But even this they did on their own
terms. Further, local curacas employed methods of resistance to imperial orders, particularly in the earlier years of colonial rule. If one
were to believe the curacas' adversaries, the royal tax collectors, the
curacas hid Indians to keep them from being recorded in the repartimiento padrones for tribute collection. On the other hand, the curacas complained vociferously about abuse their charges suffered in
the coca fields due to the relentless demands of the tax collectors. The
curacas also went to jail when they would not or could not bleed the
Indians of unattainable tax extractions.

Nor did the Europeans anticipate the Andean proclivity for mobility and migrations, a cultural tradition that harkened back to pre-
Inca times. The Spaniards called it "flight," and their draconian efforts
could not stem the flow. Indians left their European-imposed reducciones and repartimientos, opting to work on the Spanish chácaras,
haciendas, and estancias. They also left these Spanish production units
at will and in droves in order to move on to other units or return to
their ayllus. The endless rounds of padrones did not, could not stop
this wide-scale tradition of movement, but they do serve to reveal in
dramatic fashion how deeply ingrained this phenomenon had become
in the eastern Andes. There was always somewhere else to go, since
labor was always in demand. Further, the indigenous labor force on
the haciendas, chácaras, viñas, and estancias quickly became one of
multiple ethnicities, combined ethnicities, and non-ethnicities, hailing
from every corner of the Andean world and far, far beyond, mixing un-
abatedly with one another, while often still recognizing their original
ayllus and ethnicities.

Further, the Spaniards could not foresee the devastating toll Old
World disease would take upon the pathogenically vulnerable New
World populations. Their numbers dropped as drastically as the demand for their labor grew exponentially, itself a part of the relentless economic cycle driven by a growing local, regional, and highland
market demand for Mizque's many temperate and lowland products.
Confronted with an increasingly elusive indigenous labor pool and a

growing market demand, as it did throughout all of its New World colonies, Spain again looked to Africa. The purpose was not only to replace the shrinking native labor force but also to supplement it with additional skills that Africans either already possessed or could readily acquire.

Thus Spain endorsed yet another pattern in the African diaspora to the colonies. This system of human extraction wrenched thousands of victims from their west African and central African ethnic groups and transported them across the Atlantic to the port of Buenos Aires. From the port city, slave traders arranged to have their slave quotas transferred to points throughout Spanish South America, including Potosí, each stop along the way augmenting the sale price of the slave. Potosí was not the final destination for many of the African slaves, however. A good number survived the harsh overland trek and found still one more leg of the journey waiting for them—down into the eastern subpuna valleys and lowlands—increasing still again their value as a purchasable commodity. By the time African slaves were brought into Mizque, they were priced anywhere from two to five times their arrival value at Buenos Aires. They were not inexpensive sources of labor, as the slave owners themselves repeatedly testified, but they were necessary if local agricultural entrepreneurs wished to remain successful.

In the process, early on and against their will, African slaves became Mizque's third population component or root. This would have a far-reaching impact on the regional socio-economic-political systems and demographic configurations. African slaves worked in the agricultural sector—primarily in the key industries of viticulture, sugar production, and livestock, often as highly skilled labor. They were not confined to domestic service, as popular wisdom holds. African slaves were not used in coca production. They worked in the service sector as highly mobile, widely traveled recua drivers and as town criers. As runaways they no doubt adjusted to whatever job was available, with few questions asked by potential bosses. Runaway slaves—particularly skilled ones—were relentlessly pursued by their owners, even if the search continued for years. Often it was a matter of ownership priorities, with the targeted slave placed in depósito. However, slaves involved in ownership litigations could and did remain elusive, which in turn involved further costly, time-consuming pursuit. Alleged owners consistently justified their unremitting searches, declaring the slave had cost a lot of money and usually, as in wine production, had also cost the owner a lot in terms of time and energy to train the slave to become the now-skilled professional, urgently needed in production activities.

The issue of skilled labor as opposed to less-skilled labor raises its own set of contradictions in terms of measurable slave treatment and economic value of the slave. In Mizque, expensive, highly skilled runaway slaves ostensibly were not punished with the same rigor as the less-costly slaves. The valuable slave was usually placed in depósito or was allowed to stay with the more recently acquired "owner" until the case was resolved and restitution attended to. Then the slave supposedly was returned to the original owner. Even if the slave had been gone for several years, had married and resided in Mizque for a while, or even was unaccountable for a time, it simply would not make sense (in the thinking of the day) that an owner would wish to break or maim such an expensive and necessary investment. The case of the slave owner who filed a lawsuit against his mayordomo for negligence that resulted in his prized winery slave's sudden illness and ultimate death further underscores the point. Whether some other kind of psychological punishment was inflicted cannot be ascertained. Certainly, strong-willed, determined, abused slaves—especially women in domestic service—did seek and sometimes achieved release from abusive owners.

Yet the other side of the equation, the slaves who were more likely to be physically punished and abused, requires explanation. The ugly, punishing restraining devices listed in the inventories of production units that enslaved larger numbers of Africans and their descendants speak for themselves. So do the many bills of sale, whose descriptions accomplished three goals. First, there was the bill that served essentially as a disclaimer. It stated that the slave for sale suffered from illnesses, was a drunk, a liar, and a thief, an intractable runaway, and other negative descriptions. The purpose was to protect the seller and forewarn the buyer, to prevent lawsuits. And there were many lawsuits concerning slaves sold under false pretenses—who were incapacitated and near death, if not already dead—their buyers demanding their money back.

Second, this kind of disclaimer could easily cover for deliberate abuse inflicted by an owner now eager to get rid of a less-than-productive worker. Abuse in the form of physical beatings, malnutrition, and untreated illness can still affect the human organism even after the bruises and other outward signs recede. Finally, there were the bills of sale that quite candidly referred to permanent disfigurements such as broken fingers, disabled arms, a broken foot, and the like, all of which suggest at the very least neglect and possibly deliberate maiming. Again, the courts heard many cases involving slave abuse.

In all fairness, another look at the Jesuits further extends the discussion on slave treatment and the inherent contradictions of this involuntary labor system. Conspicuous sets of human restraining devices notwithstanding, documents drawn up at the time of Jesuit expulsion from their Mizque holdings inform the issue. Mizque authorities cautioned that the hundreds of slaves formerly owned by the Jesuits be well taken care of—that is, well treated, well fed, well clothed. This urging was reinforced with the reminder, "just as the Jesuits had done." In the eastern Andes, as elsewhere in the Spanish colonies, the Jesuits appeared to have treated their slaves nominally well, considering the social aberration and violation that New World slavery represented. However, two issues call for some consideration. First, the Jesuits were, among other things, astute, practical entrepreneurs—no doubt too good in their profitable agrobusiness, in the eyes of Charles III of Bourbon Spain—and harsh, abusive treatment of costly labor was not congruent with the Jesuit vision. This thinking possibly found further support in the Bourbon reform agenda, which the Mizque officials, wittingly or not, may have embraced. One of the many reform mandates called for better treatment for the shrinking pool of African slaves in the colonies. This was not humanitarian; it was merely pragmatic. The Mizque document urging that care be taken of slaves was in my opinion an anomaly and the only one of its kind that I have come across in the Mizque collection. The colonial reality placed labor—and particularly unskilled agricultural labor—close to the bottom of its ethnically, racially, and economically diverse hierarchy.

Harsh treatment and abuse were not limited to African slaves, as the hundreds of padrones de chacara testify. The response of one chacarero accused of neglecting the basic needs of his yanaconas—namely, that as far as he was concerned his yanacona could "die and go to the devil"— surely represented more than a few chacara and hacienda owners, as supported by dozens of litigations and petitions on the yanaconas' behalf. For every royal degree ordering better treatment of the yanaconas in general and of the coca workers in particular, we have repeated citations of labor/Indian abuse throughout almost the entire colonial period. However, the Indian population had its advocate in the traditional curaca or state-appointed protector or defender. That these two figures could not always be relied upon to side with the people for whom they were responsible is one of the countless contradictions that define the colonial world. However, they could and did speak out in defense of the indigenous cause when possible, or if they so desired.

The African slave had no such recourse. The telling (in more ways than one) example was the case of the Spanish employer who abused his Indian apprentice. The young apprentice claimed his employer had put him in shackles and hoisted him up to a ceiling beam and left him hanging (in front of witnesses), treating him "like a negro" (negro was synonymous with slave). Authorities quickly intervened, apprehended and incarcerated the perpetrator, who upon his eventual release was also fined, the money destined for the mistreated apprentice. It is doubtful that any action was taken when a black slave was treated in like manner. Only if the slave were willing to undergo a draconian effort and appeal formally to the court system might he or she find succor from abusive masters or mistresses.

However, there were many other opportunities to escape, flee, remove oneself, or otherwise resist a harsh or undesirable workplace situation. The characteristically Andean concept of flight played a key role in indigenous resistance, assertion, and agency, as the padrones so glaringly reveal, and African slaves followed suit. The eastern Andes served runaways well, as the evidence on cimarrones (group and individual), popular wisdom on the origins of Valle Grande, and the placement on some maps of the nearby township of Los Negros signify. Further, the people of African origins present today in the lowlands that were once part of the extensive colonial corregimiento certainly supports the discussion. The geographic settings and the dearth of willing, able-bodied labor worked in favor of the individuals, slave and free, who sought other options. The census takers tried desperately to keep up with this highly mobile, ever-growing, increasingly mixed population sector, but their efforts were largely unsuccessful. Some scholars have referred to the Andean "floating population." My work recognizes this but also closely supports a correlation posited by other scholars, who refer to a "hidden" population that Mizque officials simply could not keep under control, let alone maintain an accounting of. This could explain the puzzling absence of the term *forastero* in the Mizque padrones as well as a consistent acknowledgment of and referral to outsiders working on the chacaras by their place of birth. Those who for special reasons resisted being recorded on the chacara padrones were given permission by the authorities to be listed in the forastero padrón in town. Obviously, they had to be listed *somewhere*.

All of the Andean scholarship cited in this work involves excellent research and analysis of the indigenous populations, ethnic and non-ethnic. Analysis of the Corregimiento de Mizque adds still another important dimension to Andean history and historiography, as it addresses the issue of an African presence in the region as well as the reverberating impact of that presence on eastern Andean demography. In this context my project addresses a nuanced and controversial aspect of what is arguably an extreme form of resistance to intolerable or unacceptable conditions in the workplace and elsewhere. This resistance—conscious or unconscious—was the result of Spanish invasion and conquest and the consequent, inevitable mixing of the indigenous population with Europeans and Africans. The offspring of the mixed indigenous, European, and African unions by law assumed the legal status of the mother, and this provided an escape valve for African slaves and their slave descendants. Primarily, the union between a male slave and a female non-slave—in the Mizque documents almost always an Indian, but sometimes a mulata or a negra—produced a free mixed offspring, *immediately* labeled by the census takers and other officials as *mulato, pardo, negro* (early on synonymous with slave, later a very ambiguous, intentionally discriminating label), *zambo, or moreno.*

The labeling of indigenous and mixed populations played a crucial role in the mind-set of the colonial administration. It served as a means of tribute control—possibly one of the few quasi-viable measures apart from the fear tactics of threats and harsh treatment—that could offer some idea of the whereabouts of the working classes as well as how much tribute payment they or their land-owning bosses or mayordomos were responsible for. However, with the growing numbers of African slaves introduced into the corregimiento and the subsequent mushrooming mixed population, labeling (and nomenclature in general) took on some curious characteristics. Why for example, was there a need for a special padrón for chácara (or hacienda, estancia, or viña) mulatos? Perhaps they preferred to be on a mulato padrón and pay their own 2-peso annual tribute as a matter of status or possibly relative independence. This, of course, would save the chacarero money, especially if he or she had many mulato yanaconas. Conversely, perhaps other mulatos preferred not to be on that padrón and remained instead on the regular padrón, whereby the chacarero would have to pay the tribute for them. Even more perplexing, despite the fact that I came across other references to the mulato padrones and people expressing their desire to have their names on these records, only one mulato padrón appeared out of the hundreds of documents I examined. I was not able to locate the others.

Moreover, the Spanish colonial insistence upon labeling calls for further examination here, particularly in the context of the African and African-descended population, since the labels unequivocally confer race. First, throughout all of the padrones I studied, mulatos were clearly identified as the progeny of African (or person of African origins) and *Indian*, not white, as is commonly assumed in the scholarship. The same appears to apply to the label of *zambo* and possibly *pardo*, although this latter is less clear. There *sometimes* is a hint of status when a pardo is mentioned—caballeros pardos, soldados pardos—suggesting possible European genes or associated economic class symbols. The only other term in the racial ascriptions mentioned, *moreno*, was used in just one case. Then there is the already-discussed inconsistent use of the term *negro*, which became ambiguous over time from defining legal status (slave) to suggesting pejorative connotations in terms of color, social status, and the like.

This brings up the issue of who assigned these labels in the first place.

This is not an idle question. I found an astounding inconsistency in the ascribing of names and labels throughout the documents, including the same people in families on the same chácaras from one year to the next. Children in one yanacona family with the same mother and father were identified as a mulato and a negro. On another chácara a yanacona was considered a negra one year and a mulata the next. To make matters even more confusing for the investigator, because it occurred later rather than earlier in the time period under discussion, one man was recorded as a negro one year, while the following year or so the census takers identified him as negro esclavo. This kind of inconsistency could easily be attributed to the census takers and their retinue of lesser officials, all of whom were often replaced. The consistency lay in the very use of these particular racially construed designations and identifications. This takes on an almost caricature nature when we consider the combined use of the diminutive, which can certainly indicate affection and or youth but can easily slide into infantilization or at least a lessening of status when applied to adults, particularly when used on racial labels. Further, reducing town criers to the label of mozón has a negative, demeaning edge to it.

The fact remains that in the documents the indigenous population was always referred to as indio or india (and only once in my investigations with a diminutive attached to a given name), but not so the people of African origins. No matter how they mixed with other groups, in the eastern Andes as elsewhere throughout the Spanish colonies, in the legal system, including the courts, there was no escape from a system of nomenclature and ascriptive labeling that bound them unremittingly to their African origins and thus racial construct.

Thus, the above discussion moves well beyond caricature and into a less-than-covert discrimination based on race, and to some degree on class. The ecclesiastic court case charging Gerónimo mulato and Clara morena for concubinage further informs the discourse. It was only after more than a year of this lengthy litigation that Gerónimo was identified for the first time as mulato. The issue of how many doors were in his house and that he was a professional farrier were referred to from the onset, indicating to me a focus on class as well as race. The vicar and his clerics found far more qualifiers with which to label Clara. She was recorded as Clara morena from the onset of the trial and was also accused of concubinage. It was also noted early on that she had a house with no doors (aha!). Somewhere near midway through the litigations, her "confession" appeared. When interrogated about her name, she responded that her name was Clara López. Thereafter, court officials ascribed her every possible label to unequivocally confer or confirm her race. For the remainder of the trial, she was repeatedly referred to as la morena Clara López, Clara López negra, or Clara López mulata.

The case of cattle rancher Altamirano Gutiérrez mulato versus the Paniagua mayordomo also resonates with issues of race and class. At first glance it would appear that justice was fairly served. Upon closer scrutiny, the mulato rancher was awarded less (monetary) justice than the Paniagua mayordomo. Witnesses' statements underscore the issue. No one takes on anything Paniagua! This was clear from the outset in terms of Paniagua territoriality. The mine litigation furthers the discussion in several ways. First, it actually involved the three races—a white Spaniard, a mulato, and an Indian. Significantly, the Indian miner (now deceased; hence the question of mine proprietorship) was also an indigenous alcalde. This post conferred at least moderate status within the indigenous community, yet while he was referred to by his wife and peers as Blas, the court officials consistently referred to this adult as Blasquillo or Blasillo. Upon Blas's death the mulato had as much right to ownership of the choice vein as did the Spaniard, yet the Spaniard, who enjoyed the friendship of local prominent vecinos and key town officials (all of them Spaniards), obviously had an advantage. Again, justice weighed just enough more on the side of the Spaniard to be noticeable.

And finally there was the alférez Leiva, mulato alcalde. The post of alférez was a purchased one, that of alcalde elective, and each garnered respect. Together they must have symbolized considerable status, not to mention income and class. Yet the inescapable label defining race had to be assigned. To further complicate the interrelated issues of race, class, and encoded discrimination, the case of Hernando Martín mulato, accused of murdering Cristoval indio, reinforces the discussion. In attempting a cover-up, Hernando lied to his wife that a negro had killed the victim. This to me reflects that, in the matter of race, blackness and discrimination were so institutionalized and were such an integral part of the colonial reality that stereotyping became an acceptable leverage within the African-related population as well. While the word *racismo* (racism) was not a part of the colonial administrative lexicon, its functional equivalent was present.

Another colonial concept present from the European conquest on was the threefold notion of territoriality, boundaries, and frontiers. While the idea of territory existed among the pre-Columbian indigenous groups, that of frontiers did not. As soon as the colonial state launched its modus operandi, boundaries and frontiers became key issues within the imperial political economy. The creation of the Corregimiento de Mizque and its widely cast eastern "frontiers," established by the Europeans to fend off the lowland warriors, became part of the larger plan. These imperial demarcations were occasionally reconfigured somewhat in accordance with ecclesiastic or political dispositions at the time, but for the most part the corregimiento remained intact until the advent of the Bourbon reforms in Spain. The resultant January 1782 royal decree essentially dismantled the entire Corregimiento de Mizque and redefined it as a subordinate district of Cochabamba. Thus Mizque's decline can be explained within the same construct of shifting territoriality. Cochabamba had been recently incorporated into the territorial configuration of Santa Cruz. The intendancy of Santa Cruz was under the authority of the recently arrived Spanish intendant (a visionary in the eyes of some scholars) Francisco de Viedma.

The above sequence of events, in my view, is not the least bit coincidental. In the process, Mizque, already depopulated, weak, and vulnerable, was dealt the death blow. Judging from his acclaimed spirit of enlightenment coupled with his respective agro-economic vision for the greater eastern Andean region, Viedma could easily have had some influence over the 1782 decree. It was obviously to Viedma's advantage to see his designated intendancy flourish. In the political philosophy of the era, he may have had little compunction in overseeing the dismantling of a once economically viable region.

Granted, disease, particularly malaria, had taken a devastating toll throughout much of the 1700s. This cannot be underestimated, but factors such as the above and others must also be considered. I hope we can finally put to rest the myths about Philip of Spain imposing a ban on wine production. The ban was never enforced. Also, I found no evidence in the Cochabamba Municipal Archives or in the National Archives in Sucre of anything related to the alleged burning of the Mizque vineyards. Instead, the primary and secondary sources all point to healthy production throughout most of the period under discussion. Again, the African presence, slave and free, underestimated and unrecognized even today, played an important role in the region's economic well-being and more. In fact, Viedma himself noted Mizque's robust level of exports in the last third of the eighteenth century, which certainly suggest a still functioning labor sector. Further, his own population figures more than support this. The perpetuation of these myths does a disservice to the historical reality and reinforces the regional political-economic fissures and imbalances still present today. Cochabamba and other reconfigured districts in the intendancy became the beneficiaries of coca and other production activities that first flourished in the vast old corregimiento that was once Mizque.

The demise of the Quioma mines remains something of an enigma. The dramatic drop in Potosí mining production, however, figured far more seriously in regional economies (such as that of Mizque) than any irregular production of a local mine. The slowdown in ore production, which led to a shrinking market in Potosí and possibly La Plata, coupled with the population shifts, had an impact on Mizque's economic decline.

The Corregimiento de Mizque could have sustained itself through these adverse conditions to regain its former energy and become a viable trade partner in the now-Bourbonized Andes. It would again have required aggressive planning, effort, and above all, political support. The historical record demonstrates that this could have been achieved. However, the power and wealth, and attendant political energies, like the territorial demarcations, had once more been reconfigured by the Europeans. The forces of change created new territorialities, new power structures, and new economic centers, built upon the drive and hard work of those Blacks, Indians, and Europeans who came before. Their efforts shall not be erased or forgotten.

Glossary

ají A widely used Andean chili.

albacea Executor of an estate.

alcabala Sales tax.

alcalde Mayor of a town or city. Presides over town council.

alcalde de la Santa Hermandad Magistrate or deputy in the rural constabulary. See Santa Hermandad.

alcalde ordinario (público) Magistrate. Two per town. Usually chosen by the regidor.

alférez Ensign, standard-bearer. Close to rank of lieutenant.

alférez real Herald, municipal standard-bearer, honorary. Twice the salary of the corregidor; filled in for other important posts.

alguacil Constable.

alguacil mayor Chief constable.

almud Half an acre using half a fanega of grain for sowing.

amo Master, proprietor, overseer, Lord, stepfather, head of household.

asiento District of the mines in South America. Location of a town. Also, seat.

audiencia A high territorial or regional court in the Spanish colonies. Also refers to the region under its jurisdiction.

ayllu Andean kin unit based on collective, reciprocal functions.

Bachiller Title of person having earned the B.A. degree. Confers status.

botija In the eastern Andes, an earthen container holding roughly four to five liters.

bozal New arrival from Africa. "Unseasoned."

cabildo Municipal government.

cacicazgo Andean indigenous polity or chiefdom.

cacique Spanish term for chieftain.

camayo Outsiders serving as permanent labor. Here, specifically in the coca fields of the eastern Andes.

carga Six bushels (same as costal).

casco Main unit of a hacienda complex; also held the living quarters.

cedula An order or decree. Here, associated with a royal decree.

censo Mortgage.

cepa Stalk of a vine. Here, specifically grape.

cesto　About twenty pounds.

chácara　Modest to small agricultural unit.

chacarero　Owner of a chácara.

chicha　Beverage made from fermented, pre-masticated corn.

chuc'cho　A chill (trembling); malaria.

cimarrón　Loosely, a stray or runaway. In the New World, became quickly associated with runaway black slaves and with roving, aggressive bands of runaways and free blacks.

ciudad　City or town. Like villa, it is not a precise term.

cobranzas　Collections of debts.

cofradía　Lay brotherhood.

corregidor　Governor of a corregimiento.

corregimiento　Colonial jurisdiction or province.

costal　Six bushels, equivalent to a carga.

criollo　New World–born slave, not to be confused with creole, a New World–born Spaniard.

curaca　Andean term for indigenous chieftain.

curador　Legal guardian of minors and orphans.

demanda　Demand. An assertive request for reparation. Not a supplication for help.

depósito　A state of custody or protection, not to be confused with incarceration or punitive action.

diezmo　10 percent tithes to state/church.

encomendero　Holder of an encomienda.

encomienda　A grant of Indians awarded to a Spaniard for tribute and labor extraction in return for religious indoctrination and protection.

entrada　Entry; in the colonial context, exploration, expedition.

fanega　1.6 bushels.

fanegada　The amount of land needed to sow a fanega of grain (1.6 bushels).

flete　Pack (usually mule) team for hire.

forastero　Indian who left his or her original ayllu or community and attached to a host community, with no landholding rights; outsider.

gobernación　An administrative province or district.

hacendado　Owner of a hacienda.

hacienda　Large agricultural estate often comprising several production units.

harriero (arriero)　Occupational role of mule-team driver.

herrero　Farrier, one who shoes horses. Also called herrador.

hijo natural　A child born out of wedlock. Natural child.

hijos rectos　Direct offspring.

horro　Former black slave now free.

hospital　Combination hospital, infirmary, and temporary asylum for the poor and the transient.

huido Runaway worker, slave or free. Also connotes an act of agency and volition.

ingenio Sugar refinery.

justicia mayor Deputy of a corregidor or gobernador.

ladino Hispanicized, Spanish-speaking person of indigenous or African origins.

libre A former black slave, now free.

limosna Alms.

llacta runas Temporary migrants with close ties to their ayllus.

maese de campo Field sergeant.

mayorazgo Entailed estate retained by family for several generations.

mayordomo Steward or custodian of a private estate or a civil property.

memorial A writ.

merced A royal grant of land.

mita Work rotations assigned to repartimiento Indians. Forced draft labor.

mitimaes Quechua term for laborer-colonizer sent to distant zones.

mitimak Relating to Inca labor system.

montaña Loosely, foothills.

mozo/moza A lad, a lass.

mozón A great big lad; a label for the town criers, who were usually of African origins.

mulato A person of African and (in the eastern Andes) indigenous parentage.

natural Native-born indigenous person.

natural de Originally from; place of origin.

negro Spanish term used in the early colonial eastern Andes to mean black slave. Later used more ambiguously.

novillos Young bulls.

oidor Audiencia judge.

padrón de chácara A region-wide census designed to keep track of yanacona tributaries attached to agricultural and livestock units and ensure that their tribute payments are current.

pardo A person of African-Indian or African-European parentage. May have some class overtones.

partido An administrative district within a corregimiento made up of several parishes.

penas de camera Judicial fines.

peon Indigenous day laborer.

peso Monetary unit, usually of silver, consisting of a peso corriente (8 reales) or a peso ensayado (12 reales).

peste/pestilencia Unidentified disease or epidemic.

piezas (pieças) de esclavos Pieces or units of African slaves, each unit equivalent to one able-bodied worker.

poder Power of attorney.

pregón Public announcement made by a town crier, usually of African origins.

pregonero Town crier, usually of African origins. Often referred to in Spanish as *mozón*.

protector Legal defender, usually for the Indians.

pueblo A town where Indians were congregated for administrative and indoctrination purposes.

Quechua Official language of the Inca.

quero Ceremonial drinking vessel for chicha.

ranchería Where the yanaconas or slaves who were attached to an agricultural unit lived.

recua A pack team, usually made up of mules and driven on occasion by black slaves, but often by mulatos.

reducción Forced resettlement of dispersed Indian groups into one administrative unit in order to control, indoctrinate, and extract tribute.

regidor Municipal councilor.

repartimiento An allocation of a large indigenous unit led by a curaca (cacique) to provide tribute and/or labor to an encomendero or the crown.

rescate Term used in the eastern Andes for captive ethnic Indians sold into slavery by warring enemy tribes.

Santa Hermandad Rural constabulary, primarily for searching for and apprehending runaway slaves.

sisa Local excise tax on marketable goods.

soltero Single, unmarried person.

tasa Tax rate assigned each tributary or collection of tributaries.

tinaja Large containers holding approximately 26.7 botijas or 133.5 liters.

tutor Legal guardian of minor children and their estate.

vaquero Cowboy.

vasijas Large casks or containers for wine.

vecino Citizen and resident of a municipality.

venedizos (advenedizos) Outsider, newcomer residents, purportedly free to come and go at will.

villa Loosely akin to a township.

visita An official inspection or review, usually unexpected or unscheduled.

yanacona A pre-Inca institution of personal servitude altered by the Spaniards to indicate an indigenous servant or laborer attached to a unit of production and bound to its Spanish owner.

yungas Hot, lowland coca-producing zones of the eastern Andes. Also refers to the ethnic peoples of these regions.

zambo A persion of mixed African-Indian parentage. Also spelled çambo.

Notes

Abbreviations

AHMC-MEC   Archivo Histórico Municipal de Cochabamba, Colección de Mizque, Expedientes Coloniales (34 vols.)

AHMC-MP   Archivo Histórico Municipal de Cochabamba, Colección de Mizque, Protocolos Notariales (90 vols.)

ANB-AUDCH/CORR   Archivo Nacional de Bolivia–Audiencia de Charcas, Correspondencia

ANB-CR   Archivo Nacional de Bolivia–Catálogo Ruck

ANB-EP   Archivo Nacional de Bolivia–Escrituras Públicas

ANB-ESCHAR   Archivo Nacional de Bolivia–Escrituras de Charcas

ANB-EXP   Archivo Nacional de Bolivia–Expedientes

ANB-JMC   Archivo Nacional de Bolivia–Colección Jesuitas, Mojos y Chiquitos

ANB-M   Archivo Nacional de Bolivia–Mizque

ANB-MINAS   Archivo Nacional de Bolivia–Reales Cédulas, Cartas y Expedientes de Minas

ANB-RC   Archivo Nacional de Bolivia–Reales Cédulas

ANB-TI   Archivo Nacional de Bolivia–Tierras y Indios

CAJAS   Caja Reales de Potosí

MV-AGI   Mauricio Valcanover, Archivo General de las Indias, Sevilla

Introduction

1. TePaske, "Search for El Dorado Redux."
2. Stern, "Paradigms of Conquest."
3. Saignes, *Los Andes orientales*. See also Trouillot, *Silencing the Past*.
4. AHMC-MP, Vols. 1561–1590, 1597–1607, exp. 11.
5. See, e.g., Barnadas's pathbreaking *Charcas: Origines históricas de una sociedad colonial, 1535–1565*. Similarly, his meticulously compiled *Manual de bibliografía: Introducción a los estudios bolivianos contemporaneos, 1960–1984* remains an indispensable tool for the investigator, as is the later effort

compiled by Arze, Barragán, and Medinaceli, "Un panorama de las investigaciones históricas, 1970–1992." See also Larson's *Colonialism and Agrarian Transformation in Bolivia*, another pioneering work in which the investigator is urged to look to the still-unexplored eastern valleys for answers concerning landholding systems and labor conditions, particularly for the sixteenth century, and her "Bolivia Revisited."

6. Gordillo Claure, *El origen de la hacienda en el Valle Bajo*; Gordillo Claure, "Aportes al estudio"; Gordillo Claure, "El proceso de extinción del yanaconaje"; Gordillo Claure and del Río, *La revista de Tiquipaya (1573)*; Terrazas et al., "Epidemias históricas en Capinota," 61–85; and Rojas Vaca and Montaño, "Haciendas de Campero," 19–34. Nor would any study be complete without reference to the following works, which, because of limitations of space, are merely representative of a much larger body of contributions now available: Andrien, *Crisis and Decline*; Sempat Assadourian, *El sistema de la economía colonial*; L. G. Brockington, "Mizque: Indians and Region," "Mojos Region," "Oriente Region," "Santa Cruz: City and Region," "Tarija: City and Region," and "Yungas"; Escobari de Querejazu, *Producción y comercio*; Finot, *Historia de la conquista*; Glave and Remy, *Estructura agraria*; Harris, Larson, and Tandeter, *La participación indigena*; O'Phelan Godoy, *Un siglo de rebeliones anticoloniales*; López Beltrán, *Estructura económica*; Pease, "Una visita al obispado de Charcas 1590"; Platt, "Acerca del sistema tributario" and *Estado boliviano y ayllu andino*; Sánchez-Albornoz, *Indios y tributos* and "Mita, migraciones y pueblos"; Tandeter and Wachter, *Precios y producción agraria*; TePaske and Klein, *Royal Treasuries*, vol. 2, *Upper Peru (Bolivia)*; and Wachtel, "The Mitimas of the Cochabamba Valley."

7. Rodríguez Ostria, "Mercado interior" and *Poder central y projecto regional*.

8. The local monographs referred to include Barragán Romano, "En torno al modelo communal mercantile" and "Ayllus y haciendas en los valles orientales de Bolivia" (in a personal communication of October 2002, Barragán Romano gave me permission to cite her work); Deheza, Clavijo, and Querejazu, *Monografía de la provincia de Mizque* (see in particular chapter 4, "Breve esbozo histórico," part 2, Período Colonial, 83–119); and Rojas Vaca and Montaño, "Haciendas de Campero." More recent and welcome contributions are Presta, *Encomienda*; Meruvia Balderrama, *Historia de la coca*; and Rojas Vaca, *Población y territorio*.

9. See L. G. Brockington, "Los archivos de Mizque."

10. L. G. Brockington, "Los archivos de Mizque."

11. Burns, "Notaries, Truth, and Consequences."

1. The Landscape and Its People

1. Klein, *Bolivia*, 6–8.

2. Métraux, "Tribes," 465–67. This work also covers standard information

on the cultures (social structures, belief systems, agricultural practices) of the eastern Andean peoples. Also see Saignes, *Los Andes orientales*, ix–xvii, 36–41, 51.

3. Saignes, *Los Andes orientales*, 28.

4. Pereira Herrera et al., *Conchupata*, 37–41; and D. L. Brockington et al., *Estudios arqueológicos*, 17, 159–61.

5. Schramm, "Fronteras y territorialidad," 15–20, 24–25; and Saignes, *Los Andes orientales*, 31, 81. See chapters 5–7 of this work.

6. Saignes, *Los Andes orientales*, 16–20.

7. Saignes, *Los Andes orientales*, 6, 18, 19; and Schramm, "Fronteras y territorialidad," 7, 16. The complicated concept of "flight" will receive further attention in later chapters.

8. Saignes, *Los Andes orientales*, 6, 18, 19; Schramm, "Mosaicos," 33; González, "Visita de los Yndios," 2–3, 12; and Rojas Vaca, *Población y territorio*, 23–28, 71, 84. See also Julien, *Reading Inca History*, 4, 3–22.

9. Julien, *Reading Inca History*, 7; Saignes, *Los Andes orientales*, 27; and Métraux, "Tribes," 466–67.

10. Lockhart, *Spanish Peru*, 3–10.

11. Barnadas, *Charcas*, 32–33.

12. Barnadas, *Charcas*, 56–57.

13. Barnadas, *Charcas*, 61–65.

14. Barnadas, *Charcas*, 33–35. Barnadas notes that a number of contemporary chroniclers as well as modern scholars place the location of the siege in the Cochabamba region, but he is inclined to think it took place in the highlands.

15. Barnadas, *Charcas*, 34, 37–38, 41. The author points out that Chuquisaca (La Plata) was established at the site of a Charcas Indian village called Chukichaka, meaning bridge of silver. Also see Saignes, *Los Andes orientales*, 74; and Lockhart, *Spanish Peru*, 4.

16. Saignes, *Los Andes orientales*, 41, 45–48.

17. Saignes, *Los Andes orientales*, 56–57.

18. Saignes, *Los Andes orientales*, 62–64.

19. Saignes, *Los Andes orientales*, 62–64. Although not mentioned by the author, disease surely wrought its own havoc against the interlopers, as did the other physical hazards cited. Also, and quite significantly, Saignes, like Barnadas earlier, draws upon another idiom to explain the push eastward, using the term "westerns." Barnadas, *Charcas*, 49, 471, discussing the pacification and settlement of the region, refers to the North American push west and uses terms such as "destino manifesto" and the "frontier's way of life" to make his point. For a thorough description and analysis of internal rivalries and conflicts, see Barnadas, *Charcas*, 73ff.

20. Saignes, *Los Andes orientales*, 62–64.

21. Saignes, *Los Andes orientales*, 65–68, 85.

22. Schramm, "Mosaicos," 2–3.

23. Lockhart, *Spanish Peru*, 4–5, 8, 16; Barnadas, *Charcas*, 32–33, 46.

24. Lockhart, *Spanish Peru*, 16, 45. Here Lockhart offers the patriarch of the Paniagua de Loaysa clan, Pedro Hernández Paniagua, as an example of how good connections paved the way for a very generous encomienda. For an excellent, detailed analysis of how the system really worked see Presta, *Encomienda*.

25. See Barnadas, *Charcas*; Finot, *Historia de la conquista*; and my synthesis of Chávez's achievements in "Oriente Region" and "Santa Cruz: City and Region."

26. MV-AGI, Patronato 121, Alonzo de Chaves, fs. 1–504. Padre Mauricio Valcanover generously shared with me these family testimonies from the Archivo General de las Indias, which he was permitted to transcribe onto disk while in Sevilla. He is currently officiating in Tarata, Bolivia, and is also working on the history of the Franciscan order in South America.

27. MV-AGI, Patronato 121, and Patronato 138, Albaro de Chaves, fs. 1–67v.

28. MV-AGI, Patronato 138, Albaro de Chaves, fs. 1–67v.

29. Barnadas, *Charcas*, 323 n. 403.

30. MV-AGI, Patronato 138, Albaro de Chaves, 1–67v.

31. MV-AGI, Patronato 138, Albaro de Chaves, 1–67v, and Titulo de Corregidor a don Albaro de Chavez, 2 fs.

32. MV-AGI, Patronato 131, Caçorla, fs. 1–64v. This group of documents refers to the subject as Fernando de Caçorla Narvaez, or more simply, Fernando de Caçorla. Other documents use the alternative spelling of Hernando. This can lead to some confusion when Fernando describes the accomplishments of his son ("hijo legitimo"), also named Fernando. Fortunately, the son is often referred to as Fernando Narvaez, but one does have to be particularly careful when reading through family legacies and testimonies not to confuse sons with their fathers.

33. MV-AGI, Patronato 131, Caçorla, fs. 1–64v. For a detailed assessment and analysis of the "rebellion de Gonzalo Pizarro," see Barnadas, *Charcas*, 87–110.

34. MV-AGI, Patronato 131, Caçorla, fs. 1–64v.

35. MV-AGI, Patronato 131, Caçorla, fs. 1–64v. See also Barnadas, *Charcas*, 608, for reference to Caçorla's position as mayor of Cochabamba (formerly Oropesa). In his petitions to the crown, Caçorla used the term *Oropesa*. Also see Larson, *Colonialism*, 89–91, for a thorough assessment of Cochabamba's place in the larger market economy.

36. MV-AGI, Patronato 131, Caçorla, fs. 1–64v. The audencia repeated its recommendation on January 23, 1589, yet the first two pages of Patronato 131, fs. 1–1v, dated 1590, are merely a reiteration of all the earlier petitions

submitted by Caçorla, suggesting that authorities in Spain had not yet granted his request.

37. MV-AGI, Patronato 131, Caçorla, fs. 1–64v.

38. MV-AGI, Patronato 131, Caçorla, fs. 1–64v. See also Mujía, *Bolivia-Paraguy*, 2:406–71.

39. Barnadas, *Charcas*, 470–71.

40. MV-AGI, Patronato 131, Caçorla, fs. 1–64v.

41. MV-AGI, Patronato 131, Caçorla, fs. 1–64v; AHMC-MP, Vol. 1592, fs. 582v–85; and MV-AGI, Charcas 43, Caçorla sindico, fs. 1058–59.

42. Scholars of the region's history concur that the Paniagua family was extremely influential and have cited it as such in the literature. MV-AGI, Patronato 146, Antonio, fs. 123v–224. On the Comunero revolt see Herr, *Historical Essay*, 42.

43. MV-AGI, Patronato 146, Antonio, fs. 123v–224, and Patronato 144, Gabriel Moço, fs. 1–103v; see also Lockhart, *Spanish Peru*, 45. For an excellent account of the Paniagua clan's enterprises and affiliations see Presta, *Encomienda*, 95–138.

44. MV-AGI, Patronato 146, Antonio, fs. 123v–224.

45. MV-AGI, Patronato 144, Gabriel 2, fs. 1–103v. See also Lockhart, *Spanish Peru*, 6, and Barnadas, *Charcas*, 118–23.

46. MV-AGI, Patronato 144, Gabriel 2, fs. 1–103v, and Gabriel 4, fs. 1–171. For a helpful geneology of the Paniagua clan, see Presta, *Encomienda*, 145, fig. 4.5.

47. MV-AGI, Patronato 144, Gabriel 2, fs. 1–103v, and Gabriel 4, fs. 1–171.

48. MV-AGI, Patronato 144, Gabriel 2, fs. 1–103v.

49. MV-AGI, Patronato 144, Gabriel 4, fs. 1–171.

50. MV-AGI, Patronato 144, Gabriel 2, fs. 1–103v.

51. MV-AGI, Patronato 144, Gabriel 2, fs. 1–103v.

52. MV-AGI, Patronato 144, Gabriel 4, fs. 1–171. All of the petitions and testimonials used in this study come laden with self-serving laudatory language coupled with intense supplication. Further, the witnesses' testimonies are identical and of course unanimously in favor of the petitioner. Nevertheless, the data are supported by sufficient references and cross-references and official documents indicating rewards in the form of knighthood, government posts, encomiendas, land grants, special military or civic titles, perpetual salaries, and the like to fully support the submitted requests for further recognition. In this particular instance, grandsons Antonio and Gabriel junior provided copies of the Porco mining contracts signed by their grandfather Antonio Álvarez Meléndez and Gonzalo Pizarro.

53. MV-AGI, Patronato 144, Gabriel 4, fs. 1–171.

54. MV-AGI, Patronato 144, Gabriel 2, fs. 1–103v.

55. MV-AGI, Patronato 144, Gabriel 2, fs. 1–103v.

56. MV-AGI, Patronato 144, Gabriel 4, fs. 1–171.

57. MV-AGI, Patronato 144, Gabriel 4, fs. 1–171, and Patronato 146, Antonio, fs. 123v–224.

58. MV-AGI, Patronato 146, Antonio, fs. 123–224, Patronato 144, Gabriel 4, fs. 1–103v, and Gabriel 2, fs. 1–171.

59. MV-AGI, Patronato 146, Antonio, fs. 123v–224, and Patronato 144, Gabriel 4, fs. 1–171. For further detail on Paniagua wealth, see Presta, *Encomienda,* 114ff.

60. MV-AGI, Patronato 146, Antonio, fs. 123v–224, and Patronato 144, Gabriel 4, fs. 1–171. See also Lockhart, *Spanish Peru,* 229.

61. MV-AGI, Patronato 144, Gabriel 2, fs. 1–103v.

2. Re-creating a Region for a Colonial Market

1. Letter from the governor and cabildo of the Villa de Salinas del Río Pisuerga (Mizque) to the president of the audiencia of Charcas informing of its founding. September 20, 1603. ANB-AUDCH/CORR, Correspondencia no. 846. I chose to quote descriptions of indigenous response to the founding directly from this telling document because chapter 6 will treat in detail how, long before 1603, Indian groups were fiercely protesting European usurption of their lands. Apparently, this particular relinquishment of an indigenous holding must have been a sensitive issue because Álvaro repeatedly referred to acquiescence as the Indians "willingly" gave up two city blocks to the Franciscan monastery upon the latter's "fair" request, saying that it would not have transpired without their "consent" and that no one "expressed complaints."

2. ANB-AUDCH/CORR, Correspondencia no. 846. This letter, penned by Pedro de Lara, public and cabildo scribe, was signed by all of the newly appointed officials. During the early colonial period most official posts were elected, but over time they became open to purchase. The cost of the position usually reflected the economic potential of its district.

3. AHMC-MP, Vols. 1561–1590, 1597–1590; and Ramírez Valverde, "Visita a Pocona."

4. Mujía, *Bolivia-Paraguay,* 2:440.

5. Mujía, *Bolivia-Paraguay,* 1:348–52.

6. Mujía, *Bolivia-Paraguay,* 1:352–56.

7. Mujía, *Bolivia-Paraguay,* 1:356–60.

8. Mujía, *Bolivia-Paraguay,* 1:393.

9. Mujía, *Bolivia-Paraguay,* 1:377–84.

10. Mujía, *Bolivia-Paraguay,* 1:397.

11. For the political complexities accompanying administrative decisions on these expansion and boundary issues, see Barnadas, *Charcas,* 523–53. Andrien, *Crisis and Decline,* 17–20, stresses an early diversification in the Peruvian economy and refers to the numerous valley regions (including Cochabamba) possessing an economic "buoyancy."

12. Larson, *Colonialism*, 75–76.

13. Vásquez Machado, Mesa, and Gispert, *Manual de Historia de Bolivia*, 128.

14. See Murra's " 'El Archipelago vertical' Revisited" (3–5, 10–11), "Limits and Limitations of the 'Vertical Archipelago' in the Andes," and *The Economic Organization of the Inca State.*

15. MV-AGI, Patronato 144, Gabriel 4; see also Schramm, "Mosaicos," 35 nn. 18, 19.

16. AHMC-MP, Vol. 1597–1607, exp. 11. This detailed expediente on the Paniagua land dispute was tucked in with several consecutive years of early padrones de chacara. It spans almost fifty years and provides valuable information on agricultural production that will be presented in chapter 3.

17. Schramm, "Mosaicos," 22–23.

18. ANB-CR, 1604.III.2, nos. 890, 893, 898; ANB-CR, 1604.III.15, nos. 887, 888, 1606, no. 971; and Barnadas, *Charcas*, 470–72. In this author's words, "Mizque and its valleys, by the final quarter of the [sixteenth] century, was famous for its vineyards, wheatfields, and large herds of livestock" (*Charcas*, 351).

19. AHMC-MP, Vol. 1561–1590, exp. 2; and Ramírez Valverde, "Visita a Pocona."

20. AHMC-MP, Vol. 1561–1590, exp. 10, exp. 11, fs. 1046–47, and Vol. 1591–1598; ANB-CR, cartas, 1603, no. 845; and AHMC-MP, Vol. 1561–1590, exp. 11.

21. AHMC-MP, Vol. 1561–1590, exp. 20.

22. AHMC-MP, Vol. 1561–1590, exp. 20.

23. Sánchez-Albornoz, *Indios y tributos*, 30. See also Gade, *Nature and Culture*. I refer to this important work of historical geography a number of times in this book, particularly in chapter 7, which discusses disease and its impact at length.

24. Mujía, *Bolivia-Paraguay*, 2:699–700.

25. AHMC-MP, Vols. 1591–1598, 1599–1629, 1602, 1629–1676.

26. ANB-M, 1611, no. 6.

27. ANB-M, 1612, no. 4. These five pages of documents were badly torn and worn, with barely legible comments written in the margins. Considering the nature of the indictment on poor town management, my guess is that they were read by many of the people involved and were the subject of heated debate.

28. ANB-M, 1612, no. 4.

29. AHMC-MP, Vol. 38, leg. 1, fs. 1–84v. Unfortunately, some pages are missing, but they do not appear to have any bearing on the final result in the case involving "la" puente. Throughout the entire set of related documents, the feminine rather than the masculine article was used, suggesting perhaps an earlier custom. For example, the Spanish word for *sea* even today can have a masculine or feminine article.

30. AHMC-MP, Vol. 38, leg. 1, fs. 1–3v.
31. AHMC-MP, Vol. 38, leg. 1, f. 3v.
32. AHMC-MP, Vol. 38, leg. 1, fs. 4–4v, 5v.
33. AHMC-MP, Vol. 38, leg. 1, fs. 6v–7v.
34. AHMC-MP, Vol. 38, leg. 1, fs. 5v–6.
35. AHMC-MP, Vol. 38, leg. 1, fs. 7v, 8, and 4v.
36. AHMC-MP, Vol. 38, leg. 1, fs. 10–11v.
37. AHMC-MP, Vol. 38, leg. 1, fs. 10–11v.
38. AHMC-MP, Vol. 38, leg. 1, fs. 10–11v, 9–9v, 12v.
39. AHMC-MP, Vol. 38, leg. 1, fs. 12–13v. See also Gade, "Bridge Types in the Central Andes." According to Gade, collecting sisas to pay for bridge construction was common in the region during the colonial period.
40. AHMC-MP, Vol. 38, leg. 1, fs. 13v, 15–15v. The issue of political/territorial jurisdiction acquires additional significance in chapter 6's revisions of Viedma's 1782 population figures.
41. AHMC-MP, Vol. 38, leg. 1, fs. 15–16v.
42. AHMC-MP, Vol. 38, leg. 1, fs. 17–17v.
43. AHMC-MP, Vol. 38, leg. 1, fs. 18–18v.
44. AHMC-MP, Vol. 38, leg. 1, f. 18v.
45. AHMC-MP, Vol. 38, leg. 1, fs. 18v–20.
46. AHMC-MP, Vol. 38, leg. 1, fs. 21–23.
47. AHMC-MP, Vol. 38, leg. 1, fs. 24, 26v, 33.
48. AHMC-MP, Vol. 38, leg. 1, fs. 24–25.
49. AHMC-MP, Vol. 38, leg. 1, fs. 34, 31v, 33v, 37.
50. AHMC-MP, Vol. 38, leg. 1, fs. 38v–41.
51. AHMC-MP, Vol. 38, leg. 1, fs. 45–47v.
52. ANB-AUDCH/CORR, Correspondencia no. 845 (Carta de Fundación); AHMC-MP, Vol. 38, leg. 1, f. 42. See chapter 5 of this volume.
53. ANB-AUDCH/CORR, Correspondencia no. 845 (Carta de Fundación); AHMC-MP, Vol. 38, leg. 1, f. 42.
54. AHMC-MP, Vol. 38, leg. 1, fs. 48–49. See chapter 7 of this volume for details concerning Melo's entanglements with the law.
55. AHMC-MP, Vol. 38, leg. 1, fs. 48–49.
56. AHMC-MP, Vol. 38, leg. 1, fs. 49–50v.
57. AHMC-MP, Vol. 38, leg. 1, fs. 51v–52.
58. AHMC-MP, Vol. 38, leg. 1, fs. 52–52v.
59. AHMC-MP, Vol. 38, leg. 1, f. 53.
60. AHMC-MP, Vol. 38, leg. 1, fs. 53–54. People chosen by the cabildo to perform the tasks mentioned here were obligated to participate—it was *su obra de república* (their civic duty)—and one could not avoid it without a legitimate excuse. Failure to comply resulted in a fine. On the other hand, those selected were paid a salary for their services.

61. AHMC-MP, Vol. 38, leg. 1, fs. 55–83v.

62. Stern, "Paradigms of Conquest."

63. See, e.g., Arzans de Orsúa y Vela, *Historia de la villa imperial de Potosí,* 1:3, 8; Viedma, *Descripción geográfica*; and Viscarra, *Apuntes.* See also Bernardo de Torres, *Crónicas agustinianas del Perú,* XVII, cited in Deheza, Clavijo, and Querjazu, *Monografía,* 98–99.

3. Transforming the Land

1. AHMC-MP, Vols. 1591–1598, 1599–1629, 1602, 1629–1676; and Viscarra, *Apuntes,* 255.

2. ANB-JMC, fs. 195–280.

3. ANB-TI, 1607, EXP no. 18; and AHMC-MP, Vol. 38, 1629–1678, leg. 5. These documents were not paginated.

4. ANB-TI, 1607, EXP no. 18; and AHMC-MP, Vol. 38, 1629–1678, leg. 5. Also AHMC-MP, Vol. 1599–1629, Venta de Tierras, 1614. This volume of documents also was not paginated. The material I obtained came from eighty-one consecutive pages of documentation. For a more detailed definition of *censo,* see Presta, *Encomienda,* 261.

5. AHMC-MP, Vol. 1599–1629, Venta de Tierras, 1614. On the relation between livestock and vineyard activities, see Cushner, *Lords of the Land,* 71–73. Many of the Mizque vineyards were much larger than previously assumed. The average vineyard supported around 3,500 stalks per hectare (2.5 acres). La Calleja probably covered around 100 acres, while others ranged between 7 and 40 hectares. See Barragán Romano, "Ayllus y haciendas," 168–69.

6. AHMC-MP, Vol. 1599–1629, Venta de Tierras, 1614.

7. AHMC-MP, Vol. 1599–1629, Venta de Tierras, 1614. Unless indicated otherwise in the text, all pesos referred to are pesos corrientes.

8. AHMC-MP, Vol. 1599–1629, Venta de Tierras, 1614.

9. AHMC-MP, Vol. 1599–1629, Venta de Tierras, 1614; and AHMC-MP, Vol. 38, 1629–1678, leg. 5. By 1613, once operations were running order, Pérez's Omereque vineyard had produced 2,650 botijas of wine, which at 5 liters per botija amounted to 13,250 liters of wine. For further information on botijas and other wine container sizes and prices of wine, see Cushner, *Lords of the Land,* 125–27, 188; and Davies, *Landowners in Colonial Peru,* 63, 92–93, 223–24. While Cushner defines a botija as an earthen container holding 19 to 23 gallons and does not define *tinaja* (a much larger wine vessel) at all, Davies's far more conservative definition has a botija containing 8 liters and the larger tinaja containing 400 liters (or 50 botijas) each. Yet my 1610 Mizque data have a botija containing 4 to 5 liters and a tinaja holding 26.7 botijas (133.5 liters). These equivalents are radically lower than Cushner's and considerably lower than Davies's Peruvian prices and measures. I will stay with the ones I have for Mizque. Prices varied enormously from region to region depending on

a multitude of circumstances, as they did from one time period to another. In 1545 in Mizque, e.g., some wine was selling for 11 pesos a botija (AHMC-MP, Vol. 1591–1598, f. 1931). Also, for an excellent comparison on Mizque property values see Presta, *Encomienda*, 124–26. Presta discusses a similar (except apparently without livestock) multi-unit hacienda-chacara system belonging to the entrepreneurial genius Gabriel Paniagua de Loaysa, whose Pajiha hacienda was valued in 1583 at 34,500 pesos, considered then a good price.

10. AHMC-MP, Vol. 1561–1590, f. 1060ff.

11. AHMC-MP, Vol. 1561–1590, f. 1060ff. See also ANB-CR. By 1650, a similar hacienda system in Mizque rented for 3,000 pesos a year.

12. ANB-EXP, 1614, exp. 12, fs. 12–19v.

13. ANB-TI, 1610, no. 14, f. 1240; and AHMC-MP, Vol. 1591–1598, fs. 1937, 1938.

14. ANB-EXP, 1614, exp. 12, fs. 33–40.

15. ANB-M, 1611, no. 18; and ANB-TI, 1624, exp. 6. Also, on African slavery in Mizque, see my earlier preliminary study on the subject, "Trabajo, etnicidad y raza." Also, while the term *pieca* commonly refers to a single able-bodied male or a grouping of slaves equivalent to the labor value of one able-bodied male, *pieca* in the present context appears to refer to individual slaves, male and female.

16. AHMC-MP, Vol. 1629–1676, exp. 38, leg. 8. Significantly, in all the Mizque chacara/hacienda inventories examined in this study involving African slaves, the administrators consistently lumped the slaves together with the related agricultural equipment or household furnishings with which they were associated. Obviously, they were considered chattel.

17. AHMC-MP, Vol. 1629–1676, exp. 38, leg. 8.

18. AHMC-MP, Vol. 1605–1607, Cuentas de los menores de Encinas, fs. 3, 14v.

19. ANB-AUDCH/CORR, Correspondencia no. 845; AHMC-MP, Vol. 1605–1607, and Vol. 1605–1620, fs. 113 and 145.

20. AHMC-MP, Vol. 1605–1607, and Vol. 1605–1620, fs. 14v, 37, 125–27, 22, 133, 6v, 17.

21. AHMC-MP, Vol. 1605–1607, and Vol. 1605–1620, fs. 3–13, 37–37v; and ANB-M, Vol. 1611, no. 8, f. 14.

22. AHMC-MP, Vol. 1605–1607, and Vol. 1605–1620, fs. 34, 31, 29–29v, 32–32v, 133–33v. The categories of censos/debts, family wine production, and so forth are my own and were not organized as such in the documents. Further, my own tabulations of these thirty-one pages of accounts showed 25,102 pesos spent over the two-year (sometimes a bit more) period, some 220 pesos more than the administrators' calculations. However, I am satisfied with how close the two sets of figures are. For information pertaining to the ban on wine see Vásquez Machicado, *Catálogo descriptivo*, no. 651, 1634, 32. On the cor-

regidor who allegedly ordered the burning of Mizque vineyards, see Viscarra, *Apuntes*, 255.

23. AHMC-MP, Vol. 1605–1607, and Vol. 1605–1620, fs. 20, 21, 27, 19v, 31, 24.

24. AHMC-MP, Vol. 1605–1607, and Vol. 1605–1620, fs. 20, 21, 27, 19v, 31, 24.

25. AHMC-MP, Vol. 1605–1607, and Vol. 1605–1620, fs. 3v–5v, 36–38, 148–48v, 36.

26. ANB-M, 1633, no. 1.

27. AHMC-MP, Vol. 1561–1590, exp. 17, and Vol. 1597–1607, exps. 13, 15, 16; also, for discussion of separate units of production within a larger administrative unit or estate, see my *Leverage of Labor*.

28. AHMC-MP, Vol. 1597–1607, exps. 13, 15, 16.

29. AHMC-MP, Vol. 1597–1607, exps. 13, 15, 16. For sugar markets see Escobari de Querejazu, *Producción y comercio*, 95.

30. AHMC-MP, Vol. 1597–1607, exps. 13, 15, 16.

31. AHMC-MP, Vol. 1629–1676, Vol. 38, leg. 20, fs. 203–15v.

32. AHMC-MP, Vol. 1629–1676, Vol. 38, leg. 20, fs. 203–15v.

33. AHMC-MP, Vol. 1629–1676, Vol. 38, leg. 20, fs. 203–15v.

34. AHMC-MP, Vol. 1629–1676, Vol. 38, leg. 20, fs. 203–15v, 234–34v.

35. AHMC-MP, Vol. 1629–1676, Vol. 38, leg. 20, fs. 203–15v, 234–34v, 357, and 371v.

36. AHMC-MP, Vol. 1591–1598, f. 1930. In 1595, Juan de Paredes, vecino of Mizque, sold an estancia and cultivatable fields in the district of Taranatara for 1,800 pesos; ANB-AUDCH/CORR, Correspondencia no. 845; and AHMC-MP, Vol. 1610, fs. 380–81, 383.

37. ANB-AUDCH/CORR, Correspondencia no. 845; and AHMC-MP, Vol. 1610, fs. 380–81, 383.

38. ANB-AUDCH/CORR, Correspondencia no. 845; and AHMC-MP, Vol. 1610, fs. 380–81, 383.

39. ANB-AUDCH/CORR, Correspondencia no. 845; and AHMC-MP, Vol. 1610, fs. 380–81, 383–85; and CAJAS, 1592, no. 45, Cargo de bienes de difuntos. In 1592 nearly 11,800 pesos were returned to inheritors in Spain.

40. ANB-EXP, 1685, exp. 47, fs. 12v–14, Inventario de Bienes Robles.

41. ANB-EXP, 1685, exp. 47, fs. 14v–15v. The magueyes in Mizque are considerably larger than those grown in Mexico. Pulque, the fermented beverage produced from the maguey in Mexico, is not consumed in the region. The documents offer no clue as to why one would want thirty of these plants, and this is the only reference to them that I have encountered. We do know that maguey plants can be used as a natural fence or boundary marker.

42. ANB-EXP, 1685, exp. 47, fs. 14v–15v.

43. ANB-EXP, 1685, exp. 47, fs. 17–19. Old habits are hard to break, as

noted in chapter 2. Although Mizque was officially names Villa de Salinas del Río Pisuergo in 1603, people persisted in calling it by the original name, and still do today.

44. ANB-EXP, 1685, exp. 47, fs. 17–19.

45. AHMC-MP, Vol. 1561–1590, leg. 37, exps. 3, 6, 14, 24, and Vol. 1597–1607, leg. 39.

46. AHMC-MP, Vol. 1561–1590, leg. 37, exps. 3, 6, 14, 24, and Vol. 1597–1607, leg. 39.

47. ANB-MEC, 1616, no. 1. The six pages of documents pertaining to this case were not numbered.

48. ANB-MEC, 1616, no. 1.

49. AHMC-MP, Vol. 1599–1621.

50. AHMC-MP, Vol. 1599–1621. Two explanations come to mind here. Possibly the five Europeans did not eat much corn, or perhaps they were not full-time residents of Cauta. There is also the possibility that the Indians used the corn for making *chicha* (corn beer).

51. AHMC-MP, Vol. 1599–1621.

52. AHMC-MP, Vol. 1599–1621.

53. AHMC-MP, Vol. 1599–1621.

54. ANB-TI, 1624, exp. 6, fs. 23–26.

4. Harnessing the Resources

1. Lockhart, *Spanish Peru* (2nd ed.), 24–25, 34. Here Lockhart provides a good assessment of mayordomo salaries, to which Mizque compares quite reasonably. See also L. G. Brockington, *The Leverage of Labor*, 36–70.

2. ANB-TI, 1624, 6, fs. 23–26.

3. ANB-TI, 1624, 6, fs. 23–26.

4. ANB-M, 1611, no. 8, fs. 14–15v, 23–27. In the Abrego case the terms *mayordomo* and *administrador* were used interchangeably. There is no doubt in regard to rank or position. In this work I have tried to make the distinction between mayordomo and estate guardian, tutor, curador, and executrix as clear as possible. See chapter 2 on the categories other than mayordomo.

5. ANB-M, 1611, no. 8, fs. 34–35.

6. ANB-EXP, 1614, exp. 12, fs. 33–37.

7. AHMC-MP, Vol. 38, 1629–1676, leg. 8, f. 280.

8. AHMC-MP, Vol. 38, 1629–1676, leg. 8, fs. 1–3, 72. For Arequipa mayordomo and other wine-related information see Davies, *Landowners in Colonial Peru*, 60–62.

9. AHMC-MP, Vol. 38, 1629–1676, leg. 8, fs. 74, 251, 256.

10. AHMC-MP, Vol. 38, 1629–1676, leg. 8, fs. 251v–52.

11. AHMC-MP, Vol. 38, 1629–1676, leg. 8, fs. 252v–53.

12. AHMC-MP, Vol. 38, 1629–1676, leg. 8, fs. 266–69.

13. AHMC-MP, Vol. 38, 1629–1676, leg. 8, fs. 255–56.

14. AHMC-MP, Vol. 1580–1617, padrones de chacara; ANB-M, 1683; and AHMC-MP, Vol. 38, 1629–1674, leg. 20 (Turque).

15. ANB-EXP, 1614, exp. 12, fs. 133–36v.

16. ANB-EXP, 1614, exp. 12, fs. 133–36v.

17. AHMC-MP, Vol. 1606, f. 2353v–54, and Vol. 1619–1624, exp. 1.

18. AHMC-MP, Vol. 1605–1607, fs. 10, 37–38. Flete charges per botija of wine came to about 2 pesos each, while the transport of young bulls amounted to 1 peso each. These expenditures represent routine budget outlays in hacienda production.

19. AHMC-MP, Vol. 1605–1607, fs. 10, 37–38. I have been told that at some time, possibly in the early colonial period, a botija factory existed in Mizque, which would make sense. However, I have not been able to verify this. Also, for the collector of truly esoteric historical minutiae, containers of the same style were used to support the domes of colonial churches in La Plata and Potosí.

20. ANB-EXP, 1614, exp. 12, fs. 38–40.

21. ANB-M, 1613, no. 4.

22. ANB-M, 1613, no. 4.

23. ANB-M, 1613, no. 4. For further elaboration on the Paniagua textile activities at their Buena Vista hacienda in Mizque, see Presta, *Encomienda*, 104–5, 109. While her data indicate the obraje and hacienda as separate entities, the records I consulted simply lumped the two together, referring to the "textiles del obraje de la hacienda Buena Vista."

24. The specific origins of Viceroy Mendoza's ordinances are not clear. However, what does strike a chord is the resemblance to some of the ordinances compiled by the Mexican Mesta, the cattleman's organization that defined the rules and regulations pertaining to Mexican livestock production. See Dusenberry, *The Mexican Mesta*; L. G. Brockington, *The Leverage of Labor*, 102–3; and Bishko, "Peninsular Background."

25. Escobari de Querejazu, *Producción y comercio*, 141–52; and AHMC-MP, Vol. 38, 1629–1676, leg. 8, fs. 15–16v.

26. L. G. Brockington, "The African Diaspora."

27. AHMC-MP, Vol. 38, leg. 20. Secondary sources confirm the significance of sugar production in the region. See, e.g., Escobari de Querejazu, *Producción y comercio*, 95, 125; Viedma, *Descripción geográfica*, 163; and Viscarra, *Apuntes*, 255–56.

28. ANB-TI, f. 1232; AHMC-MP, Vol. 38, 1629–1676, leg. 8, fs. 15–16v. See also Cushner, *Lords of the Land*, 118, 122.

29. L. G. Brockington, "The African Diaspora," 213, 220–21; L. G. Brockington, "La dinámica." See also chapter 2.

30. For a useful explanation of Indian communities, labor categories, and agricultural production, including coca, see Barragán Romano, "Ayullus y

haciendas," 60–92; and specifically on coca, Ramírez Valverde, "Visita a Pocona." For yet another perspective see Gade, "Inca and Colonial Settlement" and *Nature and Culture*. Subsequent chapters will further discuss Gade's contributions to this still-controversial subject. See also González, "Visita de los Yndios," 4–11.

31. Larson, *Colonialism*, 45 n. 60.

32. ANB-EP, 1553.VI.4; and AHMC-MP, Vol. 1561–1590, exp. 13. ANB-TI, 1564.IX.16, Real cédula no. 50 and 1586, exp. 6; AHMC-MP, Vol. 1591–98; ANB-M, 1604, no. 14, 1612, no. 3, 1614, no. 1, and 1624, no. 1; and Schramm, "Archivo histórico."

33. MV-AGI, Patronato 144, Gabriel 4, fs. 1–171.

34. AHMC-MP, Vol. 1561–1590, exp. 13.

35. AHMC-MP, Vol. 1561–1590, exp. 13, and Vol. 1597–1607, exps. 13, 15, and 16. Given the historical prominence of this leaf crop, I find somewhat perplexing Viscarra's uncharacteristic silence on the issue. He refers to it only once, when quoting Viedma on Mizque's late-eighteenth-century voluminous imports of products from Cochabamba, Cliza, Santa Cruz, Valle Grande, and elsewhere. Viscarra, *Apuntes*, 257.

36. Larson, *Colonialism*, 85. Chapter 6 of this volume elaborates upon this and other related issues.

37. Viscarra, *Apuntes*, 257–58.

38. Viscarra, *Apuntes*, 254; and Viedma, *Descripción geográfica*, 83.

39. AHMC-MP, Vol. 1561–1590, exp. 17; and ANB-CR, 1588, no. 200, 1590, no. 378, and 1592, no. 441.

40. ANB-M, 1619, no. 3, f. 3.

41. ANB-M, 1619, no. 3, f. 3.

42. ANB-M, 1619, no. 3, f. 4.

43. ANB-M, 1619, no. 3, fs. 4–5v.

44. ANB-M, 1619, no. 3, fs. 8–8v.

45. ANB-M, 1619, no. 3, fs. 9v–10.

46. ANB-M, 1619, no. 3, fs. 11v–12.

47. ANB-M, 1619, no. 3, fs. 11v–12.

48. ANB-MINAS, 1688, Tomo 146, 1691, Tomo 147, fs. 1–4.

49. ANB-MINAS, 1691, Tomo 147, fs. 1–4.

50. ANB-MINAS, 1704–1705, Tomo 82, no. 638, fs. 1–12, and 1706–1707, Tomo 82, no. 639, fs. 3–5v. Reading Viscarra, *Apuntes*, 258–59, one does not get the impression that these men were "poor, struggling miners." Rather, we now know that this supplicating mode was the accepted formula of the day when individuals requested the crown's attention and consideration. Even the very wealthy Paniaguas tried to make themselves appear as paupers when requesting renumeration from the crown.

51. ANB-MINAS, 1706–1707, Tomo 82, no. 639, fs. 3–5v. Data on other

regional government posts indicate that the prices for these jobs compared favorably to major centers elsewhere. See CAJAS, 1592, no. 45, 1634, no. 261, 1612–1613, no. 139, 1650, no. 325, and 1665, no. 408.

52. Viscarra, *Apuntes*, 260–61. For analysis of the Potosí fluctuations and their repercussions, see TePaske, "Fiscal Structure"; Bakewell, *Miners of the Red Mountain*, 26–65; and Larson, *Colonialism*, 54–57, 108–9.

5. The Africans and Their Descendants

1. Lockhart, *Spanish Peru* (2nd ed.), 193–224; Bowser, *African Slave*.

2. Viedma, *Descripción geográfica*, 84, 90, 92, 94, 95, 98, 108, and 121. These references are late-colonial censuses for the region and are used by the following scholars as well. See Viscarra, *Apuntes*, 253; and Gade, *Nature and Culture*, 83, 89. Crespo, *Esclavos negros*, 31, apparently relied on a source other than Viedma. See also Palmer, *Human Cargoes*, 123–24; and Studer, *La trata de negros*, 100–101, 224–25.

3. For a critical overview of the five major African diasporas, see Palmer, "Modern African Diaspora." Also, for Black participation in the Pizarro and Almagro expeditions, see Bowser, *African Slave*, 3–5.

4. AHMC-MEC, Vol. 1613, no. 4.

5. ANB-CR, 1638, no. 382.

6. ANB-ESCHAR, 1551, f. 21. I have found that when the currency figure is not further qualified by the term *ensayado* (or as in this instance, "good money"), the value is assumed to be in pesos corrientes.

7. AHMC-MP, Vol. 1561–1590, exps. 17 and 30, and Vol. 1605–1606.

8. Lane, *Quito 1599*, 64–67.

9. ANB-M, 1610, no. 14, fs. 1204, 1219, 1237; AHMC-MP, Vol. 1606.

10. AHMC-MP, Vol. 1610, exp. 30; ANB-TI, 1624, exp. 6; AHMC-MP, Vol. 1561–1590, exp. 17, and Vol. 1597–1607, exp. 9.

11. ANB-TI, 1633–1634, exp. 6.

12. ANB-M, 1651, no. 1, fs. 3–28.

13. AHMC-MP, Vol. 1684. Contrary to popular opinion, the bishopric of Santa Cruz always functioned as the colonial seat of regional ecclesiastical power. The prelates of the bishopric usually resided in Mizque only temporarily, although on occasion they did so for extended periods of time, such as when Santa Cruz climatic conditions and periodic waves of epidemic disease forced them to the then healthier, more temperate zones of Mizque. Also, simultaneously, Mizque's population growth required an increased ecclesiastic attention that the local clerics apparently could not meet. See Viscarra, *Apuntes*, 227–36. Regarding slave ages, see Palmer, *Human Cargoes*, 120–23.

14. AHMC-MP, Vol. 1684; Palmer, *Human Cargoes*, 123–24; and Struder, *La trata*, 100–101, 224–25. When Struder offers a somewhat broader base of price variation, the price averages remained as consistent in Buenos Aires as they did in Mizque.

15. Palmer, *Human Cargoes*, 71.

16. ANB-CR, 1588, no. 344, 1592, no. 465, 1593, no. 492, 1602, no. 749, 1603, no. 839; ANB-AUDCH/CORR, 1602.IX.28; ANB-CR, 1605, no. 305, 1606, nos. 966 and 984, 1608, no. 1095, 1614, no. 1191.

17. See Adorno, *Guaman Poma*, 4–10; and Peñalosa y Mondragon, *Libro de las cinco excelencias*, 119–25, 130–32.

18. Crespo, *Esclavos negros*, 101–2.

19. *Diccionario histórico de Bolivia*, 1:465.

20. Crespo, *Esclavos negros*, 25–26; Portugal Ortíz, *La esclavitud negra*, 59–60; and Bridikhina, *La mujer negra*, 40–42.

21. AHMC-MP, Vol. 1561–1590.

22. AHMC-MP, Vol. 1597–1687, exp. 18.

23. AHMC-MP, Vol. 1597–1607, exp. 18, and Vol. 1605–1607. While doing archival research in Cochabamba and Sucre I was generally allowed to photocopy (apart from the many I copied by hand—no laptops permitted then!) a substantial number of these census documents dating from the late 1500s to the mid-1700s. Not only do they yield a wealth of information on race, ethnicity, and gender, but they also reveal familial status and kinship, places of origin, and legal status of each yanacona attached to the chacara.

24. AHMC-MP, Vol. 1561–1590, exp. 3, and exp. 17.

25. AHMC-MP, Vol. 1597–1607, exp. 18.

26. AHMC-MP, Vol. 1597–1607, exp. 18.

27. AHMC-MP, Vol. 1597–1607, exp. 18.

28. AHMC-MP, Vol. 1597–1607, exps. 9, 13, and 15, and Vol. 1561–1590, exp. 17.

29. AHMC-MP, Vol. 1597–1607, exps. 9, 13, and 15, and Vol. 1561–1590, exp. 17.

30. ANB-M, 1603, no. 6.

31. See L. G. Brockington, *The Leverage of Labor*, 110–25, 128–42. See also Berlin and Morgan, *The Slaves' Economy*, 11. Here they discuss slave participation in an "extensive internal economy," particularly livestock operations during the early settlement periods, which provides an excellent paradigm for the Mizque experience. For a discussion of the west African horse and livestock traditions see Geggus, "Sugar and Coffee Cultivation," 88.

32. ANB-M, 1603, no. 6.

33. AHMC-MP, Vol. 1610, exp. 30, and Vol. 38, 1629–1676, leg. 5.

34. AHMC-MP, Vol. 38, 1629–1676, leg. 6, 7, and 8.

35. AHMC-MP, Vol. 38, 1629–1676, leg. 8.

36. AHMC-MP, Vol. 38, 1629–1676, leg. 20.

37. AHMC-MP, Vol. 38, 1629–1676, leg. 20.

38. AHMC-MP, Vol. 38, 1629–1676, leg. 20.

39. AHMC-MP, Vol. 38, 1629–1676, leg. 20.

40. AHMC-MP, Vol. 38, 1629–1676, leg. 20.

41. AHMC-MP, Vol. 38, 1629–1676, leg. 20.

42. AHMC-MP, Vol. 38, 1629–1676, leg. 20.

43. AHMC-MP, Vol. 38, 1629–1676, leg. 20.

44. ANB-JMC, fs. 1–62, 195–280.

45. ANB-JMC, fs. 195, 208v–11.

46. ANB-JMC, fs. 206–206v.

47. ANB-JMC, fs. 247v, 208–11. Harsh labor, illness, poor nutrition, and other factors cause premature aging. Thus the age of the seventy-year-old, who in all likelihood had no birth record, could have been estimated according to his appearance.

48. ANB-JMC, fs. 247v, 208–11, 207v.

49. ANB-JMC, fs. 211–13.

50. ANB-JMC, fs. 250, 254.

51. ANB-JMC, f. 199.

52. ANB-JMC, fs. 238, 247–247v, 250, 252–53.

53. ANB-JMC, fs. 276v, 280–81v.

54. For an excellent trilogy on Jesuit economic and agricultural activities in the viceroyalty of Peru, see Cushner's *Lords of the Land, Farm and Factory*, and *Jesuit Ranches*. For Cushner's observations on post-expulsion transactions, see *Lords of the Land*, 180. For the interested scholar, Konrad's *A Jesuit Hacienda in Colonial Mexico* is also a very important contribution. In addition, see Burkholder and Johnson, *Colonial Latin America*, 275–76. In their concise synthesis of the actual expulsion, the authors note that among the many Jesuit properties in Peru alone, the royal government expropriated some fifty-two hundred slaves.

55. AHMC-MP, Vol. 1163–1730; L. G. Brockington, *The Leverage of Labor*, 126–42.

56. ANB-M, 1683; AHMC-MP, Vol. 1694–1695, leg. 15.

57. AHMC-MP, Vol. 1694–1695, leg. 15, and Vol. 1630–1730. The La Calleja padrón provides other information as well. Doña Otalla's surname (Cortés de Encina) surely reflects the widely practiced intermarriage between prominent families. Further, her La Calleja holding was possibly one of at least two or three subdivided parcels of land that once made up the vast La Calleja of the Álvarez Menéndez estate more than a century earlier. Or, equally plausible, it could have been one of several unrelated holdings throughout the region sharing the same name, such as in the case of Buena Vista.

58. AHMC-MP, Vol. 1605–1607.

59. AHMC-MP, Vol. 1597–1607.

60. AHMC-MP, Vol. 1630–1730; ANB-M, 1683.

61. ANB-M, 1683.

62. ANB-M, 1683.

63. ANB-M, 1683.

64. AHMC-MP, Vol. 1630–1730.

65. AHMC-MP, Vol. 1630–1730.

66. AHMC-MP, Vol. 1630–1730; ANB-M, 1683.

67. AHMC-MP, Vol. 1630–1730; ANB-M, 1683.

68. AHMC-MP, Vol. 1630–1730; ANB-M, 1683.

69. AHMC-MP, Vols. 1597–1607 and 1630–1730.

70. AHMC-MP, Vols. 1597–1607 and 1630–1730; ANB-M, 1683.

71. AHMC-MP, Vol. 1630–1730.

72. AHMC-MP, Vol. 1630–1730.

73. AHMC-MP, Vol. 1597–1607, and Vol. 1635, no. 5.

74. AHMC-MP, Vol. 38, 1629–1676, exps. 6–8.

75. AHMC-MP, Vol. 1597–1607, exp. 18.

76. AHMC-MP, Vol. 1597–1607, exp. 18.

77. AHMC-MP, Vol. 1597–1607, exp. 18.

78. If indeed African slaves were spared the harsh, life-threatening conditions of mine labor in the legendary *cerro rico* (rich peak) of Potosí, their toils in the royal mint, which Fray Benito neglected to mention, were far from benign (see chapter 7). Also, while both Viscarra, *Apuntes*, and Viedma, *Descripción geográfica*, write enthusiastically of Mizque's wine-production fame, neither offers specific dates for the industry's peak years (or decline). Barragán Romano, "Ayllus y haciendas," 168–69, Tables 55–57, cites dates for the famous Pererata and lesser-known Chimba wineries into the early 1700s; she, like her reader, is impressed with the extent of these huge operations.

79. ANB-TI, 1607, EC no. 18, 1624, exp. 6, fs. 2–27, and 1637, exp. 6; AHMC-MP, Vol. 38, legs. 8–21v, 34, 72–74; ANB-M, 1683, no. 3.

80. AHMC-MP, Vol. 38, legs. 6, 5, and 8, fs. 12–12v, 14, 21v, 34, 72–74.

81. AHMC-MP, Vol. 38, legs. 6, 5, and 8, fs. 12–12v, 14, 21v, 34, 72–74; ANB-JMC, fs. 204–8.

82. AHMC-MP, Vol. 1597–1607. See also Presta, *Encomienda*, 105–9. Among other things, she cites a possible fourth Paniagua livestock estancia, Uyuchama, in the valley of Mizque. She also notes the huge Paniagua Buena Vista operations were launched in the 1560s, which would obviously require access to livestock early on, and that African slaves were brought in at the outset.

83. ANB-M, 1603, no. 6, 1683, 1713, no. 12; ANB-TI, 1607, EC no. 18, 1624, exp. 6, and 1637, exp. 6; AHMC-MP, Vol. 1605–1620, f. 1780, Vol. 1605–1607, Vol. 1630–1730, Vol. 1694–1695; ANB-JMC, 1767.

84. ANB-M, 1610, no. 4, and 1683, no. 3, which notes Sebastian Ambrosio Veriti, curaca pardo of the hacienda de "Puxioni." Several mulatos are recorded on this padrón, but there is no indication of exact production activity. AHMC-MP, Vol. 1694–1695, leg. 15.

85. ANB-M, 1618, no. 3; AHMC-MP, Vol. 1630–1730.

86. ANB-M, 1645, leg. 11.

87. See, e.g., the works of George Reid Andrews (*Afro-Argentines in Buenos Aires*), Christon Archer (*Army in Bourbon Mexico*), Ben Vinson III (*Bearing Arms for His Majesty*), and Peter M. Voelz (*Slave and Soldier*), to name just a few.

88. AHMC-MP, Vols. 1561–1590, 1597–1607. Mizque continues to produce excellent cheese today. ANB-M, 1610, no. 7, 1645, no. 3, 1683, no. 3, and 1690, no. 5.

89. ANB-M, 1651, no. 1, f. 13v; Haring, *Spanish Empire in America*, 150–53, 272; and Real Academia Española, *Diccionario de la lengua Española*.

90. Crespo, *Esclavos negros*, 31. Ms. copy editor of Crespo's work missed the math error of 3.9 percent cited in the text.

91. MV-AGI, Charcas 135, 6 fs.

92. Crespo, *Esclavos negros*, 31. Here, Crespo also provided a 1793 Mizque population figure of 17,000, with the negros and mulatos making up 2,249, or 12 percent, attributed to one Alcide D'Orgbigny. This citation was not documented.

93. Viedma, *Descripción geográfica*, 90, 92, 94–95, 97–98, 104, 105, and 106.

94. Viedma, *Descripción geográfica*, 92.

95. Viedma, *Descripción geográfica*, 102, 104, 90, 98, 105, 94, and 98. See also Vázquez Machicado, *Catálogo descriptica*, no. 481, 1624, 54. For references to Chilón, Valle Grande, and Cuidad de Jesús included in the Corregimiento de Mizque's jurisdiction, see AHMC-MP, Vol. 38, leg. 1 (1630); and ANB-M, 1645, no. 3, fs. 10–19. See also Sanabria F., *Cronicario*, 18–19. In 1645, Mizque authorities complained about the shortage of mayordomos to oversee administrative issues such as the collection of tasas (and accounting of same) in these distant regions. Apparently, Mizque had not received payments or accounts from these towns between 1633 and 1640. The figures for the "padroncillo de Indios forasteros" and yanaconas in towns and nearby chacaras for 1645 appear pretty skimpy to me, as well.

96. Crespo, *Esclavos negros*, 179–81, 203; Viedma, *Descripción geográfica*, 104–6.

97. ANB-CR, 1614, no. 1191. From the crown's perspective, the case of "Joao Rodríguez Continho, Governador y Capitan General de la Conquista y Minas del Reino de Angola" underscores a somewhat different but equally pertinent issue. In 1602 he was granted a nine-year permit to import through Buenos Aires six hundred units of slaves annually. By 1605 he was under investigation for attempting to import slave units far in excess of his permit. See ANB-AUDCH/CORR, 1602.IX.28, from the Villa de San Pablo de Luanda, Angola; ANB-CR, 1606, nos. 966 and 984, 1608, no. 1095. For more on the Rodríguez Coutinho contract, see Palmer, *Slaves of the White God*, 13.

6. Indian Affairs

1. See, e.g., Barnadas, *Charcas*, 22–24; Barragán Romano, *¿Indios de arco y flecha?*; Métraux, "Tribes"; Rojas Vaca, *Población y territorio*; Saignes, *Los Andes orientales*; Casevitz, Saignes, and Taylor, *Al este de los Andes*; and Schramm, "Paces y guerras," "Fronteras y territorialidad," and *Pocona und Mizque*. Again, for an innovated assessment of Inca history, see Julien, *Reading Inca History*.

2. Schramm, "Paces y guerras," 3–5. While Schramm demonstrates a clear distinction among the ethnic groups under discussion, contemporary written reports and chronicles usually lumped these ethnicities under the almost generic label "Chiriguano."

3. Captain Joan Godoy Aguilera Papers, ANB-M, 1622, no. 2 (17 fs.), fs. 7–8v.

4. ANB-M, 1622, no. 2, fs. 8v–9v.

5. ANB-M, 1622, no. 2, fs. 8v–9v; and unnumbered petition of Captain Joan Godoy, November 24, 1622.

6. AHMC-MP, Vol. 1561–1590.

7. Schramm, "Paces y guerras," 4.

8. ANB-M, 1622, no. 2, fs. 9v–10. "Frontier" is in quotes here to remind the reader that this was a Spanish concept completely alien to the indigenous inhabitants, as explained in chapter 1.

9. ANB-M, 1622, no. 2, fs. 10v–11v.

10. ANB-M, 1622, no. 2, fs. 10v–11v; and unnumbered petition of Captain Joan Godoy, November 24, 1622.

11. ANB-M, 1622, no. 2, fs. 10v–11v.

12. ANB-M, 1622, no. 2, fs. 10v–11v.

13. ANB-M, 1622, no. 2, fs. 5–6v, 12–12v.

14. Schramm, "Paces y guerras," 7.

15. Schramm, "Archivo histórico," MEC 63.1727–1730, Vol. 1728, and MEC 74.1776–1777, Vol. 1777.

16. Léons and Sanabria, "Coca and Cocaine in Bolivia," 4.

17. Lanning, *Peru before the Incas*, 25, 74–77. Also, the pre-Columbian ceramic figurines on exhibit in the Museo Arqueológico of the Universidad Mayor de San Simón in Cochabamba, Bolivia, are depicted with the traditional wads of coca bulging their cheeks.

18. Spedding, "Coca Field as a Total Social Fact," 48–49. Léons and Sanabria's valuable, well-informed book *Coca, Cocaine, and the Bolivian Reality* consists of twelve contributions, including an excellent introductory chapter by the editors. Sanabria has a compelling, wrenching article on the Chapare, the present-day name of one of the yungas areas—Arepucho—that I discuss. Other contributors make occasional references to this area. Only Spedding acknowledges the pre-Columbian and colonial trajectory of this plant and its history, but she too focuses mainly on the La Paz region.

19. González, "Visita de los Yndios," 2–4. The more recent work of Rojas Vaca, *Población y territorio*, 54, 56–66, makes a good case for the Chuy having much earlier, deeper roots in the valley of Mizque. For an excellent assessment of regional production, see Julien, "Coca Production on the Inca Frontier," 129–60.

20. Meruvia Balderrama, *Historia de la coca*; see also Schramm, "Paces y guerras," 3–5.

21. AHMC-MP, Vols. 1591–1598, 1599–1629, 1602, 1630–1696; and Viscarra, *Apuntes*, 255.

22. This information comes from a very rich documentary source referred to as padrones de chacara. These are census-like questionnaires, supposedly taken on a yearly basis by the local corregidor or his lieutenant, always accompanied by a local cabildo scribe, in which they were to "visit" each and every chacara with the intent of keeping tabs on tribute and other payments. In truth, the padrones yield much more data than mere head counts, which will be discussed in full below.

23. González, "Visita de los Yndios," 5.

24. ANB-EP 1553.VI.4.

25. González, "Visita de los Yndios," 5.

26. Larson, *Colonialism*, 45 n. 60.

27. ANB-EP, 1553.VI.4; and AHMC-MP, Vol. 1561–1590, exp. 13. This lengthy expediente with unnumbered pages deals entirely with coca-related matters, with a good number of documents dating beyond the dates indicated on the volume's cover. Possibly the archivist who cataloged this particular group of documents considered the subject sufficiently important to keep them in one place, regardless of the extension beyond the stated time parameter. See also ANB-TI, 1564.IX.16, RC no. 50, 1584, exp. 6; AHMC-MP, Vol. 1591–98; ANB-M, 1696, no. 5.

28. AHMC-MP, Vol. 1561–1590, exp. 13.

29. For a useful explanation of Indian communities, labor categories, and agricultural production, including coca, see Barragán Romano, "Ayullus y haciendas," 60–92; and specifically on coca, Ramírez Valverde, "Visita a Pocona, 1552"; and González, "Visita de los Yndios."

30. Gade, "Inca and Colonial Settlement," 271.

31. Gade, "Inca and Colonial Settlement," 271 n. 12.

32. Ramírez Valverde, "Visita a Pocona," 273.

33. Ramírez Valverde, "Visita a Pocona," 305.

34. Ramírez Valverde, "Visita a Pocona," 305.

35. Ramírez Valverde, "Visita a Pocona," 286–90, 296. For further discussion of camayo, see Barragán Romano, "Ayllu y hacienda," 61–62.

36. Ramírez Valverde, "Visita a Pocona," 295–98.

37. Ramírez Valverde, "Visita a Pocona," 298–300.

38. Ramírez Valverde, "Visita a Pocona," 299.

39. Ramírez Valverde, "Visita a Pocona," 300.

40. Ramírez Valverde, "Visita a Pocona," 305–8.

41. AHMC-MP, Vol. 1591–98; ANB-TI, 1564.IX.16, RC no. 50.

42. AHMC-MP, Vol. 1561–1590, exp. 13; ANB-TI, 1586, exp. 6, 1588; ANB-M, 1632, no. 4, 1696, no. 5 (by now coca was selling at 14½ pesos a cesto); and ANB-EP, 1769, no. 82. See also AHMC-MP, Vol. 1585. Coca production today remains a critically divisive social and political issue. Excessive demands on indigenous community production were not limited to coca by any means. In 1585, Mizque cacique Don García Senita complained that there were not enough Indians to pay the required wine tribute, tend to the sixty thousand grape stocks, tend the sheep, or go up to La Plata.

43. AHMC-MP, Vol. 1591–1598, Vol. 1597–1607, exp. 18, Vol. 1605–1607, Vol. 1630–1730, Vol. 1694–1696; and ANB-M, Vol. 1645, leg. 11, Vol. 1683.

44. See chapter 5. See also AHMC-MP, Vol. 1597–1607.

45. AHMC-MP, Vols. 1597–1607, 1605–1607, and 1630; ANB-M, 1603, no. 2, and 1683, no. 3; ANB-TI, 1604 AM, no. 4. For the corregidor's complaint see AHMC-MP, Vol. 1580–1617 (1604).

46. See, e.g., D. L. Brockington et al., *Estudios arqueológicos*; and the above-cited works by Barnadas (*Charcas*), Barragán Romano (*¿Indios de arco y flecha?*), Métraux ("Tribes"), Casevitz, Saignes, and Taylor (*Al este de los Andes*), Rojas Vaca (*Población y territorio*), Schramm ("Paces y guerras"), et al.

47. Schramm, "Paces y guerras," 1; and Presta, *Encomienda*, 106. Also AHMC-MEC, Vol. 1576–1723 (1575) pleito de los naturals e indios del repartimiento de Mizque, 31 fs. This litigation dragged on for at least thirteen years.

48. AHMC-MEC, Vol. 1576–1723 (1575), fs. 1–3.

49. AHMC-MEC, Vol. 1576–1723 (1575), fs. 3v–5.

50. AHMC-MEC, Vol. 1576–1723 (1575), fs. 5v–7v.

51. AHMC-MEC, Vol. 1576–1723 (1575), f. 7.

52. AHMC-MP, Vol. 1597–1607. This particular volume of documents contains several consecutive years of padrones as well as litigation records dating back to 1558. In their fifty-year battle to disprove Indian property rights the Paniaguas hired scores of lawyers and scribes to *copy* past litigations and legal actions from briefs and other documents reposited in the audiencia in La Plata. Thus we have a jumble of one trial running into another, the dates of which are not always in sequence and often as not refer to earlier trials as well.

53. AHMC-MP, Vol. 1597–1607, exp. 11.

54. AHMC-MP, Vol. 1597–1607, exp. 11. Paniagua defense documents date 1558, 1559, 1560, 1561, 1563, 1568, 1570, 1584, 1587 (from the city of Panama, where Alsonso apparently turned over his holdings to half brother Gabriel), 1593, 1596, 1598, 1599, 1604, and 1605.

55. Rojas Vaca, *Población y territorio*, 144–45. The author of this brief but well-informed ethnohistorical monograph devoted a third of the work to sizable transcribed portions of the notarial and other documents he consulted in Bolivian archives. These offer the serious scholar of the region access to very useful primary data. This and the following citation are based on my readings of Rojas's transcribed documents.

56. Rojas Vaca, *Población y territorio*, 159. Further, Indian land claims persisted throughout the entire colonial period, as demonstrated in Schramm, "Archivo histórico," MEC 69. 1756–1758, Pocona; MEC 71. 1761–1766, Pocona; MEC 72. 1767–1772, Totora; MEC 73. 1773–1775, Pocona; MEC 83. 1795–1797, Chuis.

57. See, e.g., Mörner, *The Andean Past*, 38–39.

58. Espinoza, "El memorial," 117–19, 124. We are always grateful for those who came before us, uncovered obscure documents, and transcribed and published them so that we can all benefit from these otherwise "hidden" gems. Espinoza knew he had come across a treasure in the Archivo General de las Indias, which is why he chose to call the memorial a "chronicle," laden as it is with rich historical and ethnographical data.

59. Espinoza, "El memorial," 117–19, 124.

60. Espinoza, "El memorial," 117. The main memorial, transcribed on pages 128–44, consists of fifty-three capítulos (articles) signed by twenty-four curacas. The second, shorter memorial (pages 144–48) consists of sixteen capítulos signed by only one of the curacas, Don Fernando Ayavire y Velasco, cacique principal of the Charcas nation and of the repartimiento de Sacaca. The shorter memorial was addressed to Doctor Barros, formerly an oidor in the audiencia in La Plata, where he was associated with the Council of the Indies. Apparently, Barros had befriended the curacas while in the audiencia, speaking out in support of their causes whenever possible. They still felt they could trust him. The terms *cacique*, *curaca*, *cacicazgo*, and *curacazgo* are used interchangeably throughout these documents, as they are throughout the notarial and other documents studied in this project.

61. Espinoza, "El memorial," 117.

62. Espinoza, "El memorial," 128–30, capítulos 1–10.

63. Espinoza, "El memorial," 131–34, capítulos 11–20.

64. Espinoza, "El memorial," 135, capítulo 27.

65. Espinoza, "El memorial," 138, 143, capítulos 41, 51, 52.

66. Espinoza, "El memorial," Memorial II, 144, capítulo 1.

67. Espinoza, "El memorial," 145, capítulo 3.

68. Espinoza, "El memorial," 146, capítulos 5, 8.

69. Espinoza, "El memorial," 128, 132, 134, 135, 138, 143.

70. AHMC-MP, Vol. 1561–1590, leg. 37, exps. 3, 6, 14, and 24, and Vol. 1597–1607, leg. 39; and ANB-M, 1616, no. 1.

71. AHMC-MP, Vol. 38, leg. 1, fs. 45–47.

72. Lockhart, *Spanish Peru* (2nd ed.), 246.

73. Stern, "Early Spanish-Indian Accommodation"; Ramírez, *The World Upside Down*, 14–15, 39–41; and Andrien, "Early Colonial State," 124, 127–28.

74. Powers, *Andean Journeys*, 87, 107–11.

75. ANB-EP, 1553.VI.4; AHMC-MP, Vol. 1561–1590, exp. 13; ANB-TI, 1564.IX.16, RC no. 50, 1584, exp. 6; AHMC-MP, Vol. 1591–98; and ANB-M, 1696, no. 5.

76. AHMC-MP, Vol. 1561–1590, exp. 15. Like expediente 13, this one relates almost entirely to the ongoing conflicts discussed in the text.

77. AHMC-MP, Vol. 1561–1590, exp. 15.

78. ANB-TI, 1586, no. 6, and no. 9.

79. ANB-TI, 1586, no. 6, and no. 9.

80. ANB-M, 1593, no. 1; ANB-TI, 1597, exp. 9; ANB-M, 1602, no. 4.

81. AHMC-MP, Vol. 1561–1590, exp. 32.

82. Schramm, "Archivo histórico," MEC 72. 1767–1772, tribute collection, Totora, and MEC 73. 1773–1775, tribute, Pocona; and Larson, *Colonialism*, 156–59.

83. Ramírez, *The World Upside Down*, 8, 15–21; Powers, *Andean Journeys*, 108–9, 202 n.

84. AHMC-MP, Vol. 1597–1607.

85. AHMC-MP, Vol. 1630–1730; ANB-M, Vol. 1645, leg. 11.

86. AHMC-MP, Vol. 1694–1695, leg. 15.

87. Gade, *Nature and Culture*, 84–85, 86–87.

88. Sánchez Albornóz, *Indios y tributes*, 30. To arrive at my own estimate of Sánchez Albornóz's calculations, I subtracted his Totora figures from the Carangas column and added them to that of Mizque. Totora was part of the Corregimiento de Mizque until the intendency system was implemented.

89. D. L. Brockington et al., *Estudios arqueológicos*.

90. Cole, *The Potosí Mita*, 125.

91. Larson, *Colonialism*, 33.

92. AHMC-MP, Vol. 1591–1598, Vol. 1597–1607, exp. 18, Vol. 1605–1607, Vol. 1630–1730; ANB-M, Vol. 1645, leg. 11, and Vol. 1683; AHMC-MP, Vol. 1694–96.

93. Saignes, *Los Andes orientales*, 7, 21, 26, 27, 55, 82. Saignes's work is extremely helpful for the regionalist. His explanations of the geography, topography, ethnicities, and inter-ethnic relations have been indispensable for this project, and in my opinion they deserve the weight afforded primary sources.

94. Saignes, *Los Andes orientales*, 10–70, 81–148, 158, 196, 214, 222, 253–57, 297–99.

95. AHMC-MP, Vol. 1630–1730, Padron de Visita Pocona-Mizque, fs. 12–16, 44–45.

96. See also the above-mentioned works by Saignes (*Los Andes orientales*), Cole (*The Potosí Mita*), Larson (*Colonialism*), Barragán Romano ("Ayllus y haciendas"), et al.

97. Saignes, *Los Andes orientales*, 66–68.

98. L. G. Brockington, "Trabajo, etnicidad y raza."

99. ANB-M, Vol. 1683; AHMC-MP, Vol. 1694–95.

100. Saignes, *Los Andes orientales*, 59, 74, 81, 96, 101.

101. L. G. Brockington, "La dinámica," 75–104. See also chapter 2 of this volume.

102. ANB-M, Vol. 1683; AHMC-MP, Vol. 1694–95; and Saignes, *Los Andes orientales*, 101.

103. Larson, *Colonialism*, 94–95; Wightman, *Indigenous Migration*, 9–10, 19–20; and Powers, *Andean Journeys*, 7.

104. AHMC-MP, Vols. 1597–1607, 1630–1730; ANB-M, Vol. 1645, no. 11, Vol. 1683, no. 3; AHMC-MP, Vol. 1694–1695, leg. 15.

105. Barragán Romano, "Ayllus y haciendas," 131–32, 134.

106. Barragán Romano, "Ayllus y haciendas," 136.

107. ANB-M, no. 3, 1645.

108. ANB-M, no. 3, 1645.

109. Powers, *Andean Journeys*, 84–87.

110. Powers, *Andean Journeys*, 93.

7. Town, Countryside, Social Construct

1. Guaman Poma de Ayala, *Nueva crónica y buen gobierno*, 985.

2. Gade, *Nature and Culture*, 227 n. 1. Here, Gade explains the longtime existence of a native bee colony that continues to produce a honey for which Mizque remains reknown throughout the region. See also Viscarra, *Apuntes*, 209, 210–11.

3. AHMC-MP, Vol. 1599–1621; ANB-EXP, 1614, exp. 12, fs. 12–19; AHMC-MP, Vol. 1630–1730.

4. Gade, *Nature and Culture*, 86–87, 97; Viedma, *Descripción geográfica*, 83–84.

5. *Libros de baptizados, casados, y difuntos* de la Iglesia Mayor de la Villa de Salinas, 1648–1737. Padre Mauricio Valcanover generously allowed me access to these records, which are in the archives of the Iglesia Mayor de San Francisco in the presdnt-day town of Mizque.

6. *Libros de baptizados*; Gade, *Nature and Culture*, 96. Unfortunately, there exists a draconian genetic trade-off in the malaria vs. sickle-cell equation. I have personally witnessed the ravages of sickle-cell anemia once it aggressively asserts itself in young adulthood. It is a painful, progressive, debilitating, and

ultimately deadly disease. For a broader view of New World disease see Alchon, *Native Society and Disease in Colonial Ecuador*, 60, 102–3, and *A Pest in the Land*.

7. Viedma, *Descripción geográfica*, 83–84. He also discussed the wide variety of poisonous critters large and small still prevalent today in Mizque's warmer zones, such as *vinchucas* (Chagas disease) and *niguas* (water fleas that burrow into the feet and under toenails causing itching and eventually, if not treated, serious infection). See also Gade, *Nature and Culture*, 91, who refers to the unfortunate "leftovers of tertian fever."

8. Viedma, *Descripción geográfica*, 84.

9. AHMC-MP, Vol. 1605–1607, fs. 29–29v, 31, 32–32v, 34, amd Vol. 1605–1620, fs. 133–33v.

10. See Burns, *Colonial Habits*, 113. This work succinctly and eloquently explains the invaluable societal space in the colonial world occupied by the nuns and their convents. The nuns provided many services and benefits to colonial society, including the indoctrination of, and the nurturing and educating of, many of its girls and women.

11. AHMC-MP, Vol. 1605–1607, fs. 29–29v, 31, 32–32v, 34, and Vol. 1605–1620, 133–33v.

12. AHMC-MP, Vol. 1605–1607, fs. 29–29v, 31, 32–32v, 34, and Vol. 1605–1620, 133–33v.

13. AHMC-MP, Vol. 1605–1607, fs. 29–29v, 31, 32–32v, 34, and Vol. 1605–1620, 133–33v.

14. AHMC-MP, Vol. 1597–1607, exp. 18.

15. AHMC-MP, Vol. 1597–1607, exp. 18; ANB-M, 1633, no. 1.

16. ANB-M, 1616, no. 1, fs. 2–3v.

17. ANB-M, 1616, no. 1, fs. 2–3v.

18. ANB-M, 1616, no. 1, fs. 2–3v.

19. AHMC-MP, Vol. 38, leg. 1, fs. 2, 14v, 15–16, 17–17v.

20. AHMC-MP, Vol. 38, leg. 1, fs. 2, 14v, 15–16, 17–17v.

21. AHMC-MP, Vol. 1597–1607, exp. 3.

22. AHMC-MP, Vol. 1597–1607, exp. 3.

23. AHMC-MP, Vol. 1597–1607, exp. 3.

24. ANB-TI, 1624, exp. 6, 23–26, 27v.

25. AHMC-MP, Vol. 1597–1607, exp. 8.

26. AHMC-MP, Vol. 1605–1607.

27. AHMC-MP, Vol. 1597–1607, exp. 10.

28. AHMC-MP, Vol. 1561–1590, exp. 11, fs. 1047–1048.

29. ANB-EXP, 1685, exp. 47, fs. 12v–14.

30. See, e.g., Twinam, "Honor, Sexuality, and Illegitimacy"; Calvo, "The Warmth of the Hearth"; and Burns, *Colonial Habits*, 35, 121.

31. ANB-M, 1616, no. 1.

32. AHMC-MEC, Vol. 1561–1590.

33. AHMC-MP, Vols. 1599–1629, 1597–1607.

34. AHMC-MP, Vol. 1597–1607.

35. AHMC-MP, Vol. 1597–1607; ANB-M, 1619, no. 2, fs. 2–28, 30–34.

36. ANB-M, 1619, no. 2, fs. 2–28.

37. ANB-M, 1619, no. 2, fs. 2–28.

38. ANB-M, 1619, no. 2, fs. 2–28. While capital punishment did exist, more typical perhaps was the 1625 sentence issued to Indian Miguel Limancha for having killed Simón mulato in a drunken brawl. He was ordered to walk through the streets of Mizque wearing a hair shirt and with a rope around his throat and tied to his hands and feet to represent the act of justice. A town crier was to walk in his lead, publically announcing his criminal deeds, to be followed by two hundred lashes on his back. Finally, he was sentenced to two years in prison, serving in its workshop.

39. ANB-M, 1619, no. 2, fs. 2–28.

40. ANB-M, 1633, no. 1. A number of people appear to be involved in this litigation, including Captain Gabriel Encinas, though in what capacity is not entirely clear. Melo was not happy with him and accused him of "malice," possibly out of some residual rancor over the bridge affair.

41. ANB-M, 1635, no. 5.

42. ANB-M, 1635, no. 5.

43. ANB-M, 1635, no. 5.

44. ANB-M, 1635, nos. 3 and 6, 1636, no. 5.

45. ANB-M, 1609, no. 6.

46. ANB-M, 1628, no. 5.

47. ANB-M, 1628, no. 5. Restraining devices such as shackles, leg irons, collars, and chains were often associated with the production units where slaves of African origins toiled. That Melo even had such equipment at his immediate disposal suggests a wider distribution of African slave labor, or that employers used these restraints on whomever they so deemed required punishment. The former may be the more accurate than the latter, particularly in the light of Juan's protests associating the leg irons with African slavery.

48. AHMC-MP, Vol. 1605–1607.

49. ANB-M, 1698, no. 2.

50. ANB-M, 1698, no. 2.

51. MV-AGI, Charcas, 135, 6 fs.

52. This decree is cited in Portugal Ortíz, *La esclavitud negra*, 22. Similar royal orders appeared in Mexico as early as 1541. See Palmer, *Slaves of the White God*, 62–63.

53. For earlier works focusing on the Lima and coastal regions, see Lockhart, *Spanish Peru* (2nd ed.), 171–98; Bowser, *African Slave*; and Cushner, *Lords of the Land*, 81–112. Investigations that look beyond the coast and

into Andean highlands include Portugal Ortíz, *La esclavitud negro*; Crespo, *Esclavos negros*; and Bridikhina, *La mujer negra*.

54. See Blanchard, *Slavery and Abolition*, 48–50.

55. Portugal Ortíz, *La esclavitud negra*, 45.

56. Crespo, *Esclavos negros*, 117. On the disarming of the slave, see ANB-EXP, 1629, no. 4.

57. Portugal Ortíz, *La esclavitud negra*, 59, 60–61, 70–73.

58. Crespo, *Esclavos negros*, 97.

59. Crespo, *Esclavos negros*, 97.

60. Crespo, *Esclavos negros*, 97.

61. Crespo, *Esclavos negros*, 97.

62. Bridikhina, *La mujer negra*, 40–42. Other examples of harsh treatment can be found in Herrera, "Por Que No Sabenos Firmar," 256; Lane, *Quito 1599*, 67–68; and Landers, *Black Society in Spanish Florida*, 183–201. Also, I remind the reader of the Indian apprentice of Andrés Melo, who was put in leg irons and then strung up on the rafters and whipped "like a black slave" (twice, he claimed). This could suggest that such abuse of black slaves was more prevalent than the documents reveal, providing yet another reminder of the "forgotten" in history. It also glaringly testifies that abusive punishment was acceptable for black slaves but not for Indians. For Francisca's case see ANB-EXP, 1746, no. 5.

63. AHMC-MP, Vol. 13, 1604, Vol. 1605–1607, exp. 22.

64. ANB-AUDCH/CORR, 1633.IX.1.

65. ANB-M, 1651, no. 1, 1613, no. 16, 1619, no. 5, and 1674, no. 4. These cases are a sampling of what is in the Mizque Collection housed in the Archivo Nacionial de Bolivia. This collection is also the repository for most audiencia business, including court litigations. I also examined dozens of other cases originating in the regions mentioned earlier in the text: La Paz, La Plata, Potosí, Oruro, Tarija, etc., some of which are also cited in Portugal Ortíz, *La esclavitud negro*; Crespo, *Esclavos negros*; and Bridikhina, *La mujer negra*. All cases adhere to the same standard in terms of form, content, language, and procedure.

66. ANB-M, 1651, no. 1, fs. 3–28. This case, actually covering some fifty detailed pages, is relatively brief. Other court cases involving runaways and other forms of slave resistance are much longer. The documents relating to a specific case are numerous and often chronologically scrambled, making it something of an organizational challenge for the researcher. The case cited here was one of several I came across relating to ownership of highly skilled, valuable runaway slaves.

67. ANB-M, 1651, no. 1, fs. 3–28.

68. ANB-M, 1651, no. 1, fs. 3–28.

69. ANB-M, 1651, no. 1, fs. 3–28.

70. ANB-M, 1651, no. 1, fs. 3–28.

71. ANB-EXP, 1657, no. 2, fs. 1–56. See also ANB-EXP, 1656, no. 27, 1660, no. 6 and 7, 1673, no. 23, and 1693, no. 3. All concern accusation of fraudulent claims in the sale of ill or otherwise unsuitable slaves.

72. ANB-M, 1674, no. 4, 5 fs.

73. ANB-M, 1619, no. 5, 10 fs. For a detailed explanation of Mizque trade and transport routes see L. G. Brockington, "La dinámica."

74. ANB-M, 1619, no. 5, 10 fs.

75. *Black's Law Dictionary*, 5th ed.

76. Blanchard, *Slavery and Abolition*, 97; Crespo, *Esclavos negros*, 203. Although it is beyond the parameters of this work, it is of more than passing interest that Peru achieved its independence from Spain in 1824. Abolition of slavery there came much later, and only by increment, in the 1850s. Bolivia's independence from Spain occurred in 1825, but there too the abolition of slavery was a slow process, barely realized by 1851.

77. ANB-EXP, 1584, exp. 1, 1592, exp. 4, 1678, exp. 39, 1680, exp. 30, 1682, exp. 1, 1697, exp. 3197, and 1707, exp. 43, to cite a few.

78. Blanchard, *Slavery and Abolition*, 96, 103.

79. The padrones de chacara quantify the severity of the labor shortage.

80. AHMC-MP, Vol. 1561–1590; AHMC-MEC, Vol. 1591–1598, Vol. 1605–1620, fs. 1594–1599; ANB-M, 1603, no. 6.

81. AHMC-MEC, Vol. 1605–1607; ANB-M, 1618, no. 3.

82. ANB-M, 1639, no. 2, fs. 2–3v, 6v–12, 13v–15v, 18–19.

83. ANB-M, 1713, no. 12.

84. ANB-M, 1613, no. 4.

85. ANB-M, 1613, no. 4.

86. ANB-M, 1610, no. 4.

87. ANB-M, 1610, no. 4.

88. ANB-M, 1610, no. 4.

89. ANB-M, 1610, no. 4.

Bibliography

Adorno, Rolena. *Guaman Poma: Writing and Resistance in Colonial Peru*. Austin: University of Texas Press, 2000.

Alchon, Suzanne Austin. *Native Society and Disease in Colonial Ecuador*. New York: Cambridge University Press, 1991.

————. *A Pest in the Land: New World Epidemics in a Global Perspective*. Albuquerque: University of New Mexico Press, 2003.

Andrews, George Reid. *The Afro-Argentines in Buenos Aires, 1800–1900*. Madison: University of Wisconsin Press, 1980.

Andrien, Kenneth J. *Crisis and Decline: The Viceroyalty of Peru in the Seventeenth Century*. Albuquerque: University of New Mexico Press, 1985.

————. "Spaniards, Andeans, and the Early Colonial State in Peru." In *Transatlantic Encounters: Europeans and Andeans in the Sixteenth Century*, ed. Kenneth J. Andrien and Rolena Adorno, 121–48. Berkeley: University of California Press, 1991.

Archer, Christon I. *The Army in Bourbon Mexico, 1760–1810*. Albuquerque: University of New Mexico Press, 1977.

Arzans de Orsúa y Vela, Bartolomé. *Historia de la villa imperial de Potosí*. Ed. Lewis Hanke and Gunnar Mendoza. 3 vols. Providence: Brown University Press, 1965.

Arze, Silvia, Rossana Barragán, and Ximena Medinaceli. "Un panorama de las investigaciones históricas, 1970–1992." *Unitas* 13–14 (June 1994): 104–45.

Bakewell, Peter. *Miners of the Red Mountain: Indian Labor in Potosí*. Albuquerque: University of New Mexico Press, 1984.

Barnadas, Josep M. *Charcas: Origines históricas de una sociedad colonial, 1523–1565*. La Paz: Centro de Investigación y Promoción del Campesino, 1973.

————. *Manual de bibliografía: Introducción a los estudios bolivianos contemporaneos, 1960–1984*. Cuzco: Centro de Estudios Rurales Andinos "Bartolomé de las Casas," 1987.

Barragán Romano, Rossana. "Ayllus y haciendas en los valles orientales de Bolivia. Tres estudios de caso: Palca (siglo XVI), Mizque (siglo XVI–XVII), norte de La Paz (siglo XVI–XIX)." Unpublished manuscript, 1989.

———. *¿Indios de arco y flecha? Entre la historia y la arqueología de poblaciones del norte de Chuquisaca (siglos XV–XVI)*. Prologue by Gabriel Martínez. Sucre: Antropólogos del Surandino 3, 1994.

———. "El torno al modelo communal mercantile: El caso de Mizque (Cochabamba) en el siglo XVII." *Revista Chungará* 15 (December 1985): 125–41.

Berlin, Ira, and Philip D. Morgan, eds. *The Slaves' Economy: Independent Production by Slaves in the Americas*. London: Frank Case & Co., 1991.

Bishko, Charles J. "The Peninsular Background of Latin American Cattle Ranching." *Hispanic American Historical Review* 32 (1952): 491–515.

Blanchard, Peter. *Slavery and Abolition in Early Republican Peru*. Wilmington DE: Scholarly Resources, 1992.

Bowser, Fredrick P. *The African Slave in Colonial Peru, 1524–1650*. Stanford: Stanford University Press, 1974.

Bridikhina, Eugenia. *La mujer negra en Bolivia*. La Paz: Ministerio de Desarrollo Humano, Secretaría Nacional de Asuntos Étnicos, de Género y Generacionales, Subsecretaría de Asuntos de Géneros, 1995.

Brockington, Donald L., David M. Pereira Herrera, Ramón Sanzetenea Rocha, and María de los Angeles Muñoz C. *Estudios arqueológicos del período formativo en el sur-este de Cochabamba, 1988–1989*. Cuadernos de Investigación, Serie Arqueología 8. Cochabamba: Instituto de Antropológico y Museo, Universidad Mayor de San Simón, 1995.

Brockington, Lolita Gutiérrez. "The African Diaspora in the Eastern Andes: Adaptation, Agency, and Fugitive Action, 1573–1677." *The Americas* 57, no. 2 (2000): 207–24.

———. "Los archivos de Mizque: una nueva vision de las fuentes viejas." Translated by Emma María Sordo (The Mizque Collections: A New Look at Old Sources). *Anuario 1994–1995* (Archivo y Biblioteca Nacional de Bolivia) (1996): 301–5.

———. "La dinámica de la historia regional: El caso de Mizque y 'la' puente de 1630." *Historia y Cultura* (Lima: Instituto Nacional de Cultura) 22 (1994): 75–104.

———. *The Leverage of Labor: Managing the Cortés Haciendas in Tehuantepec, 1588–1688*. Durham NC: Duke University Press, 1989.

———. "Mizque: Indians and Region," "Mojos Region," "Oriente Region," "Santa Cruz: City and Region," "Tarija: City and Region," and "Yungas." *Encyclopedia of Latin American History and Culture*, editor in chief, Barbara A. Tenenbaum, 4:83b–84a, 4:89b, 4:238a–b, 5:53a–b, 5:203b–204a, 4:488a–b. New York: Scribner, 1996.

———. "Trabajo, etnicidad y raza: El afro-boliviano en el corregimiento de Mizque (1573–1787)." *Anuario* (Archivo y Biblioteca Nacional de Bolivia) (1996): 107–22.

Burkholder, Mark A., and Lyman L. Johnson, eds. *Colonial Latin America*. 4th ed. New York: Oxford University Press, 2001.

Burns, Kathryn. *Colonial Habits: Convents and the Spiritual Economy of Cuzco, Peru.* Durham NC: Duke University Press, 1999.

———. "Notaries, Truth, and Consequences." *American Historical Review* 110, no. 2 (2005): 350–79.

Calvo, Thomas. "The Warmth of the Hearth: Seventeenth-Century Guadalajara Families." In *Sexuality and Marriage in Colonial Latin America*, ed. Asunción Lavrin, 287–312. Lincoln: University of Nebraska Press, 1986.

Casevitz, F. M. Renard, Thierry Saignes, and A. C. Taylor. *Al este de los Andes: Relaciones entre las sociedades amazónicas y andinas, XV–XVII.* 2 vols. Instituto Frances de Estudios Andinos, Lima. Quito: ABYA-YALA, 1988.

Cole, Jeffrey A. *The Potosí Mita, 1573–1700: Compulsory Indian Labor in the Andes.* Stanford: Stanford University Press, 1985.

Crespo R., Alberto. *Esclavos negros en Bolivia.* La Paz: Academia Nacional de Ciencas, Talleres de Litografías, 1977.

Cushner, Nicholas P. *Farm and Factory: The Jesuits and the Development of Agrarian Capitalism in Colonial Quito, 1600–1767.* Albany: SUNY Press, 1983.

———. *Jesuit Ranches and Agrarian Development of Colonial Argentina, 1650–1767.* Albany: SUNY Press, 1983.

———. *Lords of the Land: Sugar, Wine and Jesuit Estates of Coastal Peru, 1600–1767.* Albany: SUNY Press, 1982.

Davies, Keith. *Landowners in Colonial Peru.* Austin: University of Texas Press, 1984.

Deheza, Gustavo, Juan Clavijo, and Roy Querejazu. *Monografía de la Provincia de Mizque.* Cochabamba: Centro de Investigación y Desarrollo Regional, 1987.

Diccionario histórico de Bolivia. Ed. Josep M. Barnadas, Guillermo Calvo, and Juan Teclla. 2 vols. Sucre: Grupo de Estudios Históricos, 2002.

Dusenberry, William H. *The Mexican Mesta: The Administration of Ranching in Colonial Mexico.* Urbana: University of Illinois Press, 1963.

Escobari de Querejazu, Laura. *Producción y comercio en el espacio sur andino, siglo XVII.* La Paz: Auspiciada por la Embajada de España en Bolivia, 1985.

Espinoza, Waldemar. "El memorial de Charcas 'crónica' inédita de 1582." *Revista Cantuta* 4 (1969): 117–51.

Finot, Enrique. *Historia de la conquista del oriente boliviano.* La Paz: Editorial "Juventude," 1978.

Gade, Daniel W. "Bridge Types in the Central Andes." *Annuals of the Association of American Geographers* 62, no. 1 (1972): 94–109.

———. "Inca and Colonial Settlement: Coca Cultivation and Endemic Disease in the Tropical Forest." *Journal of Historical Geography* 5, no. 3 (1979): 263–79.

———. *Nature and Culture in the Andes.* Madison: University of Wisconsin Press, 1999.

Geggus, David P. "Sugar and Coffee Cultivation in Saint Dominque and the Shaping of the Slave Labor Force." In *Cultivation and Culture: Labor and the Shaping of Slave Life in the Americas*, ed. Ira Berlin and Philip D. Morgan, 73–98. Charlottesville: University Press of Virginia, 1993.

Glave, Luís Miguel, and María Isabel Remy. *Estructura agraria y vida rural en la región andina: Ollantaytambo entre los siglos XVI–XIX*. Cuzco: Centro de Estudios Rurales Andinos "Bartolomé de las Casas," 1983.

González, Juan. "Visita de los indios churumatas e yndios charcas de Totora que todos estan en cabeza de su majestad, 1560." Transcripción e introducción por Raimund Schramm. Serie: Fuentes Primarias. La Paz: Museo Nacional de Etnografía y Folklore, 1990.

Gordillo Claure, José Miguel. "Aportes al estudio del estado colonial colonial y la economía regional: Larson-Sempat Assadourian." *Revista Estudios UMSS* 1, no. 1 (1987): 65–75.

———. *El origin de la hacienda en el Valle Bajo de Cochabamba: Coformación de la estructura agraria, 1550–1700*. Cochabamba: Universidad Mayor de San Simón, 1987.

———. "El proceso de extinción del yanaconaje en el valle de Cochabamba: Análsis de un padrón de yanaconas, 1692." In *Revista Estudios UMSS*, 29–59. Cochabamba: Universidad Mayor de San Simón: Centro de Formación e Investigación Interdisciplinaria, 1988.

Gordillo Claure, José Miguel, and Mercedes del Río. *La revista de Tiquipaya (1573): Análisis etno-demográfico de un padrón toledano*. Cochabamba: Universidad Mayor de San Simón et al., 1993.

Guaman Poma de Ayala, Felipe. *Nueva crónica y buen gobierno*. Ed. Franklin Pease. Vol. 2. Lima: Fondo de Cultura Económica, 1993.

Haring, C. H. *The Spanish Empire in America*. New York: Harcourt, Brace, 1952.

Harris, Olivia, Brooke Larson, and Enrique Tandeter, eds. *La participación indigena en los mercados surandinos: Estrategias y reproducción social, siglos XVI–XX*. La Paz: Centro de Estudios de la Realidad Económica y Social, 1987.

Herr, Richard. *An Historical Essay on Modern Spain*. Berkeley: University of California Press, 1971.

Herrera, Robinson. "Por Que No Sabemos Firmar: Black Slaves in Early Guatemala." *The Americas* 57, no. 2 (2000): 247–67.

Julien, Catherine. "Coca Production on the Inca Frontier: The Yungas of Chuquioma." *Andean Past* 5 (1998): 129–60.

———. *Reading Inca History*. Iowa City: University of Iowa Press, 2000.

Klein, Herbert S. *Bolivia: The Evolution of a Multi-ethnic Society*. New York: Oxford University Press, 1982.

Konrad, Herman W. *A Jesuit Hacienda in Colonial Mexico: Santa Lucia, 1576–1767*. Stanford: Stanford University Press, 1980.

Landers, Jane. *Black Society in Spanish Florida*. Urbana: University of Illinois Press, 1999.

Lane, Kris E. *Quito 1599: City and Colony in Transition*. Albuquerque: University of New Mexico Press, 2002.

Lanning, Edward P. *Peru before the Incas*. Englewood Cliffs NJ: Prentice-Hall, 1967.

Larson, Brooke. "Bolivia Revisited: New Directions in North American Research in History and Anthropology." *Latin American Research Review* 23, no. 1 (1988): 63–89.

———. *Colonialism and Agrarian Transformation in Bolivia: Cochabamba, 1550–1900*. Princeton: Princeton University Press, 1988.

Léons, Madeline Barbara, and Harry Sanabria. "Coca and Cocaine in Bolivia: Reality and Policy Illusion." In *Coca, Cocaine, and the Bolivian Reality*, ed. Madeline Barbara Léons and Harry Sanabria, 1–46. Albany: SUNY Press, 1977.

Lockhart, James M. *Spanish Peru, 1532–1560: A Colonial Society*. Madison: University of Wisconsin Press, 1968.

———. *Spanish Peru, 1532–1560: A Colonial Society*, 2nd ed. Madison: University of Wisconsin Press, 1994.

López Beltran, Clara. *Estructura económica en una sociedad colonial: Charcas en el siglo XVII*. La Paz: Centro de Estudios de la Realidad Económica y Social, 1988.

Meruvia Balderrama, Fanor. *Historia de la coca: Las Yungas de Pocona y Totora (1550–1900)*. La Paz: Plural Editores, 2000.

Métraux, Alfred. "Tribes of the Eastern Slopes of the Bolivian Andes." In *Handbook of South American Indians*, vol. 2, *Tropical Forest Tribes*, ed. Julian H. Steward, 465–67. Bureau of American Ethnology Bulletin 143. Washington DC: Smithsonian Institution, 1948.

Mörner, Magnus. *The Andean Past: Land, Societies, and Conflicts*. New York: Columbia University Press, 1985.

Mujía, Ricardo. *Bolivia-Paraguay*. 10 vols. La Paz: Editorial de "El Tiempo," 1914.

Murra, John V. *The Economic Organization of the Inca State*. Greenwich CN: Greenwood Press, 1980.

———. " 'El Archipelago vertical' Revisited." In *Andean Ecology and Civilization: An Interdisciplinary Perspective on Andean Ecological Complementarity*, ed. Shozo Masuda, Izumi Shimada, and Craig Morris, 3–14. Tokyo: University of Tokyo Press, 1985.

———. "The Limits and Limitations of the 'Vertical Archipelago' in the Andes." In *Andean Ecology and Civilization: An Interdisciplinary Perspective on Andean Ecological Complementarity*, ed. Shozo Masuda, Izumi Shimada, and Craig Morris, 15–19. Tokyo: University of Tokyo Press, 1985.

New Velázquez Spanish and English Dictionary. Clinton NJ: New Win Publishing, 1999.

O'Phelan Godoy, Scarlette. *Un siglo de rebeliones anticoloniales: Peru y Bolivia, 1700–1783.* Cuzco: Centro de Estudios Rurales Andinas "Bartolomé de las Casas," 1988.

Palmer, Colin A. "Defining and Studying the Modern African Diaspora." *Perspectives* (American Historical Association newsletter) 36, no. 6 (1998): 1, 22–25.

————. *Human Cargoes: the British Slave Trade to Spanish America, 1700–1739.* Urbana: University of Illinois Press, 1981.

————. *Slaves of the White God: Blacks in Mexico, 1570–1650.* Cambridge: Harvard University Press, 1976.

Pease, Franklin, ed. "Una visita al obispado de Charcas 1590." *Humanidades* 3 (1969): 89–125.

Peñalosa y Mondragon, Benito Fr. *Libro de las cinco excelencias del Español que despueblan a España su major postencia de dilatación . . .* Pamplona: Carlos de Labayen, 1629.

Pereira Herrera, David M., María de los Angeles Muñoz, Ramón Sanzetenea Rocha, and Donald L. Brockington. *Conchupata: Un panteón formativo temprano en el valle de Mizque (Cochabamba), Bolivia.* Cuadernos de Investigación, Serie Arqueología 7. Cochabamba: Instituto de Antropología y Museo, Universidad Mayor de San Simón, 1992.

Platt, Tristan. "Acerca del sistema tributario pre-Toledano en el Alto Perú." *Advances* 1 (1978): 33–44.

————. *Estado boliviano y allyu andino: Tierra y tributo en el norte de Potosí.* Lima: Instituto de Estudios Peruanos, 1982.

Portugal Ortíz, Max. *La esclavitud negra en las épocas colonial y nacional de Bolivia.* La Paz: Instituto Boliviano de Cultura, 1977.

Powers, Karen Viera. *Andean Journeys: Migration, Ethnogenesis, and the State in Colonial Quito.* Albuquerque: University of New Mexico Press, 1995.

Presta, Ana María. *Encomienda, familia, y negocios en Charcas colonial (Bolivia): Los encomenderos de La Plata, 1550–1600.* Lima: Instituto de Estudios Peruanos/Banco Central de Reserva de Peru, 2000.

————, ed. *Espacios, étnias y fronteras: Atenuaciones políticas en el sur de Tawantinsuyo, siglos XV–XVIII.* Sucre: Antropólogos del Surandino 4, 1995.

Ramírez, Susan Elizabeth. *The World Upside Down: Cross-Cultural Contact and Conflict in Sixteenth-Century Peru.* Stanford: Stanford University Press, 1996.

Ramírez Valverde, María, transcriber. "Visita a Pocona 1557." *Historia y Cultura* (Lima: Instituto Nacional de Cultura) 4 (1970): 269–308.

Real Academia Española. *Diccionario de la lengua Española.* 21st ed. 2 vols. Madrid: Editorial Espaso Cape, SA, 1996.

Rodríguez Ostria, Gustavo. "Mercado interior, liberalismo y conflictos regionales: Cochabamba y Santa Cruz (1880–1932)." *Revista de Historia y Cultura* 18 (October 1990): 79–80.

———. *Poder central y proyecto regional, Cochabamba y Santa Cruz en los siglos XIX y XX*. Cochabamba: Instituto Latinoamericano de Investigaciones Sociales, 1993.

Rojas Vaca, Hector Luís. *Población y territorio: Una perspectiva histórica, Mizque y Ayopaya*. Cochabamba: Centro de Comunicación y Desarrollo Andino, 2001.

Rojas Vaca, Hector Luís, and Claudio Montaño. "Haciendas de Campero: Crisis y expansión." Cochabamba: Universidad Mayor de San Simón, Centro de Formación e Investigación Interdisciplinaria, 1987.

Saignes, Thierry. *Los Andes orientales: Historia de un olvido*. Cochabamba: Centro de Estudios de la Realidad Económica y Social, 1985.

Sanabria F., Hernando. *Cronicario de la cuidad de Jesús y Montes Claros de los caballeros*. La Paz: Publicaciones de la Fundación Ramón D. Gutiérrez de Santa Cruz de la Sierra, Empresa Editora "Urquizo, LTDA," 1971.

Sánchez-Albornoz, Nicolás. *Indios y tributos en el Alto Peru*. Lima: Instituto de Estudios Peruanos, 1978.

———. "Mita, migraciones y pueblos: Variaciones en el espacio y en el tiempo, Alto Peru, 1573–1692." *Historia Boliviana* 3, no. 1 (1983): 31–59.

Schramm, Raimund. "Archivo histórico de Cochabamba: Indice de documentos sobre indios y tierras (siglos XVI, XVII, XVIII)." *Revista Andino* 8, no. 1 (1990): 187–236.

———. "Fronteras y territorialidad repartición étnica y política colonizadora en los Charcas (valles de Ayopaya y Mizque)." *Jarbuch Für Geschichte: Von Staat, Wirtschaft, und Gesellschaft Lateinamericas* 30 (1993): 1–25.

———. "Mosaicos etno-históricos del valle de Cliza (valle alto cochabambino), siglo XVI." *Historia y Cultura* (La Paz: Sociedad Boliviana de Historia) 18 (October 1990): 3–42.

———. "Paces y guerras, coca y sal: Recursos naturales y planteamientos étnicos en el Anti de Pocona (corregimento de Mizque), siglos XVI–XVII." Unpublished paper, 1990.

———. *Pocona und Mizque: Die Umgestaltung einer indianescken gesellschaft im Kolonialsn Peru (Charcas)*. Köln: Weimar: Böhalu Verlag, 1999.

Sempat Assadourian, Carlos. *El sistema de la economia colonial: Mercado interno, regiones, y espacio económico*. Lima: Instituto de Estudios Peruanos, 1982.

Spedding, Alison L. "The Coca Field as a Total Social Fact." In *Coca, Cocaine, and the Bolivian Reality*, ed. Madeline Barbara Léons and Harry Sanabria, 47–70. Albany: SUNY Press, 1997.

Stern, Steve J. "Early Spanish-Indian Accommodation in the Andes." In *The Indian in Latin American History: Resistance, Resilience, and Accultura-*

tion, ed. John E. Kicza. Jaguar Books on Latin America, no. 1:23–52. Rev. ed. Wilmington DE: Scholarly Resources, 2000.

———. "Feudalism, Capitalism, and the World System." *American Historical Review* 93, no. 4 (1988): 829–72.

———. "Paradigms of Conquest: History, Historiography, and Politics." *Journal of Latin American Studies: The Colonial and Post Colonial Experience* (Quincentenary Supplement) 24 (1992): 1–34.

Studer, Elena F. S. de. *La trata de negros en Río de la Plata durante el siglo XVIII*. Buenos Aires: Universidad de Buenos Aires, 1958.

Tandeter, Enrique, and Nathan Wachter. *Precios y producción agraria: Potosí y Charcas en el siglo XVIII*. Buenos Aires: Estudios Centro de Estudios de Estado y Sociedad, 1983.

TePaske, John J. "The Fiscal Structure of Upper Peru and the Financing of Empire," In *Essays in the Political, Economic, and Social History of Colonial Latin America*, ed. Karen Spalding, 69–94. Newark: University of Delaware Press, 1984.

———. "The Search for El Dorado Redux: Gold Production in New Granada, New Spain, and Peru, 1521–1810." Paper presented at the annual meeting of the Virginia-Carolinas Colonial Latin American history seminar, Charleston, SC, April 1993.

TePaske, John J., and Herbert Klein. *The Royal Treasuries of the Spanish Empire in America*, vol. 2, *Upper Peru (Bolivia)*. Durham NC: Duke University Press, 1982.

Terrazas, Israel, et al. "Epidemias históricas en Capinota durante los siglos XVII–XIX: Años 1672–1868." Cochabamba: Universidad Mayor de San Simón, Centro de Formación e Investigación Interdisciplinaria, 1988. 61–85.

Torres, Bernardo de. *Crónicas agustinianas del Perú*, XVII. Cited in Deheza, Clavigo, and Querejazu, *Monografía*, 98–99.

Trouillot, Michel Ralph. *Silencing the Past: Power and the Production of History*. Boston: Beacon Press, 1995.

Twinam, Ann. "Honor, Sexuality, and Illegitimacy in Colonial Spanish America." *Sexuality and Marriage in Colonial Latin America*, ed. Asunción Lavrin, 118–49. Lincoln: University of Nebraska Press, 1986.

Vásquez Machado, Humberto, José de Mesa, and Teresa Gispert. *Manual de Historia de Bolivia*. La Paz: Gispert y Cia. SA Libreros Editores, 1963.

Vásquez Machicado, José. *Catálogo descriptivo del material del Archivo de Indias referente a la historia de Bolivia (Sevilla, 1933)*. 5 vols. La Paz: Ministerio de Educación y Cultura, Instituto Boliviano de Cultura, 1989.

Viedma, Francisco A. *Descripción geografía y estadística de la provincia de Santa Cruz de la Sierra*. 1836. Cochabamba: Editorial Los Amigos del Libro, 1969.

Vinson, Ben, III. *Bearing Arms for His Majesty: The Free-Colored Militia in Colonial Mexico*. Stanford: Stanford University Press, 2001.

Viscarra, Eufronio. *Apuntes para la historia de Cochabamba: Casos históricos y tradiciones de la ciudad de Mizque*. 1907. Cochabamba: Editorial Los Amigos del Libro, 1967.

Voelz, Peter M. *Slave and Soldier: The Military Impact of Blacks in the Colonial Americas*. New York: Garland, 1993.

Wachtel, Nathan. "The Mitimas of the Cochabamba Valley: The Colonization Policy of Huayna Capac." In *The Inca and Aztec States*, ed. George Collier, Renato Rosaldo, and John Wirth, 199–235. New York: Academic Press, 1982.

Wightman, Ann M. *Indigenous Migration and Social Change: The Forasteros of Cuzco, 1570–1720*. Durham NC: Duke University Press, 1990.

Index

Abrego y Figueroa, Gen. Álvaro, 80–81, 102, 108
abuse of slaves, 279–81, 319n47
acculturation of the curacas, 206–14
African diaspora, 130–31
Agicha, Curaca Don Juan, 212–13
agricultural products, 51–53, 77–78; coca, 90–91, 116–19; corn, 81, 98–99, 304n50; prices of, 81–83, 301nn9–10, 305n18; and proliferation of estates, 78–84; sugar plantations, 107–8, 115–16. *See also* vineyards
Álfaro, Francisco de, 43–44
Allallona silver mine, 119–20
Almagro, Diego de, 20, 21–22
Altamirano, Licenciado, 47
Álvares de Toledo y Gatico, Francisco, 134
Álvarez Meléndez, Antonio, 35–37, 38
Álvarez Meléndez, Cristoval, 89
Álvarez Meléndez, Joan, 89–91, 118, 132, 141; *mulato* slaves owned by, 161
Álvarez Meléndez, Julio, 240
Álvarez Meléndez, Leonor, 35, 39
Andrada, Manuel de, 70
Angola, María, 164
Angola, Ylario, 164
Antonius, Bishop, 177
Aponte, Antonio, 186
Aquino, Pedro de, 99
Arapa, Curaca Don Pedro, 97, 118
architects and carpenters of Mizque, 63–65

Archivo Histórico Municipal de Cochabamba, 4–5, 288
Archivo Nacional de Bolivia, 4–5, 288, 320n65
Arepucho coca fields, 183–85
Argumedo, Pedro, 53
Arias, Miguel, 271
Arias, Paula, 160, 165
Arias Dávila, Pedro, 35
Atahualpa, 19–20
Avila, Leonarda de, 172
Ayavire Y Velasco, Curaca Don Fernando, 204–5

Barnadas, Josep M., 20, 21, 26
Barragán, Rossana, 230
Bentura Mauricio, Juan, 165
Berbesi, Hernando, 161, 164, 167
Berbesi, Salvador, 160, 164
Betancourt, Matías de, 55
Blanchard, Peter, 267
Bowser, James, 129
bridge, the Río Grande: Andrés de Melo's supervision of, 69–72; bids to build, 63–65, 241; conflicts and regional interests over, 72–74; donations collected for, 65–69; funds for, 58–61; implications for surrounding towns, 58, 241–43; Indians used to construct, 64, 69; inspections during the construction of, 69–71; need for, 56–57; proposal for building, 55–56; regional contributions toward building, 60–62; yanaconas and, 228

Buena Vista chácara. *See* Paniagua de
 Loaysa, Gabriel
Buenos Aires, 131, 134, 136, 179, 279,
 311n97

Cabeza de Vaca, Fernando, 260
Cabeza de Vaca, Isodoro Veraga, 271
Cabrera, Andrés, 210
caciques, 96–98. *See also* estates
Calderón, Antonio, 57, 91, 159
Calderón, Juan, 173
Cañete, Viceroy, 24
Cano de Manzano, Joseph, 120–25
Caño de Paredes, Juan, 111–12, 244
Capagasa, Francisco, 148
Çarate, Pedro de, 240
Carrasco, Bartolomé, 109
Casa de la Moneda, 137
Cassanga, Antón, 270
Cauta chácara, 98–100
Cazorla, Hernando de, 25
Cazorla, Luis, 30
Cazorla de Guevara, Juan, 242
Cazorla Narváez, Fernando de, 27–31;
 church founded by, 50; slaves owned
 by, 134
censuses: ambiguities of, 165–70, 313n22;
 categories of slaves recorded in, 158–
 65; curacas, 213–14; *forasteros*,
 229–30; migration patterns and, 215–
 16; of slaves and their descendants,
 176–80; yanaconas, 220–28
Cereso de Aponte, Balthasar, 166
Cerrato, Antonio, 264–65
Céspedes y Abrego, Pedro, 43
Cevita, Curaca Don Miguel, 210
chácaras. See estates
Chalguani hacienda, 152–56, 158
Champi, Governor Don Pedro, 231–32
Chan, Gerónimo, 272–74, 285–86
Charcas province, 45–48
Chare, Martín, 140, 166
Charles I, King of Spain, 20
Chávez, Álvaro de, 25–27, 50–51
Chávez, Francisco de, 25–27

Chávez, Ñuflo de, 21, 25–27, 47
children: inheritances of, 246–48; legal
 rights of illegitimate, 246–47; of
 slaves, 167–69
Chiriguano Indians, 182, 203; ethnicity
 and ethnic identities, 217–18;
 Fernando de Cazorla Narváez attacks
 on, 29–30; Ñuflo de Chávez family
 attacks on, 25; settlement in the
 Mizque region, 22, 24; Spanish
 attacks on, 182–86
Chirima, Curaca Don Pedro, 96, 190
Choque, Andrés, 253–54
Chuquioma coca fields, 183–85, 194–95
churches. *See* Roman Catholic Church
Chuy Indians, 198–201, 205, 217–19
Cibita, Miguel, 270
cimarrones. See runaway slaves
Cisneros, Bernardo de, 120–23
Ciudad de Jesús del Valle Grande, 177–78
civic projects in the Mizque region, 50–51
civil wars, 23, 28, 35–36
Clemente, Bernabe, 163, 173
Clemente, Francisco, 160, 163
climate of Mizque, 15–16, 101, 234–35
coca production, 90–91, 116–19,
 313n27; attacks on Indians working
 in, 183–85; battles over control of,
 186–97; closing of fields involved in,
 194–95; curacas and, 209; health and,
 189–92; during Inca control, 187,
 189; levels, 192, 314n42; slave labor
 used in, 195–97; working rotations,
 190–91
cohabitation and marriage, 272–74, 285
Cole, Jeffrey, 215
common people and the courts, 255–58
Congo, Francisco, 159
Congo, Juan, 159
Congo, Pedro, 166
Copachuncho hacienda, 89–91, 141
corn production, 81, 98–99, 304n50
Cortés, Gen. Bartolomé, 91, 104, 111;
 mules and slaves owned by, 115;
 slaves owned by, 143–47, 171

Cortés, Luisa, 104, 107
Cortés de Encinas, Otalla, 160
Corzo, Francisco, 142
Cosio, Diego de, 264
Cota, Antonio, 219
Cota, Catalina, 256–57
cowboys, 269–72
Crespo, Alberto, 137, 176–77, 179
curacas: acculturation and demise
    of, 206–14; census recording of,
    213–14; demands made by, 201–6;
    inheritances, 244–45; litigation
    against, 209–10; protests against
    abusive treatment, 211–12; slaves
    and land owned by, 207–8; taxes on,
    208–9. *See also* Indians
Cushner, Nicholas P., 158

Dávalos de Zárate, Juan, 44, 212
demands: made by curacas to the
    Spaniards, 201–6
disease in the Mizque region, 49–50,
    211–12, 278–79, 295n19, 309n47;
    and environmental changes, 235–37;
    leishmaniasis, 189–92; malaria,
    235–37, 287–88, 317–18n6
Durán, María, 91

economy, Mizque. *See* trade
Encinas, Gabriel de, 43, 53, 60, 111, 250;
    children of, 84–85, 238–41; expenses
    of, 87–88; hacienda owned by, 84–89;
    houses of, 88–89; income of, 85, 87;
    lifestyle of, 238–41; livestock owned
    by, 85–86; mayordomos of, 102–3;
    slaves owned by, 133, 140
Encinas Saavedra, Francisco, 85–89, 110
encomendero system, 24–25
environment, Mizque: ravages of disease
    and, 235–37
Episana estate, 142–44
Escalante, Pedro de, 177–78
Esclavos negros en Bolivia, 176
Espinoza, Waldemar, 201–2
estancias. *See* estates

estates: Copachuncho, 89–91; Episana,
    142–44; income of successful, 85, 87,
    92–93; Jesuit, 78; La Calleja, 80–84;
    livestock of, 85–86, 89–90, 92, 110–
    11, 111–15; mayordomos, 102–8,
    304n54; Oloy, 84–89; outmigration
    from, 140–41; production costs, 87–
    88; proliferation and rapid turnover
    of, 78–84; slaves as inventory at,
    79, 83–84, 103, 108, 115, 139–40,
    142–47, 171, 180, 302nn15–16;
    successful, 84–96; tax appraisals,
    148–50; transfers, 142–44; Tucuma,
    93–96; Tucuma Baja, 94–96; Turque
    and Tuyota, 91–93, 143–47; wine
    production, 92–93, 108–15. *See also*
    caciques
ethnicity and ethnic identity: census
    records of, 215–16; of different Indian
    groups, 217–19; *huidos*, 219–26;
    lowland peoples, 219–27; migration
    patterns and, 214–15; Raché, 226–27;
    surnames revealing, 216–17; *yancona*,
    167–70, 219–26

families of the Mizque region, 25, 77;
    Fernando de Cazorla, 25, 27–31,
    134; Gabriel Paniagua de Loaysa, 26,
    28, 31–42, 49; Ñuflo de Chávez, 21,
    25–27
Fernández, Juan, 213
Ferrufino, Augustín, 85, 87, 102; slaves
    owned by, 159
forasteros, 228–33, 283. *See also*
    outsiders among Indians
Franciscans: testimonies on coca-worker
    abuse, 190, 192–93, 194
Francisco de Morales, Juan, 94
Fresnada y Zúñiga, Bernardo de la, 100,
    102, 103, 263; slaves owned by, 133,
    170–71; will of, 245

Gade, Daniel W., 189, 235–36
Gaita de Mendoza, Pedro, 98
Galarsa, Felipe, 213

Gallegos, Francisco, 200
García, Bartolomé, 142
García de Robles, Felipe, 94
García Morato, Miguel, 69, 71, 91
Garimbola, Diego, 148
Garro, Domingo, 166
Garro, Isabel, 166
Gasca, Pedro de la, 24, 40, 41
geography and prehistory of Mizque,
   2–3, 15–19
Godoy Aguilera, Capt. Joan, 183–86
Gómez Arnalde, Francisco, 53–55
Gómez Leal, Juan, 119–20
González, María, 78–79
González de la Torre, Juan, 94
Guadalcassar, Enríquez de, 59
Guanca, Curaca Lorenzo, 213–14
Guaraní Indians, 217–19
Guarayo, Curaca Don Alonzo, 97–98,
   210, 241–42, 247–48
Guarayo Indians, 217–19
Gutiérrez, Altamirano, 111–15, 120, 142,
   174, 271, 286
Gutiérrez Caro, Antonio, 124

haciendas. *See* estates
health and lifestyles of the wealthy,
   237–41. *See also* disease in the
   Mizque region
Hernández, Francisca, 99
Hernández, Juan, 99
Hernández, Pedro, 174, 199
Hernández, Rodrigo, 98–100
Hernández Girón, Francisco, 33
Hernández Paniagua, Pedro, 118, 132.
   See also Panigua de Loaysa, Pedro
   Fernández
hinterland-highland trade routes, 45–48,
   275–76
huidos, 220–26, 263, 268

illegitimate children, 246–47
Inca occupation of Mizque, 18–19, 27,
   117, 181, 214–15, 235, 275; coca
   production during, 187, 189; ethnicity

of people under, 217–19; lasting
   influence of, 49
income: caciques, 97; mayordomos,
   102–4; vineyards and haciendas,
   85–87, 92–93
Indians: acculturation and demise of,
   206–14; alliances created by, 23–24;
   categorization of, 140–41, 283–85;
   Chiriguano, 22, 24, 25, 29–30, 182–
   86, 203, 217–19; Christianization of,
   24, 49–50, 205–6, 275; Chuy, 198–
   201, 205, 217–19; coca production
   and taxes on, 34, 117–18, 187–97;
   construction work performed by,
   53–54, 211; disease among, 189–92,
   211–12, 278–79, 287–88, 317–18n6;
   ethnicity and ethnic identity, 214–28;
   formal requests to the Spanish,
   201–6; grain production by, 49;
   inheritances, 247–48; Isla de la Puna,
   27; land holdings, 197–201, 314n52;
   litigation against and incarceration of,
   209–10; migration patterns, 214–15,
   230–31; mining work by, 120–23;
   Mizque population, 51; names, 216;
   outsider, 228–33, 283; Pocona,
   117–18, 142, 177, 183–85, 188;
   protests against abusive treatment,
   211–12; Raché, 226–27; Spanish
   attempts to control, 181–86; Spanish
   defeat of, 19–22; vineyard work
   by, 105; wealthy, 205–6; Yunga,
   118–19, 217–19, 226–27. *See also*
   curacas
indigenous people. *See* Indians
Isla de la Puna, 27
Isodoro Belzu, Manuel, 179

Jesuits, 275; Chalguani slaves, 152–56,
   158; and slaves, 150–58, 172, 281;
   vineyards owned by, 78, 150–51,
   309n54
Juan de Paredes, Maese del Campo, 43,
   53
Julien, Catherine, 19

Juri Indians, 217–19
Justino de O'Campo, Juan, 124

labor: Indian, 3–54, 49, 105, 117–18, 120–23, 140–41, 188, 189, 211; skilled, 280; yanacona, 159–65; yunga, 118–19. *See also* slaves and their descendants
La Calleja vineyard, 80–84, 103–6; curacas, 213–14; diseases affecting workers at, 235–36
land and labor administration: agricultural products and, 51–53; caciques, 96–98; chácara Cauta, 98–100; chácara censuses in, 158–65; challenges and civic projects, 50–55; after death, 243–48; European settlement acceleration in, 48–50, 298n1; Indian holdings in, 197–201, 314n52; legal issues regarding, 198–201, 248–54; *mulatos* and, 174–75; Paniagua de Loaysa family and, 33–34, 37–40, 197–201; and rapid proliferation and turnover of estates in Mizque, 79–84; regional expansion in the Charcas interior and, 45–48; and the Río Grande bridge, 72–74; successful haciendas, 84–96
Lane, Kris, 132–33
La Plata: and the bridge across the Río Grande, 55–71, 72–73, 243; -Potosí market, 46–48, 288; slaves of, 259–65; wine trade, 109, 110
Lara, Pedro de, 53
Lascano Argumedo, Pedro, 44
la Sierra, Bernardo, 94
Layasa, Curaca Don Diego, 199
legal issues and courts: common people and, 255–58; curacas and, 209–10; inheritances, 242; land ownership, 198–201; livestock, 111–15; magistrates and, 175–76; marriage and cohabitation, 272–74, 285; mining claims, 120–23; mixed families, 160, 285; murder, 250–52,

286–87, 319n38; slaves, 258–69, 282; wills and inheritances, 242, 243–48
leishmaniasis disease, 189–92
León y Terán, Antonia de, 136
Lima-Cuzqueños, 20
livestock, 85–86, 89–90, 92, 110–11; cowboys and, 269–72; legal battles and regulations, 111–15, 305n24; mule teams, 115–16; production and regulations, 113–14; recua mules, 110–11; slave labor and, 142–43, 172–74
Llano, Juan de, 57
Loaysa, Gabriel, 90
Lockhart, James, 32, 129, 206
López de Arora, Sebastian, 109
lowlands, eastern Andean, 1–2, 185; indigenous ethnicities of, 219–27

Macías, Francisco de, 161
Macías Torrico, Francisco, 44, 142
Macompabomba, Francisco, 133
magistrates, 175–76
Malaga, Francisco, 174
Malaga, Julio de, 104
malaria, 235–37, 287–88, 317–18n6
Manso, Andrés, 28, 47
Manuel de Medina, Joseph, 166
marriage and cohabitation, 272–74, 285
Martín, Gonzalo de, 45
Martín, Hernando, 250–52, 286
Martínez de Sandagarda, Domingo, 136
Mauricio Chiminea, Juan, 160, 165
mayordomos, 102–8, 304n54, 311n95; legal problems, 111–15, 211–12; recua trips, 110–11
Medellín, Julia, 245–46
Mejía de Illescas, Juan, 124–25
Melo, Andrés de: criminal charges against, 254–55; land disputes with Elvira de Valenzuela, 252–54; land disputes with Gabriel de Encinas, 89; lawsuit filed by, 252; Río Grande bridge and, 64, 69–72, 241
Mendoza, Encomendero, 191

Mendoza, García de, 45–46
Mendoza, Lope de, 49
Meneses, Diego de, 47
Menesses, Paulo de, 183–84
Mercado, Juan, 123
Merubia, Juana, 160
Mesa, Pedro de, 172
Métraux, Alfred, 16, 17
migration patterns, 214–15, 230–31
Min de Cetona, Gonzalo, 198
mining: Allallona silver, 119–20; court
    battles over, 120–25; early, 119–20;
    Indian labor in, 120–23; Potosí silver,
    1, 3, 22, 36, 73–74, 129–30, 188, 288;
    Quioma silver, 119, 288; royal mints,
    137–38, 310n78; and the search for
    gold, 24; Spanish encouragement of,
    123–25. *See also* trade
mints, royal, 137–38, 310n78
Miro, Bernarda, 245
Mizque region: agricultural products,
    51–53, 77–78, 77–84, 90–91, 107–8,
    115–19, 304n50, 305n18; architects
    and carpenters of, 63–65; caciques
    of, 96–98; chácaras of, 98–100;
    Chiriguano of, 22, 24, 25; civil wars,
    23, 28, 35–36; climate of, 15–16, 101,
    234–35; courts, 111–15; cowboys
    of, 269–72; diseases, 49–50, 189–90,
    211–12, 235–37, 278–79, 295n19,
    317–18n6; early European settlement
    in, 37–38, 275–76, 298n1; economy,
    45–48, 108–16, 117–18, 275–78;
    European imposed classifications on,
    17–18; explorations and the search
    for gold in, 24; *forasteros* of, 228–33;
    geography and prehistory, 2–3, 15–
    19; Inca occupation of, 18–19, 27, 49,
    117, 181, 235, 275; indigenous people
    of, 16–18, 22–25, 51; lowlands of,
    15–16; migration patterns, 214–15,
    230–31; modern districts in area of,
    15; official founding and renaming
    of villa of, 43–45; proliferation and
    rapid turnover of estates, 78–84;

prominent families of, 24–42, 77;
    and the Río Grande river, 21, 55–71,
    241–43; Spanish population, 51;
    subpuna valleys of, 16–17; successful
    haciendas of, 84–96; traditional
    literature pertaining to, 3–5, 275. *See
    also* Villa de Salinas del Río Pisuerga
Mojo Indians, 217–19
Montesclaros, Marques de, 177
Montesinos, Percival, 211
Morena, Clara, 272–74, 285–86
Morocossi Indians, 217–19
Mosanga, Francisco, 148
Moya Indians, 217–19
mulatos: categorization of, 140–41, 165,
    283–85; cohabitation between, 272–
    74, 285; court cases involving, 111–
    15, 120; cowboy, 270; land ownership
    by, 174–75; murder of, 250–52, 286–
    87, 319n38; populations, 177–78;
    recording of, 140–41, 159–65; slaves,
    28, 156–57, 159–65, 172–73, 178–79;
    yanacona, 159–65, 167–69, 285. *See
    also* slaves and their descendants
mule teams, 110–11, 115–16
Muñoz, Juan, 213
murders, 250–52, 286–87, 319n38
Murra, John V., 48
Musinga, Felipe, 148

Narváez, Agustín de, 270
Narváez, Fernando de, 28
Narváez, Luís de, 28
Navarrette, Estevan, 111–14, 120, 271
Nodar, Alonzo de, 244
Nueva Asunción, 21
Ñunez Bela, Blasco, 27–28
Nuñez Lorenzo, Maese de Campo, 56–57
Nuñez Vila, Blasco, 36

Ogate, Lorenzo, 212
Ojeda, Gabriel de, 179
Oloy hacienda, 84–89; lifestyle at,
    239–41; livestock, 110–11; slaves at,
    140, 160; winemaking at, 110

Orozco, Melchor, 190, 193–94
outmigration from estates, 140–41. See
    also *forasteros*
outsiders among Indians, 228–33, 283
Ovando, Francisco, 160

Pacheco, Lorenzo, 109
Pacsima, María, 241–42, 247–48
Paez de Laguna, Joan, 184
Palmer, Colin, 134–35, 136
Panama, Gracía de, 249
Paniagua, Bernardo de, 162
Paniagua de Loaysa, Antonio, 32, 38–41,
    49; court cases involving, 111–15,
    198–201; relationships with Indians,
    198
Paniagua de Loaysa, Gabriel, 26, 28,
    210, 240; children of, 38–42; coca
    production and, 118; as corregidor of
    Cuzco, 34, 37–38; family influence
    and power, 31–32, 40–42, 49; land
    holdings of, 33–34, 38–40, 93;
    livestock of, 271–72; *mulato* slaves
    owned by, 161; relationships with
    Indians, 197–98; slaves owned by,
    140, 166, 172
Paniagua de Loaysa, Gabriel, Jr., 38–42
Paniagua de Loaysa, Pedro Fernández,
    32–33, 36, 118, 132, 199
Paraguayan Europeans, 20–22
pardos. See *mulatos*; slaves and their
    descendants
Paredes, Alonso de, 94
Paredes, Juan de, 93–96, 240
Paredes, María de, 94
Paredes de Hinojosa, Gonzalo, 197
Peñalosa y Mondragon, Benito, 137, 170
Peraza Betancourt, Rodrigo, 57–58
Perero Barrantes, Francisco, 44
Pérez, Diego, 108
Pérez, Pablo, 78–80
Pérez de Calahorra, Juan, 47
Peru (Viceroyalty of): African diaspora
    in, 130–31; location of la Villa de
    Mizque in, 2–3; lowlands of the

eastern Andes in, 1–2, 185, 219–27,
    234–35; Paraguayan Europeans in,
    20–22; search for gold in, 24; silver
    mines, 1, 3, 22, 36, 73–74, 119,
    129–30; Spanish conquest of, 1–2,
    19–25, 181; traditional literature on,
    3–5. See also Mizque region
Phelipe García, Diego, 107
Philip, King of Spain, 47–48, 182–83,
    288
Philip II, King of Spain, 110, 117, 170,
    189, 259
Philip III, King of Spain, 137
Picón, Juan, 244
Pila, Constable de la, 70–71
Pinelo de Ayala, Joan, 80–81, 103
Pizarro, Francisco, 19–20, 19–22, 35
Pizarro, Gonzalo, 21–22, 27, 32, 35–36
Pizarro, Hernando, 21–22
Pocona Indians, 117–18, 142; African
    population among, 177; coca
    production and, 183–85, 188;
    curacas, 211–12; Indian attacks on,
    183–85
Pojo Indians, 200
Polanco y Velasco, Antonio, 94
Poma de Ayala, Guaman, 234–35
Ponce de León, Joseph, 122
Ponce de León, Luisa, 83–84, 171
populations. See censuses
Portocarrera, Fernando, 211
Portugal, Diego de, 59, 141
Potosí, La Villa Imperial de: and the Río
    Grande bridge, 73–74; silver mines,
    1, 3, 22, 36, 129–30, 188, 288; slave
    population, 177; wine trade, 109, 110
Powers, Karen Viera, 207, 232
Presta, Ana María, 197
prices: slave, 131–36, 311n97; wine,
    81–83, 301nn9–10, 305n18
Pucura, Battle of, 33

Quintela Salazar, Diego de, 86
Quioma silver mines, 119, 288
Quiros, Pedro de, 49

Quíroz de Ávila, Pedro, 198

Quispe, Salvador, 257–58

Raché Indians, 226–27

Ramírez, Juan, 174, 208

Ramírez de Romagera, Juan, 270

Ramo de Tierras y Indios and Expedientes, 5

Ramón, Juan de, 141

Ramón, Miguel de, 110

recua mules, 110–11

Río Grande river, 21; bridge built across, 55–71

Rivas, Sebastian de, 46

Rivera, Francisco de, 55

Rivera, Juan de, 91–93

Robles, Domingo de, 174, 178

Robles, Juan de, 174

Robles y Palma, Josepha de, 94–96

Rodríguez de Herrera, Juan, 71

Rodríguez Ostria, Gustavo, 4

Roldán, Cristobal, 139

rolls, slave, 143–49

Roman Catholic Church, the: Cazorla family and, 50; Christianization of Indians, 24, 49–50, 205–6, 275; and coca field workers, 192–93; hospitals and education provided by, 49, 189; and slaves, 150–58; vineyards and sugar haciendas owned by, 78

Romero, Pascual, 271

Romero del Castillo, Matheo, 156

Rosas, Juan de, 162

Rubio Betancourt, Bernardo, 124

Ruíz de Herrera, Juan, 55

runaway slaves, 140–41, 162–64, 260–65, 268–69, 279–80, 282–83, 320n66

Saenz de Soto, Matías, 265

Saez Ortíz, Mateo, 134

Saignes, Thierry: on ethnicity of Indians, 217, 220; on the subpuna valleys, 16–17; works on Mizque, 1–2

Salazar, Felix de, 271

Salazar, Pedro de, 98, 99

Salazar Negrete, Gerónimo de, 163

Saldaña, Juan de, 55, 98, 242, 248

Sanabria F., Hernando, 178

Sandoval y Rojas, Cristobal de, 55

San Juan del Oro, 22

San Lorenzo de la Barranca, 134–35

Santa Cruz region, 29–30, 33, 244, 287, 307n13; population growth, 51; slave trade, 134–35; taxes in, 61

Santo Domingo, 132

Santos Ugarte, Juan, 120, 121–24

Schramm, Raimund, 17–18, 186, 187

Sepulveda, Miguel de, 109

Sermeno, Juárez, 198–200

sickle-cell anemia, 317–18n6

Sisa, Ana, 163

slaves and their descendants, 2, 5–6, 104; abuse of, 279–81, 319n47; and the African diaspora, 130–31; and the chácara censuses, 158–70; children of, 167–69; cimarrone, 261–66; coca production by, 195–97; countries of origin, 147–48; cowboy, 269–72; dehumanized by owners, 132–33; female, 148–49; health of, 309n47; as inventory sold with estates, 79, 83–84, 103, 108, 115, 139–40, 142–47, 171, 180, 302nn15–16; involved in livestock production, 142–43, 172–74; and the Jesuits, 150–58, 172; laws affecting, 258–69, 282; as magistrates, 175–76; mortality rates, 236; *mulato*, 28, 156–57, 159–65, 178–79; names, 141, 148, 166–67; occupational patterns, 170–76; owned by curacas, 207–8; population figures for, 176–80; prices, sales, and traffic, 131–36, 179–80, 279–80, 311n97; rolls, 143–49, 151–52; royal mints and, 137–38, 310n78; runaway, 140–41, 162–64, 260–65, 279–80, 282–83, 320n66; theft of, 266–67; as town criers, 175; used in attacks on the Chiriguano, 29–30; at vineyards,

132, 138, 170–72; working conditions
of, 136–50. *See also* labor; *mulatos*
Solís, Gonzalo de, 244
Soría, Jerónimo de, 137
Spaniards, the: atrocities committed
by, 26; classifications imposed on
Mizque by, 17–18, 219–20, 226–27,
283–85; coca production and, 117,
186–97; environmental difficulties
faced by, 23; gold and silver mining
and, 123–25, 129–30; importance of
Mizque region to, 45–48, 275–76;
relationships between Indian curacas
and, 201–6
Spanish, the: attempts to control
indigenous people, 181–86, 276;
conquest of Peru, 19–22; population
in Mizque, 51; wars with Paraguayan
Europeans, 19–22
Suárez de Figueroa, Hernando, 25
sugar plantations, 107–8, 115–16; slaves
on, 142–49
surnames, Indian, 216–17

Tablares, Juan de, 55
taxes, 59–60; curacas and, 208–9; mining,
124–25; and slave rolls, 148–50
theft of slaves, 266–67
Toledo, Francisco de, 29, 33–34, 48,
50; and the curacas, 202–3; on
land ownership, 51; on livestock
production and regulations, 113–14;
mint established by, 137
Tordoya, Francisco de, 266–67
Torres, Rodrigo de, 104–5
Torres de la Calancha, Pedro de, 44, 53;
and the bridge across the Río Grande
river, 58–59
Torricos, Melchor, 271
Tovar, Pedro López, 104–7, 110
town criers, 175
trade: coca, 117–18, 186–97; hinterland-
highland routes, 45–48, 275–76;
La Plata-Potosí market, 46–48; by
successful haciendas, 84–96; sugar,

115–16; wine, 108–15. *See also*
mining
Trejo, Ana de, 99
Trejo, Fernanda de, 99
Trejo, María, 98–100
Trejo de la Cerda, Juan, 102
Troche del Vallejo, Antonio, 43
Trouillot, Michel-Rolph, 2
Tucuma Baja hacienda, 94–96
Tucuma hacienda, 93–96
Turque sugar plantation, 107–8; slave
rolls, 143–47, 151–52
Turumaya, Curaca Don Francisco, 68,
206
Turumaya, Curaca Don Hernando,
190–92

Uminchipa, Barbola de, 174

Valdés, Pedro de, 211
Valenzuela, Elvira de, 249, 252–54
Valenzuela, Gerónima, 251–52
Valenzuela, Juan, 240, 248–55
Valenzuela, Juan de, 271
Valle de Chilón, 61
Valverde, Bishop, 27
Vargas de Toldeo, Juan de, 44, 200
Vega, Diego de la, 262
Velasco, Viceroy Luís de, 38, 43, 209
Velazco, Pedro, 78–79
Venegas, Diego de, 262
Verdugo de Ángulo, Mayor, 35, 38, 39,
53; coca production and, 118; wine
production and, 90
Viedma, Francisco, 177, 214, 237, 288
Villa de Mizque. *See* Villa de Salinas del
Río Pisuerga
Villa de Salinas del Río Pisuerga:
acceleration of settlement process
in, 48–50; administrative challenges
and civic projects, 50–55; founding
of, 43–45; land ownership records,
51–53; leadership, community action,
and bridge building, 55–71; officials
of, 43–44; regional expansion and

Villa de Salinas del Río Pisuerga
(*continued*)
    territorial shifts, 45–48; rented houses
    in, 81; taxes, 59–60; water fountain,
    59–60. *See also* Mizque region
Villapando, Gerónimo de, 173, 272–74,
    274
Villaroel, Jacinto, 104, 107
vineyards: at La Calleja, 80–84,
    103–6, 108–9, 170–71; slaves
    working at, 132, 138, 170–72;
    wine prices and, 81–83, 301n9–
    10, 305n18; wine production of,
    92–93, 108, 301nn9–10. *See also*
    estates
Viriti, Jacinto, 162–63
Viscarra, Eufronio, 101, 119

water: fountain, Mizque, 59–60; rights,
    242
wealthy, the: curacas, 205–6; lifestyles
    and health of, 237–41; wills and
    inheritances of, 242, 243–48
wills and inheritances, 242, 243–48

winemaking. *See* agricultural products;
    vineyards
World Upside Down, The, 208

Xaqui Xaguana, Battle of, 32, 36
Xaraxuri, Curaca Don Diego, 190
Ximénez de Obeido, Joan, 69–71

yanaconas: abuse of, 282; categorization
    of, 167–70, 219–20, 285; census
    recordings of, 220–28; coca produc-
    tion and, 196; differentiated from
    African slaves, 159–65; inheritances,
    246; lifestyles of, 240; outsiders
    among, 229–30; and the Río Grande
    river bridge, 228
Yrigo, Joan, 102, 103
Yunga Indians, 118–19, 217–19, 226–27
Yupanqui, Capac, 235

zambiahgos. *See* slaves and their
    descendants
zambos. *See* slaves and their descendants
Zaragún, Luís, 261